West Academic Publishing's Law School Advisory Board

PRINCIPLES OF EMPLOYMENT LAW

Second Edition

Ann C. Hodges
Professor of Law
University of Richmond

Rafael Gely
James E. Campbell Missouri Endowed Professor of Law
University of Missouri–Columbia

for

THE LABOR LAW GROUP

CONCISE HORNBOOK SERIES™

WEST ACADEMIC PUBLISHING

Printed in the United States of America

ISBN: 978-1-68328-359-1

To my late husband Stan Meyer, our children, Deb and Chuck, Elizabeth and Keith, and Lisa, and our precious grandchildren, Rory and Eirnin.

—ACH

To my wife Yoko Frances Ito-Gely and our three very special children Sebastian, Yumiko and Pablo.

—RG

Preface

The employment relationship is increasingly regulated by law. For many years, the employment relationship was primarily contractual, with terms and conditions of employment set by agreement of the parties. The law of the workplace was labor law, which dealt chiefly with union organizing and collective bargaining. The 1960s saw the enactment of statutes prohibiting employment discrimination, dividing the law of the workplace into the subjects of labor law and employment discrimination law. The enactment of federal employment discrimination statutes and the decline of collective bargaining, along with changing conditions in the economy and the workplace, unleashed a plethora of employment regulation through both statute and common law, leading to a dynamic and rapidly developing body of law now known as employment law.

Employment law does not incorporate only relatively new statutes and claims, however. It includes laws enacted in the early twentieth century such as workers' compensation statutes and the Fair Labor Standards Act governing minimum wage, overtime and child labor. In addition, it overlaps in many areas with the traditional subjects of labor and employment discrimination law. This book will assist anyone interested in the study of today's workplace in understanding the laws that govern its operations. The traditional subjects of labor law and employment discrimination are not a focus of the book, although discussion of these laws is included where they overlap with the concepts covered. Employee benefits law, sometimes the subject of a separate course in the curriculum, is included in the employment laws covered here.

The book is designed to provide a basic understanding of employment law and is a useful supplement to any of the current employment law casebooks. It does not follow the structure of any one book, but rather is divided into seven substantive chapters. Chapter 1 discusses the question of who is an employee and who is an employer, a centrally important issue for almost all areas of employment law. Chapter 2 follows with an analysis of the employment-at-will doctrine and job security claims, an area of law that has developed exponentially in the last 35 years through both statutory and common law. Chapter 3 focuses on privacy, autonomy and dignity in the workplace, a topic that includes speech and association claims as well as legal challenges to intrusive employment practices. While most of the book concentrates on legal claims commonly filed by employees against employers, Chapter 4 analyzes the claims that employers may have against employees including, for example, claims relating to intellectual property rights and violations of the duty of loyalty. Chapter 5 discusses the increasing number of employment terms and benefits that are either directly mandated by law, like the minimum wage, or strongly encouraged and regulated by law, such as pensions. Chapter 6, reviews the laws relating to workplace health and safety. The final chapter addresses the increasingly important issue of the use of arbitration to resolve employment disputes.

Employment law seeks to balance the rights and interests of employers, employees and society. To understand employment law, it is essential to understand the interests of each of these groups. This theme runs through each of the chapters. Additionally, we have attempted to do the following:

(1) Provide a basic understanding of the existing law. In areas governed by state law, we have provided examples to illustrate the range of legal approaches in the states.

(2) Highlight areas of the law where there is disagreement among the courts in legal interpretation and explain the rationales underlying those varying interpretations.

(3) Demonstrate how the law has evolved in response to changes in the workplace.

(4) Point out major criticisms of existing law and direct readers to further resources to explore those critical perspectives.

(5) Provide cross references to other sections to show the interrelatedness of the various areas of employment law.

(6) Relate each subject area to labor and employment discrimination law, where relevant, to assist the reader in attaining a fuller understanding of the law of the workplace.

The authors wish to thank the members of the Labor Law Group for their support and editorial review and their co-authors on the first edition, Peggie R. Smith and Susan J. Stabile, whose work remains an important part of the second edition. Additionally, we wish to thank our research assistants for their excellent work: Lisa A. Allen and Adam F. Wall at the University of Richmond School of Law; and Samantha Groark and Michele Moyer at the University of Missouri.

Foreword

The Labor Law Group had its origins in the desire of scholars to produce quality casebooks for instruction in labor and employment law. Over the course of its existence, the hallmarks of the Group have been collaborative efforts among scholars, informed by skilled practitioners, under a cooperative nonprofit trust in which royalties from past work finance future meetings and projects.

At the 1946 meeting of the Association of American Law Schools, Professor W. Willard Wirtz delivered a compelling paper criticizing the labor law coursebooks then available. His remarks so impressed those present that the Labor Law Roundtable of the Association organized a general conference on the teaching of labor law to be held in Ann Arbor in 1947. The late Professor Robert E. Mathews served as coordinator for the Ann Arbor meeting, and several conferees agreed to exchange proposals for sections of a new coursebook that would facilitate training exemplary practitioners of labor law. Beginning in 1948, a preliminary mimeographed version was used in seventeen schools; each user supplied comments and suggestions for change. In 1953, a hardcover version was published under the title *Labor Relations and the Law*. The thirty-one "cooperating editors" were so convinced of the value of multicampus collaboration that they gave up any individual claims to royalties. Instead, those royalties were paid to a trust fund to be used to develop and "provide the best possible materials" for training students in labor law and labor relations. The Declaration of Trust memorializing this agreement was executed November 4, 1953, and remains the Group's charter.

The founding committee's hope that the initial collaboration would bear fruit has been fulfilled. Under Professor Mathews's continuing leadership, the Group's members produced *Readings on Labor Law* in 1955 and *The Employment Relation and the Law* in 1957, edited by Robert Mathews and Benjamin Aaron. A second edition of *Labor Relations and the Law* appeared in 1960, with Benjamin Aaron and Donald H. Wollett as coeditors of the book and cochairs of the Group, and a third edition was published in 1965, with Jerre S. Williams at the helm.

In June 1969 the Group, now chaired by William P. Murphy, sponsored a conference to reexamine the labor law curriculum. Practitioners and full-time teachers, including nonmembers as well as members of the Group, attended the meeting, held at the University of Colorado. In meetings that followed the conference, the Group decided to reshape its work substantially. It restructured itself into ten task forces, each assigned a unit of no more than two hundred pages on a discrete topic such as employment discrimination or union-member relations. An individual teacher could then choose two or three of these units as the material around which to build a particular course. This multiunit approach dominated the Group's work throughout much of the 1970s under Professor Murphy and his successor as chair, Herbert L. Sherman, Jr.

As the 1970s progressed and teachers refined their views about what topics to include and how to address them, some units were dropped from the series while others increased in scope and length. Under Professor Sherman's leadership, the Group planned a new series of six enlarged books to cover the full range of topics taught by labor and employment law teachers. Professor James E. Jones, Jr., was elected chair in 1978, and he shepherded to completion the promised set of six full-size, independent casebooks. The Group continued to reevaluate its work and eventually decided that it was time to convene another conference of law teachers.

In 1984 the Group, now chaired by Robert Covington, sponsored another general conference to discuss developments in the substance and teaching of labor and employment law, this time in Park City, Utah. Those discussions and a subsequent working session led to the conclusion that the Group should devote principal attention to three new conventional length coursebooks, one devoted to employment discrimination, one to union-management relations, and one to the individual employment relationship. In addition, work was planned on more abbreviated coursebooks to serve as successors to the Group's earlier works covering public employment bargaining and labor arbitration.

In 1989, with Alvin Goldman as chair, the Group met in Breckenridge, Colorado, to assess its most recent efforts and develop plans for the future. In addition to outlining new coursebook projects, the Group discussed ways to assist teachers of labor and employment law in their efforts to expand conceptual horizons and perspectives. In pursuit of the latter goals it cosponsored, in 1992, a conference held at the University of Toronto Faculty of Law at which legal and nonlegal specialists examined alternative models of corporate governance and their impact on workers.

When Robert J. Rabin became chair in 1996, the Group and a number of invited guests met in Tucson, Arizona, to celebrate the imminent fiftieth anniversary of the Group. The topics of discussion included the impact of the global economy and of changing forms of representation on the teaching of labor and employment law, and the impact of new technologies of electronic publishing on the preparation of teaching materials. The Group honored three of its members who had been present at the creation of the Group, Willard Wirtz, Ben Aaron, and Clyde Summers. The Group next met in Scottsdale, Arizona, in December 1999, to discuss the production of materials that would more effectively bring emerging issues of labor and employment law into the classroom. Among the issues discussed were integration of international and comparative materials into the labor and employment curriculum and the pedagogical uses of the World Wide Web.

Laura J. Cooper became chair of the Group in July 2001. In June 2003, the Group met in Alton, Ontario, Canada. The focus there was on "labor law on the edge"—looking at doctrinal synergies between workplace law and other legal and social-science disciplines—and "workers on the edge"—exploring the legal issues of highly compensated technology workers, vulnerable immigrant employees, and unionized manufacturing employees threatened by foreign competition. The Group also heard a report from its study of the status of the teaching of labor and employment law in the nation's law schools and discussed the implications of the study for the Group's future projects. Members of the Group began work on the casebook on international labor law at this meeting. During Professor Cooper's term, the Group also finished its popular reader *Labor Law Stories*, which examines the stories behind many of the most important American labor law cases.

In July 2005, Kenneth G. Dau-Schmidt became the chair of the Labor Law Group. Shortly after his election, the Group held a meeting in Chicago with nationally recognized practitioners to discuss how best to teach students about the practice of labor law in the new global economy of the information age. The outline that resulted from this meeting served as the basis for *Labor Law in the Contemporary Workplace*. Following the Chicago meeting, the Group met several times to work on new editions of its books and develop new projects: June 2006 in Saratoga Springs, New York; June 2007 in St. Charles, Illinois; and June 2010 in Arrowhead, California. Group projects that grew out of or benefited from these meetings include *International Labor Law: Cases and Materials on Workers' Rights in the Global Economy* and *A Concise Hornbook on Employment Law*. The Group also hosted: a November 2007 symposium on the problems of low-wage workers, the proceedings of which were published in the *Minnesota Law Review*; a February 2009 symposium on the American Law Institute's Proposed Restatement of Employment Law, the proceedings of which were published in the *Employee Rights and Employment Policy Journal*; and a November 2010 symposium on labor and employment law policies under the Obama administration, the proceedings of which were published in the *Indiana Law Journal*.

Marion Crain became chair of the Group at the beginning of 2011. That same year, the Group sponsored a one-day conference on the crisis confronting public-sector employment, the proceedings of which were published in the *ABA Journal of Labor and Employment Law*. In 2011 the Group also hosted a meeting of experts in Chicago to consider the ongoing Restatement of Employment Law project. In June 2012, the Group met in Asheville, North Carolina, and approved the formation of an editorial policy committee charged with establishing policies to ensure that the Group's products continue to reflect its tradition of close collaboration and high standards. The Asheville meeting served as the genesis for a labor arbitrator training workshop for academics in Chicago in December 2012. In February 2013, the Group cosponsored a symposium at the University of California–Irvine School of Law on alternatives to the Wagner Act and employment law models of workplace protection. The proceedings of the conference, called "Re-imagining Labor Law: Building Worker Collectivities After the NLRA," will be published in the *UC Irvine Law Review*. In June 2014, the Group met in Ithaca, New York.

Steve Befort and Melissa Hart became Co-Chairs of the Group at the beginning of 2015. In that year, Group members voted to approve a partnership between the Group and the Chicago-Kent Law School to oversee the publication of the Employee Rights and Employment Policy Journal. In December 2016, the Group met in Los Angeles, California.

At any one time, roughly twenty-five to thirty members are actively engaged in the Group's work; this has proven to be a practical size, given the challenges of communication and logistics. Coordination and editorial review of the projects are the responsibility of the executive committee, whose members are the successor trustees of the Group. Governance is by consensus; votes are taken only to elect trustees and to determine whom to invite to join the Group. Since 1953, more than eighty persons have worked on Group projects; in keeping with the original agreement, none has ever received anything more than reimbursement of expenses.

The Labor Law Group currently has nine books in print. West Academic has published *Public Sector Employment: Cases and Materials* (Third Edition) by Martin H. Malin, Ann C. Hodges, Joseph E. Slater, and Jeffrey Hirsch; *Principles of Employment Law* (Second edition) by Ann C. Hodges and Rafael Gely; *Labor Law in the Contemporary Workplace* (Second edition) by Kenneth G. Dau-Schmidt, Martin H. Malin, Roberto L. Corrada, Christopher David Ruiz Cameron, and Catherine L. Fisk; *Disability Law: Cases and* Materials, by Stephen F. Befort and Nicole Buonocore Porter;

International Labor Law: Cases and Materials on Workers' Rights in the Global Economy by James Atleson, Lance Compa, Kerry Rittich, Calvin William Sharpe, and Marley S. Weiss; *Employment Discrimination Law: Cases and Materials on Equality in the Workplace* (Eighth Edition) by Dianne Avery, Maria L. Ontiveros, Roberto L. Corrado, Michael L. Selmi, and Melissa Hart; *ADR in the Workplace* (Third Edition) by Laura J. Cooper, Dennis R. Nolan, Richard A. Bales, and Stephen F. Befort; and *Legal Protection for the Individual Employee* (Fifth Edition) by Kenneth G. Dau-Schmidt, Matthew W. Finkin and Robert N. Covington. Foundation Press has published *Labor Law Stories*, edited by Laura J. Cooper and Catherine L. Fisk.

The Labor Law Group

Executive Committee

Stephen Befort
Co-Chair
University of Minnesota

Melissa Hart
Co-Chair
University of Colorado–Boulder

Richard A. Bales
Ohio Northern University

Ruben Garcia
University of Nevada–Las Vegas

Jeffrey Hirsch
University of North Carolina

Cynthia Nance
University of Arkansas–Fayetteville

Nicole Buonocore Porter
University of Toledo

Kerry Rittich
University of Toronto

Noah Zatz
University of California–Los Angeles

Editorial Policy Committee

Members

Steven D. Anderman
University of Essex

Harry W. Arthurs
York University (Emeritus)

Rachel Arnow-Richman
University of Denver

James B. Atleson
State University of New York–Buffalo (Emeritus)

Dianne Avery
State University of New York–Buffalo

Richard A. Bales
Ohio Northern University

Stephen Befort
University of Minnesota

Adele Blackett
McGill University

Alfred W. Blumrosen
Rutgers University (Emeritus)

Christopher David Ruiz Cameron
Southwestern Law School

Lance Compa
Cornell University

Laura Cooper
University of Minnesota

Roberto L. Corrada
University of Denver

Robert N. Covington
Vanderbilt University (Emeritus)

Marion G. Crain
Washington University–St. Louis

Kenneth G. Dau-Schmidt
Indiana University–Bloomington

Cynthia Estlund
New York University

Martin H. Malin
Illinois Institute of Technology, Chicago–Kent College of Law

Mordehai Mironi
University of Haifa

Robert B. Moberly
University of Arkansas

Charles J. Morris
Southern Methodist University (Emeritus)

Cynthia Nance
University of Arkansas–Fayetteville

Dennis R. Nolan
University of South Carolina (Emeritus)

Maria L. Ontiveros
University of San Francisco

Angela Onwuachi-Willig
University of Iowa

Nicole Buonocore Porter
University of Toledo

Robert J. Rabin
Syracuse University (Emeritus)

Kerry Rittich
University of Toronto

Brishen Rogers
Temple University

Cesar Rosado
Illinois Institute of Technology, Chicago–Kent College of Law

Alvaro Santos
Georgetown University

George Schatzki
Arizona State University (Emeritus)

Michael Selmi
George Washington University

Calvin W. Sharpe
Case Western Reserve University

Eileen Silverstein
University of Connecticut (Emerita)

Summary of Contents

Table of Contents

PRINCIPLES OF EMPLOYMENT LAW

Second Edition

Chapter 1

DEFINING THE EMPLOYMENT RELATIONSHIP

Work is everywhere. It pervades almost all our waking time. One would think that, given the pervasiveness of work in our lives, the legal system would be able to answer clearly some very basic questions, such as what makes someone an employee or an employer. As the discussion in the following sections illustrates the answers to these questions are far from clear.

In part, the difficulty in answering what seem at first glance relatively straightforward questions lies in the fact that the answers are contextually specific. Legislatures and courts do not care about who an employee is or who an employer is in the abstract, but only in the context of a specific law, policy or doctrinal issue. Thus, not only do the definitions of the terms "employee" and "employer" vary from statute to statute, but even within a particular statute courts might adopt more expansive or limited definitions depending on the particular issue involved.

§ 1.1 Who Is an Employee?

1.1.1 The Employee Versus the Independent Contractor

At the heart of employment law rests the relationship between an employer and its employees. However, the question frequently arises as to whether workers properly fit within the category of employee or whether they fall within some other category. This other category is commonly described as self employed or independent contractor. As discussed below, various commentators have challenged the traditional employee-independent contractor distinction, arguing that it fails to capture the myriad of work relationships existing today. For now, however, the following discussion focuses on this traditional distinction and explains its implications for employment law.

1.1.1.1 What Is at Stake?

In the United States, federal as well as state statutes treat employees differently than independent contractors. Employees, but not independent contractors, enjoy minimum wage and overtime protection under the Fair Labor Standards Act (FLSA),[1] anti-discrimination protection under Title VII of the Civil Rights Act of 1964,[2] leave under the Family and Medical Leave Act (FMLA),[3] pension and benefit protection under the Employee Retirement Income Security Act (ERISA),[4] safety and health protection under the Occupational Safety and Health Act (OSH Act),[5] benefits under workers' compensation systems,[6] and compensation under unemployment insurance programs.[7]

1.1.1.2 Determining a Worker's Status

In some instances, the question of whether a worker is an employee or an independent contractor yields relatively intuitive conclusions. For example, a salesperson at a local clothing store who provides service to customers, reports to the store manager, wears a

---

1 29 U.S.C. §§ 201 et seq. See, e.g., Shultz v. Hinojosa, 432 F.2d 259, 263 (5th Cir. 1970) (finding that because the worker was an employee, and not an independent contractor, he was entitled to protection under the FLSA).

2 42 U.S.C. §§ 2000e et seq. See, e.g., Wilde v. County of Kandiyohi, 15 F.3d 103, 104 (8th Cir. 1994) (stating that "Title VII protects workers who are 'employees,' but does not protect independent contractors").

3 29 U.S.C. §§ 2601 et seq. See, e.g., Nichols v. All Points Transp. Corp., 364 F.Supp.2d 621, 634 (E.D. Mich. 2005) (finding a truck driver to be an independent contractor and thus not entitled to FMLA leave).

4 29 U.S.C. §§ 1001 et seq. See Nationwide Mut. Ins. Co. v. Darden, 503 U.S. 318, 323 (1992) (using the common law test to distinguish between "employee" and "independent contractor" under ERISA).

5 29 U.S.C. §§ 651 et seq. See, e.g., Melerine v. Avondale Shipyards, Inc., 659 F.2d 706, 710–11 (5th Cir. 1981) (stating that OSHA regulations apply only to "an employer's own employees" and not "third persons," such as independent contractors).

6 See, e.g., Atchison v. Boone Newspapers, Inc., 981 So.2d 427, 431 (Ala. Civ. App. 2007) (stating that Alabama's workers' compensation law only applies where the claimant is an employee, not an independent contractor); Hix v. Minn. Workers' Comp. Assigned Risk Plan, 520 N.W.2d 497, 502 (Minn. Ct. App. 1994) (commenting that the Minnesota Workers' Compensation Act does not apply to persons who are independent contractors as defined by administrative rules); Alaska Pulp Corp. v. United Paperworkers Int'l Union, 791 P.2d 1008, 1012 (Alaska 1990) (commenting that employees as opposed to independent contractors are eligible for workers' compensation benefits under the Alaska Workers' Compensation Act).

While most workers benefit from being classified as an employee under a workers' compensation statute, at other times classification as an employee can prove a hindrance. This is especially true in cases where workers want to avoid the workers' compensation system and pursue a tort claim against their employers because of the possibility of recovering greater damages, including punitive damages. Because the laws only apply to employees, if a worker is not an employee, the worker is free to pursue such a claim. See infra Section 6.1 ("Workers' Compensation").

7 See, e.g., Zubi Advertising Serv., Inc. v. Dep't of Labor, 537 So.2d 145 (Fla. Dist. Ct. App. 1989) (holding that because individuals performing in radio and television commercials were not employees but independent contractors, the appellant advertising agency was not obligated to pay their unemployment compensation tax); Tomlin v. Cal. Employment Comm'n, 30 Cal.2d 118, 122, 180 P.2d 342, 345 (1947) (stating that "the relationship contemplated by the Unemployment Insurance Act has been held to be that of employer and employee, an independent contractor not being within the scope of its provisions").

uniform or nametag, is provided a schedule at the beginning of the week and receives a regular check as compensation is likely to be deemed an "employee" under most statutory frameworks. At the other end, a painter who, after quoting a price is hired by the store manager to paint the store, who buys all the necessary materials and utilizes his own equipment, who brings an assistant to complete the work and who at the end of the day makes $1500 in profit, after paying his helper and covering all costs, is likely an independent contractor.

However, determining a worker's status is not always so straightforward. The determinations depend both on the circumstances of a given work relationship and on the particular employment law statute at issue. Courts rely upon three main tests to assess whether a worker is an employee or an independent contractor: the common law test, the economic reality test, and a hybrid test that combines elements of both the common law test and the economic reality test.[8]

1.1.1.2.1 The Common Law Test

The common law test incorporates traditional agency law principles[9] which rely heavily on the level of control that a company exercises over the manner and means by which a worker performs her job.[10] Under this test, an employment relationship exists if the putative employer reserves the right to control not only the result to be achieved, but also the means to be used to attain the result.[11] By contrast, an independent contractor relationship exists where the putative employer " 'reserve[s] only the right to control the ends to be achieved.' "[12] In assessing the level of control, courts accord

---

[8] See, e.g., Frankel v. Bally, Inc., 987 F.2d 86, 89 (2d Cir. 1993) (listing the three tests). For useful discussions of the tests, see Lewis Maltby & David Yamada, Beyond "Economic Realities": The Case for Amending Federal Employment Discrimination Laws to Include Independent Contractors, 38 B.C. L. Rev. 239, 247–53 (1997); Mitchell H. Rubinstein, Our Nation's Forgotten Workers: The Unprotected Volunteers, 9 U. Pa. J. Lab. & Emp. L. 147, 161–70 (2006).

[9] Restatement (Second) of Agency § 220(2).

[10] See, e.g., NLRB v. United Ins. Co., 390 U.S. 254, 256 (1968) (applying general agency principles to determine whether an individual is an employee or independent contractor); N. Am. Van Lines, Inc. v. NLRB, 869 F.2d 596, 599 (D.C. Cir. 1989) (stating that "[i]n applying traditional agency law principles, the NLRB and the courts have adopted a right-to-control test"); In re Morton, 284 N.Y. 167, 172, 30 N.E.2d 369, 371 (1940) (observing that the distinction between an employee and an independent contractor turns on the "right of control over the [worker] in respect of the manner in which his work is to be done").

[11] See, e.g., Cobb v. Sun Papers, Inc., 673 F.2d 337, 340 (11th Cir. 1982) (when "an employer has the right to control and direct the work of an individual, not only as to the result to be achieved, but also as to the details by which that result is achieved, an employer/employee relationship is likely to exist").

[12] C.C. Eastern, Inc. v. NLRB, 60 F.3d 855, 858 (D.C. Cir. 1995) (quoting Twin City Freight, Inc., 221 N.L.R.B. 1219, 1220 (1975)).

considerable weight to the amount of supervision that the putative employer has a right to exercise over the worker.[13]

While control is the "essential ingredient" of the common law test,[14] the test relies on several other factors as well.[15] As stated by the Supreme Court in *Nationwide Mutual Insurance Co. v. Darden*,[16] these factors include:

> the skill required; the source of the instrumentalities and tools; the location of the work; the duration of the relationship between the parties; whether the hiring party has the right to assign additional projects to the hired party; the extent of the hired party's discretion over when and how long to work; the method of payment; the hired party's role in hiring and paying assistants; whether the work is part of the regular business of the hiring party; whether the hiring party is in business; the provision of employee benefits; and the tax treatment of the hired party.[17]

Courts rely on the common law test to determine a worker's status in various employment-related statutes, most notably ERISA (the statute at issue in *Darden*),[18] the National Labor Relations Act (NLRA),[19] the Federal Insurance Contributions Act,[20] and the Federal Unemployment Tax Act.[21]

1.1.1.2.2 The Economic Reality Test

The Supreme Court articulated the economic reality test in *NLRB v. Hearst Publications, Inc.*[22] to determine the status of an employee under the NLRA. The Court highlighted the importance of

---

13 See, e.g., NLRB v. Friendly Cab Co., 512 F.3d 1090, 1096–97 (9th Cir. 2008).

14 SIDA of Haw., Inc. v. NLRB, 512 F.2d 354, 357 (9th Cir. 1975).

15 Restatement (Second) of Agency § 220(2).

16 503 U.S. 318, 322 (1992).

17 Id. at 323–24 (quoting Cmty. for Creative Non-Violence v. Reid, 490 U.S. 730, 751–52 (1989)).

18 See, e.g., Darden, 503 U.S. at 323; Speen v. Crown Clothing Corp., 102 F.3d 625, 631 (1st Cir. 1996).

19 29 U.S.C. §§ 151 et seq. See, e.g., NLRB v. United Ins. Co. of Am., 390 U.S. 254, 256 (1968).

20 26 U.S.C. §§ 3101 et seq. The Federal Insurance Contributions Act (FICA) establishes a payroll tax that is imposed on both employers and employees to help fund Social Security benefits and Medicare. For the purpose of FICA, § 3121(d)(2) of the Internal Revenue Code of 1954 expressly adopts the common law test for determining the existence of the employer-employee relationship.

21 26 U.S.C. §§ 3301 et seq. The Federal Unemployment Tax Act (FUTA) imposes a payroll tax on employers to help provide payments of unemployment compensation to workers who have lost their jobs. For the purpose of FUTA, § 3306(i) of the Internal Revenue Code of 1954 expressly adopts the common law test for determining the existence of the employer-employee relationship.

22 322 U.S. 111 (1944).

focusing on the economic circumstances of the working relationship to determine whether the worker was dependent on the putative employer for work. If dependency existed, then the worker was an employee.[23]

While the economic reality test was short-lived for NLRA purposes,[24] it has gained renewed life under several other statutes, especially the FLSA.[25] Building on the Court's pronouncement in *Hearst Publications*, courts have held that the test's critical inquiry should focus on whether the worker "is economically dependent on the business to which he renders service . . . or is, as a matter of economic [reality], in business for himself."[26]

Courts typically apply a "totality of the circumstances"[27] approach to evaluate the economic reality test that includes consideration of the following factors:

> 1) the degree of the putative employer's right to control the manner in which the work is to be performed; 2) the worker's opportunity for profit or loss depending upon managerial skill; 3) the worker's investment in equipment or materials required for his task, or his employment of helpers; 4) whether the service rendered requires a special skill; 5) the degree of permanence of the working relationship; 6) whether the service rendered is an integral part of the alleged employer's business.[28]

Courts have repeatedly emphasized that these factors are not exhaustive[29] and that the presence or absence of any one factor is not

---

23 Id. at 128–29.

24 Congress expressed its clear disapproval of the *Hearst* decision and its use of the economic reality test in enacting the Taft-Hartley Amendments. 29 U.S.C. §§ 141 et seq; see also Richard R. Carlson, Why the Law Still Can't Tell an Employee When it Sees One and How it Ought to Stop Trying, 22 Berkeley J. Emp. & Lab. L. 295, 321–25 (2001) (discussing the congressional response to *Hearst*).

25 See, e.g., Tony & Susan Alamo Found. v. Sec'y of Labor, 471 U.S. 290, 301 (1985) (stating that the "test of employment under the [FLSA] is one of 'economic reality' "); Schultz v. Capital Int'l Sec., Inc., 460 F.3d 595, 601 (4th Cir. 2006) (stating that "[i]n determining whether a worker is an employee covered by the FLSA, a court considers the 'economic realities' of the relationship between the worker and the putative employer"); Martin v. Selker Bros., Inc., 949 F.2d 1286, 1293 (3d Cir. 1991) (observing that "the Supreme Court has emphasized that the courts should look to the economic realities of the relationship in determining employee status under the FLSA") (referencing Rutherford Food Corp. v. McComb, 331 U.S. 722, 730 (1947)).

26 Henderson v. Inter-Chem Coal Co., 41 F.3d 567, 570 (10th Cir. 1994) (internal quotation marks omitted).

27 Dole v. Snell, 875 F.2d 802, 805 (10th Cir. 1989).

28 Donovan v. DialAmerica Mktg., Inc., 757 F.2d 1376, 1382 (3d Cir. 1985), cert. denied, DialAmerica Mktg., Inc. v. Brock, 474 U.S. 919 (1985) (quoting Donovan v. Sureway Cleaners, 656 F.2d 1368, 1370 (9th Cir. 1981)).

29 See, e.g., DialAmerica, 757 F.2d at 1382; Selker Bros., 949 F.2d at 1293.

dispositive.[30] "The [factors] are aids—tools to be used to gauge the degree of dependence of alleged employees on the business with which they are connected. It is *dependence* that indicates employee status."[31] Also, many of the factors used in the economic reality test are the same as those used in the common law test. However, the economic reality test, because it adopts a "totality of the circumstances" approach, accords less weight to the control factor than does the common law test.

Donovan v. DialAmerica Marketing, Inc.[32] usefully highlights application of the economic reality test. DialAmerica, a company that sold magazine subscription renewals, hired "home researchers" to find the telephone numbers of individuals whose subscriptions had expired or were near expiration.[33] The company provided the researchers with cards that contained information relevant to a subscriber whose telephone number was needed. The researchers, working at home, located the telephone numbers of the persons listed, wrote the numbers on the cards as instructed by DialAmerica, and returned the completed cards to DialAmerica's office.[34] DialAmerica compensated the researchers on a piece-rate basis for each completed card. However, the compensation received by the researcher plaintiffs, when computed on an hourly basis, was less than that required by the FLSA.

DialAmerica claimed that the researchers were not employees under the FLSA but were independent contractors, an assessment shared by the district court. In reaching this conclusion, the district court placed considerable weight on the control factor, observing that DialAmerica had little control over the manner in which the researchers did their work because they were able to work at their own pace, to work when they desired, and to work under whatever conditions they desired.[35] The district court sharply contrasted the company's lack of control over the home researchers with that of the company's "in-house" researchers who labored under "direct and constant supervision."[36]

Under the common law test, with its emphasis on direct control and supervision, the lower court's analysis might have survived

---

30 See, e.g., Usery v. Pilgrim Equip. Co., 527 F.2d 1308, 1311 (5th Cir. 1976); DialAmerica, 757 F.2d at 1382, Selker Bros., 949 F.2d at 1293; Ricketts v. Vann, 32 F.3d 71, 74 (4th Cir. 1994) (citing Haywood v. Barnes, 109 F.R.D. 568, 587 (E.D.N.C. 1986)).

31 Pilgrim Equip. Co., 527 F.2d at 1311 (emphasis in original).

32 757 F.2d 1376.

33 Id. at 1379.

34 Id. at 1380.

35 Id.

36 Id.

appellate review. Yet, as the Third Circuit Court of Appeals held, the analysis did not comport with the economic reality test. As to the issue of control, the appellate court observed that because a lack of direct supervision is inherent to home work, this fact was not dispositive in determining the researchers' status under the FLSA.[37] Factors that did indicate that the researchers were employees included their negligible investment in materials or equipment for the job, a small opportunity for profit and loss, the largely unskilled nature of the job, the relative permanence of their working relationship, and the provision of services that were an integral part of DialAmerica's business.[38]

With respect to the last factor, which considers whether the service rendered is an integral part of the alleged employer's business, the inquiry properly focuses on the nature of the work performed by the workers and not on the percentage of total work that they accomplish.[39] As long as the work performed represents an "essential part" of the alleged employer's business, this factor weighs in favor of employee status.[40] In other words, work can qualify as integral even if the worker performs very little of it.[41]

Two other factors merit some additional discussion.

The permanence of the working relationship factor has been particularly difficult to apply, especially as it relates to seasonal workers. Several FLSA cases have involved transient work forces, such as migrant farm workers, and have considered whether the transient quality of the work undermines the permanency of the working relationship.

Courts have generally taken the view that in evaluating the permanency factor in such cases, the seasonal nature of the work is not dispositive.[42] Instead, courts have found a sufficiently permanent

---

[37] DialAmerica, Inc., 757 F.2d at 1384.

[38] Id. at 1383.

[39] Id. at 1385.

[40] Id. See also Brock v. Superior Care, Inc., 840 F.2d 1054, 1061 (2d Cir. 1988) (the services of nurses "are the most integral part" of a business that refers health-care personnel, primarily nurses, to individual patients, hospitals and other health care institutions); Harper v. Wilson, 302 F.Supp.2d 873, 879–80 (N.D. Ill. 2004) (work of person responsible for supervising security guards is integral to alleged employer in the business of providing security guards).

[41] In *DialAmerica*, for example, the telephone numbers located by the home researchers accounted for only 4 percent to 5 percent of the total number of telephone numbers required by the company. DialAmerica, Inc., 757 F.2d at 1385. However, the home researchers' work—locating phone numbers—was deemed integral to DialAmerica's business because the work fit within the company's primary purpose of locating subscriber phone numbers. Id.

[42] See, e.g., Sec'y of Labor v. Lauritzen, 835 F.2d 1529, 1537 (7th Cir. 1987), cert. denied, Lauritzen v. McLaughlin, 488 U.S. 898 (1988) (observing that "[m]any seasonal businesses necessarily hire only seasonal employees, but that fact alone does

relationship where workers return to a farm from season to season.[43] Thus, in *Secretary of Labor v. Lauritzen*,[44] the Seventh Circuit observed that the fact that migrant farmers returned to the alleged employer year after year indicated permanency. Some courts also consider, for purposes of the permanency inquiry, whether the relationship between the workers and the alleged employer is exclusive.[45] In *Charles v. Burton*,[46] the court held that the permanency factor weighed against a determination that the workers were employees because, although they had returned to the defendant's farm for a couple of years, they had worked for another farm during the season as well.

Another factor that has received increased attention relates to the concept of entrepreneurial opportunity. Both the common law test and the economic realities test involve inquiries into the extent to which the putative employee enjoys the opportunity to exercise entrepreneurial skill to manage the job in a manner that would affect potential losses or profits. The Restatement of Employment Law has incorporated the concept fully.[47] An interesting question that has emerged in cases dealing with this factor is whether, in deciding if the putative employee exercises enough entrepreneurial control to no

---

not convert seasonal employees into seasonal independent contractors"); Haywood v. Barnes, 109 F.R.D. 568, 589 (E.D.N.C. 1986) (commenting that the "fact that the plaintiffs and the farm labor contractors worked only for the [defendant's farm] on a seasonal basis does not vitiate the essential permanency of the relationship with the defendants").

[43] See, e.g., Lauritzen, 835 F.2d at 1537 (stating that "[o]ne indication of permanency . . . is the fact that it is not uncommon for the migrant families to return year after year"). But see Donovan v. Brandel, 736 F.2d 1114, 1117 (6th Cir. 1984) (commenting that the return of migrant workers "is no more indicative of the employment relationship than when a businessman repeatedly uses the same subcontractors due to satisfaction with past performance").

[44] Lauritzen, 835 F.2d at 1537.

[45] See, e.g., Luna v. Del Monte Fresh Produce (Southeast), Inc., 13 Wage & Hour Cas.2d (BNA) 883 (N.D. Ga. Mar. 19, 2008) (indicating that the permanency factor is satisfied where workers labored exclusively for defendant and returned for multiple seasons); Barrientos v. Taylor, 917 F.Supp. 375, 384 (E.D. N.C. 1996) (stating that " 'the relationship is permanent to the extent that the migrants worked only for defendants during the season' ") (quoting Haywood v. Barnes, 109 F.R.D. 568, 589 (E.D. N.C. 1986)); see also Cavazos v. Foster, 822 F.Supp. 438, 444 (W.D. Mich. 1993) (noting that the relationship between the migrant laborers and the defendant was exclusive and that the laborers "tend[ed] to return to [the defendant's] employment year after year").

[46] 169 F.3d 1322 (11th Cir. 1999).

[47] "An individual renders services as an independent businessperson and not as an employee when the individual in his or her own interest exercises entrepreneurial control over important business decisions including whether to hire and where to assign assistant, whether to purchase and where to deploy equipment, and whether and when to provide service to other customers." Restatement of Employment Law, § 1.01(b).

longer be considered an employee, actual as opposed to apparent control must be established.[48]

In addition to the FLSA, courts routinely invoke the economic reality test in employment cases arising under the FMLA,[49] the OSH Act,[50] and the Employee Polygraph Protection Act (EPPA).[51] Courts have also applied the economic reality test in the context of Title VII,[52] the Age Discrimination in Employment Act (ADEA),[53] and the Americans with Disabilities Act (ADA).[54] It must be noted, however, that courts do not always agree on the appropriate test to use to evaluate a worker's status under some of these statutes. In addition, a preference for a given test can change over time. Consider, for

---

48 See FedEx Home Delivery, 361 N.L.R.B. No. 55 (2014) (finding that in deciding whether drivers were employees covered under the National Labor Relations Act, actual but not theoretical entrepreneurial opportunity was relevant).

49 See, e.g., Demers v. Adams Homes of Nw. Fla., Inc., 155 Lab.Cas. (CCH) P35,363 (M.D. Fla. Nov. 7, 2007) (stating that "[w]hen determining whether one is an 'employee' under the FMLA, courts apply the same test used with regard to the Fair Labor Standards Act. . . . That test is the 'economic realities' test."); Nichols v. All Points Transp. Corp. of Mich., Inc., 364 F.Supp.2d 621, 630 (E.D. Mich. 2005) (concluding that the economic reality test is the appropriate test for determining whether workers are "employees" covered by the FMLA because "the FMLA incorporates, by reference, the definition of 'employee' found in the FLSA").

50 See, e.g., Loomis Cabinet Co. v. OSHRC, 20 F.3d 938, 941–42 (9th Cir. 1994) (approving the use of the economic reality test to determine if an employment relationship exists under the OSH Act); see also Van Buren-Madawaska Corp., 13 OSH Cas. (BNA) 2157, 2158–61 (1989) (using the economic reality test to determine the employee status of workers in a road construction company that contracts services to landowners); Griffin & Brand of McAllen, Inc., 6 OSH Cas. (BNA) 1702, 1703 (1978) (noting the use of the economic reality test to determine if an employment relationship exists for purposes of the OSH Act).

51 29 U.S.C. §§ 2001 et seq. See also Watson v. Drummond Co., 436 F.3d 1310, 1316 (11th Cir. 2006) (stating that because of "the substantial similarity between the definitions of 'employer' in the EPPA and in the FMLA and the FLSA, we find the economic reality test appropriate [to the EPPA] as well"); id. (observing that "[t]he economic reality test has . . . been the prevailing approach for courts determining whether a polygraph examiner is an 'employer' for the purposes of the EPPA").

52 See, e.g., Armbruster v. Quinn, 711 F.2d 1332, 1340 (6th Cir. 1983) (overruled on other grounds); Dean v. American Fed'n of Gov't Employees, Local 476, 509 F.Supp.2d 39, 54 (D.D.C. 2007) (stating that for purposes of determining employee status under Title VII, "the D.C. Circuit has instructed that courts should engage in an 'analysis of the "economic realities" of the work relationship,' which involves 'consideration of all of the circumstances surrounding the work relationship' ") (quoting Spirides v. Reinhardt, 613 F.2d 826, 831 (D.C. Cir. 1979)). But see Maltby & Yamada, supra note 8, at 250 (stating that "the factor of economic dependence has been marginalized or even swept aside by courts that have claimed to adopt the economic realities test" in the context of federal discrimination statutes).

53 29 U.S.C. §§ 621 et. seq. See, e.g., Schmidt v. Ottawa Med. Ctr., P.C., 322 F.3d 461, 463 (7th Cir. 2003) (stating that "[t]o determine whether an organization has enough 'employees' to qualify as an 'employer' under the ADEA, we have . . . decided that the economic realities of the workplace, rather than mechanical adherence to state-law corporate forms, shall define the relationship between the parties").

54 42 U.S.C. §§ 12101 et seq. See, e.g., Hollingsworth-Hanlon v. Alliance Française, No. 97 C 6841, 1998 WL 341630, at *3 (N.D. Ill. June 24, 1998) (adopting the economic reality test in the context of the ADA).

example, that the preferred test used by some courts to determine employee status under Title VII and the ADEA has shifted from the common law test to the economic reality test to the hybrid test.[55]

The rise of the on-demand, or gig economy, has provided yet another context in which to apply the economic realities test. The gig economy refers to economic arrangements in which companies provide online platforms to help individuals sell products and services to each other.[56] Companies such as Uber and Lyft are noted as common examples. Are the individuals who sign up to become drivers with these types of companies, employees or independent contractors? A recent case involving Uber provides some insight into how courts are applying the test in this context.

In *O'Connor v. Uber Technologies*,[57] a group of Uber drivers claimed that they were employees and not independent contractors and thus were eligible for various statutory protections under the California Labor Code. In denying Uber's motion for summary judgment, on the ground that the issue involved a mixed question of law and fact that was to be decided at trial, the court noted the importance of the issue of control, but also referred to set of "secondary indicia" relevant to the employee/independent contractor determination.[58] The secondary indicia included the factors usually considered when applying the economic realities test. Interestingly, the court concluded by casting doubt as to whether the existing test is likely to provide a satisfactory answer in this context. In particular the court noted that the existing test "evolved under an economic model very different from the new 'sharing economy,' " and that some of the factors the test considers are outmoded, while other factors such as "the proportion of revenues generated and shared by the respective parties, their relative bargaining power, and the range of alternatives available to each" are ignored.[59]

1.1.1.2.3 The Hybrid Test

The hybrid test combines elements of both the common law test and the economic reality test. Most of the federal circuits have had occasion to adopt the hybrid test in some employment law contexts,[60] especially in employment discrimination cases under Title VII and

---

[55] See Maltby & Yamada, supra note 8, at 248–252.

[56] See Benjamin Means & Joseph Seiner, Navigating the Uber Economy, 49 U.C. Davis Law Review 1511 (2016).

[57] 82 F. Supp. 3d 1133 (N.D. Cal. 2015).

[58] Id. at 1139.

[59] Id. at 1153.

[60] See, e.g., Wilde v. County of Kandiyohi, 15 F.3d 103, 105 (8th Cir. 1994) (commenting that "nearly every appellate court has applied a test described as a hybrid of the common-law test and the economic realities test").

the ADEA.[61] Courts using this test consider the economic realities of the working relationship but generally accord particular weight to the putative employer's right to control the work.[62] As a result, the line between the hybrid test and the common law test can be extremely murky.[63] As the Tenth Circuit observed in *Lambertsen v. Utah Dep't of Corrections*, the blurring of the two tests reflects that they both emphasize the right of the putative employer to control the means and manner by which the work is performed while simultaneously allowing for consideration of other factors.[64]

Assuming a substantive difference does exist between the application of the two tests, commentators have suggested that the Supreme Court's 1993 decision in *Darden* may have led some courts to retreat from their use of the hybrid test in employment discrimination cases.[65] The *Darden* Court held that when a statute, such as ERISA, does not usefully define the term "employee," the definition should accord with common law agency principles.[66] Because the Court's interpretation of the definition of "employee" in ERISA appears largely identical to the definition of "employee" in Title VII[67] and the ADEA,[68] some lower courts have concluded that

---

[61] See Stephen F. Befort, Revisiting the Black Hole of Workplace Regulation: A Historical and Comparative Perspective of Contingent Work, 24 Berkeley J. Emp. & Lab. L. 153, 167 (2003) (commenting that "[d]uring the 1970s and 1980s, most federal courts of appeal adopted a 'hybrid' test for determining employee status under federal discrimination statutes"); Maltby & Yamada, supra note 8, at 250 (commenting that the hybrid test "became the favored standard for claims under both Title VII and the ADEA").

[62] See, e.g., Lambertsen v. Utah Dep't of Corr., 79 F.3d 1024, 1028 (10th Cir. 1996). See also Befort, supra note 61, at 167 (commenting that "[u]nder the hybrid approach, courts examine the economic realities of the work relationship, but with particular emphasis on 'the employer's right to control the "means and manner" of the worker's performance' ") (internal citation omitted); Katherine V.W. Stone, Legal Protections for Atypical Employees: Employment Law for Workers without Workplaces and Employees without Employers, 27 Berkeley J. Emp. & Lab. L. 251, 280 (2006) (commenting that the hybrid test "uses a multi-factored economic realities test but gives particular weight to the employer's right to control the employee's work").

[63] Maltby & Yamada, supra note 8, at 254 (noting the substantial similarity between the hybrid test and the common law test); Rubinstein, supra note 8, at 168–69 (stating that "[s]everal circuits . . . have noted that there is 'little discernible difference between the hybrid test and the common law agency test' ") (quoting Frankel v. Bally, Inc., 987 F.2d 86, 90 (2d Cir. 1993)).

[64] 79 F.3d 1024, 1028 (10th Cir. 1996).

[65] See, e.g., Befort, supra note 61, at 167; Maltby & Yamada, supra note 8, at 253.

[66] Darden, 503 U.S. at 322–23 (citing Cmty. for Creative Non-Violence v. Reid, 490 U.S. 730, 739–40 (1989)).

[67] See, e.g., Lambertsen, 79 F.3d at 1028; Kellam v. Snelling Personnel Servs., 866 F.Supp. 812, 814 (D. Del. 1994), aff'd, 65 F.3d 162 (3d Cir. 1995).

[68] Frankel, 987 F.2d at 90.

they must apply a common law test to determine employee status under these statutes as well.[69]

1.1.1.3 Critical Appraisals of the Employee/Independent Contractor Distinction

The various tests used to determine employee status have prompted considerable criticism from both the courts and commentators. Some of the criticism reflects the unpredictability of the tests, which in turn highlights their open-ended nature. With so many factors incorporated into each test, it is exceedingly difficult to predict how a judge will ultimately decide.[70] Also, to the extent that application of different tests to the same fact pattern often leads to the same outcome, it has been suggested that the time has arrived to scrap the various tests and develop one uniform approach to determine employee status.[71]

Some critics of the existing legal distinction between employee and independent contractor have taken aim at the emphasis on supervisory control that undergirds the common law test and the hybrid test.[72] They argue that even as some workers do not technically qualify as employees, because they are not subject to supervisory control, this fact should not matter if they depend on

---

[69] See Maltby & Yamada, supra note 8, at 250 (collecting cases).

[70] See, e.g., Carlson, supra note 24, at 361 (observing that "the control test sometimes leads to uncertain results, because an employer's control over one aspect of the employment relationship may be offset by a lack of control over some other aspect"); Hiroshi Motomura, Comment, Employees and Independent Contractors Under the National Labor Relations Act, 2 Indus. Rel. L.J. 278, 295 (1977) (commenting that the right-to-control test has failed to yield "a coherent, well-formulated set of principles for distinguishing independent contractors and employees").

[71] See, e.g., EEOC v. Zippo Mfg. Co., 713 F.2d 32, 35–36 (3d Cir. 1983) (stating that the lack of a universal approach "breeds ambiguity and confusion requiring courts to assess a broad spectrum of facts in their quest to clarify and determine who is and who is not an employee"); Report & Recommendation of the Commission on the Future of Worker-Management Relations 36, 38 (1994) (proposing the adoption of a unitary "economic realities" test for defining employee status to be "appl[ied] . . . across the board in employment and labor law"); Jonathan P. Hiatt, Policy Issues Concerning the Contingent Work Force, 52 Wash. & Lee L. Rev. 739, 750 (1995) (arguing that "there should be a single definition applicable in all employment and labor law contexts that would recognize the distinction between an employee and an independent contractor in a more direct, less manipulable manner").

[72] See, e.g., Michael C. Harper, Defining the Economic Relationship Appropriate for Collective Bargaining, 39 B.C. L. Rev. 329, 335 (1998) (observing that the right-to-control test enables employers "to exclude from the Act's coverage workers, such as traveling sales personnel, delivery drivers and taxicab drivers, whose mobility makes direct supervision infeasible"); Hiatt, supra note 71, at 749–50 (discussing how companies engaged in contract hiring manipulate the control test); Marc Linder, Towards Universal Worker Coverage Under the National Labor Relations Act: Making Room for Uncontrolled Employees, Dependent Contractors, and Employee-Like Persons, 66 U. Det. L. Rev. 555, 594–96 (1989) (discussing how taxi companies manipulate the control test to deny collective bargaining rights to leased taxi drivers).

their putative employer for their economic well-being.[73] A proposed solution to help address this concern is to create a *dependent contractor* category that would confer employment rights on workers who are "economically so dependent on the entities for which they work that they are effectively precluded from competing as capital accumulators."[74] Such an approach recognizes that even though some workers may not fit the traditional definition of an employee, they also do not possess the type of skill, capital, or bargaining power that characterizes independent contractors.

1.1.2 Individuals Who Cannot Be Employed

Some individuals are prohibited from entering into an employment relationship. The reasons vary depending on the type of individual involved. In this section we discuss two kinds of individuals who cannot be considered "employees."

1.1.2.1 Children

A variety of federal and state laws impose limits on the employability of children. These laws are generally intended to protect the educational opportunities of youths and to prohibit their employment in jobs and under conditions detrimental to their general welfare.

At the federal level, for example, the FLSA regulates the employment of children.[75] Under the FLSA the employment of children under the age of 14 is generally prohibited, while children ages 14 and 15 are allowed to work in some limited types of jobs

---

[73] See, e.g., Marc Linder, Dependent and Independent Contractors in Recent U.S. Labor Law: An Ambiguous Dichotomy Rooted in Simulated Statutory Purposelessness, 21 Comp. Lab. L. & Pol'y J. 187, 201 (1999) ("As long as employers control the working conditions that workers want improved, why should it matter whether they tell them how to work?"); Carlson, supra note 24, at 299 ("The difficulty of defining 'employee' . . . leads to what ought to have been the first question for legislators: why should employee status matter at all?").

[74] Linder, supra note 72 at 601; see also Maltby & Yamada, supra note 8, at 266 (suggesting the use of the dependent contractor category in the context of discrimination statutes such that some independent contractors would be covered); Charles J. Morris, A Blueprint for Reform of the National Labor Relations Act, 8 Admin. L.J. Am. U. 517, 562 (1994) (recommending coverage of dependent contractors under the NLRA to apply to "individuals [who] exhibit a dependent economic relationship to a single company not unlike that of wage-earners"); Henry H. Perritt, Jr., Should Some Independent Contractors Be Redefined as "Employees" Under Labor Law?, 33 Vill. L. Rev. 989, 1032–34 (1988) (discussing the "dependent contractor" concept in Canadian law); Stone, supra note 62, at 284 (arguing in favor of an "expansive definition of 'employee'" that would encompass "dependent independent contractors" for purposes of various employment laws including unemployment insurance, workers' compensation, minimum wage, family and medical leave, and discrimination protection).

[75] A more detailed description of the FLSA's child labor provisions can be found infra in Section 5.1.2.2.3.

outside of school hours. The employment of children between the ages of 16 and 17 is lawful except in occupations deemed to be hazardous as classified by the Secretary of Labor.[76] Every state has also enacted child labor laws as well.[77] When both the FLSA and a state law apply, the law setting the higher standards must be observed.

Despite the general prohibition on employing children, the employment of children is widespread in certain industries, since both federal and state laws provide plenty of opportunities for lawful child employment. The rationale for allowing the employment of young children is in part the belief that children benefit from some kind of work experience, particularly when such experience occurs in fairly safe environments and under the supervision of someone who cares for the child, such as a parent. The safety of employment in family businesses, however, has been challenged by recent data. A report by the Bureau of Labor Statistics concludes that regardless of industry, children employed in family businesses face a significantly higher risk of injury as compared to other youths.[78]

The fact that in general children cannot be legally employed, however, has not precluded courts from finding that a child is a covered employee for purposes of other statutes. For example, a finding that the child is covered under worker's compensation laws allows children injured at work to collect benefits under the state's workers' compensation program without proof of employer negligence.[79]

In addition to the protections provided under both federal and state law, employment contracts with children could be challenged on contract common law principles. For example, contracts involving children could be voided on grounds of incapacity. The contractual incapacity argument has been raised in cases involving challenges by minors to employment contracts requiring them to arbitrate employment disputes.[80]

---

76 29 U.S.C. § 203(1).

77 See, e.g., Ala.Code 1975 § 25 8–36; Conn. Gen. Stat. Ann. § 31–23. For a useful summary of the various state child labor laws see, Selected State Child Labor Standards Affecting Minor Under 18 in Non-Farm Employment as of January 1, 2017, available at https://www.dol.gov/whd/state/nonfarm.htm.

78 U.S. Dept. of Labor, Bureau of Statistics, Report on the Youth Labor Force 58 (2000).

79 See, e.g., Jensen v. Sport Bowl Inc., 469 N.W.2d 370, 373 (S.D. 1991).

80 See, e.g., Sheller by Sheller v. Frank's Nursery & Crafts, Inc., 957 F.Supp. 150 (N.D. Ill. 1997); Stroupes v. Finish Line, Inc., No. 1:04–cv–133, 2005 WL 5610231 (E.D. Tenn. Mar. 16, 2005).

1.1.2.2 Undocumented Workers

Another group of individuals who are not allowed employment are undocumented workers. Unlike the prohibitions regarding child labor, the laws regarding undocumented workers are intended not for their own well-being, but for the economic protection of other workers. In particular, prohibiting the employment of undocumented workers limits the available labor pool, likely protecting the wages of U.S. workers.

The Immigration Reform and Control Act (IRCA), which applies to all employers, regardless of size or industry, prohibits employers from knowingly hiring or retaining workers who are "unauthorized aliens."[81] IRCA provides civil penalties (ranging from $250 to $2,000 for each worker hired and up to $10,000 for subsequent violations),[82] where a person hires, recruits or refers for a fee "for employment in the United States an alien knowing the alien is an unauthorized alien." IRCA also provides for a criminal fine of $3,000 and six months imprisonment, in cases involving a pattern or practice of violations.[83]

IRCA requires employers to ask employees to provide proof that they are either citizens or aliens allowed to work within the U.S. Although the employer is required to obtain and keep documents establishing the individual's legal status, the employer is not required to check the authenticity of the documents. Courts have noted that the legislative history of IRCA indicates that Congress intended to minimize the burden and the risk placed on the employer in the verification process.[84]

Despite IRCA's efforts to minimize the employment of undocumented workers, many undocumented workers do work. There exist strong pernicious incentives for the hiring of undocumented workers. Undocumented workers might be perceived to be less likely to complain about lower wages, violations of employment laws, and generally poor working conditions. Accordingly, employers might prefer to hire undocumented workers, particularly in certain industries. Thus, an issue that has become increasingly contentious is the applicability of various employment laws to undocumented workers. In *Hoffman Plastic Compounds Inc.*

---

[81] Immigration Reform and Control Act of 1986, 8 U.S.C. §§ 1324a et seq.

[82] Id. at § 1324a(e)(4)(a).

[83] Id. at § 1324a(f)(1).

[84] See, e.g., Collins Food Intl., Inc. v. INS, 948 F.2d 549 (9th Cir. 1991) (finding that an employer's failure to check the back of a social security card presented by a prospective employee, does not amount to constructive knowledge of the individual's illegal status).

v. NLRB,[85] the U.S. Supreme Court significantly limited the protections available to undocumented workers under the National Labor Relations Act (NLRA).[86] According to the Court, awarding back pay to an undocumented worker who was terminated for engaging in statutorily protected union organizing activity was contrary to federal immigration policy as expressed in IRCA.

The application of the Court's reasoning in *Hoffman* to other federal statutes and even to other remedies under the NLRA is unclear. The Court in *Hoffman* did not overrule an earlier decision in which the Court had found that undocumented workers are considered "employees" for purposes of the NLRA,[87] and thus it would appear to be the case that such workers are entitled to other protections and remedies under the NLRA.

Lower courts that have considered the issue have refused to extend the *Hoffman* rationale to actions under the FLSA. For example, in *Lucas v. Jerusalem Cafe.*,[88] the court held that undocumented restaurant workers were not precluded from seeking relief under the FLSA on unpaid minimum wage and overtime claims. Similarly, the Wage and Hour Division of the Department of Labor has indicated its intent to enforce the various laws over which it has jurisdiction without regard to the immigration status of the individual claimant, given that one of the key concerns the Supreme Court expressed in *Hoffman*—the awarding of back pay "for years of work not performed, for wages that could not lawfully have been earned"—does not apply to claims where the work has been actually performed.[89]

Courts have been similarly reluctant to extend the rationale in *Hoffman* to employment discrimination actions under Title VII. Courts taking this limited view of *Hoffman* point out that, unlike the NLRA, Title VII depends heavily on private enforcement, which would be less effective if back pay remedies were to be precluded.[90]

At the state level, the issue of whether an employee's undocumented status affect their ability to enforce workplace protective legislation has faced a variety of responses. While undocumented employees have been permitted to pursue certain

---

[85] 535 U.S. 137 (2002).

[86] 29 U.S.C. §§ 151 et seq.

[87] Sure-Tan, Inc. v. NLRB, 467 U.S. 883 (1984).

[88] 721 F.3d 927 (8th Cir. 2013).

[89] U.S. Dept. of Labor Fact Sheet #48, Application of U.S. Labor Laws to Immigrant Workers: Effect of Hoffman Plastics Decision on Laws Enforced by the Wage and Hour Division (Jan. 13, 2002, revised July 2008).

[90] See, e.g., Rivera v. NIBCO Inc., 384 F.3d 822 (9th Cir. 2004), cert. denied, 544 U.S. 905 (2005).

claims against employers,[91] their ability to pursue workers' compensation claims have been questioned.[92]

In addition to the federal law issues discussed above, the status of undocumented workers as employees is increasingly being affected by state law. In recent years, states and local governments have become actively involved in enacting regulations regarding the employability of undocumented workers by state contractors. Various state laws prohibit the employment of undocumented workers in state financed projects,[93] imposing a variety of penalties on employers who violate such laws.[94]

§ 1.2 Who Is an Employer?

Not everyone who works is an employee, and not everyone who pays for the services of another is an employer. The answer to the question of who is an employer, however, is critical in delineating the reach of a statute and in assigning liability for violations of the law. As in the case of defining who is an employee, the answer depends on the particular context, as different statutes define the term differently.

The definition of the term employer is primarily litigated in two types of situations. First, in some cases it is not clear whether a worker within an organization should be classified as an "employee" or an "employer." Second, sometimes there might be more than one "employer" and thus liability for statutory violations might fall on more than one entity.

---

91 See Tyson Foods. Inc. v. Guzman, 116 S.W. 3d. 233 (Tex. App. 2003) (rejecting employer's argument that the worker's immigration status precluded an award for damages due to loss earning capacity).

92 See Reinforced Earth Company v. Workers' Compensation Appeal Board, 810 A. 2d 99 (Pa, 2002) (holding that while an injured undocumented worker was entitled to medical benefits, temporary total disability benefits could be terminated due to immigration statues).

93 For example, a Colorado statute makes it illegal for a state agency to "enter into or renew a public contract for services with a contractor who knowingly employs or contracts with an illegal alien to perform work under the contract or who knowingly contracts with a subcontractor who knowingly employs or contracts with an illegal alien to perform work under the contract," Colo. Rev. Stat. Ann. § 8–17.5–102(1). Similarly, a Pennsylvania statute provides that "No person shall knowingly employ, or knowingly permit, the labor services of an illegal alien" on state financed projects. 43 Pa. Const. Stat. § 166.3.

94 For example, under Tennessee's law, employers that employ undocumented workers are barred from contracts with the state for a one-year period. Tenn. Code Ann. tit. 12 ch. 3, 309(c). Pennsylvania law requires state contractors violating the prohibition to repay the loan or grant and prevents them from receiving another grant or loan for two years. 43 Pa. Const. Stat. § 166.5.

1.2.1 The Employee/Employer Distinction

As discussed in the previous sections, sometimes it is difficult to decide whether individuals are "employees" or "independent contractors," or whether they cannot be deemed at all to be employees, because of their age (as in the case of children) or their undocumented status. Yet another distinction which at times becomes problematic is whether individuals are to be considered "employers" rather than "employees."

That is the case, for example, in situations involving individuals with ownership interest in a firm, such as partners.[95] One context in which the definition of the term employer is of critical importance is in cases involving the "small" employer exemption. Most federal and state employment laws exempt from coverage small employers. For example, Title VII covers only employers with more than fifteen employees,[96] and the Age Discrimination in Employment Act applies only to employers with twenty or more employees.[97]

Thus, it sometimes becomes critical to determine whether an employer employs the statutorily required number of employees, so as to be covered by a particular statute. This was the question raised in *Clackamas Gastroenterology Associates v. Wells*,[98] where the plaintiff was terminated from her job with the defendant, a medical clinic organized as a professional corporation under state law. The plaintiff brought suit alleging unlawful discrimination on the basis of disability under the Americans with Disabilities Act (ADA). The defendant moved for summary judgment, arguing that it was not an "employer" and thus not a "covered entity" within the meaning of the ADA because it did not have the requisite "15 or more employees for the 20 weeks required by the statute."[99] The basis for this argument, according to the defendant, was that its four physician-shareholders should not be counted as employees for purposes of determining whether the defendant was a covered entity.

Relying on the "economic reality" test, the defendant successfully argued before the federal district court that its four-physician shareholders should be regarded as "partners" and not as "employees" within the meaning of the ADA.[100] The U.S. Court of

---

95 See, e.g., EEOC v. Sidley Austin Brown & Wood, 315 F.3d 696 (7th Cir. 2002), (discussing whether partners at a law firms were employees for purposes of the Age Discrimination in Employment Act). See also, Leonard Bierman & Rafael Gely, So, You Want to Be a Partner at Sidley & Austin?, 40 Hous. L. Rev. 969 (2003).

96 42 U.S.C. § 2000e(b).

97 29 U.S.C. § 630(b).

98 538 U.S. 440 (2003).

99 Id. at 442.

100 Id.

Appeals for the Ninth Circuit reversed, finding that the four-physician shareholders could not be treated as partners due to the professional corporation status of their practice.[101] The Supreme Court, however, reversed and remanded, adopting instead the EEOC's guidelines on the issue of who is an employee and when partners qualify as employees. The EEOC guidelines, which the Court noted properly focus on the "touchstone" issue of control, rely on six key factors: (1) whether the organization can hire or fire the individual or set the rules and regulations of the individual's work; (2) whether and to what extent the organization supervises the individual's work; (3) whether the individual reports to someone higher in the organization; (4) whether and to what extent, the individual is able to influence the organization; (5) whether the parties intended that the individual be an employee, as expressed in written agreements or contracts; and, (6) whether the individual shares in the profits, losses, and liabilities of the organization.[102]

In adopting the EEOC's approach, the Court noted that neither individual job titles, nor the existence of an "employment agreement" will be determinative, and instead, "all the incidents of the relationship" ought to be considered.[103] The Court remanded the case to the Ninth Circuit, noting that while several of the factors considered under the EEOC guidelines supported the finding that the four physician shareholders were not employees, contrary evidence existed on the record.[104]

1.2.2 Multiple Potential Employers

It is possible for an employee to have more than one employer. Although not entirely a recent development, the cases involving multiple employers have become more common as new work arrangements have developed during the transition of the U.S. economy from manufacturing to service, and more recently to an information-based economy. The adoption of innovative staffing arrangements, such as the use of temporary workers or leased employees, has become increasingly common, as has the subcontracting of certain types of jobs. Where an employment dispute arises in situations involving these types of employment arrangements it becomes critical to determine which of the various employers with whom the employee has a relationship is responsible to the employee.

---

101 Id. at 443.

102 EEOC Compliance Manual § 605:0009.

103 Clackamas, 538 U.S. at 451.

104 Id.

In cases involving leased and temporary workers, courts have generally applied the common law right of control test typically used in the context of the employee/independent contractor question. For example, *Black v. Employee Solutions, Inc.*,[105] involved a leased employee arrangement under which the defendant agreed to hire the employees of a trucking company, provide those employees with workers' compensation coverage, and lease them back to the trucking company. In an action to collect unpaid wages under the state's wage laws, the court found that the defendant was not the employer of the leased employees. The Court noted that no evidence was introduced that the defendant "scheduled, directed or supervised" the leased employees, but instead was only involved in processing the payroll data supplied by the trucking company.

A different and likely more protective approach is used in cases involving violations of the Fair Labor Standards Act (FLSA). In the FLSA context, the issue tends to arise in situations in which an employee clearly has an employment relationship with one employer (the "intermediary" employer), but it is also apparent from the circumstances that the employee is economically dependent on another employer involved in the work (the potential joint employer). In this situation, also known as "vertical" joint employment, the putative joint employer contracts with the intermediary employer to provide workers and possibly to perform some personnel functions such as payroll. The putative employer, however, exercises control over the employee and benefits from the employee's effort. In these cases, the employee may seek to hold both employers liable, particularly if the immediate employer has few resources to pay any judgment.

In determining a joint employment relationship exists, the focus is on the economic realities of the relationships between the employee and the putative joint employer. In assessing the nature of the relationship, courts rely on a series of factors reminiscent of the economic realities factors used (e.g., "whether the alleged employer (1) had the power to hire and fire the employees, (2) supervised and controlled employee work schedules or conditions of employment, (3) determined the rate and method of payment, and (4) maintained employment records.")[106]

---

[105] 725 N.E. 2d 138 (Ind. App. 2000).

[106] See Bonnette v. Cal. Health & Welf. Agency, 704 F.2d 1465 (9th Cir. 1983). In 2017, the Fourth Circuit adopted a different test for determining whether two entities should be treated as joint employers. The new test rejects the "economic realities"-focused test and instead incorporates six other factors: "(1) Whether, formally or as a matter of practice, the putative joint employers jointly determine, share, or allocate the power to direct, control, or supervise the worker, whether by direct or indirect means; (2) Whether, formally or as a matter of practice, the putative joint employers

The joint-employer principle has also been adopted under other employment laws. Department of Labor regulations incorporate the joint-employer principle for purposes of the Family and Medical Leave Act.[107] The Equal Employment Opportunity Commission has adopted an approach similar to that under the FLSA.[108]

jointly determine, share, or allocate the power to—directly or indirectly—hire or fire the worker or modify the terms or conditions of the worker's employment; (3) The degree of permanency and duration of the relationship between the putative joint employers; (4) Whether, through shared management or a direct or indirect ownership interest, one putative joint employer controls, is controlled by, or is under common control with the other putative joint employer; (5) Whether the work is performed on a premises owned or controlled by one or more of the putative joint employers, independently or in connection with one another; and (6) Whether, formally or as a matter of practice, the putative joint employers jointly determine, share, or allocate responsibility over functions ordinarily carried out by an employer, such as handling payroll; providing workers' compensation insurance; paying payroll taxes; or providing the facilities, equipment, tools, or materials necessary to complete the work." Salinas v. Commercial Interior, Inc., 2017 WL 360542 (4th Cir. 2017).

[107] 29 C.F.R. § 825.106.

[108] U.S. Dept. of Labor, Enforcement Guidance: Application of EEO Laws to Contingent Workers Placed by Temporary Employment Agencies and Other Staffing Firms (Dec. 3, 1997).

Chapter 2

JOB SECURITY

For over a century, employees have fought to obtain some form of job security protection. In response, employers have pushed back to limit any encroachments arguing that they should have the unconstrained ability to terminate employees at will. At times, the battle has been fought, literally, on factory shop floors.[1] At other times, the struggle has been fought in the legislative and judicial arenas.[2]

Over the years, legislatures and courts have intervened, at times expanding and at other times limiting the extent of job security protections available to employees. When expanding these protections, courts and legislatures have emphasized the centrality of work in people's lives and the inequality of bargaining power between employers and employees. By contrast, when rejecting attempts by employees to expand their job security rights, courts and legislatures have focused on the need for employers to have the flexibility necessary to manage employees with minimal judicial or legislative interference.

Finding the appropriate policy has been a difficult task, resulting in a complex system of statutes and common law doctrines that places a myriad of restrictions on the ability of employers to terminate their employees at will, but which also embraces the principle of limited governmental intervention in workplace matters. This chapter discusses the three major components of that system: the employment-at-will doctrine; job security protections enacted by statute; and common law job security doctrines.

§ 2.1 The Employment-at-Will Doctrine

Historically, under the employment-at-will doctrine employers were free to terminate the employment relationship "for good cause

---

[1] See Paul Le Blanc, A Short History of the U.S. Working Class: From Colonial Times to the Twenty-First Century, 45–52 (1999) (describing the efforts by the Knights of Labor and other early labor organizations to improve their members' working conditions); Daniel Nelson, Origins of the Sit-Down Era: Worker Militancy and Innovation in the Rubber Industry, 1934–1938, 331–60 in Daniel J. Leab, (ed.), The Labor History Reader (1999) (describing workers' efforts to improve working conditions in the rubber industry).

[2] See Robert A. Gorman & Matthew W. Finkin, Labor Law Analysis and Advocacy 1–8 (2013) (describing the various legal doctrines used by employers to limit the ability of workers to form labor organizations).

or for no cause, or even for bad cause without thereby being guilty of an unlawful act."[3]

An early marker in the development of the at-will doctrine was the publication of Horace G. Wood's 1877 treatise.[4] In his treatise Wood announced: "With us the rule is inflexible, that a general or indefinite hiring is prima facie a hiring at will, and if the servant seeks to make it out a yearly hiring, the burden is upon him to establish it by proof."[5] Although the validity of Wood's assertion that in 1877 the at-will presumption represented the dominant rule in the United States is questionable,[6] it is clear that after the publication of Wood's treatise, the doctrine quickly spread throughout the country.[7]

Over the next several decades, in an environment where "commerce was King [and] laws were tailored to facilitate business,"[8] the at-will doctrine flourished.[9] The doctrine was consistent with the prevailing view of allowing employers unfettered discretion in hiring and firing.[10] Although initially the doctrine was based on notions of freedom of contract, it quickly became grounded on the idea that employers should be allowed to manage their affairs as they wished.[11] During this period, courts embraced the at-will doctrine, turning it from a rebuttable presumption into "a substantive limitation whereby the employment relationship was conclusively at will."[12] Courts at times refused to enforce informal employment contracts, even though it was clear that the parties intended something other than an at-will relationship.[13]

The at-will doctrine is commonly described as a default rule. This implies that unless the parties have agreed that the contract

---

[3] Payne v. Western & Atlantic Railroad, 81 Tenn. 507, 523, 49 Am.Rep. 666 (1884). See also Greene v. Oliver Realty, Inc., 363 Pa.Super. 534, 543, 526 A.2d 1192, 1196 (1987).

[4] Wood, A Treatise on the Law of Master & Servant (1877).

[5] Id. at § 134, p. 272.

[6] See, e.g., Jay M. Feinman, The Development of the Employment At Will Rule Revisited, 23 Ariz. St. L. J. 733 (1991); Theodore J. St. Antoine, You're Fired!, 10 Hum. Rts. Q. 32 (1982).

[7] As to the reasons for the rapid adoption of the doctrine see, e.g., Richard A. Bales, Explaining the Spread of At-Will Employment as an Inter-jurisdictional Race-to-the-Bottom of Employment Standards, 75 Tenn. L. Rev. 453 (2008); Andrew P. Morriss, Exploding Myths: An Empirical and Economic Reassessment of the Rise of Employment At-Will, 59 Mo. L. Rev. 679 (1994).

[8] Greene, 363 Pa.Super. at 544, 526 A.2d at 1196.

[9] Id.

[10] Id.

[11] Id. at 544, 526 A.2d. at 1197.

[12] Id.

[13] See Skagerberg v. Blandin Paper Co. 197 Minn. 291, 266 N.W. 872 (1936) (finding an offer for permanent employment to be nothing more than a contract at will). See also Henry H. Perritt, Employee Dismissal Law and Practice 6 (1984).

will last for a specific duration, or that the employer will only dismiss the employee for cause, or a statute makes it illegal for the employer to terminate employment relationship for a particular reason, the employment relationship is at will.

While as noted above, at some point in our history (perhaps in the late 1800s and early 1900s) it might have been accurate to state that most employees could be terminated for any reason without having recourse to legal relief, that period was short lived and it seems unlikely to be accurate today. Legislatures, initially at the federal level and eventually at the state level, began to enact statutes limiting the ability of employers to fire employees by making certain kinds of terminations illegal. Courts also began to use a variety of common law doctrines to provide employees some measure of job security protection.

Thus, it is clear that currently employers do not enjoy an absolute right to terminate employees regardless of the reason. Instead it is more accurate to conclude that states are providing, along a spectrum, different levels of job security for employees. Some employers face few restrictions, either because they do not fall under the coverage of specific federal employment laws (e.g., small employers) or because they operate in states in which few protections have been adopted either via legislation or by the judiciary. Other employers face a greater set of restrictions, and thus are fairly limited in their ability to terminate employees at will.

In spite of this, courts continue to refer to the at-will doctrine as the default rule. This framework has made it more difficult for employees challenging their dismissals to obtain relief as their claims are seen as contrary to the status quo. When reading the cases and materials in this area, readers are encouraged to think about how the outcome of the cases might vary if the at-will presumption was not there.

§ 2.2 Statutory Protections

Since the first half of the 1900s, federal and state legislatures have enacted a variety of job security protections, constraining the ability of employers to terminate employees. For example, in 1935 Congress enacted the National Labor Relations Act,[14] providing employees the right to form labor unions and to bargain collectively, and prohibiting employers from firing employees for exercising their rights under the statute. In 1964, Congress further limited the ability of employers to terminate employees, by making it illegal for employers to make employment decisions based on race, sex and

---

[14] 29 U.S.C. §§ 151 et seq.

other protected characteristics.[15] Further protections were enacted over the ensuing 40 years, including, for example, protections against employment decisions based on age,[16] disability,[17] and certain family obligations.[18] These statutes also include anti-retaliation protections, making it illegal for employers to take adverse employment action against employees who exercise their statutory rights.

Many state and local governments have also enacted job security protections.[19] These laws vary in scope. Some protect employees against firing for specific activities, such as Alabama's statute prohibiting employers from taking action against employees for being in lawful possession of a firearm,[20] and the Illinois statute outlawing discrimination against employees who smoke on their own time off the employer's premises.[21] Other statutes prohibit discriminating against an employee for "participation in lawful activity off the employer's premises during nonworking hours."[22] Perhaps more forcefully and in direct challenge to the employment-at-will doctrine, Montana enacted legislation prohibiting employers from terminating employees without "good cause."[23] All these legislative efforts limit the ability of employers to terminate the employment relationship, by exposing the employer to liability if the decision to terminate is statutorily prohibited.

§ 2.3 Common Law Protections

In addition to the extensive set of protections enacted by statute, courts in every state have afforded employees protections against termination by relying on a variety of contract-based and tort-based common law doctrines. Starting in 1959 courts in most states began to use fairly traditional common law principles to limit the ability of employers to terminate employees at will. *Petermann v. Teamsters Local 396*,[24] is illustrative. *Petermann* involved the firing of an employee for refusing to provide false testimony before a state

---

[15] Title VII, Civil Rights Act, 42 U.S.C. §§ 2000e–2000e–17.

[16] Age Discrimination in Employment Act, 29 U.S.C. §§ 621–634.

[17] Americans with Disabilities Act, 42 U.S.C. §§ 12101–12213.

[18] Family and Medical Leave Act, 29 U.S.C. §§ 2601–2653.

[19] See James O. Castagnera, Patrick J. Cihon, & Andres P. Morris, Overview of State Laws, 1 Termination of Employment § 2.1 (2017).

[20] 2013 Ala. Acts 283, § 4(c)(2).

[21] 820 Ill. Comp. Stat. Ann. 55/5(a), (b) (Westlaw, current through P.A. 99–502 of the 2016 Reg. Session).

[22] E.g., N. Dakota Cent. Code § 14.02.4–03. The North Dakota statute requires the lawful off-duty activity, not to be "in direct conflict with the essential business-related interests of the employer."

[23] See Mont. Code Ann. §§ 39–2–901–39–2–914. See infra Section 2.7.1 for a detailed discussion of the Montana statute.

[24] 174 Cal.App.2d 184, 344 P.2d 25 (1959).

legislative committee. The court recognized a cause of action for wrongful discharge, holding that the employees who are discharged for reasons contrary to public policy could seek judicial relief.

Over the last 50 years courts have continued to create new common law-based job security protections: (1) contract-based protections, wherein employees challenge their firings on the grounds that the employer has breached an express or implied promise; and, (2) tort-based protections, like the *Petermann* case, in which employees have used traditional tort doctrines to obtain relief following an adverse employment action.

§ 2.4 Contract Based Protections

Employers and employees can enter oral or written contracts, expressly providing job security protections. Courts have also found implied promises of job security based on communications between the parties (e.g., employee handbooks) and the parties' behavior.

2.4.1 Express Contract

Contractual job security protections can arise in situations where: (1) the employer promises not to terminate the employment relationship except for good cause; or (2) the employer promises to hire the employee for a specific/definite period of time. These promises, which might be made independently or in combination, indicate the parties' intent to enter an employment relationship which incorporates some level of job security[25]

2.4.1.1 Just-Cause Contracts

Express written just-cause employment contracts are common among unionized workers in the United States. Almost every collective bargaining agreement includes a provision limiting the employer's ability to terminate employees except for just cause. Such provisions are enforced via the grievance-arbitration process, which is also a common feature of most collective bargaining agreements. Outside the unionized workplace, express written just-cause contracts are less common.[26]

For those employees who do not have written employment agreements, the circumstances under which they can be fired or can quit may be inferred from other written documents or oral

---

[25] Rooney v. Tyson, 91 N.Y.S. 2d 616, 697 N.E. 2d 571 (1998).

[26] See generally Robert Sprague, Invasion of the Social Networks: Blurring the Line Between Personal Life and The Employment Relationship, 20 U. Louisville L. Rev. 1, 19 (2011). Employee handbooks and employment manuals can serve as the basis of a just-cause express contract to the extent that the handbook or manual includes a specific just-cause provision. Handbooks and manuals can also serve as the basis for implied just-cause provisions, see infra Section 2.4.2.1.

statements that may evidence the parties' understanding as to the terms of employment. Cases in which employees have alleged some form of just-cause protection tend to involve statements (either written or oral) that are suggestive of such protection, but which rarely amount to a direct just-cause provision. The key factual determination in such cases hinges on the interpretation of the statement that arguably provides some form of job security.

For example in *Hetes v. Schefman & Miller Law Office*,[27] the plaintiff challenged her dismissal arguing that at the time of her hiring, the employer had made statements that her job was safe as long as "she did a good job." The court of appeals concluded that the jury could have construed the oral representation as a promise to discharge for just cause. In *Shebar v. Sanyo Business Corp.*,[28] the court reversed a grant of summary judgment in favor of the employer, where the company's president told the plaintiff that the company "had never fired, and never intended to fire, a corporate employee whose rank was manager or above," and that he "had a job for the rest of [his] life."[29]

Some courts have expressed concern about finding that such statements are sufficient evidence of intent to create a just-cause employment relationship. For instance, some courts have found statements of this kind to constitute "puffery" and "expressions of hope for a long relationship," which should not be equated with a promise for just-cause employment.[30]

Employers, with varying degrees of success, have raised three basic arguments in cases where employees claim to operate under a just-cause contract: (1) arguments regarding the specificity of the language; (2) arguments regarding the lack of consideration; and (3) arguments regarding the statute of frauds.

In order to successfully establish a just-cause relationship, employees have to show that the employer intended to create a just-cause contract.[31] Employers have argued that this requirement should be strictly construed.[32] For example, in *Rowe v. Montgomery*

---

[27] 152 Mich.App. 117, 118, 393 N.W.2d 577, 578 (1986).

[28] 111 N.J. 276, 282, 544 A.2d 377, 380 (1988).

[29] Id. at 282, 544 A.2d at 380.

[30] Broussard v. Caci Inc.-Federal, 780 F.2d 162, 163 (1st Cir. 1986). See also Rodden v. Savin Hill Enterprises, 33 Mass.L.Rptr. 442 (2016).

[31] See, e.g., Gunderson v. Alliance of Computer Professionals, 628 N.W.2d 173 (Minn. App. 2001); Thompson v. St. Regis Paper Co., 102 Wash.2d 219, 685 P.2d 1081 (1984).

[32] See, e.g., Rodden v. Savin Hill Enterprises, 33 Mass. L. Rptr. 442 (Sup. Ct. 2016); Muscarella v. Milton Shoe Mfg. Co., 352 Pa.Super. 158, 507 A.2d 430 (1986); Hillesland v. Federal Land Bank Ass'n of Grand Fork, 407 N.W.2d 206 (N.D. 1987).

Ward & Co.,[33] at the time the plaintiff was hired as a sale associate, a manager told her that "as long as [employees] generated sales and were honest . . . they had a job at Wards," and that "about the only way that you could be terminated would be if you failed to make your draw."[34] The court noted that "statements of job security must be clear and unequivocal to overcome the presumption of employment at will" and concluded that the statements involved in this case did not clearly indicate the intent to form a contract for permanent employment.[35]

In addition to requiring clear and definite language, some courts have indicated that for a promise of just-cause employment to be valid, the employee must provide additional consideration beyond simply performing the duties the employee was hired to do.[36] The additional consideration requirement arguably helps to clarify the intent of the parties, by making it clear that the parties were bargaining about the promise of job security.[37]

Finally, in some states employers may assert the statute of frauds to prohibit enforcement of an oral just-cause contract. The statute of frauds bars enforcement of an oral contract that cannot be fully performed within one year from the time the contract was formed.[38] If the employer promised not to fire without just cause more than one year before firing the employee, the statute of frauds would forbid enforcement of the contract in a minority of states. Most states, however, treat oral just-cause employment agreements as capable of being performed within a year because the employer might cease to do business, or either party might terminate the employment within the year.[39] Therefore, the statute of frauds is usually not a defense to enforcement of an oral just cause contract. [40]

---

[33] 437 Mich. 627, 632, 473 N.W.2d 268, 270 (1991).

[34] Id. at 632, 473 N.W.2d at 270.

[35] Id. at 643, 473 N.W.2d at 275.

[36] See, e.g., Murphree v. Alabama Farm Bureau Insurance Co., 449 So.2d 1218 (Ala. 1984); Moody v. Bogue, 310 N.W.2d 655 (Iowa App. 1981).

[37] See, e.g., Buffaloe v. United Carolina Bank, 366 S.E. 2d 918, 89 N.C. App. 693 (N.C. App. 1988). Notice that while the additional consideration requirement has been enforced in cases involving express oral promises of job security, it has been abandoned in cases involving employee handbooks and manuals. See infra Section 2.4.2.1.

[38] Restatement (Second) of Contracts § 110.

[39] See, e.g., Ohanian v. Avis, 779 F.2d 101 (2d Cir. 1985) (finding that because a lifetime/just-cause contract could be performed within a year, it was not within the statute of frauds and thus it was enforceable, even though it was not in writing).

[40] See, e.g., Audiovox Corp. v. Moody, 737 S.W.2d 468 (Ky. App. 1987); UPS v. Rickert, 996 S.W.2d 464 (Ky. 1999). The Supreme Court of Virginia continues to require a writing before enforcing permanent/lifetime employment contracts. See Falls v. Virginia State Bar, 240 Va. 416, 397 S.E.2d 671 (1990) (stating that absent a contract provision so providing, the employee's death, resignation or discharge for

2.4.1.2 Specific Duration Contracts

A second type of promise that could defeat the employment-at-will presumption involves not a promise of just-cause or lifetime employment, but instead a promise of employment for a specific period of time.

Chiodo v. General Waterworks Corp.,[41] offers an example of a specific duration contract. In *Chiodo*, the plaintiff sold his business to defendant, with the understanding that defendant would hire the plaintiff for a ten year period. Three years after the sale, the defendant fired the plaintiff, and the plaintiff sued for breach of contract. The court found that even though the employment contract did not explicitly incorporate a "just cause" provision, such provision could be implied. According to the court, when entering a specific duration contract, the parties must have intended the employee to provide "honest, faithful and loyal service in accordance with his ability."[42]

The *Chiodo* case illustrates the likely consequences of a specific duration contract. First, a promise to hire an employee for a specific time period carries with it a just-cause standard, similar to a contract in which the employer agrees only to terminate the employee for just cause. Second, absent proof of just cause, the employer is bound to retain the employee for the duration of the agreed upon time period, even if it is economically burdensome to the employer to do so.[43] The rationale is that by agreeing to hire the employee for a specific period of time, the employer has assumed the risk of economic downturns, and the court should enforce such a promise. Thus, to the extent that a specific duration contract incorporates by implication a just-cause standard, and also protects the employee against terminations based on economic reasons, specific duration contracts appear to provide a greater degree of job security than the type of contracts discussed in the prior section, express just-cause contracts.

As illustrated in the *Chiodo* case, specific duration contracts clearly limit the *employer's* ability to terminate the employee, since the employer has made an implicit promise not to terminate the employee except for just cause, and also agreed to provide employment to the employee for the specified time period. Do specific duration contracts impose similar obligations on the *employee*? Suppose that the plaintiff in *Chiodo* had decided to quit after only a

---

cause did not constitute performance and therefore the contract could not be performed within a year).

[41] 17 Utah 2d 425, 413 P.2d 891 (1966).

[42] Id. at 426, 413 P.2d at 892.

[43] See, e.g., Boundy v. Arnold Haviland Co., 33 Ohio App.3d 156, 514 N.E.2d 931 (1986); Greene, 363 Pa.Super. 534, 526 A.2d 1192 (1987).

couple of years, having received a more attractive job offer elsewhere. Would an employee in such a situation be liable to the employer for breach? While as a practical matter those cases might be rare, since the employer might easily find a replacement for the employee, the rationale of *Chiodo* suggests that the employee will similarly be in breach in such a case. For example, a Wisconsin state court found that a speech therapist who resigned her position during a one-year contract, was liable for damages equal to the cost of hiring a replacement therapist where the reason for quitting her position was to take a competing job closer to her home.[44] In applying this reasoning, courts have been guarded, by for example, refusing to award lost profits and the recoupment of training costs.[45]

Sometimes it might not be clear whether the employment contract is for a specific period of time. For example, in a number of cases, plaintiffs have attempted to establish the existence of a specific duration contract by relying on the fact that their rate of pay was expressed in a yearly figure. This type of evidence standing alone has generally not been found to be sufficient to establish a definite duration contract.[46] However, in conjunction with other evidence such as the inclusion of additional terms involving a specific time period, rate of pay evidence has been found to be helpful in establishing the parties' intent to enter a definite duration contract.[47]

2.4.1.3 What Is Just Cause?

Once the employee establishes that the employment contract included some measure of job security either by means of a just-cause contract or a contract for a specific time period, the court needs to decide whether the employer had just cause to discharge the employee.[48] Unless the parties' contract specifically defines just cause (an unlikely occurrence), the court is left to craft a definition.

In unionized workplaces, where collective bargaining agreements frequently include just-cause provisions, labor

---

[44] Handicapped Children's Educ. Bd. v. Lukaszewski, 112 Wis.2d 197, 332 N.W.2d 774 (1983).

[45] See Med+Plus Neck and Back Pain Center v. Noffsinger, 726 N.E. 2d 687, 311 Ill. App. 3d 853.

[46] See, e.g., Crawford v. David Shapiro & Co., 490 So.2d 993 (Fl. App. 3 Dist. 1986); Gatins v. NCR Corp., 180 Ga.App. 595, 349 S.E.2d 818 (1986); Dalton v. Union Bank of Switzerland, 520 N.Y.S.2d 764, 134 A.D.2d 174 (1987).

[47] See, e.g., Maines v. Davis, 491 So.2d 1233 (Fla. App. 1st Dist. 1986).

[48] As it has traditionally been the case in the context of labor arbitration cases, where just-cause provisions are common, NC-DSH v. Service Employees Intern. Union Loc. 1107, 2011 WL 1362297 (Dist. Ct. Nev. 2011), courts regularly place the burden of proof in the employer. See e.g., Meehan v. American Media Intern., 214 N.C. app. 445, 712 S.E. 2d 904 (N.C. App. 2011); Turner v. Allstate Insurance Co., 902 F. 2d 1208 (6th Cir. 1990).

arbitrators have developed substantial case law defining just cause.[49] Courts facing the task of defining just cause in the non-unionized sector have relied on the case law developed in the unionized sector. Generally, just cause will be evaluated from an objective standard, thus requiring the employer to demonstrate more than a subjective dissatisfaction with the employee's performance.[50]

Cases involving dismissals based on off-the-job misconduct present some unique considerations. On the one hand, the fact that the alleged misconduct does not relate to the employees' job duties will appear to make it difficult for the employer to establish just cause.[51] On the other hand, where the employee's off-duty conduct affects legitimate employer interests, courts have found just cause to terminate the employees.[52]

An important consideration in evaluating whether a dismissal satisfies the just-cause standard is whether the employee actually engaged in the behavior for which she is being terminated. Courts are divided. The majority of courts have found just cause where the employer reasonably believed that the employee had committed the alleged misconduct, even if the employer turns out to be mistaken.[53] A minority of courts require the employer to establish that the employee actually engaged in the misconduct which led to the termination.[54]

2.4.2 Implied Contract

Representations made by employers regarding job security, disciplinary procedures, and other employee privileges, may be treated as enforceable provisions creating job security protection for employees. These implied-contract protections can arise from employer communications, including oral statements, written

49 See Roger I. Abrams & Dennis R. Nolan, Toward a Theory of "Just Cause" in Employee Discipline Cases, 85 Duke L. J. 594 (1985).

50 See, e.g., McKnight v. Simpson's Beauty Supply, Inc. 86 N.C.App. 451, 358 S.E.2d 107 (1987).

51 See Camille L. Hébert, Employee Privacy Law, § 13–46 (2008).

52 See, e.g., Conway Inc. v. Ross, 627 P.2d 1029 (Alaska 1981) (finding that bar owner lacked good cause to terminate employment contract of topless stripper for engaging in one act of prostitution on her own time, at her own place and through her own contacts); Deegan v. City of Mountain View, 72 Cal.App.4th 37, 84 Cal.Rptr.2d 690 (1999) (upholding the disciplinary action imposed by the city's appeals board on an employee who had used improper language, shouted to a member of the public and misrepresented his authority). See infra Section 3.2.6 for a detailed discussion of off-duty conduct issues.

53 See, e.g., New England Stone v. Conte, 962 A. 2d 30 (2009); Almada v. Allstate Ins. Co., 153 F.Supp.2d 1108 (D. Ariz. 2000); Towson University v. Conte, 384 Md. 68, 862 A.2d 941 (2004); Life Care Centers of America v. Dexter, 65 P.3d 385 (Wyo. 2003).

54 See, e.g., Kern v. Palmer College of Chiropractic, 757 N.W. 2d 651 (2008); Raymond v. Int'l Business Machines Corp., 954 F.Supp. 744 (D. Vt. 1997).

memoranda, and policies expressed in employee handbooks and manuals. Implied contract protections may also arise from the parties' behavior.

2.4.2.1 The Case of Employee Handbooks

With the advent of bureaucratic human resource management, the use of employee handbooks or manuals has become common practice in most businesses.[55] Employee manuals serve a variety of functions, including communicating the firm's policies and reminding employees about the firm's preferences and expectations. Employee manuals also convey practical information such as available employee benefits. Regardless of what function the handbook performs, it is clear that handbooks communicate information to employees, and that they have become a staple of today's workplace.

In a majority of jurisdictions, employees have successfully claimed that promises made in employee manuals and handbooks may give rise to an action for breach of an implied contract.[56] *Woolley v. Hoffmann-La Roche*,[57] is illustrative. Shortly after being hired, the plaintiff received an employee manual intended to serve as "a practical and operating tool in the equitable and efficient administration of [the company's] employee relations program."[58] Five of the eight pages in the manual were devoted to the issue of employment termination, and described in detail the various types of terminations (e.g., layoffs, discharge due to performance, disciplinary discharge, retirement and resignation). After being terminated the plaintiff sued, arguing that he could be fired only for cause, and only after the procedures outlined in the manual had been followed. The Supreme Court of New Jersey reversed the lower court's dismissal of the plaintiff's complaint, concluding that the jury could find the manual to constitute a binding commitment by the employer. In particular, the court found that although the manual did not directly make a just-cause promise, such a promise was implied from the fact that the manual provided an exclusive list of grounds for termination and the procedure to be followed in case of termination. Other courts have followed this reasoning, finding for example that a description of the standards of behavior and performance expected of employees

---

[55] See J. Hoult Verkerke, An Empirical Perspective on Indefinite Term Employment Contracts: Resolving the Just Cause Debate, 1995 Wisc. L. Rev. 837, 861–69 (1995).

[56] Only nine jurisdictions have explicitly rejected, or declined to rule on the employee manual exception. See Kenneth G. Dau-Schmidt & Timothy A. Haley, Governance of the Workplace: The Contemporary Regime of Individual Contract, 28 Comp. Lab. L & Pol'y J. 313, 344 (2006–2007).

[57] 99 N.J. 284, 491 A.2d 1257 (1985).

[58] Id. at 287, 491 A.2d at 1259.

can be construed as adopting a just-cause standard.[59] Courts have also found that where a manual includes a reference to a probationary period, such reference could mean that following such period, the employee can be fired only for cause.[60] As in the case of oral just-cause contracts, however, courts are likely to require that the promises made in the manual be definite and clear, and that they represent directives as opposed to mere guidelines.[61]

Woolley and its progeny appear to create a significant problem for employers who would like to adopt a handbook, but who fear that the handbook will create a binding contract limiting their ability to terminate employees. The court in *Woolley* recognized this concern and explicitly provided employers with a way out. "[I]f the employer, for whatever reason, does not want the manual to be capable of being construed by the court as a binding contract, there are simple ways to attain that goal. All that need be done is the inclusion in a very prominent position of an appropriate statement that there is no promise of any kind by the employer . . . that the employer continues to have the absolute power to fire anyone with or without good cause."[62]

Thus, employers can, by means of a disclaimer, prevent the claim that the manual was intended to create a just-cause employment relationship. To be effective, courts have required the disclaimer to be conspicuous, communicated to the employee in definite, unequivocal and clear language, and to be prominently displayed.[63] Using large print, distinctive font or some other noticeable mark will likely satisfy the conspicuousness requirement.[64]

The communication requirement is met where the disclaimer is signed by the employee or the employee otherwise acknowledges that

---

59 See, e.g., Jones v. Lake Park Care Center, 569 N.W. 2d 369 (Iowa 1997); Havill v. Woodstock Soapstone Co. 783 A. 2d 423; 172 Vt. 625 (2001); Cisco v. King, 205 S.W. 3d 808; 90 Ark. App. 207 (Ct. App. Ark 2005).

60 See, e.g., Wiskotoni v. Michigan Nat. Bank-West, 716 F.2d 378 (6th Cir. 1983); Norris v. Filson Care Home Ltd., No. 89–CA–0599–MR, 1990 WL 393903 (Ky. Ct. App. Jan. 26, 1990).

61 See, e.g., DeFosse v. Cherry Elec. Products, 156 Ill.App.3d 1030, 1035, 510 N.E.2d 141, 144 (2 Dist. 1987) (stating that the language of the policy statement must contain a promise clear enough that an employee would reasonably believe that an offer has been made); Nork v. Fetter Printing Co., 738 S.W.2d 824 (Ky. App. 1987) (same).

62 Woolley, 99 N.J. at 309,491 A.2d at 1271.

63 See, e.g., Britton v. ITT Technical Institute, 2014 WL 1568684 (N.D. Ill. 2014); Hicks v. Methodist Medical Center, 229 Ill.App.3d 610, 593 N.E.2d 119 (1992).

64 See, e.g., Ramirez v. The GEO Group, Inc., 655 F. Supp. 2d 1170 (D. Colo. 2009); Kuhl v. Wells Fargo Bank, 281 P. 3d 716 (Wyo. 2012).

she received and read the statement.[65] This requirement is met, for example, when the disclaimer is part of the employment application form which the employee might sign and return to the employer.[66] The communication requirement also is satisfied where the employee acknowledges via email to have read and reviewed the document.[67]

Courts have also required that the statement be definite, unequivocal and clear. The disclaimer is likely to be found inoperative where it is written in overly legal terms, not readily (or easily) understood by an average employee.[68] Similarly, courts are likely to ignore the disclaimer where the manual is ambiguous. For example, in *Dillon v. Champion Jogbra, Inc.*,[69] in addition to a typical disclaimer ("The policies and procedures contained in this manual constitute guidelines only. They do not constitute part of an employment contract. . . ."),[70] the manual contained a specific progressive discipline system. In reversing the grant of summary judgment for the employer, the Vermont Supreme Court noted that where the manual was itself ambiguous regarding the employees' at-will status, and the employer's employment practices were inconsistent with an at-will employment arrangement, the question of whether the employee's at-will status has been modified should be left to the jury.

Companies frequently modify employee handbooks. Among the provisions employers might seek to modify are those related to job security, including any language that might suggest that employees will be terminated only for cause. Employees have argued that employers may not eliminate promises of job security by simply revising the handbook without paying consideration. Courts have taken three different approaches to this problem.

First, courts in some states allow employers to modify the just-cause provisions of an employee manual with few, if any

---

[65] See, e.g., David v. Nordstrom, 755 F. 3d 1089 (9th Cir. 2014).

[66] See, e.g., Butler v. Walker Power, Inc., 137 N.H. 432, 629 A.2d 91 (1993).

[67] Patterson v. Raymours Furniture Co., 96 F.Supp.3d 71 (Dist. Ct. E.D. NY, 2015). The issue of acknowledging changes to employee handbooks via email has also come up in cases where the employers have adopted arbitration provisions. See Brondyke v. Bridgeport Educ. Inc., 985 F.Supp.2d 1079 (Dist. Ct. S.D. Iowa, 2013) (finding that the employer had communicated its offer to the employee, where the employee received an email alerting her that the company's employee handbook had been updated, that the attachment to the email contained a new binding arbitration provision, and that it was important that employees read the document in its entirety).

[68] See, e.g., Nicosia v. Wakefern Food Corp., 136 N.J. 401, 643 A.2d 554 (1994).

[69] 175 Vt. 1, 819 A.2d 703 (2002).

[70] Id. at 3, 819 A.2d at 705.

constraints.[71] Of the states that allow employers a fairly free hand in modifying employee handbooks, three do so on the grounds that the unilateral contract theory allows employers to make a new offer (e.g., changing a just-cause relationship into an at-will relationship) which employees could accept by coming back to work and continuing to perform their job functions.[72] Several other courts have given employers substantial flexibility to modify manuals on the grounds that such flexibility is needed so that employers can meet changing business conditions.[73] For example, in *Govier v. North Sound Bank*,[74] the employer sought to modify a promise of permanent employment, with language permitting either party to terminate the contract upon 20 days' written notice. The plaintiff refused to sign the new agreement and she was fired. The court found that the employer was permitted to amend the manual unilaterally and that the new policy was effective upon giving actual notice to the employees.

At the other extreme, some courts have treated manual modifications from a bilateral contract perspective, strictly requiring compliance with the elements of contract formation. *Demasse v. ITT Corp.*[75] represents the most restrictive view. Under this approach, a modification will be effective only where: (1) an offer is made to modify the contract; (2) the employee assents to the offer; and, (3) the modification is supported by consideration.

An offer was found to exist where the handbook was the only statement of the terms and conditions of employment, it made clear that all employees were to be made aware of its provisions, and it specifically dealt with the manner of terminating an employee.[76] More generally, an offer has been defined as "a promise to the employee that, if the employee worked for the company, his or her employment would thereafter be governed by those oral or written statements, or both."[77]

In interpreting the assent and consideration requirements, the court in *Demasse* made clear that continuing employment after

---

71 See David Slawson, Unilateral Contracts of Employment: Does Contract Law Conflict with Public Policy? 10 Tex. Wesleyan L. Rev. 9, 10 (2003) (identifying eleven jurisdictions that have taken this view).

72 Sadler v. Basin Elec. Power Coop., 431 N.W.2d 296 (N.D. 1988); Ryan v. Dan's Food Stores, Inc., 972 P.2d 395 (Utah 1998); Progress Printing Co., v. Nichols, 244 Va. 337, 421 S.E.2d 428 (1992).

73 See Slawson, supra note 71 at 11.

74 91 Wash.App. 493, 957 P.2d 811 (1998).

75 194 Ariz. 500, 984 P.2d 1138 (1999).

76 Thompson v. King Entertainment Co., 674 F. Supp. 1194 (Dist. Ct. E.D. Va. 1987).

77 Torosyan v. Boehringer Ingelheim Pharmaceuticals, Inc., 234 Conn. 1, 13, 662 A.2d 89, 96 (1995).

announcement of the handbook modification would not constitute consideration. According to another court, "When an employer issues an employment manual that substantially interferes with an employee's legitimate expectations about the terms of employment, however, the employee's continued work after notice of those terms cannot be taken as conclusive evidence of the employee's consent to those terms.[78]

A few courts have adopted a compromise approach focusing on the reasonableness of the notice provided to employees. Under this view, the employer can modify the handbook if it provides the employee with reasonable notice of the intention to modify the terms of employment.[79] In order to satisfy the reasonable notice requirement, the employer must give actual notice. For example, in *Gaglidari v. Denny's Restaurants Inc.*, the court found that the employer did not satisfy the reasonable notice requirement by leaving copies of the revised policy manual in the employees' lounge.[80] It would appear that to satisfy the reasonable notice requirement, the employer also must give the notice with reasonable advanced time.[81]

2.4.2.2 Implied-in-Fact Contracts

Not only can promises of job security be implied from employee handbooks, but some courts have held that such promises can arise from the overall conduct of the parties. Unlike the cases discussed above in Section 2.4.1.1, involving the creation of just-cause contracts based on the employer's oral representations, implied-in-fact contracts can arise both from the parties' statements, and from other factors, such the duration of the employment relationship and the employee's job performance. When raising this claim, employees argue that the parties' behavior creates a just-cause employment contract.

A seminal case raising this argument is *Pugh v. See's Candies*.[82] After working for the defendant for 32 years, in the course of which the plaintiff moved from a dishwasher to an executive position, he was fired without explanation. The plaintiff challenged his

---

78 Id., 234 Conn. at 19, 662 A.2d at 99. See also Torosyan v. Boehringer Ingelheim Pharmaceuticals, Inc., 234 Conn. 1, 662 A.2d 89 (1995) (finding that to be effective a modification requires an offer and an acceptance).

79 See, e.g., Asmus, 23 Cal.4th 1, 999 P.2d 71; In Re Certified Question, 432 Mich. 438, 443 N.W.2d 112 (1989); Hogue v. Cecil I. Walker Machinery, 189 W.Va. 348, 431 S.E.2d 687 (1993).

80 117 Wash.2d 426, 815 P.2d 1362 (1991).

81 See Asmus, 23 Cal.4th at 18, 999 P.2d at 81 (finding a 60-day notice period reasonable).

82 116 Cal.App.3d 311, 171 Cal.Rptr. 917 (1981).

termination, claiming the existence of a just-cause, implied-in-fact contract. The California Court of Appeals agreed, noting that in determining whether there exists such a contract courts should look at a variety of factors such as the personnel policies of the employer, the employee's longevity of service, actions and communications reflecting expectations of continued employment, and industry practices.[83] In particular, the court found that the duration of the plaintiff's employment, the commendations and promotions he had received, the apparent lack of criticism of his work, and the assurances of continued employment he was given, all suggested the existence of a just-cause employment contract.[84]

While more recently the California Supreme Court appears to have limited the extent of *Pugh*,[85] courts in other states have adopted its reasoning at least to some extent. Various courts look at factors such as those listed in *Pugh* to decide whether an implied contract exists.[86] For example, in *Kestenbaum v. Pennzoil Co.*,[87] the court found the existence of a just-cause contract on the basis of oral statements made by employer at the time of hiring, the acknowledgement by the employer of a policy to dismiss employees only for a good reason, and statements made in the insurance benefits manual consistent with the aforementioned policy.

2.4.3 Promissory Estoppel

Sometimes employees who have been terminated might not be able to identify the type of factors that could establish the existence of an implied-in-fact just-cause contract. For example, an employee might not enjoy the length of service of the plaintiff in *Pugh*, or perhaps the employee cannot point to any statements of job security which might give rise to a just-cause type of contract. The doctrine of promissory estoppel provides a possible avenue of relief in cases where neither an express nor implied just-cause contract can be established.

Promissory estoppel allows courts to enforce promises that induce reasonable detrimental reliance even in the absence of an

---

83 Id. at 925.

84 Id. at 927.

85 See Guz v. Bechtel National, Inc., 24 Cal.4th 317, 341, 8 P.3d 1089, 1104 (2000) (finding that longevity of service alone cannot form the basis of an implied-in-fact just-cause contract).

86 See, e.g., Kestenbaum v. Pennzoil Co., 108 N.M. 20, 766 P.2d 280 (1988) (focusing on statements made at time of hiring, statements by management acknowledging a just-cause promise, and statements in insurance benefits manual); Berube v. Fashion Centre, Ltd., 771 P.2d 1033 (Utah 1989) (finding that an implied just-cause promise may arise from the conduct of the parties, personnel policies, and practices of the particular industry).

87 Kestenbaum, 108 N.M. at 26, 766 P.2d at 286.

enforceable contract supported by consideration. The Restatement (Second) of Contracts provides that "A promise which the promisor should reasonably expect to induce action or forbearance on the part of the promise [. . .] and which does induce such action or forbearance is binding if injustice can be avoided only by enforcement of the promise."[88]

An example of the application of the promissory estoppel doctrine in the employment context is *Grouse v. Group Health Plan*.[89] Having received a job offer from the defendant, the plaintiff gave up his existing job and also rejected a competing offer. The defendant reneged on the job offer and decided to hire someone else, before the plaintiff was able to start his new position, however. The plaintiff could not point to any statements or circumstances suggesting the existence of a just-cause contract, and consequently was not able to pursue either an express or implied-in-fact breach of contract cause of action.[90] The court, however, allowed the plaintiff to pursue his promissory estoppel claim. According to the court, where the defendant knew that to accept its offer plaintiff had to quit his current position, it was reasonable for the plaintiff "to assume he would be given a good faith opportunity to perform his duties."[91]

Although the rationale advanced in *Grouse* has been followed by other courts,[92] some courts have questioned the applicability of promissory estoppel in this context, arguing that the central finding in *Grouse*—that prospective employees have a right to assume they will be given a good faith opportunity to perform—is entirely inconsistent with the at-will doctrine.[93] Other courts, while accepting the doctrine in principle, have limited its application, by, for example, strictly construing the elements of promise and reliance.[94]

---

[88] Restatement (Second) of Contracts § 90.

[89] 306 N.W.2d 114 (Minn. 1981).

[90] In fact the court noted that "[o]n these facts no contract exists because due to the bilateral power of termination neither party is committed to performance and the promises are, therefore, illusory." Id. at 116.

[91] Id.

[92] See, e.g., Goff-Hamel v. Obstetricians & Gynecologists, P.C., 256 Neb. 19, 588 N.W.2d 798 (1999); Tersigni v. General Tire, 91 Ohio App.3d 757, 633 N.E.2d 1140 (1993); Korslund v. DynCorp Tri-Cities Services, Inc., 121 Wash.App. 295, 88 P.3d 966 (2004).

[93] See, e.g., White v. Roche Biomedical Laboratories, Inc., 807 F.Supp. 1212 (D.S.C. 1992); Rosatone v. GTE Sprint Communications, 761 S.W.2d 670 (Mo. Ct. App. 1988); Heinritz v. Lawrence University, 194 Wis.2d 606, 535 N.W.2d 81 (1995).

[94] See, e.g., Pepsi-Cola General Bottlers, Inc. v. Woods, 440 N.E.2d 696 (Ind. App. 1982) (rejecting a promissory estoppel argument on grounds that the plaintiff's decision to leave her prior job based on employer's promise of an at-will contract did not satisfy the reliance requirement); Soderlun v. Public Service Co. of Colorado, 944 P.2d 616, 620 (Colo. Ct. App. 1997) (finding that to satisfy the promise requirement the statement made by the employer "must either disclose a promissory intent or be

2.4.4 Covenant of Good Faith and Fair Dealing

The Restatement (Second) of Contracts provides that "[e]very contract imposes upon each party a duty of good faith and fair dealing in its performance and its enforcement."[95] In a typical contract case, application of this principle might lead the court to conclude that a party's uncooperative and inflexible attitude amounts to breach of contract, for example.[96] While the implied covenant of good faith and fair dealing has been widely accepted as a matter of general contract law, its application to the employment context has been limited.[97] A minority of courts have held that firing an employee in circumstances that defeat an employee's reasonable expectation of continued employment violates the implied covenant of good faith and fair dealing.

However, most courts have held that when employment is at will a firing is not contrary to the covenant of good faith and fair dealing because no such covenant exists with regard to termination of an at-will agreement. For example, in *Murphy v. American Home Products*,[98] the plaintiff was fired for reporting accounting improprieties to top management. In challenging his dismissal, the plaintiff argued that his job duties required him to disclose any accounting improprieties he discovered, and thus, the employer's decision to fire him for having done his job amounted to a failure to act in good faith.[99] The court rejected the plaintiff's argument explaining that where the plaintiff was clearly an employee at will, "it would be incongruous to say that an inference may be drawn that the employer impliedly agreed to a provision which would be destructive of his right of termination. The parties may by express agreement limit or restrict the employer's right of discharge, but to

---

one that the employee could reasonably conclude constituted a commitment by the employer"); DeKoning v. Flower Mem. Hospital, 82 Ohio Misc.2d 20, 676 N.E.2d 614 (Comm. Pl. 1996) (finding that employer's statements that plaintiff could be fired for certain policy violations did not create a promise to or contract right in continued employment).

[95] Restatement (Second) of Contracts § 205. The Uniform Commercial Code adopts the same principle, U.C.C. § 1–304.

[96] See, e.g., Benefit Mgmt. of Maine, Inc. v. Allstate Life Ins. Co., 993 F.2d 1530 (1st Cir. 1993).

[97] A survey of state law identifies twenty-one jurisdictions as having applied the good faith and fair dealing principle to employment contracts, and thirty jurisdictions as not recognizing the principle at all in the employment context. See Dau-Schmidt & Haley, supra note 56 at 346–478.

[98] 58 N.Y.2d 293, 448 N.E.2d 86 (1983).

[99] Id. at 304, 448 N.E.2d at 91.

imply such a limitation from the existence of an unrestricted right would be internally inconsistent."[100]

The majority of courts have refused to adopt the covenant of good faith argument, at least when defined as broadly as suggested by the plaintiff in *Murphy*.[101] Some courts have implied a covenant of good faith and fair dealing requirement in employment contracts, but have defined the term narrowly.[102] Courts adopting this narrower view view the good faith covenant as a way of preventing employers from interfering with the ability of employees to enjoy benefits they have already earned. For example, in *Fortune v. NCR*,[103] the plaintiff, a salesperson working partially on commissions, was dismissed shortly after negotiating a multi-million dollar sale. Under the plaintiff's employment contract, his commissions depended on whether he was involved in the sale and whether he was assigned to the customer at the time of the installation. Because of his dismissal, the plaintiff was prevented from receiving the maximum amount of commissions to which he would otherwise be entitled if he had remained employed until the contract was fully performed.

In finding in favor of the plaintiff, the court held that employment contracts contain an implied covenant of good faith and fair dealing, and that a termination not made in good faith would constitute a breach of such covenant.[104] The court, however, interpreted the reach of the good faith covenant narrowly, defining the extent of the obligation it was imposing on the employer as that of not doing anything which would have the effect of destroying or interfering with the right of the other party to receive the fruits of the contract.[105]

---

[100] Id. at 304–05, 448 N.E.2d at 91. Other courts have expressed similar concerns. See, e.g., Morriss, 241 Kan. 501, 518, 738 P.2d 841, 851; Sanchez v. The New Mexican, 106 N.M. 76, 78, 738 P.2d 1321, 1324 (1987); Breen v. Dakota Gear & Joint Co., 433 N.W.2d 221, 224 (S.D. 1988).

[101] Only twenty-one jurisdictions have allowed the good faith covenant argument. Of those 21, nine either limit the type of recovery available or the circumstances in which the argument can be raised. See Dau-Schmidt & Haley, supra note 56, at 347.

[102] See, e.g., Carbone v. Atlantic Richfield Co., 204 Conn. 460, 471, 528 A.2d 1137, 1142 (1987) (limiting cause of action to situations involving a discharge intended to deprive employee of earned compensation); Kravetz v. Merchants Distributors Inc., 387 Mass. 457, 463, 440 N.E.2d 1278, 1281 (1982) (limiting damages to recovery of compensation earned for past services); Keiger v. Citgo, 326 S.C. 369, 374, 482 S.E.2d 792, 794 (App. 1997) (finding that a covenant of good faith and fair dealing is implied where the at-will relationship is altered by the existence of an employee manual, for example).

[103] 373 Mass. 96, 364 N.E.2d 1251 (1977).

[104] Id. at 104, 364 N.E.2d at 1257.

[105] Id. at 105, 364 N.E.2d at 1257. Various other courts have adopted this interpretation. See, e.g., Hall v. Farmers Insurance Exchange, 713 P.2d 1027 (Okla. 1985).

Notice that by narrowly defining the duty arising from the covenant of good faith and fair dealing, courts that adopt this view avoid the incongruity which worried the *Murphy* court. Under the *Fortune* definition of good faith, the employer continues to be free to terminate the employee for any reason, but will not be able to deprive the employee of benefits already earned.

§ 2.5 Tort Based Protections

Tort law has long been a source of protection for employees seeking relief after being fired. This section examines some of the key tort theories of liability used by employees in wrongful discharge cases, including the tort of wrongful discharge, the tort of intentional infliction of emotional distress and the tort of intentional interference with contractual relations. The tort of defamation is discussed, infra, in Section 3.2.1 of Chapter 3.

2.5.1 Discharge in Violation of Public Policy

The tort of wrongful discharge in violation of public policy was first articulated in the 1959 case of *Petermann v. International Brotherhood of Teamsters Local 396.*[106] Petermann, who worked for a local union, filed an action against the union, alleging that the union fired him for failing to comply with a union directive to give false testimony before a legislative committee.

The California Court of Appeal reversed the trial court's entry of judgment against Petermann on the pleadings. The court held that while an employment of no fixed duration is generally terminable at the will of either party, the employer's right to discharge an at-will employee may be limited by public policy considerations. The court also observed that the term public policy was intended to convey " 'that principle of law which holds that no citizen can lawfully do that which has a tendency to be injurious to the public or against the public good. . . .' "[107] The court further stated:

> The threat of criminal prosecution would, in many cases, be a sufficient deterrent upon both the employer and the employee, the former from soliciting and the latter from committing perjury. However, in order to more fully effectuate the state's declared policy against perjury, the civil law, too, must deny the employer his generally unlimited right to discharge an employee whose employment is for an unspecified duration, when the reason

---

[106] 174 Cal.App.2d 184, 344 P.2d 25 (1959).

[107] Id. at 188, 344 P.2d at 27 (quoting Safeway Stores v. Retail Clerks Int'l Ass'n, 41 Cal.2d 567, 575, 262 P.2d 721, 726 (1953)).

for the dismissal is the employee's refusal to commit perjury.[108]

Most courts have recognized the tort of wrongful termination in violation of public policy.[109] A handful of courts have refused to do so, primarily on the grounds that allowing employees to bring a wrongful discharge claim will seem to undermine the employment-at-will doctrine and that such choice should be left to resolution at the hands of the state legislature.[110]

2.5.1.1 What Is Public Policy?

A critical step in making the wrongful discharge against public policy argument involves defining the policy that is at odds with the employer's decision to terminate the affected employee. The term "public policy," however, has proven difficult to define.[111]

Given the indeterminate nature of public policy, some courts have adopted a narrow approach to determine which sources of public policy are adequate to support a cause of action for the tort of wrongful discharge. Under this approach, courts allow only those claims that are anchored to an important public policy based on either a statutory or a constitutional provision, and which provide a clear and compelling mandate. Courts endorsing this limitation generally treat administrative regulations as statutory sources because they are promulgated pursuant to a legislative grant of authority by a government agency and have the force of law.[112] As explained by the California Supreme Court, a narrow approach acknowledges that the legislative branch is the proper forum to

---

[108] Id. at 188–89, 344 P.2d at 27.

[109] See State Rulings Chart, Bloomberg BNA Individual Employment Rights Law (showing that as of 2017 the following states had not recognized the tort of wrongful discharge: Alabama, Florida, Georgia, Louisiana, Maine, New York, and Rhode Island).

[110] Murphy v. American Home Products Corp., 58 N.Y.2d 293, 448 N.E.2d 86 (1983).

[111] Various judicial opinions have described public policy as "amorphous," "nebulous," and "vague." See, e.g., Hinrichs, 352 So.2d 1130, 1131 ("vague"); Green v. Ralee Eng'g Co., 19 Cal.4th 66, 99, 960 P.2d 1046, 1067 (1998) ("amorphous"); Carl v. Children's Hosp., 702 A.2d 159, 163 (D.C. App. 1997) ("nebulous" and "vague"); Simmons v. Newton, 178 Ga. 806, 812, 174 S.E. 703, 707 (1934) ("vague and undefinable"); Mistishen v. Falcone Piano Co., 36 Mass. App. Ct. 243, 245, 630 N.E.2d 294, 295 (1994) ("amorphous"); Rothrock v. Rothrock Motor Sales, 810 A.2d 114, 117 (Pa. Super. 2002) ("nebulous").

[112] See, e.g., Green, 19 Cal.4th at 72, 960 P.2d at 1049 (stating that "statutorily authorized regulations that effectuate the Legislature's purpose to ensure commercial airline safety are 'tethered to' statutory provisions"); Mehrer v. Diagnostic Imaging Ctr., P.C., 157 S.W.3d 315, 319 (Mo. Ct. App. 2005) ("To trigger the policy exception, the Missouri Supreme Court has stated that the reasons for the employee's discharge must implicate 'a constitutional provision, a statute, or a regulation based upon statute.' ") (quoting Luethans v. Washington Univ., 894 S.W.2d 169, 171 n.2 (Mo. 1995)).

decide what public policy is. [113] The preference for a narrow approach also recognizes an employer's general ability to discharge employees without cause and it respects the need for employers to have broad discretion in making managerial decisions.[114] In addition, a narrow approach may be fairer to employers in that "[t]he employer is bound, at a minimum, to know the fundamental public policies of the state and nation as expressed in their constitutions and statutes; so limited, the public policy exception presents no impediment to employers that operate within the bounds of law."[115]

Others courts have adopted a broad approach to evaluate whether a given source is sufficient to support a public policy claim. Courts that use this more expansive approach allow policy to originate in non-legislative sources including judicial decisions.[116] Some courts have gone even further to hold that a professional code of ethics may contain an expression of public policy.[117]

Located at the outer limits of the tort are cases where courts have held that public policy rests on broad societal interests that are moored to neither legislative nor recognized non-legislative sources. *Wells v. Ormet Corp.*[118] illustrates the point. Mark Wells worked as a general foreman for a division of the Ormet Corporation. Ormet terminated him in connection with events surrounding the cancellation of an overtime shift. When five employees scheduled to work the shift did not report to work, the shift had to be cancelled. The general manager suspended the five employees, convinced that they had collaborated to shut the plant down, prompting the union to request a formal hearing. At the hearing, Wells testified that he did not believe the five employees had acted pursuant to a concerted plan. Three days later, Ormet discharged him. Wells filed an action for violation of the tort of wrongful discharge. The lower court dismissed the complaint, concluding that no clear public policy protected a manager's expression of personal opinions that may conflict with the corporation's position. The appellate court reversed,

---

[113] See, e.g., Green, 19 Cal.4th at 80, 960 P.2d at 1071.

[114] See id. at 79–80, 960 P.2d at 1054.

[115] Gantt v. Sentry Ins., 1 Cal.4th 1083, 1095, 824 P.2d 680, 688 (1992). See also Wholey v. Sears, Roebuck & Co., 370 Md. 38, 46, 803 A.2d 482, 501 (2002); Wadsworth v. State, 275 Mont. 287, 306, 911 P.2d 1165, 1176 (1996); Tudor v. Charleston Area Med. Ctr., Inc., 203 W.Va. 111, 124, 506 S.E.2d 554, 567 (1997).

[116] See, e.g., Parnar v. Americana Hotels, Inc., 65 Haw. 370, 652 P.2d 625 (1982); Cloutier v. Great Atlantic & Pac. Tea Co., 121 N.H. 915, 922, 436 A.2d 1140, 1144 (1981); Pierce v. Ortho Pharm. Corp., 84 N.J. 58, 417 A.2d 505 (1980); Gardner v. Loomis Armored, 128 Wash.2d 931, 913 P.2d 377 (1996).

[117] See, e.g., Pierce, 84 N.J. at 71, 417 A.2d at 512; Boyle v. Vista Eyewear, Inc., 700 S.W.2d 859, 871 (Mo. Ct. App. 1985); LoPresti v. Rutland Reg'l Health Servs., 177 Vt. 316, 327, 865 A.2d 1102, 1112 (2004). See generally John Bourdeau & Barbara J. Van Arsdale, 81 Am. Jur. 2d 56 (2017).

[118] No. 97–CV–99, 1999 WL 159231 (Ohio Ct. App. Mar. 17, 1999).

however, holding that "[t]he public policy in the case sub judice consists of various established interests of society as a whole. These broad societal interests include a fair workplace, truthful grievance proceedings, job stability for long-term employees, and economic productivity."[119]

2.5.1.2 Public Versus Private Concerns

The *public* part of the public policy concept is intended to protect the actions of an employee when the actions promote policies that affect the general public and not the personal or proprietary interests of either the employer or employee.[120] Stated differently, the tort of wrongful discharge operates to vindicate the public interest by prohibiting employers from acting in a manner contrary to public policy. As a result, courts do not recognize the claim where the interest implicated by a discharge is purely private rather than general public concern.

Consider, for example, the facts of *Campbell v. Ford Industries, Inc.*[121] The employee-stockholder was terminated after he requested information to uncover an alleged scheme by the defendants to force him to sell his stock. Because he was legally entitled to request the information, he claimed that the exercise of this right leading to his discharge violated public policy. The court disagreed, explaining that "[a]lthough there may be reasons of public policy why the stockholders of a corporation should have the right to examine its books and records, the primary basis for that right is not one of public policy, but the private and proprietary interest of stockholders, as owners of the corporation."[122]

The distinction between a private interest and a public interest is not always readily apparent in the case law, however. Consider the facts of *Bowman v. State Bank of Keysville*,[123] a case which, similar to *Campbell*, involved a claim of termination for exercising shareholder rights. The plaintiffs in *Bowman* were bank employees who also owned shares of common stock in the bank. The bank terminated them for failing to vote their stock in accordance with the

---

[119] Id.

[120] See, e.g., Clark v. Modern Group Ltd., 9 F.3d 321, 331–32 (3d Cir. 1993); Foley v. Interactive Data Corp., 47 Cal.3d 654, 670–71, 765 P.2d 373, 380 (1988); Palmateer, 85 Ill.2d 124, 130 (1981); Hayes v. Eateries, Inc., 905 P.2d 778, 786–87 (Okla. 1995).

[121] 274 Or. 243, 546 P.2d 141 (1976).

[122] Id. at 250–51, 546 P.2d at 145 (footnote omitted). See also Perry v. Sears, Roebuck & Co., 508 So.2d 1086, 1090 (Miss. 1987) (refusing to recognize the tort but also stating that such recognition would not help plaintiff as "[a]ny wrong he has suffered appears to be private, rather than public"); Hayes, 905 P.2d at 786–87 (finding that the action of an employee who was terminated for reporting the illegal conduct of a co-worker did not implicate a public interest but the private interest of the employer).

[123] 229 Va. 534, 331 S.E.2d 797 (1985).

directives of the bank's management. The Virginia Supreme Court held that the terminations violated public policy because a state statute guaranteed stockholders the right to cast one vote for each share of stock held, without fear of intimidation.[124]

How does one explain the contrasting outcomes in *Campbell* and *Bowman*? One theory is that the right to vote one's stock freely without duress from corporate management is of greater public importance than the right to access shareholder information. Perhaps, but this distinction is not obvious and not particularly compelling, especially since shareholder information can play a vital role in one's ability to make an informed decision with respect to voting. Assuming *Campbell's* reasoning is correct, arguably voting shares freely is as much of "a private and proprietary interest of stockholders" as is accessing shareholder information. Likewise, if *Bowman's* rationale is correct, accessing shareholder information appears on par with voting freely since both rights were statutorily conferred. The cases reveal that while courts have made clear that the tort is designed to vindicate public interests and not personal interests, the line between public and private can be difficult to discern.

To help combat this difficulty, and to help ensure that a discharge truly implicates a public policy, many courts require the policy to be "clear and compelling," "fundamental," "well-defined and established," "substantial," or of similar quality.[125] If a policy does not meet this high standard, a risk exists that the policy may not be one that affects the public in a meaningful fashion. Such a risk can be present even when the claimed source of the public policy is a legislative source. As one commentator observes: "Although public policy is most obviously embodied in the legislative enactments, not every legislative enactment embodies public policy; only those which protect the public or promote the public interest qualify."[126]

Consider, for example, *Franklin v. Swift Transportation Company*.[127] Swift terminated Franklin, a truck driver, for his refusal to drive a truck that did not contain in it an original proof of

---

124 Id. at 540, 331 S.E.2d at 801.

125 See, e.g., DeSoto v. Yellow Freight Sys., Inc., 957 F.2d 655, 659 (9th Cir. 1992) ("fundamental"); Lloyd v. AMF Bowling Ctrs., Inc., 195 Ariz. 144, 146, 985 P.2d 629, 631 (1999) ("substantial and fundamental"); City of Green Forest v. Morse, 316 Ark. 540, 546, 873 S.W.2d 155, 159 (1994) ("substantial and well-established"); Sullivan v. Delta Air Lines, 58 Cal.App.4th 938, 942, 68 Cal.Rptr.2d 584 (1997) ("substantial and fundamental"); Shrout v. TFE Group, 161 S.W.3d 351, 354 (Ky. App. 2005) ("fundamental and well-defined"); Burk v. K-Mart Corp., 770 P.2d 24, 29 (Okla. 1989) ("clear and compelling").

126 Bourdeau & Van Arsdale, supra note 117, § 59.

127 210 S.W.3d 521 (Tenn. 2006).

registration, called an IRP cab card. The card indicates that the vehicle is properly registered to operate in multiple jurisdictions. Although the company supplied Franklin with a copy of the IRP cab card, the original was missing. Because a Tennessee regulation requires that the original IRP cab card be kept in the vehicle, Franklin argued that Swift terminated him in violation of public policy because he refused to engage in an illegal act. The court disagreed and concluded that Franklin's refusal to drive the truck in violation of a regulation did not implicate an important and fundamental public policy. The court based its decision on the de minimis nature of the regulatory violation, stating that there was no allegation that the truck was not properly registered and observing that the violation did not implicate the health, safety or welfare of the public.

2.5.1.3 Elements of a Successful Claim

In order to succeed on a wrongful discharge claim, many courts hold that an employee must establish three basic elements: (1) she was engaged in conduct protected by a clearly defined public policy; (2) dismissing the employee would jeopardize or undermine the public policy; and (3) a causal link existed between the employee's conduct and the discharge to indicate that the employer terminated the employee because of the latter's participation in the protected conduct. Some courts also add a fourth element, namely that there was no other justification for the termination.[128] These elements have been identified as the clarity element, the jeopardy element, the causation element, and the absence-of-justification element, respectively.[129] The jeopardy element, in particular, makes it clear that to succeed on a public policy claim, plaintiffs must do more than simply reference a source of public policy. They must prove that the discharge undermines the public policy reflected in the source.[130]

Despite the argument advanced by some plaintiffs that the tort should be extended to apply to retaliation other than discharge, such as demotions, courts have generally refused to extend it.[131] Most courts have been willing, however, to apply the tort to situations involving constructive discharges.[132] A constructive discharge occurs

---

[128] See, e.g., Davis v. Horton, 661 N.W.2d 533, 535 (Iowa 2003); Clifford v. Cactus Drilling Corp., 419 Mich. 356, 368, 353 N.W.2d 469, 474 (1984); Gardner, 128 Wash.2d at 941, 913 P.2d at 382.

[129] Henry H. Perritt, Jr., Workplace Torts: Rights and Liabilities § 3.7 (1991). See generally Bourdeau & Van Arsdale, supra note 117, § 54.

[130] See id. § 61.

[131] See Dau-Schmidt & Haley, supra note 56 at 346–478.

[132] See, e.g., Colores v. Bd. of Trustees, 105 Cal.App.4th 1293, 130 Cal.Rptr.2d 347 (2003); Wells v. Town of Plainfield, No. CV020068211, 2005 WL 375293 (Conn. Super. 2005); Tony v. Elkhart County, 851 N.E.2d 1032 (Ind. Ct. App. 2006); Bell v. Dynamite

when an employer renders the employee's working conditions so intolerable that the employer effectively forces the employee to quit the job. Whether an employer constructively discharged an employee depends on whether a reasonable person would have resigned rather than endure the conditions.[133]

2.5.1.4 Activities Protected by the Tort

Several distinct categories of employee activities routinely serve as the basis for a claim of wrongful discharge in violation of public policy: (1) refusing to engage in illegal conduct; (2) performing a public obligation; (3) exercising a legal right or privilege; and (4) reporting a statutory violation for the public's benefit.[134] These four categories, while common in judicial opinions, are not rigid. Some courts have expanded the list and others have applied the tort to fewer categories.[135]

2.5.1.4.1 Refusing to Engage in Illegal Conduct

Courts generally permit employees to maintain a public policy cause of action for refusing to engage in illegal conduct. As expressed by the *Petermann* court, employees should not have to decide between violating the law and retaining their jobs. Allowing employers to condition employment on an employee's commission of an illegal act would "encourage criminal conduct upon the part of both the employee and employer and . . . is patently contrary to the public welfare."[136]

Foods, 969 S.W.2d 847 (Mo. Ct. App. 1998). See generally Whitt v. Harris Teeter, Inc., 165 N.C.App. 32, 40–41, 598 S.E.2d 151, 157 (2004) (stating that "ten of the eleven states to consider whether such a claim is cognizable have extended the public policy exception to prohibit constructive discharge"). The Restatement of the Law Third Employment Law § 5.01(c) also recognizes the availability of the tort in cases involving constructive discharge. However, the Restatement expresses no view "on whether public-policy claims based on adverse employer actions falling short of discharge or constructive discharge (termed here "wrongful discipline") should be actionable."

133 See, e.g., Bell, 969 S.W.2d at 851.

134 See, e.g., Wagner v. City of Globe, 150 Ariz. 82, 88, 722 P.2d 250, 256 (1986); Sterling Drug, Inc. v. Oxford, 294 Ark. 239, 245, 743 S.W.2d 380, 382 (1988); Green, 19 Cal.4th at 76, 960 P.2d at 1051; Boyle, 700 S.W.2d at 873–75; Touchard v. La Z-Boy, Inc., 148 P.3d 945, 948–49 (2006).

135 See, e.g., Martin Marietta Corp. v. Lorenz, 823 P.2d 100, 107 (Colo. 1992) (including as a fifth category "the employee's performance of an act that public policy would encourage under circumstances where retaliatory discharge is supported by evidence of employer's bad faith, malice, or retaliation"); Makovi v. Sherwin-Williams Co., 316 Md. 603, 611, 561 A.2d 179, 182–83 (1989) (describing the division of the public policy exception into three categories of cases); Senseney v. Miss. Power Co., 914 So.2d 1225, 1228 (Miss. App. 2005) (applying the tort in cases where the employee is terminated for refusing to engage in an illegal act and for exposing an employer's illegal act); Spierling v. First Am. Home Health Servs., 737 A.2d 1250, 1252 (Pa. Super. 1999) (limiting the tort to three narrowly defined exceptions).

136 Petermann, 174 Cal.App.2d at 189, 344 P.2d at 27.

Courts have applied the essential reasoning of *Petermann* to hold that employees have stated a claim of wrongful discharge when they were terminated for refusing to falsify records in violation of the law,[137] refusing to endanger the health and safety of the public in violation of the law,[138] refusing to engage in illegal price-fixing schemes,[139] refusing to commit perjury,[140] refusing to pollute coastal waters in violation of federal law,[141] and refusing to commit an act that might violate indecent exposure laws.[142]

Courts are split over whether the employer must actually demand that the employee violate a law or whether it is sufficient that the employee reasonably believes that her employer is asking her to violate a law. In *Clark v. Modern Group Ltd.*,[143] Clark, the employer's chief financial officer, believed incorrectly that the company's method of reimbursing employees for auto expenses violated federal tax laws. When Clark refused to sign tax forms certifying the expenses, the company fired him. In his action for discharge in violation of public policy, Clark argued that an "employee need show only a reasonable belief in the illegality of the requested activity. . . ."[144] In rejecting this argument, the court held that to permit the claim would only protect Clark's interests, not the

---

137 See, e.g., Russ v. Pension Consultants Co., Inc., 182 Ill.App.3d 769, 131 Ill.Dec. 318, 538 N.E.2d 693 (1st Dist. 1989) (employee alleged he was terminated for refusing to backdate pension plans in violation of federal law); Trombetta v. Detroit, T. & I. R.R., 81 Mich.App. 489, 265 N.W.2d 385, 388–89 (1978) (employee refused to falsify pollution control records in violation of state law); Coman v. Thomas Mfg. Co., Inc., 325 N.C. 172, 381 S.E.2d 445 (1989) (employee claimed he was discharged for refusing to falsify truck driving logs that federal regulations required him to maintain). See generally 82 Am. Jur. 2d Wrongful Discharge § 109.

138 See, e.g., Sarratore v. Longview Van Corp., 666 F.Supp. 1257 (N.D. Ind. 1987) (refusing to participate in an illegal scheme to set back odometers); Boyle, 700 S.W.2d 859 (refusing to obey employer's orders to manufacture eyeglasses that did not meet specifications issued by the FDA); Silver v. CPC-Sherwood Manor, 84 P.3d 728 (Okla. 2004) (refusing to serve food while suffering from an intestinal infection in violation of state public health codes). See generally Bourdeau & Van Arsdale, supra note 117, § 56.

139 See, e.g., Levito v. Hussman Food Serv. Co., Civ. A. No. 89–5967, 1990 WL 1426 (E.D. Pa. Jan. 8, 1990); Haigh v. Matsushita Elec. Corp. of Am., 676 F.Supp. 1332 (E.D. Va. 1987); McNulty v. Borden, Inc., 474 F.Supp. 1111 (E.D. Pa. 1979); Tameny v. Atlantic Richfield Co., 27 Cal.3d 167, 164 Cal.Rptr. 839, 610 P.2d 1330 (1980). See generally Bourdeau & Van Arsdale, supra note 117, § 56.

140 See, e.g., Donovan on Behalf of Anderson v. Stafford Constr. Co., 732 F.2d 954 (D.C. Cir. 1984); Petermann, 174 Cal.App.2d 184, 344 P.2d 25; Cronk v. Intermountain Rural Elec. Ass'n, 765 P.2d 619 (Colo. Ct. App. 1988). See Bourdeau & Van Arsdale, supra note 117, § 56.

141 See, e.g., Sabine Pilot Serv., Inc. v. Hauck, 687 S.W.2d 733, 734–35 (Tex. 1985).

142 See, e.g., Wagenseller v. Scottsdale Memorial Hosp., 147 Ariz. 370, 710 P.2d 1025 (1985) (superseded in part by Ariz. Rev. Stat. Ann. § 23–1501).

143 9 F.3d 321 (3d Cir. 1993).

144 Id. at 328.

public's since "[a] company acting within the law is presumed to pose no threat to the public at large."[145]

In contrast to the *Clark* decision, some courts allow the tort in situations where the employee only has a reasonable belief that the activity in which she refuses to participate is illegal.[146] Consider the facts in *Allum v. Valley Bank*.[147] Allum, a bank loan officer, claimed that he was terminated for refusing to grant loans which he *believed* violated federal law. In reversing the lower court's ruling in favor of the bank, the Supreme Court of Nevada held that "a claim for tortious discharge should be available to an employee who was terminated for refusing to engage in conduct that he, in good faith, reasonably believed to be illegal."[148]

Some state legislatures have eliminated the uncertainty involved with establishing a public policy claim based on refusing to engage in illegal activity by enacting a law that prohibits employers from dismissing employees for such conduct.[149] For example, the Tennessee Public Protection Act[150] provides that "No employee shall be discharged or terminated solely for refusing to participate in, or for refusing to remain silent about, illegal activities."[151] Whether such laws preclude a tort remedy for wrongful discharge depends on the legislative intent of each statute.[152]

2.5.1.4.2 Performing a Public Obligation

Employees may have a viable claim for the tort of wrongful discharge when an employer terminates them for performing a public obligation. *Nees v. Hocks*[153] provides a classic illustration of the tort in this context. The employer fired the plaintiff because of her service on a jury and her refusal to try to evade such service. In ruling for the plaintiff, the court observed that:

> the jury system and jury duty are regarded as high on the scale of American institutions and citizen obligations. If an employer were permitted with impunity to discharge an employee for fulfilling her obligation of jury duty, the jury

145 Id. at 331–32. See also Reese v. Tom Hesser Chevrolet-BMW, 413 Pa.Super. 168, 604 A.2d 1072 (1992).

146 See Dau-Schmidt & Haley, supra note 56 at 346–478.

147 114 Nev. 1313, 970 P.2d 1062 (1998).

148 Id. at 1324, 970 P.2d at 1068. See also Wagenseller, 147 Ariz. at 380, 710 P.2d at 1035 (holding that a discharge for refusing to commit an act "which might" violate the law may provide the basis for a wrongful discharge claim).

149 See, e.g., Tenn. Code Ann. § 50–1–304; Mich. Comp. Laws § 15.362.

150 Tenn. Code Ann. § 50–1–304.

151 Id. § 50–1–304(a).

152 See infra Section 2.5.1.5.

153 272 Or. 210, 536 P.2d 512 (1975).

> system would be adversely affected. The will of the community would be thwarted. For these reasons we hold that the defendants are liable for discharging plaintiff because she served on the jury.[154]

Other public obligation activities that courts have protected include cooperating in official investigations[155] and testifying in official proceedings.[156]

The same rationale has been applied in cases in which the employee is terminated for violating a work rule when taking actions to save an innocent bystander. In *Gardner v. Loomis Armored Inc.*,[157] the driver of an armored car was fired for violating a company rule prohibiting drivers from leaving their vehicles. The driver was waiting in the car at a scheduled stop, when he observed the bank manager running out of the building pointing to a man who was armed with a knife and chasing her. The driver got out of the car, eventually assisting in subduing the attacker. Noting the well-defined public policy "encouraging citizens to rescue persons from life threatening situations,"[158] the Supreme Court of Washington found in favor of plaintiff, on the grounds that discharging the plaintiff for leaving the truck to save a woman from an imminent life threatening situation violated public policy.[159]

2.5.1.4.3 Exercising a Legal Right or Privilege

Courts commonly recognize the availability of a public policy cause of action for employees whose employers terminated them for exercising a legal right or privilege. *Frampton v. Central Indiana Gas Co.*[160] illustrates this third category of public policy cases. The plaintiff alleged that her employer terminated her for filing a workers' compensation claim after she was injured on the job. In evaluating plaintiff's claim for retaliatory discharge against the employer, the court observed that:

---

[154] Id. at 219, 536 P.2d at 516. See also Reuther v. Fowler & Williams, Inc., 255 Pa.Super. 28, 31–32, 386 A.2d 119, 120 (1978).

[155] See Bourdeau & Van Arsdale, supra note 117, § 98 (collecting cases).

[156] Id. § 105 (collecting cases).

[157] 128 Wash.2d 931, 913 P.2d 377 (Wash. 1996).

[158] 128 Wash.2d at 950, 913 P.2d at 387.

[159] Other courts have been less receptive to this type of claim. See e.g., Bruley v. Village Green Mgmt. Co., 592 F.Supp.2d 1381 (M.D. Fla. 2008), aff'd, 333 F. App'x 491 (11th Cir. 2009) (holding that a leasing agent who was discharged for failing to follow established procedures in case of emergency and for having a firearm on the employer's property did not have a claim for wrongful discharge against public policy although he responded to a shooting on the property and provided life-saving aid to the victim.)

[160] 260 Ind. 249, 297 N.E.2d 425 (1973).

> [i]f employers are permitted to penalize employees for filing workmen's compensation claims, a most important public policy will be undermined. The fear of being discharged would have a deleterious effect on the exercise of a statutory right. Employees will not file claims for justly deserved compensation—opting, instead, to continue their employment without incident. The end result, of course, is that the employer is effectively relieved of his obligation.[161]

Consequently, the court held that the termination clearly contravened public policy. Since *Frampton* was decided in 1973, numerous other courts have used the tort to protect employees wrongfully discharged for filing workers' compensation claims.[162]

Other activities that fit within this category, and which some courts have protected, include exercising the right of free speech,[163] refusing to take a polygraph test,[164] hiring an attorney to pursue a claim against one's employer,[165] filing for bankruptcy,[166] and exercising their constitutional or statutory rights to bear arms.[167]

2.5.1.4.4 Reporting a Statutory Violation

Employees may find protection in the tort of wrongful discharge following a termination for reporting an employer's illegal conduct to supervisors or outside officials. This type of protected activity is commonly known as whistleblowing. When applied to whistleblowing, the tort reflects the idea that individuals should not be subject to reprisals for performing a civic duty by reporting

---

[161] Id. at 251–52, 297 N.E.2d at 427.

[162] See, e.g., Leach v. Lauhoff Grain Co., 51 Ill.App.3d 1022, 366 N.E.2d 1145 (1977); Murphy v. City of Topeka-Shawnee County Dep't of Labor Servs., 6 Kan.App.2d 488, 630 P.2d 186 (1981); Sventko v. Kroger Co., 69 Mich.App. 644, 245 N.W.2d 151 (1976); Clanton v. Cain-Sloan Co., 677 S.W.2d 441 (Tenn. 1984); contra Meeks v. Opp Cotton Mills, Inc. 459 So.2d 814 (Ala. 1984); Kelly v. Miss. Valley Gas Co., 397 So.2d 874 (Miss. 1981).

[163] See Novosel v. Nationwide Ins. Co., 721 F.2d 894, 896 (3d Cir. 1983) (finding that employee, terminated for refusing to participate in a lobbying effort, had stated a sufficient cause of action for the tort of wrongful discharge based on public policy expressed in the First Amendment and the Pennsylvania Constitution). But see Drake v. Cheyenne Newspapers, Inc., 891 P.2d 80 (Wyo. 1995) (dismissing plaintiff's public policy claim for wrongful termination where plaintiff argued that he was exercising free speech by refusing to wear anti-union buttons).

[164] Perks v. Firestone Tire & Rubber Co., 611 F.2d 1363 (3d Cir. 1979).

[165] See Bourdeau & Van Arsdale, supra note 117, § 87.

[166] Id. § 92.

[167] Stewart v. FedEx, 114 A.3d 424 (2015) (finding that that termination of employee for possessing firearm in the glove compartment of his car while on employer's premises did not violate public policy, so as to fall within public policy exception to at-will employment doctrine); Hoven v. Walgreen Co., 751 F.3d 778 (6th Cir. 2014) (finding that employee's termination for exercising his rights of self-defense, defense of others, and to carry a concealed weapon, in connection with the firing of his handgun, did not violate public policy).

violations of statutes, rules, and regulations that affect the public's health, safety, and general welfare.[168] Courts have recognized public policy claims on behalf of employees who were discharged for reporting various illegal activities engaged in by employers including overloading trucks in violation of state law,[169] violating federal laws pertaining to nuclear power plants,[170] violating state pharmacy rules,[171] stealing property,[172] employing undocumented workers,[173] and violating safety codes.[174]

Courts are split over whether an employee, in order to maintain a tort action for wrongful discharge, must report the violation externally. External whistleblowing occurs when an employee reports the violation to external, third-party authorities. By contrast, internal whistleblowing refers to a report made internally, within a company, to a superior.[175] While some courts insist on external whistleblowing,[176] others recognize a whistleblowing tort based on either internal or external reporting.[177]

The argument in favor of requiring external whistleblowing is that it helps to ensure that recognition of the wrongful discharge tort will serve to vindicate the public's interests. As expressed by the Supreme Court of Nevada, when a plaintiff reports illegal activity only to his superiors, and does not contact appropriate outside authorities, he acts solely in a private manner that does not benefit the public as a whole.[178]

In contrast to this view, courts that protect internal whistleblowing argue that such an approach appropriately gives

---

168 Palmer v. Brown, 242 Kan. 893, 900, 752 P.2d 685, 689 (1988).

169 Shaw v. Russell Trucking Line, Inc., 542 F.Supp. 776 (W.D. Pa. 1982).

170 Howard v. Zack Co., 264 Ill.App.3d 1012, 202 Ill.Dec. 447, 637 N.E.2d 1183 (1994).

171 Kalman v. Grand Union Co., 183 N.J. Super. 153, 443 A.2d 728 (1982).

172 Vermillion v. AAA Pro Moving & Storage, 146 Ariz. 215, 704 P.2d 1360 (Ariz. App. 1985).

173 Jie v. Liang Tai Knitwear Co., 89 Cal.App.4th 654, 107 Cal.Rptr.2d 682 (2001).

174 See, e.g., Morse v. Sarah Tuxis Residential Servs., Inc., No. CV 960252481S, 1996 WL 548179 (Conn. Super. Sept. 20, 1996); Love v. Polk County Fire Dist., 209 Or.App. 474, 487, 149 P.3d 199, 206 (2006).

175 See, e.g., Porter v. Reardon Mach. Co., 962 S.W.2d 932, 937 (Mo. Ct. App. 1998). See generally Lisa R. Lipman et al., 2–6 Employee Rights Litigation: Pleading and Practice § 6.03(2)(b) (2007).

176 See, e.g., Zaniecki v. P. A. Bergner & Co., 143 Ill.App.3d 668, 97 Ill.Dec. 756, 493 N.E.2d 419 (1986); King v. Marriott Int'l, Inc., 160 Md.App. 689, 866 A.2d 895 (2005); Wiltsie v. Baby Grand Corp., 105 Nev. 291, 774 P.2d 432 (1989).

177 See, e.g., Liberatore v. Melville Corp., 168 F.3d 1326 (D.C. Cir. 1999); Murcott v. Best Western Int'l, 198 Ariz. 349, 9 P.3d 1088 (2000); Shea v. Emmanuel Coll., 425 Mass. 761, 682 N.E.2d 1348 (1997); Brenneke v. Dep't of Mo., VFW, 984 S.W.2d 134 (Mo. Ct. App. 1998).

178 Wiltsie, 774 P.2d 432.

management an opportunity to resolve the wrongdoing through internal channels.[179] In addition, the point has been made that internal whistleblowing may save public resources by avoiding "needless public investigations of matters best addressed internally in the first instance."[180]

As in the cases involving the employee being fired for refusing to commit an illegal act, whistleblowing cases require courts to decide whether the employee must demonstrate that the employer actually engaged in illegal activity or whether the employee need only have a reasonable belief that the employer did so. Courts differ on this issue although the majority approach appears to be that an employee need only establish that she had a reasonable belief that the employer engaged in illegal activity.[181]

Most states have whistleblower statutes that prohibit employers from terminating employees in retaliation for reporting illegal activity.[182] While some statutes are general, others apply only to public employees.[183] In addition, a few states have subject-matter specific statutes that apply to certain occupational groups such as healthcare employees.[184] Courts have interpreted some whistleblower statutes to protect whistleblowers only if they have a reasonable basis in fact and/or law for believing that the employer was engaged in an illegal act.[185]

At the federal level, the Whistleblower Protection Act[186] protects federal employees who make disclosures indicating illegal or improper government activities. Various other federal statutes also contain provisions that protect employees who blow the whistle.[187]

---

179 See, e.g., Murcott, 198 Ariz. at 358, 349, 9 P.3d at 1097; Liberatore, 168 F.3d at 1331 (quoting Belline v. K-Mart Corp., 940 F.2d 184, 187 (7th Cir. 1991)).

180 Sullivan v. Mass. Mut. Life Ins. Co., 802 F.Supp. 716, 724–25 (D. Conn. 1992).

181 See Lipman et al., supra note 175, § 6.03(2)(b).

182 See National Conference of State Legislatures, State Whistleblower Laws, available at http://www.ncsl.org/research/labor-and-employment/state-whistleblower-laws.aspx.

183 See, e.g., Ala. Code § 36–26A–1; Alaska Stat. § 39.90.100; Colo. Rev. Stat. Ann. § 24–50.5–101; Del. Title 29 § 5115; Ill. 20 ILCS 415/19c.1; Utah Code Ann. § 67–21–1.

184 See, e.g., Massachusetts Healthcare Whistleblower Statute, Mass. Gen. Laws ch. 149, § 187(b)(1); Missouri Health Care Whistleblower Protection Act, Mo. Ann. Stat. § 191.908; Vermont Healthcare Whistleblowers Protection Act, Vt. Stat. Ann. tit. 21, § 507.

185 See, e.g., Maine Whistleblowers' Protection Act, 26 Me. Rev. Stat. Ann. tit. 26, § 831(1)(A); see also Kulch v. Structural Fibers, Inc., 78 Ohio St. 3d 134, 677 N.E.2d 308 (1997) (interpreting Ohio's Whistleblower Statute to incorporate a reasonable belief standard).

186 5 U.S.C. § 2301(b)(9).

187 See generally Stephen Kohn, Concepts and Procedures in Whistleblower Law 79–118 (2001) (discussing federal statutory protection for whistleblowers).

2.5.1.5 *Preclusion*

An applicable federal or state statute may preclude actions for the tort of wrongful discharge if the statute prohibits retaliatory discharge for the conduct at issue and provides an exclusive remedy. Federal law may also preempt such causes of action.[188]

2.5.1.5.1 *Exclusivity Concerns*

If a federal or state statute provides the exclusive remedy for addressing the alleged public policy violation, the statute bars an employee from maintaining a wrongful discharge tort action.[189] *Ohlsen v. DST Industries, Inc.*[190] illustrates the point. The employer discharged the plaintiff, a truck driver, for refusing to make a trip with another driver. He refused to do so because the other assigned driver abused alcohol. Plaintiff filed a public policy claim based on the Michigan Occupational Safety and Health Act (MOSHA) and his right under the statute to protest unsafe working conditions. The court dismissed the claim because the MOSHA expressly prohibited retaliatory discharges and provided an exclusive remedy to employees who established a violation of the statute.[191]

By contrast, in *Nelson v. Productive Alternatives, Inc.*,[192] the court held that the Minnesota Whistleblower Act did not preclude an employee from maintaining a public policy claim. The employee alleged that he was terminated because of his actions as a member of a non-profit corporation which was also his employer. The court held that the whistleblower statute, although it provided a remedy for the discharge, did not displace a tort action for wrongful discharge. The contrasting decisions in these two cases reflect not only substantive differences between the statutes but also the courts' determination of whether the statutes provide an exclusive remedy. Because this question is one of legislative intent, court decisions may vary considerably even among cases that involve similar statutes.[193]

When evidence indicates that the legislature did not prescribe a statute that prohibits retaliatory discharge as an exclusive remedy, courts must decide whether to permit a claim for wrongful discharge in violation of public policy. This decision involves a consideration of whether the statutory remedy for the alleged violation is adequate. If an adequate remedy exists, allowing a common law action to proceed is unnecessary. In evaluating the adequacy of a statutory

---

[188] See Bourdeau & Van Arsdale, supra note 117, § 184.

[189] See generally id. § 9.03(1)(b).

[190] 111 Mich.App. 580, 314 N.W.2d 699 (1981).

[191] Id.

[192] 696 N.W.2d 841 (Minn. Ct. App. 2005).

[193] See Bourdeau & Van Arsdale, supra note 117, § 184.

remedy, courts consider various factors including the availability of a private cause of action under the statute, the comprehensiveness of the remedy, and the ability to appeal an administrative decision under the statute to a court.[194] For example, because the Occupational Safety and Health Act does not provide employees a private action to challenge retaliatory acts in federal court,[195] some courts have allowed plaintiffs to maintain an action for the tort of wrongful discharge.[196] By contrast, many courts that have decided the adequacy issue in the context of antidiscrimination statutes have concluded that the available statutory remedies are adequate, and have consequently refused to allow plaintiffs to maintain an action for the tort of wrongful discharge.[197] Some courts have reached the opposite conclusion, however.[198]

Several courts have confronted the question of whether antidiscrimination statutes preclude a wrongful discharge tort action against an employer that is not covered by the statute because of its size. For example, in *Weaver v. Harpster & Shipman Financial Services*,[199] the plaintiff pointed to the Pennsylvania Human Relations Act (PHRA) as the source of public policy to support her tort claim for wrongful discharge against her former employer for alleged sexual harassment. The Pennsylvania Human Relations Commission had earlier denied the plaintiff's PHRA complaint against the employer because the employer had less than four employees and thus did not qualify as a covered "employer" under the PHRA. In reversing the lower court's ruling for the defendant employer, the Superior Court of Pennsylvania observed that "[t]o prevent an employee who is alleging sexual harassment from pursuing her claim in court only because her employer has less than four employees appears a direct contravention of a clear public policy

---

194 American Law Institute, Restatement of the Law Third Employment Law § 5.01(d).

195 See infra Section 6.2.6.2 for discussion of the right against retaliation protected by the Occupational Safety and Health Act.

196 See, e.g., Flenker v. Willamette Indus., 266 Kan. 198, 967 P.2d 295 (1998). See also D'Angelo v. Gardner, 107 Nev. 704, 819 P.2d 206 (1991) (finding an adequate remedy under the Nevada Occupational Safety and Health Act).

197 See, e.g., Clinton v. State ex rel. Logan County Election Bd., 29 P.3d 543 (Okla. 2001).

198 See, e.g., Chamberlin v. 101 Realty, Inc., 915 F.2d 777 (1st Cir. 1990); Mayse v. Protective Agency, Inc., 772 F.Supp. 267 (W.D.N.C. 1991); Wynn v. Boeing Military Airplane Co., 595 F.Supp. 727 (D. Kan. 1984); Rojo v. Kliger, 52 Cal.3d 65, 276 Cal.Rptr. 130, 801 P.2d 373 (1990); Schuster v. Derocili, 775 A.2d 1029 (Del. 2001); Insignia Residential Corp. v. Ashton, 359 Md. 560, 755 A.2d 1080 (Md. 2000); Drinkwalter v. Shipton Supply Co., 225 Mont. 380, 732 P.2d 1335 (1987); Gandy v. Wal-Mart Stores, Inc., 117 N.M. 441, 872 P.2d 859 (1994); Howell v. Whitehurst Co., No. L–05–1154, 2005 WL 3078196 (Ohio Ct. App. Nov. 18, 2005); Collier v. Insignia Fin. Group, 981 P.2d 321 (Okla. 1999).

199 885 A.2d 1073 (Pa. Super. 2005).

on grounds both quixotic and arbitrary."[200] While some courts have echoed the basic holding in *Weaver*,[201] others have not.[202]

2.5.1.5.2 *Preemption Concerns*

Employees may also be precluded from pursuing a tort action for wrongful discharge if federal law preempts the action. The preemption defense often arises in the context of the Employee Retirement Income Security Act (ERISA)[203] and federal labor legislation. ERISA contains an especially broad preemption provision by which the federal law supersedes any and all state laws insofar as they may now or hereafter relate to any employee benefit plan.[204] In *Ingersoll-Rand Co. v. McClendon*,[205] the United States Supreme Court held that ERISA preempted a Texas wrongful discharge tort action, where the employer's alleged reason for discharge was to avoid contributing to the plaintiff's pension fund. The Court concluded that ERISA's express language evinced a clear congressional intent to preempt state common law actions that claimed unlawful discharge to prevent the attainment of benefits under an ERISA-covered plan. However, courts have held that ERISA does not preempt an action for wrongful discharge where the employer was not motivated by a desire to interfere with plaintiff's ERISA-protected benefits.[206]

The Supreme Court's decision in *Lingle v. Norge Division of Magic Chef, Inc.*[207] is central to any discussion of preemption of wrongful discharge tort actions in the context of federal labor laws. *Lingle* held that § 301 of the Labor Management Relations Act (LMRA)[208] does not preempt state tort actions for retaliatory discharge of unionized employees covered by a collective bargaining

---

[200] Id. at 1077.

[201] See, e.g., Kittle v. Cynocom Corp., 232 F.Supp.2d 867 (S.D. Ohio 2002) (applying Ohio law); Molesworth v. Brandon, 341 Md. 621, 672 A.2d 608 (App. 1996); Roberts v. Dudley, 140 Wash.2d 58, 993 P.2d 901 (2000).

[202] See, e.g., Jennings v. Marralle, 8 Cal.4th 121, 32 Cal.Rptr.2d 275, 876 P.2d 1074 (1994); Thibodeau v. Design Group One Architects, 260 Conn. 691, 802 A.2d 731 (2002); Brown v. Ford, 905 P.2d 223 (Okla. 1995).

[203] 29 U.S.C. §§ 1001 et seq. See infra Section 5.3 for further discussion of ERISA.

[204] See infra Section 5.3.5.3 for further discussion of ERISA preemption.

[205] 498 U.S. 133 (1990).

[206] See, e.g., Campbell v. Aerospace Corp., 123 F.3d 1308 (9th Cir. 1997).

[207] 486 U.S. 399 (1988).

[208] 29 U.S.C. § 185(a). Section 301(a) of the Labor Management Relations Act provides:

> Suits for violation of contracts between an employer and a labor organization representing employees in an industry affecting commerce as defined in this Act, or between any such labor organizations, may be brought in any district court of the United States having jurisdiction of the parties, without respect to the amount in controversy or without regard to the citizenship of the parties.

agreement (CBA) that prohibits discharge absent good cause. The purpose of the § 301 preemption provision in the LMRA is to ensure that federal law, and not state law, will be the basis for interpreting the substantive provisions of CBAs. The Court explained that the facts in *Lingle* did not implicate the preemption concerns of § 301 because resolution of Lingle's state tort claim did not require an interpretation of the CBA. If, however, a plaintiff's state claim does depend on such an interpretation, preemption may apply.[209]

2.5.1.6 In-House Attorneys and the Tort of Wrongful Discharge

A number of wrongful discharge cases have involved attorneys who claim retaliatory discharge against their former employers. At issue is whether an attorney's status as in-house counsel should preclude a tort action for wrongful discharge because proof of the claim may result in the disclosure of privileged attorney-client communications.[210] Two leading cases on the subject, with divergent outcomes, are *Balla v. Gambro, Inc.*[211] and *General Dynamics Corp. v. Superior Court.*[212]

Balla involved in-house counsel for Gambro, Inc., a company that distributed kidney dialysis equipment manufactured by Gambro Germany. Balla, the in-house counsel, was discharged as a result of his efforts to stop Gambro from selling defective dialyzers in violation of federal law. While acknowledging that Gambro terminated Balla in contravention of a clearly mandated public policy, the Illinois Supreme Court concluded that the attorney-client relationship barred Balla from maintaining a tort action for wrongful discharge in violation of public policy.

The court held that because Balla was required under the Rules of Professional Conduct to report Gambro's intention to sell the defective dialyzers, the underlying public policy at issue—"protecting

---

209 See generally Lipman et al., supra note 175, § 6.03; Jane Byeff Korn, Collective Rights and Individual Remedies: Rebalancing the Balance After Lingle v. Norge Division of Magic Chef, Inc., 41 Hastings L.J. 1149 (1990).

210 For in-depth discussions of the tort of wrongful discharge in the context of attorneys, see H. Lowell Brown, The Dilemma of Corporate Counsel Faced with Client Misconduct: Disclosure of Client Confidences or Constructive Discharge, 44 Buff. L. Rev. 777 (1996); Nancy Kubasek et al., The Social Obligation of Corporate Counsel: A Communitarian Justification for Allowing In-House Counsel to Sue for Retaliatory Discharge, 11 Geo. J. Legal Ethics 665 (1998); Todd Myers, The In-House Attorney Employment Dilemma, 6 Kan. J.L. & Pub. Pol'y 147 (1997); Symposium, The Role of the General Counsel: Ethical Dilemmas of Corporate Counsel, 46 Emory L.J. 1011 (1997).

211 145 Ill.2d 492, 584 N.E.2d 104 (1991).

212 7 Cal.4th 1164, 876 P.2d 487 (1994).

the lives and property of citizens"—was already adequately safeguarded.[213]

By contrast, in *General Dynamics*, the California Supreme Court held that an attorney's status as an in-house counsel did not preclude him from maintaining a tort action for discharge in violation of public policy. The attorney in the case, Andrew Rose, claimed that his former employer, General Dynamics, terminated him for various reasons, all of which were in violation of public policy.[214]

The court highlighted the dilemma that may confront in-house attorneys such as Rose who are "forced to choose between the demands of the employer and the requirements of a professional code of ethics. . . ."[215] The court observed that the *Balla* court's suggestion that in-house counsel could avoid the dilemma by voluntarily withdrawing from the position was unrealistic because, absent the ability to maintain an action for wrongful discharge, in-house attorneys "will almost always find silence the better part of valor."[216] The court explained why silence was a more likely response of in-house counsel relative to outside counsel:

> [U]nlike their in-house counterparts, outside lawyers enjoy a measure of professional distance and economic independence that usually serves to lessen the pressure to bend or ignore professional norms. . . . [T]he distinguishing feature of the in-house attorney is a virtually complete dependence on the good will and confidence of a single employer to provide livelihood and career success.[217]

Given this reality, the court concluded that in-house counsel faced with a choice between the demands of an employer and the requirements of an ethical code were not precluded from maintaining a tort action for wrongful discharge. In deference to the concerns about attorney-client confidentiality raised by *Balla* and other courts, however, the court limited application of the tort to claims that would not require a breach of the attorney-client privilege.[218]

---

213 Balla, 145 Ill.2d at 501, 584 N.E.2d at 108.

214 The reasons included Rose's involvement in an investigation into employee drug use at General Dynamics; his complaint concerning the company's failure to investigate the bugging of the office of the chief of security (allegedly a criminal offense); and his advice to company officials that General Dynamics was possibly violating the FLSA, a violation that might cost the company several hundred million dollars in backpay claims. General Dynamics, 7 Cal.4th at 1171, 876 P.2d at 490–91.

215 Id. at 1182, 876 P.2d at 498.

216 Id. at 1188, 876 P.2d at 502.

217 Id. at 1182, 876 P.2d at 498.

218 See also Heckman v. Zurich Holding Co. of Am., 242 F.R.D. 606, 608 (D. Kan. May 8, 2007) (allowing plaintiff to maintain her retaliatory discharge claim against defendants and to reveal confidential information under Rule 1.6(b)(3) to the extent

As between the holdings in *Balla* and *General Dynamics*, the overwhelming majority of courts that have considered the issue have followed *General Dynamics* and have permitted in-house attorneys to bring a tort action for retaliatory discharge against their former employers/clients so long as doing so does not interfere with their duty of confidentiality.[219] In part, this trend has been facilitated by changes to the Model Rules of Professional Responsibility, permitting attorneys to disclose confidential client communications in order to establish a claim in a controversy between the lawyer and the client.[220]

In the aftermath of various accounting scandals in the early 2000s, and in the context of the Sarbanes-Oxley Public Company Accounting Reform and Investor Protection Act of 2002, the Securities Exchange Commission issued rules for attorneys practicing before the commission that require lawyers to report "evidence of a material violation" up the corporate ladder, potentially all the way to the corporate board, and even to reveal confidential information to the commission where necessary to prevent a violation of the law likely to cause substantial injury to the financial interest or property" of investors.[221]

2.5.2 Intentional Infliction of Emotional Distress

The Restatement (Second) of Torts defines the tort of intentional infliction of emotional distress (IIED) as extreme and outrageous conduct that intentionally or recklessly causes severe emotional distress.[222] An IIED claim requires proof of the following elements: (1) extreme and outrageous conduct; (2) intent to cause, or disregard of a substantial probability of causing, severe emotional distress; (3)

---

necessary to establish such claim); Burkhart v. Semitool, Inc., 2000 MT 201, 5 P.3d 1031 (2000) (holding that the plain language of Montana's Wrongful Discharge from Employment Act required recognition of an in-house counsel's rights to maintain a wrongful discharge action under the Act); Parker v. M & T Chem., Inc., 236 N.J. Super. 451, 566 A.2d 215 (App. Div. 1989) (holding that the attorney-client relationship did not preclude an attorney's retaliatory discharge claim under the New Jersey whistleblower statute); Crews v. Buckman Labs. Int'l, Inc., 78 S.W.3d 852, 862 (Tenn. 2002) (holding that in-house counsel may bring a common-law action for retaliatory discharge resulting from counsel's compliance with a provision of the Code of Professional Responsibility that represents a clear and definitive statement of public policy).

219 See Heckman, 242 F.R.D. at 608 (listing cases).

220 Burkhart v. Semitool, Inc., 300 Mont. 480, 5 P.3d 1031 (Mont. 2000) (citing to Rules of Professional Conduct 1.6, in finding that in-house counsel's wrongful discharge action against employer-client is contemplated by the professional conduct rule that permits an attorney to reveal confidential attorney-client information to establish a claim in a controversy between the lawyer and the client).

221 17 C.F.R. § 205.3.

222 Restatement (Second) Torts § 46.

a causal connection between the conduct and injury; and (4) severe emotional distress.

Courts have established a very high bar for plaintiffs to succeed on an IIED claim.[223] The element of extreme and outrageous conduct, which forms the gravamen of the claim, is especially challenging for employees. As an initial matter, the standard of outrageousness can often be difficult to satisfy because the phrase "extreme and outrageous conduct" is vague and subjective.[224] Courts attempting to apply the standard typically begin by referencing the Restatement (Second) of Torts which defines "extreme and outrageous" as conduct that

> has been so outrageous in character and so extreme in degree, as to go beyond all possible bounds of decency, and to be regarded as atrocious, and utterly intolerable in a civilized community. Generally, the case is one in which the recitation of the facts to an average member of the community would arouse his resentment against the actor and lead him to exclaim, "Outrageous!"[225]

Such conduct does not include "insults, indignities, threats, annoyances, petty oppressions or other trivialities."[226]

Of particular importance in employment settings, an employer is not liable for the tort if it has done no more than to insist upon its legal rights in a permissible way.[227] *State Farm Mutual Automobile Insurance Co. v. Novotny*[228] illustrates this point. Novotny worked as a claims adjuster for the employer which was also her insurer. When Novotny filed a claim with the employer for damages to the fender and door of her car, a co-worker arranged for the body shop to paint the entire car at no additional charge. Upon discovering the free paint

---

[223] See Frank J. Cavico, The Tort of Intentional Infliction of Emotional Distress in the Private Employment Sector, 21 Hofstra Lab. & Emp. L.J. 109, 112–13 (2003).

[224] See, e.g., Wilson v. Monarch Paper Co., 939 F.2d 1138, 1142 (5th Cir. 1991) (describing the phrase as "amorphous"); Sommers v. Household Int'l, Inc., No. 98 C 4539, 1999 WL 1285858, at *8 (N.D. Ill. Dec. 30, 1999) (describing the phrase as "inherently ambiguous in character"); State Farm Mut. Auto. Ins. Co. v. Novotny, 657 So.2d 1210, 1213 (Fl. Dist. Ct. App. 1995) (describing the phrase as " 'highly subjective' " and " 'extremely mutable' "); Bevan v. Fix, 2002 WY 43, ¶ 19 n.7, 42 P.3d 1013, 1021 n.7 (Wyo. 2002) (describing the phrase as "vague, subjective, and value-laden").

[225] Restatement (Second) Torts § 46, cmt. (d).

[226] Id.

[227] See, e.g., Stewart v. Matthews Indus., 644 So.2d 915 (Ala. 1994); Mintz v. Bell Atl. Sys. Leasing Int'l, 183 Ariz. 550, 905 P.2d 559 (1995); Stanton v. Tulane Univ., 777 So.2d 1242 (La. App. 2001); Mason v. U.S. Fidelity & Guaranty Co., 69 Ohio App.3d 309, 590 N.E.2d 799 (1990); House v. Hicks, 218 Or.App. 348, 179 P.3d 730 (2008). See generally Restatement (Second) Torts § 46, cmt. (g).

[228] 657 So.2d 1210, 1213 (Fl. Dist. Ct. App. 1995).

job, the employer interviewed several of its employees, including Novotny, at a local motel. The employer questioned Novotny at the motel for 45 minutes until she admitted that she had accepted the free paint job. The employer then gave her a choice of resigning or being terminated. While being driven back to work by one of the interviewers, Novotny began crying and threatened to commit suicide. She was eventually seen by a psychiatrist. After resigning, Novotny filed an IIED claim against her employer. Although the jury awarded Novotny damages at trial, the appellate court reversed. The appellate court held that the employer had a legal right to investigate the paint job and to terminate Novotny.

An employer's ability to exercise its legal rights in a permissible way is especially relevant when an employment relationship is at will. Courts have observed that because employers are ordinarily entitled to terminate at-will employees, such a termination, without more, cannot constitute the type of extreme and outrageous conduct necessary to establish an IIED claim.[229]

Although courts do not regard the fact of discharge by itself as outrageous, an employee may recover on an IIED claim if an employer terminates an employee in an outrageous manner.[230] In such instances, courts remain vigilant in insuring that the challenged employer's conduct was truly outrageous and not a garden-variety employment dispute. Consider, for example, the facts of *Dean v. Ford Motor Credit Co.*[231] The employee, a terminated office clerk who occasionally worked as a cashier processing incoming checks, pointed to several incidents to support her IIED claim including evidence that when she expressed an interest in transferring to a higher-paying position she was told that " 'women usually don't go into that department.' "[232] Plaintiff also offered evidence that the employer selected a lesser qualified male for the position and that the employer assigned her a heavier workload relative to other clerks. Although these incidents were insufficient to constitute extreme and outrageous conduct, the plaintiff prevailed on evidence that the employer had placed checks in her purse so as to make her appear to be a thief. This latter conduct, concluded the

---

[229] See, e.g., Novosel v. Sears, Roebuck & Co., 495 F.Supp. 344 (E.D. Mich. 1980); M.B.M. Co. v. Counce, 268 Ark. 269, 596 S.W.2d 681 (1980); Mendlovic v. Life Line Screening of Am., Ltd., 173 Ohio App.3d 46, 877 N.E.2d 377 (2007); Hoflund v. Airport Golf Club, 2005 WY 17, 105 P.3d 1079 (2005).

[230] See, e.g., M.B.M. Co., 268 Ark. at 280–281, 596 S.W.2d at 688; Agarwal v. Johnson, 25 Cal.3d 932, 603 P.2d 58 (1979); Patton v. J.C. Penney Co., 301 Or. 117, 719 P.2d 854 (1986); Wornick Co. v. Casas, 856 S.W.2d 732 (Tex. 1993).

[231] 885 F.2d 300 (5th Cir. 1989).

[232] Id. at 303.

court, sufficed to take the case "beyond the realm of an ordinary employment dispute and into the realm of an outrageous one."[233]

In determining whether certain conduct is extreme and outrageous, courts generally consider the context and the relationship between the parties. Doing so has occasionally led courts to adopt contrasting approaches in IIED claims arising in the workplace. Some courts adopt a so-called "strict approach"[234] in which they suggest that employees should expect a certain level of unpleasantness in the workplace. The rationale for this approach seems to rest on the view that an employer requires wide latitude to properly operate its business and that many of the disciplinary acts required in managing employees such as evaluating, criticizing, and demoting them, are necessarily unpleasant from the employee's perspective.[235]

Other courts, adopting a more employee-oriented approach, insist that the employment relationship may "produce a character of outrageousness that otherwise might not exist."[236] The rationale behind this approach can be traced to the Restatement (Second) of Tort's comment that "the extreme and outrageous character of the conduct may arise from an abuse by the actor of a position, or a relation with the other, which gives him actual or apparent authority over the other, or power to affect his interests."[237] Consequently, some courts maintain that because of the power that employers exercise over employees, an employer's abuse of that power may be a factor in assessing outrageousness.[238] In *Wigginton v. Servidio*,[239] for

---

233 Id. at 307. See also Wilson v. Monarch Paper Co., 939 F.2d 1138 (5th Cir. 1991) (the incident which made the employer's conduct extreme and outrageous was requiring a 30-year executive to spend most of his time cleaning up after former subordinates).

234 See, e.g., Sterling v. Upjohn Healthcare Servs., Inc., 299 Ark. 278, 280, 772 S.W.2d 329, 330 (1989); GTE Sw., Inc. v. Bruce, 998 S.W.2d 605, 612 (Tex. 1998).

235 See, e.g., Johnson v. Merrell Dow Pharms., Inc., 965 F.2d 31, 34 (5th Cir. 1992); GTE Sw., 998 S.W.2d at 612; Sterling, 299 Ark. at 280, 772 S.W.2d at 330.

236 Bridges v. Winn-Dixie Atlanta, Inc., 176 Ga.App. 227, 230, 335 S.E.2d 445, 448 (1985); see also Pavilon v. Kaferly, 204 Ill.App.3d 235, 245, 561 N.E.2d 1245, 1251 (1990); Blong v. Snyder, 361 N.W.2d 312, 316 (Iowa App. 1984); White v. Monsanto Co., 585 So.2d 1205, 1209–10 (La. 1991); Travis v. Alcon Labs., Inc., 202 W.Va. 369, 376–77, 504 S.E.2d 419, 426–27 (1998).

237 Restatement (Second) Torts § 46, cmt. (e).

238 See, e.g., Pavilon, 204 Ill.App.3d at 245–46, 561 N.E.2d at 1251; Ky. Fried Chicken Nat'l Mgmt. Co. v. Weathersby, 326 Md. 663, 677, 607 A.2d 8, 15 (1992); see also Coleman v. Housing Auth. of Americus, 191 Ga.App. 166, 169, 381 S.E.2d 303, 306 (1989) (commenting that the workplace "by its very nature, . . . provides an environment more prone to . . . occurrences [of IIED] because it provides a captive victim who may fear reprisal for complaining, so that the injury is exacerbated by repetition, and it presents a hierarchy of structured relationships which cannot easily be avoided").

239 324 N.J. Super. 114, 734 A.2d 798 (App. Div. 1999).

example, the appellate court held that the lower court erred in dismissing an employee's IIED claim based on her supervisor's offensive racial slur. The court observed that "[s]tandards of decency and civility are different in the workplace. . . ."[240] While courts following a strict approach might use this observation to argue that employees should expect a certain amount of vile language in the workplace, the *Wigginton* court held that an employer has a higher duty than a stranger to avoid inflicting emotional distress, and that a supervisor's act in using a racial slur may contribute to a finding of outrageous conduct.

2.5.3 Intentional Interference with Contractual Relations

The tort of intentional interference with contractual relationships occurs when a third party improperly induces a party to break a valid contract that it has with another party. In the employment context, the tort historically served to protect the interests of employers in situations where Employer A claims that Employer B improperly interfered with Employer A's relationship with its employees. The claimed interference frequently involved an allegation that Employer B enticed the employees to leave Employer A's business and work instead for Employer B.[241] Over the years, courts in most states have also recognized the tort to protect an employee in situations where a third party improperly causes the employee's discharge or otherwise interferes with the employee's legitimate employment expectations. The third party may include the employee's co-worker or supervisor,[242] a former employer,[243] or a party who has a business relationship with the employee's employer.[244]

Most courts have made it clear that the tort, as applied to employment contracts, is not limited to contracts for a definite duration but protects at-will contracts as well. The Restatement (Second) of Torts echoes this position, observing that until an at-will employment contract is terminated, it is "valid and subsisting, and

---

240 Id. at 131, 734 A.2d at 807.

241 See, e.g., Ryan, Elliott & Co. v. Leggat, McCall & Werner, Inc., 8 Mass.App Ct. 686, 396 N.E.2d 1009 (1979).

242 See, e.g., Henderson v. Early, 555 So.2d 130 (Ala. 1989); Wagenseller v. Scottsdale Memorial Hosp., 147 Ariz. 370, 710 P.2d 1025 (1985); Sorrells v. Garfinckel's, Brooks Bros., Miller & Rhoads, Inc., 565 A.2d 285 (D.C. Cir. 1989).

243 See, e.g., Stebbins & Roberts, Inc. v. Halsey, 265 Ark. 903, 582 S.W.2d 266 (1979).

244 See, e.g., Hurst v. Ala. Power Co., 675 So.2d 397 (Ala. 1996); Pinger v. Behavioral Sci. Ctr., Inc., 52 Ohio App.3d 17, 556 N.E.2d 209 (1988).

the defendant may not improperly interfere with it."[245] However, some courts diverge from this view.[246]

Proof of the tort requires the following elements: (1) the existence of a valid contractual relationship; (2) knowledge of the relationship on the part of the interferer; (3) intentional interference inducing or causing a breach or termination of the relationship; (4) the interference was improper; and (5) resulting damages.[247] The most important element of the tort is the requirement of improper interference. While some courts hold that the plaintiff has the burden to establish that there was intentional interference *and* that the interference was improper,[248] others conclude that after the plaintiff establishes intentional interference, the defendant has an affirmative defense to demonstrate that it was justified in interfering with the relationship.[249] The Restatement (Second) of Torts lists various factors relevant to determining whether a given action constitutes improper interference, including the following: the nature of the actor's conduct, the actor's motive, the interests sought to be advanced by the actor, and the relations between the parties.[250]

As a general rule, only a third party, separate from the contracting parties, can be liable for tortious interference with contractual relationships.[251] Consequently, in instances where the

---

245 Restatement (Second) of Torts, § 766, cmt. g.

246 See, e.g., Jenkins v. Boise Cascade Corp., 141 Idaho 233, 108 P.3d 380 (2005) (observing that the grant of summary judgment for the employer on the employee's claim of tortious interference with contract was proper since the employee was an at-will employee and could be terminated with or without cause); Mendonca v. Tidewater, Inc., 939 So.2d 1280 (La. 2006) (observing that because an employee was at-will and he lacked a legally protected interest, he could not satisfy the required elements to maintain a claim for intentional tortious interference with contract).

247 The tort is closely analogous to interference with prospective contractual relations. The key difference between the two torts is that the tort of intentional interference with contractual relationships applies when a contract is already in existence while the tort of interference with prospective contractual relations applies in situations where a contract has not yet been formed but there is a reasonable expectation that one will be formed. See, e.g., Thompson Coal Co. v. Pike Coal Co., 488 Pa. 198, 412 A.2d 466 (1979).

248 See, e.g., Wagenseller, 147 Ariz. at 388, 710 P.2d at 1043 (stating that "the plaintiff bringing a tortious interference action must show that the defendant acted improperly").

249 See, e.g., Pegram v. Hebding, 667 So.2d 696, 701 (Ala. 1995) (noting that "[j]ustification for the interference is an affirmative defense that has to be pleaded and proved by the defendant"); Stebbins & Roberts, Inc., 265 Ark. at 907, 582 S.W.2d at 268 (observing that after the plaintiff satisfies a prima facie burden, the burden passes to the defendant "to show that its interference was justified").

250 Restatement (Second) of Torts, § 767.

251 See, e.g., Piekarski v. Home Owners Sav. Bank, 956 F.2d 1484 (8th Cir.), cert. denied, 506 U.S. 872, 113 S.Ct. 206 (1992); O'Neill v. ARA Serv., Inc., 457 F.Supp. 182 (E.D. Pa. 1978); Fregara v. Jet Aviation Bus. Jets, 764 F.Supp. 940 (D.N.J. 1991). But see Elliott v. Shore Stop, Inc., 238 Va. 237, 246, 384 S.E.2d 752, 757 (1989) (reversing the trial court's dismissal of plaintiff's action for intentional tortious interference

employee claims interference by a supervisor or a co-worker, most courts hold that as agents of the employer, such defendants cannot be liable for tortious interference as long as they were acting within the scope of their official employment duties. Where defendants were acting outside the scope of their employment and with actual malice, however, courts typically regard the interference by a supervisor or co-worker as improper.[252]

For instance, the employee in *Sorrells v. Garfinckel's, Brooks Bros., Miller & Rhoads, Inc.*[253] worked as a cosmetics sales representative for Garfinckel's until she was terminated. Sorrells claimed that her supervisor had intentionally undermined her employment relationship and that this action culminated in her termination. The court observed that since the supervisor was not a party to the contract between Garfinckel's and Sorrells, she could be found liable for tortious interference with that contract. The evidence indicated that the supervisor knew that Sorrells depended on telephone sales to perform her job, yet refused to allow Sorrells to use the telephone while permitting other employees to do so; that she ridiculed Sorrells and the products that she sold in front of customers; that she denied Sorrells use of a doctor-recommended stool to sit on out of spite and with the intent to cause Sorrells physical pain; and that she had requested on several occasions that Garfinckel's fire Sorrells. This evidence was sufficient to support the jury's finding that the supervisor had acted with malicious intent to interfere with Sorrells' contract.

While the Restatement (Second) of Torts opts to use the language of improper interference instead of privilege or justification, some courts, including the District of Columbia Court of Appeals in *Sorrells*, use these terms interchangeably or instead describe their decisions using only these latter terms, especially if the court holds that the defendant has an affirmative defense to establish that its conduct was proper. Thus in *Sorrells*, the supervisor was unable to prove that her conduct was legally justified or privileged.

Under the Restatement (Second) of Torts, a showing of actual malice is not required in order to pin liability on supervisors for tortious conduct performed outside of the scope of their employment duties. However, as a practical matter, many courts follow the

---

against her employer, the court held that "an action in tort exists against those who conspire to induce a breach of contract and that such rule will be applied to hold one liable . . . for conspiring to breach his own contract").

[252] See, e.g., Henderson v. Early, 555 So.2d 130 (Ala. 1989); Hickman v. Winston County Hosp. Bd., 508 So.2d 237 (Ala. 1987); Sorrells v. Garfinckel's, Brooks Bros., Miller & Rhoads, Inc., 565 A.2d 285 (D.C. Cir. 1989); Alba v. Sampson, 44 Mass.App.Ct. 311, 690 N.E.2d 1240 (1998).

[253] 565 A.2d 285.

approach in *Sorrells* and assign liability to supervisory employees only upon a showing of actual malice, the definition of which includes ill will, hostility, and personal spite.[254] As the Supreme Judicial Court of Massachusetts explained, assigning "liability to corporate officials only when their actions are motivated by actual, and not merely implied, malice has particular force because 'their freedom of action directed toward corporate purposes should not be curtailed by fear of personal liability.' "[255]

§ 2.6 Reform Efforts and the At-Will Doctrine

Although the law governing the employment relationship has evolved considerably over the years, its patchwork quality has led many commentators to argue in support of a comprehensive and uniform legislative approach to replace the different and often competing state judicial approaches to the employment-at-will doctrine.[256] This section briefly overviews three efforts to reform the employment-at-will doctrine as well as a proposal to clarify the many state standards governing the doctrine.

2.6.1 The Montana Wrongful Discharge from Employment Act

Montana offers a distinctive statutory approach to providing employees with greater job security. Since 1987, the Montana Wrongful Discharge from Employment Act (WDFEA)[257] has provided comprehensive protection for employees by prohibiting dismissals without "good cause." Montana is the only state to have established a "good cause" standard for dismissal of employees who lack an employment contract with a specific duration.[258]

---

[254] See, e.g., Pegram v. Hebding, 667 So.2d 696 (Ala. 1995); Jones v. Lake Park Care Ctr., 569 N.W.2d 369 (Iowa 1997).

[255] Gram v. Liberty Mut. Ins. Co., 384 Mass. 659, 663–64, 429 N.E.2d 21, 24 (1981) (quoting Steranko v. Inforex, Inc., 5 Mass.App.Ct. 253, 273, 362 N.E.2d 222, 235 (1977)). See also Alba, 44 Mass.App.Ct. at 314, 690 N.E.2d at 1243 (observing that "[i]n the employment and discharge context, the law of this jurisdiction seeks to protect a corporate official's freedom of action by requiring proof that the official acted with actual malice").

[256] See, e.g., Theodore J. St. Antoine, The Making of the Model Employment Termination Act, 69 Wash. L. Rev. 361 (1994); Theodore J. St. Antoine, A Seed Germinates: Unjust Discharge Reform Heads Toward Full Flower, 67 Neb. L. Rev. 56, 76 (1988); Lawrence E. Blades, Employment At Will vs. Individual Freedom: On Limiting the Abusive Exercise of Employer Power, 67 Colum. L. Rev. 1404 (1967); Ann C. McGinley, Rethinking Civil Rights and Employment At Will: Toward a Coherent National Discharge Policy, 57 Ohio St. L.J. 1443 (1996); Jack Stieber & Michael Murray, Protection Against Unjust Discharge: The Need for a Federal Statute, 16 U. Mich. J.L. Reform 319 (1982–1983).

[257] Mont. Code Ann. § 39–2–901.

[258] For a history of the WDFEA, including an overview of court cases that led to the enactment of the statute, see Bradley T. Ewing et al., The Employment Effects of

The WDFEA prohibits private employers from terminating employees under the following circumstances: (1) the discharge was in retaliation for the employee's refusal to violate public policy or for reporting a violation of public policy; (2) the discharge was not for good cause and the employee had completed the employer's probationary period of employment; or (3) the employer violated the express provisions of its own written personnel policy.[259]

Two definitional sections of the WDFEA are worth highlighting. First, the WDFEA defines "discharge" to include constructive discharge.[260] However, constructive discharge does not apply to situations where an employee quits as a result of an employer's refusal to promote, to improve wages, or to improve other terms and conditions of employment.[261] Second, the WDFEA defines good cause to mean "reasonable job-related grounds for dismissal based on a failure to satisfactorily perform job duties, disruption of the employer's operation, or other legitimate business reason."[262]

Under the WDFEA, a wrongfully discharged employee may be awarded lost wages and benefits,[263] and, in limited cases, punitive damages.[264] The WDFEA allows either party to offer arbitration as a means of resolving a wrongful discharge dispute.[265] While neither party is required to accept a proposal to arbitrate, if the offer is declined and the party offering arbitration prevails in litigation, she is entitled to reasonable attorney's fees from the date of the offer.[266] An offer to arbitrate is the only mechanism in the WDFEA that may allow a party an opportunity to receive attorney's fees.[267]

In 1989, the Montana Supreme Court upheld the constitutionality of the WDFEA.[268] Although the WDFEA provides substantial protection for at-will employees, critics point out that it suffers from several limitations, including disallowing damages for pain and suffering and emotional distress, limiting the recovery of

---

a "Good Cause" Discharge Standard in Montana, 59 Indus. & Lab. Rel. Rev. 17 (2005); Arthur S. Leonard, A New Common Law of Employment Termination, 66 N.C. L. Rev. 631 (1988).

259 Mont. Code Ann. § 39–2–904.

260 Id. § 39–2–903(2).

261 Id. § 39–2–903(1).

262 Id. § 39–2–903(5)

263 Id. § 39–2–905(1) (limiting lost wages and benefits "for a period not to exceed 4 years from the date of discharge").

264 Id. § 39–2–905(2).

265 Id. § 39–2–914(1).

266 Id. § 39–2–914(4).

267 See Marc Jarsulic, Protecting Workers from Wrongful Discharge: Montana's Experience with Tort and Statutory Regimes, 3 Empl. Rts. & Employ. Pol'y J. 105, 109 (1999).

268 See Meech v. Hillhaven W., 238 Mont. 21, 776 P.2d 488 (1989).

punitive damages to claims for a violation of public policy, hinging the collection of attorney's fees on an offer to arbitrate, and leaving it to the employer's discretion to define the length of the probationary period for employees who can be terminated absent good cause.

2.6.2 The Model Employment Termination Act

In 1991, the National Conference of Commissioners on Uniform State Laws proposed the Model Employment Termination Act (META)[269] for adoption by state legislatures. The Act, similar to the WDFEA, represents a compromise position between the interests of employers and employees. It provides employees with good cause protection against discharge while limiting the scope of available remedies. Whereas the Montana statute provides fairly broad coverage of employees and employers,[270] META limits its coverage to private employers with at least five employees[271] and applies only to employees who have worked for a covered employer for at least a year and who have worked a minimum number of hours during the 26-week period preceding the termination.[272]

META's central substantive provision prohibits employers from discharging employees absent "good cause."[273] The Act allows the parties to waive the requirement of good cause if they execute an agreement that guarantees the employee a minimum severance pay allowance that reflects the employee's length of service.[274]

META provides for arbitration of claims by state-appointed arbitrators.[275] While the WDFEA allows for voluntary arbitration if agreed to by both parties, META provides that either party can demand arbitration.[276] Available remedies for successful claimants include reinstatement,[277] back pay, reimbursement for lost

---

[269] Model Employment Termination Act, 7A U.L.A. 421 (1999) [hereinafter referred to as META]. For a discussion of the Act from its reporter, see St. Antoine, The Making of the Model Employment Termination Act, supra note 256; St. Antoine, A Seed Germinates, supra note 256.

[270] The Montana Wrongful Discharge from Employment Act does, however, exclude from its protection employees who work under a written contract for a specified term and employees covered by a collective bargaining agreement. Mont. Code Ann. § 39–2–912.

[271] META § 1(2).

[272] Id. § 3(b) (providing that an employee must work at least 520 hours during the 26-week period preceding the termination).

[273] Id. § 3(a); see also id. § 1(4) (defining "good cause").

[274] Id. § 4(c).

[275] Id. § 6(a) & (b).

[276] Id. § 5(a) & (c).

[277] Id. § 7(b)(1).

benefits,[278] and attorney's fees.[279] Severance pay is also available in lieu of reinstatement.[280] Finally, META, like the Montana statute, prohibits an award for pain and suffering, emotional distress, defamation, fraud, punitive or compensatory damages.[281]

In proposing META, the National Conference of Commissioners on Uniform State Laws hoped to eliminate the disjointed employment framework that currently exists as a result of states adopting differing approaches to modifying the employment-at-will doctrine. To date, however, no state has adopted META.[282]

2.6.3 The American Law Institute's Restatement of the Law Third, Employment Law

In 2015, the American Law Institute (ALI) published the Restatement (Third) of Employment Law.[283] The Restatement includes nine chapters which address the existence of the employment relationship, the termination of employment contracts, issues of compensation and benefits, principles of tort liability for tortious acts to employees, the tort of retaliation in violation of public policy, other tort actions like defamation, wrongful interference and misrepresentation, principles of privacy and autonomy, employee obligations and restrictive convenants, and remedies.

Unlike the Montana law and META, both of which aim to protect employees from arbitrary dismissal, the Restatement does not seek to provide employees with any substantive rights. Instead, similar to other Restatements, it represents an effort to clarify and simplify the existing law. The attempt to do so in the area of employment law has provoked some controversy, with commentators expressing the view that such an enterprise is premature as the law governing the employment relationship is in a state of flux, so much so that any effort to codify it may prove counterproductive.[284]

---

278 Id. § 7(b)(2).

279 Id. § 7(b)(4).

280 Id. § 7(b)(3).

281 Id. § 7(d). Section 905(3) of the Montana Wrongful Discharge from Employment Act provides for the exclusion of recovery for pain and suffering, emotional distress, and compensatory damages.

282 For an insightful critique of the Act, see Kenneth A. Sprang, Beware the Toothless Tiger: A Critique of the Model Employment Termination Act, 43 Am. U. L. Rev. 849 (1994).

283 American Law Institute, Restatement of the Law Third Employment Law (2015) [hereinafter Restatement of Employment Law]. Although labeled the "Third" Restatement, there does not currently exist a Restatement of Employment Law.

284 See, e.g., Mathew W. Finkin et al., Working Group on Chapter 2 of the Proposed Restatement of Employment L: Employment Contracts: Termination, 13 Emp. Rts. & Emp. Pol'y 93 (2009); Rachel Arnow-Richman, Response to Working

Some of the controversy has focused on the status of the employment relationship vis-à-vis the employment-at-will doctrine. The Restatement states that the default rule is an at-will employment relationship, and treats the contract and tort modifications discussed earlier in this chapter as "exceptions" to this default rule.

As discussed supra in Chapter 2, Montana is the only state that has legislatively changed the default rule from at-will employment to job security absent good cause to terminate. Yet because most other states have also moved away from the at-will default rule through the use of the common law, some critics have expressed the view that it may be misleading to state, as does the Restatement, that "courts in 49 states recognize the principle that the employment is presumptively an at-will relationship."[285] Arguably so many exceptions presently exist to the at-will doctrine that the exceptions may have swallowed the rule. Part of the concern is that the Restatement's classification of common law erosions of the at-will rule as "exceptions" and its apparent failure to appreciate the magnitude of those exceptions may halt the evolution of employment law in some jurisdictions and may lead other jurisdictions to abandon various common law protections that they currently afford employees.[286]

Group on Chapter 2 of the Proposed Restatement of Employment Law: Putting the Restatement in its Place, 13 Employee Rts. & Emp. Pol'y J. 143, 143 (2009).

[285] Restatement of Employment Law, § 2.01.

[286] See Robert A. Hillman, Drafting Chapter 2 of the ALI's Employment Law Restatement in the Shadow of Contract Law: An Assessment of the Challenges and Results, 100 Cornell L. Rev. 1341 (2015), for a discussion of the criticisms and responses to the project.

Chapter 3

PRIVACY, AUTONOMY AND DIGNITY IN THE WORKPLACE

Like other areas of employment law, the laws relating to workplace privacy, autonomy and dignity seek to balance the rights and interests of employers, employees and society. Employers want to control their property and manage their workforces in order to operate a profit-making enterprise or, in the case of government employers, to provide services to the public efficiently and effectively. To operate efficiently, employers want to investigate and monitor both applicants and employees to insure that they are, or will be, honest and productive. Employers[1] and employees have interests in free speech and association. Employees want to protect their personal information and control its use. Additionally, employees have an interest in being free from employer intrusion into their private lives. Employees also have an interest in autonomy, in having the freedom to make significant decisions about their lives without interference. Finally employees want to be treated with dignity and respect in the workplace.

Societal interests overlap those of employers and employees. Efficient and productive businesses serve the public and enable American enterprises to compete in the global marketplace, providing jobs for citizens. Society also seeks efficient government services, effective use of tax dollars, and democratic participation by citizens. Protecting employee rights, both to warn about dangerous or unlawful employer conduct and to contribute to the public debate based on their specialized knowledge, benefits society. Additionally, there are societal norms, such as privacy, dignity and autonomy for all citizens, which are often reflected in state and federal constitutions, statutes, and the common law. These laws determine when the interests of employers, employees and society become legal rights subject to protection and how they are balanced with the rights and interests of the other party and society.

---

[1] The Supreme Court has recognized that organizations have speech and associational interests. See, e.g., Boy Scouts of America v. Dale, 530 U.S. 640 (2000). Employer speech and associational interests are uncertain, complex, confusing and in many cases problematic, however. See Paul Secunda, The Solomon Amendment, Expressive Associations, and Public Employment, 54 UCLA L. Rev. 1767 (2007).

§ 3.1 Protections Regarding Speech and Association

The primary source of the rights of speech and association is the First Amendment to the U.S. Constitution which provides: "Congress shall make no law respecting an establishment of religion, or prohibiting the free exercise thereof; or abridging the freedom of speech, or of the press; or the right of the people peaceably to assemble, and to petition the Government for a redress of grievances." The Fourteenth Amendment made the First Amendment applicable to the states.[2] Employees frequently have invoked the First Amendment in employment cases. Of course, only the actions of public employers constitute state action sufficient to invoke the direct protection of the Constitution.[3] Constitutional protection may be extended to private sector employees, however, through a state constitution,[4] a state statute,[5] or state common law.[6] In addition to First Amendment protection, certain kinds of workplace speech and association are protected by statute.

3.1.1 Constitutional Protection for Speech

Government employees have invoked the First Amendment to challenge employer interference with their rights to speak both within and outside of the workplace. While government employees do not forego their speech rights when they become public employees, the speech rights of government employees are more limited than those of other citizens. In *Pickering v. Board of Education*,[7] the Supreme Court established a balancing test to determine when government employers may restrict the speech of their employees. The Court in *Pickering* recognized that a public employer has an interest in the efficient operation of government that may justify restricting employee speech. Accordingly, the court must balance these interests to determine when an employer may limit the speech of an employee to further the interests of the government.

---

[2] Gitlow v. New York, 268 U.S. 652, 666 (1925).

[3] Martin H. Malin, et al., Public Sector Employment 61 (3d ed. 2016).

[4] Cal. Const. Art. 1, § 1; Luck v. Southern Pac. Transp. Co., 218 Cal.App.3d 1, 17–19, 267 Cal.Rptr. 618, 627–29 (1990) (holding private employers bound by California constitutional privacy provision and finding drug testing violated employee's constitutional rights.)

[5] N.J. Stat. Ann. § 10:6–2 (providing cause of action under New Jersey law against a person who deprives another of "substantive due process or equal protection rights, privileges or immunities secured by the Constitution or laws of the United States").

[6] As discussed further in Section 3.1.1, the First Amendment has been used as the public policy supporting a claim of wrongful discharge in the private sector. See, e.g., Novosel v. Nationwide Ins. Co., 721 F.2d 894 (3d Cir. 1983).

[7] 391 U.S. 563 (1968).

The test set forth by the *Pickering* Court requires an initial determination of whether the employee speech at issue relates to a matter of public concern. This determination is based on the "content, form and context" of the employee's speech, "as revealed by the whole record."[8] If the speech relates to a matter of public concern, the court must then balance the employee's interest in making the statement against the employer's interest in providing efficient government service. Among the factors that weigh in the balance are the manner, time and place of the speech and the context of the dispute over the speech.[9] The level of disruption that the speech causes or might cause in the workplace is an important factor on the government's side of the balance.[10] In determining whether speech is disruptive, the court relies on what the employer reasonably believed the employee said in situations where the substance of the speech is in dispute.[11]

The Supreme Court has found the following to be matters of public concern: speech to a coworker by a clerk in the constable's office regarding the assassination attempt on President Reagan;[12] speech by a teacher to her principal alleging racial discrimination in the school district;[13] a questionnaire distributed to coworkers by an assistant district attorney regarding pressure on employees to work in the political campaigns of favored candidates;[14] speech to a radio station by a teacher regarding a school district's policy on teacher dress and appearance;[15] and a letter to a newspaper written by a

---

[8] Connick v. Myers, 461 U.S. 138, 148–49 (1983). The public concern requirement was also applied to a petition clause case involving an employee grievance over termination and a complaint about overtime pay. Borough of Duryea v. Guarnieri, 564 U.S. 379 (2011). The Court said that the case could easily have been filed as a speech case and so no different test should be applied. Id. at 387–88, 393.

[9] Rankin v. McPherson, 483 U.S. 378, 388 (1987).

[10] Connick v. Myers, 461 U.S. at 151–52.

[11] Waters v. Churchill, 511 U.S. 661, 675–78 (1994).

[12] Rankin v. McPherson, 483 U.S. at 386–87 (finding statement to coworker in discussion of the policies of President Reagan and his attempted assassination that "if they go for him again, I hope they get him" was a matter of public concern as a part of the "robust" debate on public issues).

[13] Givhan v. Western Line Consol. Sch. Dist., 439 U.S. 410, 412–14 (1979) (finding school teacher's complaints to principal about alleged racial discrimination in employment practices protected by First Amendment, although made privately rather than publicly).

[14] Connick v. Myers, 461 U.S. at 149 (finding employee's general complaints about office morale and supervision were not matters of public concern where the speech arose from a private employment dispute rather than an effort to bring poor performance of government functions to the attention of the public, but complaints about pressure to work in political campaigns were a matter of public concern in light of the importance of the constitutional right involved and public interest in merit-based, rather than patronage-based, employment).

[15] Mt. Healthy City Sch. Dist. Bd. of Educ. v. Doyle, 429 U.S. 274, 284 (1977) (agreeing with district court that call to radio station about teacher dress code was protected by First Amendment).

teacher regarding school funding decisions.[16] On the other hand, a police officer who made and sold sexually explicit videos in a generic police uniform was not speaking on a matter of public concern because his speech did not qualify as a legitimate news interest to the public.[17]

In 2006, the Supreme Court further limited the protection of employees' speech, ruling in *Garcetti v. Ceballos*[18] that speech pursuant to official duties was not citizen speech entitled to constitutional protection. Ceballos was a deputy district attorney who wrote a disposition memorandum recommending dismissal of charges against a criminal defendant because his investigation revealed that the police affidavit used to obtain the search warrant contained misrepresentations. Ceballos subsequently testified at a hearing on a defense motion challenging the warrant, but the court rejected the challenge and the district attorney proceeded with the prosecution. Ceballos was later reassigned, transferred, and denied a promotion, allegedly in retaliation for his actions relating to the case. The Supreme Court held that the speech relating to the search warrant was pursuant to his official duties however, and therefore not protected by the First Amendment. The Court concluded that where the employee is not speaking as a citizen, but rather as an employee, the First Amendment is not implicated and courts should refrain from interfering with the employer's supervision of the employee.

In *Lane v. Franks*,[19] the Court addressed the issue of the context of the speech as a factor in determining whether the employee was speaking as an employee or a citizen. Despite warnings from his boss not to take action, Lane fired a state representative who was paid by a government agency he directed, but who was not working. The representative sued and threatened to have Lane terminated. Lane later testified at a grand jury hearing and two criminal trials of the representative and was subsequently terminated. The Supreme Court held that Lane's testimony was protected because it was "outside the scope of his ordinary job duties."[20] Although the speech concerned his employment, that was insufficient to render it employee speech. A concurrence emphasized that the case did not resolve the question of the *Garcetti* doctrine's application to

---

[16] Pickering v. Board of Educ., 391 U.S. at 571–72 (holding that teacher's comments on school funding were a matter of public concern because they were of substantial concern to the public and related to a subject on which public debate is important).

[17] See City of San Diego v. Roe, 543 U.S. 77, 84 (2004).

[18] 547 U.S. 410 (2006).

[19] 134 S.Ct. 2369 (2014).

[20] Id. at 2378.

testimony by employees who regularly engaged in such activity as a part of their job.[21]

As a result of *Garcetti*, many lower court decisions have focused on whether employee speech was made pursuant to the employee's official duties, a determination that has not proved to be an easy one for the courts.

There is an additional category of speech protection for government employees. When the speech has no relationship to the workplace, it is pure citizen speech and the government has an insufficient interest in restricting it.[22] Under this rule, the Court struck down a law banning federal employees from receiving compensation for speeches or articles made outside the workplace on matters unrelated to their employment.[23] But in the case of the police officer who made sexually explicit videos in a police uniform and sold them, the Court held that he was not engaged in speech unrelated to the workplace, although the conduct occurred outside of work and on his own time.[24] Because the employee intentionally exploited his role as a police officer in the videos in a way that harmed his employer, the Court concluded that his activity was not unrelated to work.[25]

Consider the following example: A police officer observes her partner abusing a suspect during an arrest for assault and battery. The arrest takes place outside the suspect's home. If the officer reports the abuse to her superior in the police department and as a result is transferred to the night shift in a dangerous and crime-ridden precinct, does she have a claim under the First Amendment? Clearly the speech is related to the workplace. Under *Garcetti,* the first question is whether the report is an official duty of the officer. Suppose the job description for police officers includes a requirement to report all improper activity of other officers to the commanding officer. Such a provision would seem to doom a First Amendment claim based on *Garcetti*. Yet a citizen observing the arrest could make the same complaint, and the Court has made it clear that government employees do not check their rights to speak as citizens at the workplace door. In *Skrutski v. Marut*,[26] the district court denied a summary judgment motion and allowed a police officer's First Amendment case to proceed to trial where the officer contended that

---

21 Id. at 2383–84.

22 United States v. National Treasury Employees Union, 513 U.S. 454 (1995).

23 Id. Among the members of the class challenging the ban were a mail handler who lectured on the Quaker religion, an aerospace engineer who spoke about black history, and a microbiologist who reviewed dance performances for radio and television. Id. at 461.

24 City of San Diego v. Roe, 543 U.S. at 81.

25 Id.

26 2006 WL 2660691 (M.D. Pa.)

he acted as a citizen in reporting the misconduct of fellow officers, despite the fact that the departmental regulations incorporated in his job description required him to make such reports. The court concluded that if a citizen had observed similar misconduct by the officers, the citizen could have made the same complaints as Officer Skrutski, thus distinguishing the case from *Garcetti* where no citizen could have engaged in analogous speech.[27] After the trial, however, the court of appeals reversed a jury verdict in favor of the officer, finding he was acting as a supervisor and reporting up the chain of command.[28]

In *Matthews v. City of New York*,[29] the district court found an officer's complaint to high ranking officials about a ticket quota system that he believed was impairing community relationships to be unprotected employee speech. The district court relied on a Patrol Guide that imposed on all officers a duty to report any corruption or other misconduct. The Second Circuit reversed however, finding the speech was not part of his job description or "every day work."[30] The court applied a functional approach, finding that reporting on policy issues was not part of his job. Similarly, the Fourth Circuit in *Hunter v. Town of Mocksville* found a genuine issue of fact as to whether officers were acting as citizens when they reported corruption, fraud and racism in the police department to the governor, noting such a report was not part of their daily duties.[31]

Suppose no policy or job description required the officer to report misconduct. Should the court find an inherent job requirement to report misconduct by other officers? If so, the officer loses. *Wilson v. Tregere* supports this conclusion, finding that a chief deputy sheriff has a duty to report any action that he believes violates law.[32]

Suppose the officer reports the matter to the newspaper rather than to her superior officers, fearing a cover-up if she uses official channels. Certainly it is not her job to report misconduct to the newspaper.[33] This would get the officer over the hurdle created by

---

27 Id. at *10.

28 288 F. App'x 803, 806–07 (2d Cir. 2008).

29 779 F.3d 167 (2d Cir. 2015).

30 Id. at 174.

31 789 F.3d 389, 399 (4th Cir. 2015).

32 787 F.3d 322, 325 (5th Cir. 2015) (relying on a Louisiana attorney general's opinion that a sheriff has a duty to enforce all laws even where others also have a duty).

33 See Rohr v. Nehls, No. 04–C–477, 2006 WL 2927657 (E.D. Wis. Oct. 11, 2006) (concluding that because the deputy sheriff bypassed the official complaint channels, his complaints regarding the sheriff were not unprotected under *Garcetti*). Cf. Haynes v. City of Circleville, 474 F.3d 357 (6th Cir. 2007) (finding that since the employee's complaint was made solely to his supervisor, and not in a public forum, he was speaking as an employee).

Garcetti, but a report to the media without an initial attempt to resolve the matter internally might be found to be sufficiently disruptive to the efficiency and effectiveness of the police department that the employer's interests would outweigh the officer's First Amendment rights. Would the result be different if the officer first made an official report to her superior and then, when no action was taken, gave a copy of the report to the newspaper? Similar facts in *Andrew v. Clark*, led the district court to dismiss the case, finding that an employee cannot invoke First Amendment protection by releasing an official complaint to the media.[34] The court of appeals, however, found that there was a material issue of fact as to whether the initial memorandum was pursuant to official duties or citizen speech, remanding the case to the district court for further proceedings.[35]

What if the officer reported instead to her union? In *Dahlia v. Rodriguez*, the court found that a report to superiors about abusive interrogation was not protected, but allowed the officer to proceed on his claim that he was retaliated against when he complained to his union that his boss threatened him for reporting the abusive interrogation.[36] The court found no job duty to report to the union, a separate entity from the police department.

If the officer's official report is not protected by the First Amendment because of *Garcetti*, suppose that she testifies pursuant to a subpoena in a civil lawsuit brought by the assault victim against the abused suspect and, in the course of her testimony, mentions the excessive force used by her fellow officer in the arrest. If the unwanted job transfer is in retaliation for her testimony, rather than any official report, she is likely to be protected.[37] If she can show that the protected speech was a part of the employer's motivation, to avoid liability the employer must show that it would have transferred her for legitimate reasons in the absence of the protected speech.[38]

---

[34] 472 F. Supp. 2d 659 (D. Md. 2007).

[35] 561 F. 3d 261, 266 (4th Cir. 2009).

[36] 735 F.3d 1060, 1077 (9th Cir. 2013).

[37] See Morales v. Jones, 494 F.3d 590 (7th Cir. 2007) (finding that a police officer's testimony about official misconduct in a deposition in an unrelated lawsuit was not part of his official duties and remanding for a determination whether his transfer was in retaliation for the protected deposition testimony or the unprotected report of the misconduct to the district attorney, which was part of his official duties). *Lane v. Franks*, decided after *Morales*, would also support protection since testifying in a civil claim would not be part of her job duties. The *Lane* concurrence, however, suggests that if her testimony was in the criminal proceeding that arose from the arrest, the result might be different as police officers regularly testify in criminal proceedings.

[38] See Mt. Healthy City Sch. Dist. Bd. of Educ. v. Doyle, 429 U.S. 274 (1977) (establishing the proof framework for cases in which both the plaintiff's protected

Social media is creating new issues relating to free speech of government employees. In *Bland v. Roberts*, the court held that clicking "like" on the Facebook page of a political candidate constituted speech.[39] The court pointed to the consequences of the click, including the appearance of the campaign and candidate photo on the employee's page, the appearance of the employee on the campaign's page as one who liked it, and the notice of the "like" on the news feeds of the employee's friends.[40]

Off-duty blogging by government employees has also raised issues of free speech. In *Munroe v. Central Bucks School District*,[41] a teacher's blog commented on academic integrity, the school district's grading process, and lack of student effort, in addition to extensive personal writings. Her blog also became the subject of extensive media coverage and resulted in interviews of the teacher in national media. The court found that the teacher was speaking on matters of public concern, but in balancing interests concluded that the extensive negative comments about students, resulting in parents and students objecting to being in her class, outweighed her interests. Among factors weighing heavily in the balance were the fact that the public concern aspects of the blog were not predominant and the importance of public trust in public school teachers.

The Michigan Appellate Court reached a similar result in a case of an assistant attorney general who blogged about the gay president of University of Michigan Student Assembly and his "radical homosexual agenda".[42] After the blog became public, the employee gave television interviews that identified his government position. Examining the contents of the blog posts, the court found them of limited public concern since much of the focus was the sexual orientation of the student and his friends. Thus, the government's justification for terminating the employee need not be as weighty. The court found the government's interest outweighed that of the employee since the postings and subsequent media interest created a "public relations crisis" for the agency, including condemnations from the city council and state civil rights agency questioning the ability of the department of the attorney general to achieve its mission.[43] Further, one of the department's initiatives was a

---

speech and another legitimate reason motivated the employer to take action against the employee).

[39] 730 F.3d 368, 385–86 (4th Cir. 2013). The district court, however, had found that it was not speech. Id. at 384–85.

[40] Id. at 385–86.

[41] 805 F.3d 454 (3d Cir. 2015).

[42] Shirvell v. Michigan Dep't of Attorney Gen'l, 866 N.W.2d 478, 484, 505 (Mich. App. 2015).

[43] Id. at 502–03.

campaign against cyber-bullying, which the court concluded was undermined by the employee's blog posts.[44]

Like government employees, independent contractors who have contracted to perform work for the government, have First Amendment protection for their speech. In *Board of County Commissioners v. Umbehr*,[45] the Court held that the First Amendment protects independent contractors from the termination of at-will government contracts in retaliation for their protected speech. The Court concluded that the *Pickering* balancing test used in employee cases should also be used in independent contractor cases to determine whether a contract termination violates the First Amendment. The government's interests as a contractor are balanced against the independent contractor's interests in free speech.

Private sector employees have attempted to use the First Amendment as a source of public policy supporting a tort claim for wrongful discharge in violation of public policy.[46] In *Novosel v. Nationwide Ins. Co.*,[47] the plaintiff succeeded. There, the Third Circuit Court of Appeals, applying Pennsylvania law, held that the employee stated a claim for wrongful discharge based on allegations that he was fired for refusing to lobby for legislation supported by his employer and for privately stating his opposition to the legislation. *Novosel* has subsequently been limited to its facts, however.[48] Other courts have rejected the use of federal constitutional provisions as public policies in wrongful discharge cases filed by private sector employees who are not directly protected by the provisions.[49] These courts reason that the public policy underlying the First Amendment is a limitation on the power of government to restrict speech, not a public policy limiting interference with speech by private employers.[50]

---

[44] Id. at 503–04.

[45] 518 U.S. 668, 670 (1996).

[46] For further discussion of wrongful discharge claims, see Section 2.6.1.

[47] 721 F.2d 894 (3d Cir. 1983).

[48] See Fraser v. Nationwide Mut. Ins. Co., 352 F.3d 107, 112–13 (3d Cir. 2003), as amended (Jan. 20, 2004) (predicting that the Supreme Court of Pennsylvania would not find a violation of public policy based on the First Amendment if there is no state action and stating *Novosel* is limited to its facts).

[49] See, e.g., Edmondson v. Shearer Lumber Prods., 139 Idaho 172, 75 P.3d 733 (2003) (finding private sector employee has no cause of action for termination based on exercise of constitutional right of free speech); Barr v. Kelso-Burnett Co., 106 Ill.2d 520, 478 N.E.2d 1354 (1985) (same); Grzyb v. Evans, 700 S.W.2d 399 (Ky. 1985) (finding no cause of action for wrongful discharge in violation of public policy based on constitutional right of association).

[50] See, e.g., Barr v. Kelso-Burnett, 106 Ill.2d at 527–28, 478 N.E.2d at 1357.

3.1.2 Constitutional Protection for Association

Government employees have a right to freedom of association which arises from the due process clause of the Fourteenth Amendment's protection of liberty and from the First Amendment's protection of the rights of speech and assembly.[51] The associational right that arises from the protection of liberty relates to an individual's interest in maintaining intimate human relationships.[52] The First Amendment right relates to association for the purposes of engaging in other rights protected by the First Amendment such as speech, assembly, petitioning for the redress of grievances, and religion.[53] Cases raising both issues have arisen in the context of public employment.[54]

An example of a case implicating the liberty interest is *Matusick v. Erie County Water Authority*.[55] There, the court found that the harassment of the employee on the basis of his interracial relationship, which ripened into marriage, violated his right to association.

Most of the cases involving public sector employees, however, allege violations of the associational interests under the First Amendment. For example, in *Shelton v. Tucker*,[56] the Supreme Court found that the plaintiffs' constitutional rights to association were violated by the public employer's requirement that employees disclose all organizational memberships as a condition of their employment by any public educational institution in Arkansas.

As in the case of free speech rights, the government's interests in fit and competent employees and efficient government service may justify intrusions on the associational interests of employees. Courts are split on the question of whether the *Pickering* test applied in free speech cases also applies to cases involving associational rights.[57] Some courts have applied the *Pickering* test to associational rights cases, requiring that the association of the employee relate to a

---

[51] See Roberts v. United States Jaycees, 468 U.S. 609, 622 (1984); Erwin Chemerinsky, Constitutional Law: Principles and Policies 1155 (3d ed. 2006).

[52] 468 U.S. at 617–18.

[53] Id.

[54] Alex B. Long, The Troublemaker's Friend: Retaliation Against Third Parties and the Right of Association in the Workplace, 59 Fla. L. Rev. 931, 937 (2007).

[55] 757 F.3d 31 (2d Cir. 2014)

[56] 364 U.S. 479 (1960).

[57] Hudson v. Craven, 403 F.3d 691 (9th Cir. 2005) thoroughly discusses the circuit split.

matter of public concern.[58] Other courts have refused to limit associational rights to matters of public concern.[59]

Not surprisingly, associational cases relating to political affiliation and activity have been particularly prevalent in the public workplace. The constitutional right to association limits the government's ability to prefer employees with a particular political affiliation (patronage employment) to those situations where "party affiliation is an appropriate requirement for effective performance of the public office involved."[60] Thus, in most cases only high level government employees in policy-making positions may be appointed or terminated based on their membership in, or loyalty to, a political party. This protection for employees not only prevents termination or refusal to hire based on party affiliation or support, but also other actions such as promotions, discipline, recalls from layoff, or job transfers.[61]

The Constitution does permit restrictions on the political activity of government employees, however. The Hatch Act, which bars federal employees from running for partisan political office and from engaging in political activity while on duty,[62] has survived constitutional challenge.[63] In *U.S. Civil Service Commission v. National Association of Letter Carriers*, the Court upheld the Hatch Act's broad limitations on political activity based on the following

---

[58] See, e.g., Merrifield v. Bd. Of Comm'rs of Santa Fe, 634 F.3d 1073 (10th Cir. 2011) (finding that hiring an attorney to contest discipline is protected by the right of association but did not meet the public concern test); Balton v. City of Milwaukee, 133 F.3d 1036 (7th Cir. 1998) (applying the test and rejecting the employee's claim though indicating some concern about the test's impact in the case of private associations).

[59] See, e.g., Hatcher v. Board of Pub. Educ., 809 F.2d 1546 (11th Cir. 1987). In *Hatcher,* a school principal claimed that she suffered retaliation for her protest against a school closing that resulted in her job loss. Her associational rights claim was based upon her association with a minister and school board member whom she brought to a meeting about her job. The court found that the *Pickering* test's public concern requirement would limit the private associational rights at issue in this case, and refused to apply the *Pickering* test.

[60] Branti v. Finkel, 445 U.S. 507, 518 (1980) (finding that political party affiliation is not an appropriate consideration for the job of assistant public defender whose job is to represent indigent criminal defendants and serve the interests of the client).

[61] Rutan v. Republican Party, 497 U.S. 62, 74–75 (1990) (applying rule of *Branti v. Finkel* to adverse employment actions other than termination, finding that such actions raise the same First Amendment concerns).

[62] 5 U.S.C. §§ 7321–26. Among other restrictions, the law also bars use of "official authority" to affect the results of elections and strictly limits solicitation of campaign contributions. 5 U.S.C. § 7323.

[63] See United States Civil Serv. Comm'n v. National Ass'n of Letter Carriers, 413 U.S. 548 (1973). Notably, the case upheld more onerous restrictions than currently exist, as Congress has since amended the statute to loosen the restraints on employee political activity. The provisions at issue in *Letter Carriers,* which have since been abandoned, barred employees from taking "an active part in political management or in political campaigns." 413 U.S. at 550.

government interests: (1) guaranteeing that the law is administered as intended by Congress rather than at the whim of a political party; (2) preventing politicians from using government employees to build political machines; and (3) making sure that government employees are free to vote as they choose and are not compelled to engage in political activity by their bosses.[64] While the latter two objectives are in accord with the restrictions on patronage employment, some have suggested that the Hatch Act prohibitions on political activity interfere with the political process as much as patronage employment and should be subject to greater scrutiny by the courts on First Amendment grounds.[65] Following the federal Hatch Act, many states passed "Little Hatch Acts" to restrict the political activities of state government employees, laws which have also survived constitutional challenge.[66] The federal Hatch Act also imposes limitations on the political activity of state employees whose positions are funded with federal funds.[67]

The right of association has been held to encompass the right of public employees to join a union.[68] This constitutional right does not extend to employees the right to have the union represent them in grievance procedures or collective bargaining, however.[69] Thus, states can prohibit collective bargaining by public employees and public employers can refuse to entertain employee grievances submitted by union representatives, unless compelled to do so by statute.[70]

---

[64] Letter Carriers, 413 U.S. at 564–66.

[65] Rafael Gely & Timothy D. Chandler, Restricting Public Employees' Political Activities: Good Government or Partisan Politics?, 37 Houston L. Rev. 775, 821–22 (2000).

[66] See Broadrick v. Oklahoma, 413 U.S. 601 (1973) (upholding the constitutionality of Oklahoma's Little Hatch Act). See also Claussen v. Pence, 826 F.3d 381 (7th Cir. 2016) (upholding an Indiana law requiring employees to resign before taking elected office in the government body where they are employed, finding a legitimate government interest in avoiding self-dealing, corruption and the appearance of both); Redemske v. Romeoville, 85 Ill.App.3d 286, 406 N.E.2d 602 (1980) (holding that a municipal government has the authority to enact local laws restricting the political activities of municipal officers and employees)..

[67] See 5 U.S.C. §§ 1501–08.

[68] See McLaughlin v. Tilendis, 398 F.2d 287 (7th Cir. 1968); Atkins v. City of Charlotte, 296 F. Supp. 1068 (W.D.N.C. 1969).

[69] Smith v. Arkansas St. Hwy. Employees, Local 1315, 441 U.S. 463 (1979).

[70] See, e.g. Va. Code § 40.1–57.2 (prohibiting collective bargaining by public employers and employees); Va. Code §§ 2.2–1001, 2.2–3000 to 3008 (directing establishment of grievance procedure for state employees); N.C. Gen. Stat. § 95–98 (stating that collective bargaining agreements between public employers and unions are void as against public policy).

3.1.3 Statutory Protection

3.1.3.1 Private Sector Labor Law

The National Labor Relations Act (NLRA) provides statutory associational rights for rank and file private sector employees[71] working for employers in interstate commerce.[72] Section 7 of the NLRA protects the right of employees "to form, join or assist labor organizations" and "to engage in other concerted activities . . . for other mutual aid or protection."[73] It also protects the right to refrain from such activity.[74] This associational protection is enforced through a series of prohibitions on employer and union interference with such activities.[75] The statute is administered by an independent government agency, the National Labor Relations Board (NLRB), with decisions enforceable in the federal appellate courts. Employees may lose their protection for these associational rights if they try to bypass an existing union selected by the majority of the employees and deal directly with their employer, however.[76]

Less well-known is the statute's protection of the associational rights of employees who act without a formal union. When employees act in concert to seek some change in their terms and conditions of employment, such activity is protected under § 7 and any employer retaliatory action violates the NLRA.[77] The protection of the NLRA requires concert, i.e., some connection with other employees, unless the employee is invoking a right contained in a collective bargaining agreement negotiated by a union.[78]

Suppose, for example, that employee John, a truck driver, believes that because the employer has been cutting back on maintenance of the trucks in its fleet to save money, the trucks that

---

71 Excluded from the protection of the NLRA are supervisors, managers, independent contractors, agricultural and government employees. See 29 U.S.C. §§ 152(2), 152(3) and 152(11); NLRB v. Bell Aerospace Co. Div. of Textron, Inc., 416 U.S. 267, 275 (1974).

72 29 U.S.C. §§ 151–69.

73 29 U.S.C. § 157.

74 Id.

75 29 U.S.C. § 158.

76 Emporium Capwell Co. v. W. Addition Cmty Org., 420 U.S. 50 (1975) (upholding discharge of employees who bypassed their union and attempted to pressure the employer to deal with the protesting employees directly, because they believed the union was not effectively dealing with employer discrimination,).

77 See NLRB v. Washington Aluminum Co., 370 U.S. 9 (1962) (finding employer unlawfully terminated employees who walked off the job to protest extremely cold working conditions).

78 See NLRB v. City Disposal Systems, Inc., 465 U.S. 822 (1984) (finding individual employee who invoked a right contained in the collective bargaining agreement was engaged in concerted activity because the contract was the product of the employees concerted activity).

he must drive are unsafe. If he has a union contract that gives him the right to refuse to drive unsafe trucks, his individual refusal to drive the truck is protected by the NLRA and he cannot be lawfully disciplined or terminated.[79] On the other hand, if he has no union and, as an individual, he refuses to drive the truck, he has no statutory protection and can be terminated for insubordination.[80] If however, he consults other drivers and they agree that they will all refuse to drive the unsafe trucks, John's action is concerted and protected, and any discipline will be unlawful, so long as the employer is aware of the concerted nature of the protest. Similarly, an employee who acts as spokesperson for a group[81] or solicits group support, even unsuccessfully,[82] is protected.

Protected concerted activity need not relate exclusively to the employees' own working conditions. The Supreme Court has found that passing out a union newsletter urging employee support for a minimum wage increase and opposition to right to work laws is protected.[83]

Even where activity is clearly concerted and for mutual aid or protection, employees can lose their statutory protection when their protest has an unlawful or improper objective or uses unlawful or improper means. Illegal conduct and attempts to force an employer to violate the law are clearly unprotected.[84] More difficult is determining when the employees' lawful conduct is so disloyal or damaging to the employer that it is unprotected. The NLRB uses a balancing test to make this determination and as with many

---

79 See id.

80 See Meyers Industries, 281 N.L.R.B. 882 (1986), aff'd sub nom., Prill v. NLRB, 835 F.2d 1481 (D.C. Cir. 1987) (finding that employee Prill, who refused to drive a truck that state authorities agreed was unsafe, was not engaged in concerted activity because his actions had no connection with those of other employees, although they were also concerned about truck safety). The employee might have a claim for retaliation under OSHA. See Section 6.2.6.2 infra.

81 See, e.g., NLRB v. Guernsey-Muskingum Elec. Cooperative, Inc., 285 F.2d 8 (6th Cir. 1960) (holding that where employees discussed problem and agreed to approach management about it, their failure to formally designate spokesperson did not deprive the employee who discussed the complaints with management of protection from termination).

82 See, e.g., Circle K Corp., 305 N.L.R.B. 932 (1991), enf'd, 989 F.2d 498 (6th Cir. 1993) (finding employee who wrote a letter to other employees soliciting their support to improve wages and working conditions was engaged in concerted activity even in the absence of support from other employees). See also Wyndham Resort Dev. Corp., 356 NLRB 765 (2011) (finding an employee who protested a change in the employee dress code in the presence of other employees was initiating group action although he had not previously consulted coworkers, emphasizing that he used terminology such as "us" and "we".)

83 Eastex, Inc. v. NLRB, 437 U.S. 556 (1978).

84 See, e.g., NLRB v. Fansteel Metallurgical Corp., 306 U.S. 240 (1939) (violence to employer property unprotected); American News Co., 55 N.L.R.B. 1302 (1944) (strike to compel employer to violate wage controls during war unprotected).

balancing tests, it is not always easy to determine how the balance is struck in particular cases. Conduct that is deemed excessively damaging to the employer may be unprotected.[85] Additionally, where conduct is deemed particularly abusive or disloyal to the employer, the NLRB may find that the impact outweighs the employees' rights.[86] Further, intermittent work stoppages have been found unprotected, with the NLRB and courts suggesting that employees may work or strike but not insist on working on their own terms.[87]

To prevail on a claim of discrimination based on concerted activity, employees must show that the retaliatory employer knew that the activity was concerted, sometimes a difficult task. That challenge is sometimes easier in the world of social media where concerted activity often takes place online. The NLRB has found protected activity in social media posts about working conditions.[88] The agency has also found unlawful some employer social media policies, which may chill employees in the exercise of their Section 7 rights.[89] For example, in *Costco Wholesale Corp.*, the NLRB found unlawful a policy which prohibited posting material which would damage the employer's reputation, concluding it was likely to chill the employees in criticizing their working conditions.[90] By way of contrast, the opinion pointed out that rules prohibiting malicious or abusive communication would be lawful as such conduct is not protected. Similarly, a rule requiring courtesy and respect to fellow employees and barring language which injures the image of the employer was unlawful.[91]

---

[85] See NLRB v. Marshall Car Wheel Co., 218 F.2d 409 (5th Cir. 1955) (finding unprotected a walkout which occurred when molten metal was in equipment and would cause serious damage if left there).

[86] See, e.g., NLRB v. IBEW, Local 1229, 346 U.S. 464 (1953) (finding that employees who distributed leaflet to employer's customers disparaging the product during a labor dispute lost their protection because the conduct was disloyal, noting that the leaflet did not mention the labor dispute). Cf. Sierra Publishing Co. v. NLRB, 889 F.2d 210 (9th Cir. 1989) (finding that employees did not lose protection where they stated that the treatment of employees might affect the quality of the product).

[87] See NLRB v. Montgomery Ward & Co., 157 F.2d 486, 496 (8th Cir. 1946) (finding that employees who refused to handle certain orders because of a strike at another plant engaged in unprotected activity, as they could not work on their own terms).

[88] See, e.g., Design Technology Group LLC, 359 NLRB No. 96 (2013).

[89] See National Labor Relations Board, The NLRB and Social Media, https://www.nlrb.gov/news-outreach/fact-sheets/nlrb-and-social-media (containing links to official memos and cases involving social media). Among the concerns of the agency are policies that limit disclosure of confidential information, policies that bar disparagement of the employer, and policies that prohibit discussion of the employer, all of which may discourage employees from discussing their terms and conditions of employment.

[90] 358 NLRB No. 106 (2012).

[91] Karl Knauz Motors, Inc., 358 NLRB No. 164 (2012).

A common though unlawful provision in many employer policies is a ban on discussion of wages among employees. The NLRB has held that such policies interfere with employees' rights to engage in concerted activity, since a ban on discussing their pay will certainly frustrate efforts to challenge employer pay practices.[92] The widespread use of such policies suggests a lack of awareness of the applicability of the law among employers and employees in nonunion workplaces.

Some commentators have suggested that the NLRA rights offer a vehicle for nonunion employees to challenge employer power and accomplish change in the workplace more quickly and at lower cost than litigation under other existing statutes.[93] Employees have utilized § 7 rights to challenge workplace discrimination, unlawful pay practices, and other illegal actions by employers.[94]

Remedies under the NLRA are limited to those that make the employees whole for losses, which in a typical discharge case will be reinstatement with back pay, reduced by what the employee earned or could have earned elsewhere. Remedies for other actions such as threats or unlawful rules are orders to cease and desist and rescind unlawful rules, with no monetary penalty. Compensatory and punitive damages are not available. Coupled with the often lengthy litigation process, these remedies often prove to be little deterrent to determined employers.

3.1.3.2 Public Sector Labor Laws

The majority of states have enacted legislation providing some or all state and local government employees with the statutory right to join or assist unions and to engage in collective bargaining.[95] In the federal sector, union activity is protected by the Civil Service Reform Act, which covers all federal employees except for supervisors, members of the armed forces, and employees in certain specified agencies.[96] Employees of the Tennessee Valley Authority

---

[92] See Jeannette Corp. v. NLRB, 532 F.2d 916 (3d Cir. 1976) (enforcing NLRB decision that employer rule against discussing wages was unlawful).

[93] William Corbett, Waiting for the Labor Law of the 21st Century: Everything Old is New Again, 23 Berkeley J. Emp. & Lab. L. 259, 277–278 (2002).

[94] See North Carolina Prisoner Legal Servs. Inc., 351 N.L.R.B. 464, 467 (2007) (finding that filing a class sex discrimination charge and petitioning the employer's board of directors regarding complaints of sex discrimination constituted protected concerted activity); Triangle Tool & Eng'g, Inc., 226 N.L.R.B. 1354, 1357 (1976) (finding employee complaints to the Department of Labor regarding overtime pay protected); Garage Mgt. Corp., 334 N.L.R.B. 940, 951 (2001) (finding cooperating in an OSHA investigation protected).

[95] See Malin, et al., supra note 3, at 349; Richard C. Kearney & David G. Carnevale, Labor Relations in the Public Sector 58–77 (3d ed. 2001).

[96] 5 U.S.C. § 7103(a)(3).

bargain through New Deal legislation[97] and Postal Service employees are covered by the NLRA.[98] Transportation security officers have the right to bargain pursuant to authorization from the director of the agency.[99]

Legislation enacted after September 11, 2001 restricted the collective bargaining rights of employees in the newly created Department of Homeland Security and the Department of Defense. Labor unions challenged the regulations issued pursuant to the legislation, resulting in a decision striking down some of the restrictions on bargaining for Homeland Security employees,[100] but upholding the time-limited restrictions for Department of Defense employees.[101] The legislation permitted bargaining for civilian workers in the Department of Defense after November 2009.[102]

3.1.3.3 Other State Laws

In addition to the statutes discussed above protecting the rights of employees to engage in union and concerted activity, some states have enacted other laws protecting employees' speech and associational rights. For example, California and Louisiana prohibit discrimination by private employers based on political activity, echoing the First Amendment protection for public sector employees.[103] These two statutes protect the rights of employees to engage in political activity, including both supporting and becoming candidates. Illinois protects the rights of local government and school district employees to be free from pressure to participate in political activity and from restraint on their own political activity.[104] Connecticut prohibits all employers from discharging employees for the exercise of their First Amendment rights under the U.S. Constitution if their actions do not interfere with their work performance or employment relationship.[105] Additionally, state

---

97 Kearney & Carnevale, supra note 95, at 52.

98 Postal Reorganization Act, 39 U.S.C. § 1209(a).

99 Malin, et al., supra note 3, at 390.

100 See National Treasury Employees Union v. Chertoff, 452 F.3d 839 (D.C. Cir. 2006).

101 American Federation of Government Employees v. Gates, 486 F.3d 1316 (D.C. Cir. 2007); see Joseph Slater, Homeland Security vs. Workers' Rights? What the Federal Government Should Learn from History and Experience, and Why, 6 U. Pa. J. Lab. & Emp. Law 295 (2004).

102 486 F.3d at 1326.

103 See Cal. Lab. Code § 1101; La. Rev. Stat. § 23:961; Davis v. Louisiana Computing Corp., 394 So.2d 678 (La. Ct. App. 1981) (upholding damages for employee fired for running for office by employer who feared antagonizing public officials who might withhold business).

104 50 Ill. Comp. Stat. § 135/10.

105 Conn. Gen. Stat. § 31–51q.

constitutional provisions may protect speech and associational rights.[106]

§ 3.2 Protection from Intrusive Employment Practices

Employers, both public and private, have legitimate interests in investigating, testing and monitoring applicants and employees, on and off the job. Employers desire to hire and retain the most productive workers. Once hired, they want to insure that employees are working effectively and efficiently. Employers seek healthy employees to reduce absenteeism and insurance costs. Additionally, employers are concerned about potential liability for injury caused by employees. Further, employers want to prevent loss of confidential information, including trade secrets, and breaches of computer security. Finally, when a workplace problem occurs, such as missing inventory, employers investigate to determine the cause of the loss. All of these matters have the potential to affect profitability and efficiency, motivating employers to utilize various monitoring, investigatory and testing methods to minimize current and future problems with employees.

Employers may also engage in such activity with improper motives, such as voyeurism, discrimination, curiosity, and countering employee efforts to unionize.[107] Even where employer motives are legitimate, however, employer practices may intrude on employee privacy interests. As previously noted, employees want to protect and control the use of their personal information and personal space. Additionally, employees desire to be free from regulation or surveillance on, but most importantly off, the job. Finally, employees have an interest in expressing their autonomy through their activities, associations, dress, and appearance. The Restatement of Employment Law adopted in 2015 recognizes these interests in privacy and autonomy.[108] These employee interests often clash with legitimate employer interests, necessitating reconciliation by law or agreement.

Recent technological changes have exacerbated employee privacy concerns. Increasingly sophisticated monitoring, surveillance and testing technology is available to employers at steadily decreasing cost. Such technology allows employers to engage in

---

106 See, e.g., Ala. Const. Art. I, § 4; Cal. Const. Art. 1, §§ 2, 3.

107 See Dennis R. Nolan, Privacy and Profitability in the Technological Workplace, 24 J. Lab. Res. 207, 215–16 (2003).

108 Restatement of Employment Law §§ 7.02–7.05, 7.08. For a critique of the Restatement's chapter on privacy and autonomy, see Matthew W. Finkin, Chapter 7: Privacy and Autonomy, 21Employee Rts and Employment Pol'y J. (forthcoming 2017).

continual monitoring of employees in situations that previously required supervisory observation. Technology also has increased the employer's ability to obtain and retain information about employees, not only in the workplace, but also in their private lives. In addition to increased monitoring of employees, the availability of new tests for genetic susceptibility to many diseases and conditions facilitates employer discrimination on genetic grounds. The law is developing in response to these changes but in many areas, it is in its infancy.[109]

3.2.1 Background Investigations

In addition to the various forms of testing discussed in Section 3.2.5 infra, employers engage in background investigations to evaluate potential employees. Criminal background checks and reference checks are common,[110] and employers increasingly utilize internet searches, including social media.[111] Depending on the job, the employer may also do a credit check.[112] Legal restrictions on the use of such methods are limited, although there is a growing movement to limit the use of criminal background checks by employers. Social media and internet searches are treated in Section 3.2.3.

---

109 See Katherine V.W. Stone, From Widgets to Digits: Employment Regulation for the Changing Workplace (2004) (describing the impact of technological change on the workplace and the laws relating to employment and recommending changes in the law to adapt to the new workplace); William A. Herbert, The Electronic Workplace: To Live Outside the Law You Must Be Honest, 12 Employee Rts. & Employment Pol'y J. 49 (2008) (discussing the limited legal response to the increasing use of computer technology in the workplace and arguing for a comprehensive approach); Matthew W. Finkin, Second Thoughts on a Restatement of Employment Law, 7 U. Pa. J. Lab. & Employment L. 279, 280–81 (2005) (suggesting that the wide-ranging legal issues relating to employee privacy are seriously in need of legislative action); S. Elizabeth Wilborn, Revisiting the Public/Private Distinction: Employee Monitoring in the Workplace, 32 Ga. L. Rev. 825, 826–30 (1998) (discussing the increase in employer use of monitoring, surveillance and health screening and the lack of protection for privacy available to private sector employees).

110 HireRight Annual Employment Screening Benchmark Report, 2015 edition, at 17, http://hosteddocs.ittoolbox.com/2015-employment-screening-benchmark-report_final.pdf.

111 A 2016 survey by Career Builder found that 60 percent of employers search social networking sites for information about applicants, while 59 percent use internet search engines. Use of social media searches has increased 500 percent in the last ten years. Career Builder, Press Release, April 28, 2016, available at http://www.careerbuilder.com/share/aboutus/pressreleasesdetail.aspx?sd=4%2f28%2f2016&siteid=cbpr&sc_cmp1=cb_pr945_&id=pr945&ed=12%2f31%2f2016. A different survey in 2015, however, found that 64% of employers avoided social media searches to prevent discovering information about candidates that might make them vulnerable to discrimination charges. HireRight, supra note 110, at 18. For further discussion of the risks of social media searches, see Eric D. Bentley, The Pitfalls of Using Social Media Screening for Job Applicants, 29 A.B.A. J. Lab. & Emp. L. 1 (2013).

112 Id. at 17 (showing 34% of surveyed employers conduct credit checks).

3.2.1.1 References

The scope of reference checks varies by the job. In some cases, few references are contacted, while in others, especially employment involving access to confidential information or national security data, the investigation is far more extensive. Reference checking is lawful and can be an effective method of obtaining information for evaluation purposes. One difficulty that sometimes arises is the inability to obtain useful information because previous employers and references fear lawsuits. To some extent the fear is exaggerated, because the number of lawsuits actually filed based on references is quite small and the number of successful lawsuits even smaller.[113] It is difficult for a potential employee to learn why he or she has not been hired, and more difficult still to obtain evidence about specific information provided to prospective employers. Without such information, a lawsuit is highly unlikely. Nevertheless, as a result of litigation phobia, employers sometime choose to provide to potential employers only limited information about former employees, such as the jobs held and the dates of employment.

The legal actions most feared by former employers are tort-based defamation claims. The tort of defamation consists of two separate torts: slander and libel. Slander refers to oral defamation while libel involves written defamation. To prevail on such a claim, a former employee must establish the following elements which apply to both torts: (1) a false and defamatory statement published without privilege to a third party; (2) made with some fault by the publisher; and (3) causing damage to the plaintiff as a result of the statement.[114] A defamatory statement is one that harms the reputation of another. Statements that clearly satisfy this standard tend to subject an individual to hatred, ridicule or contempt, or tend to reflect unfavorably upon a person's morality or integrity. Such statements have included, for example, a charge that an employee sexually abused his own daughter,[115] a comment that an employee held racist attitudes,[116] a claim that an employee committed larceny,[117] and an assertion that an employee was a drug user.[118] To qualify as a defamatory communication, an untruthful statement need only have

---

113 Steven L. Willborn & Ramona L. Paetzold, Employer (Ir)rationality and the Demise of Employment References, 30 Am. Bus. L.J. 123 (1992).

114 Restatement (Second) of Torts § 558.

115 See, e.g., Brown v. Farkas, 158 Ill.App.3d 772, 511 N.E.2d 1143 (1986).

116 See, e.g., Brownsville v. Pena, 716 S.W.2d 677 (Tex. App. 1986).

117 See, e.g., Sunshine Invs. v. Brooks, 642 So.2d 408 (Ala. 1994).

118 See, e.g., Houston B. & T. R. Co. v. Wherry, 548 S.W.2d 743 (Tex. App. 1976).

"a general tendency" to harm another's reputation; actual harm is not required.[119]

As for damages, a plaintiff's reputational injury may be presumed in cases that involve defamation to an individual in his or her business, trade or profession.[120] This presumption establishes defamation per se, allowing the plaintiff to recover general damages, which a court will award without evidence of the actual harm incurred.[121] If, however, the harm to reputation cannot be presumed, because it is not apparent, the plaintiff must allege and prove special damages[122] in order to recover.[123] She must specifically show the harm caused by the statement. Thus an employee who loses a job as a result of a defamatory reference and who can show harm to her business, trade or profession will not have to prove special damages. On the other hand, special damages will have to be proved if the harm is more general and she simply cannot find another job.[124]

Constitutional law has superimposed additional requirements on the defamation tort because of First Amendment considerations. In *Gertz v. Robert Welch*,[125] the Supreme Court suggested in dicta that opinions are constitutionally protected speech so that defamation claims must be based on statements of fact, not opinion. Although many courts read *Gertz* as creating a clear dichotomy between fact and opinion in defamation law, the Court subsequently clarified in *Milkovich v. Lorain Journal Co.* that no such distinction

---

119 Restatement (Second) of Torts § 559, cmt. d.

120 Id. at § 573. Slander or libel relating to an individual in his or her business, trade or profession is defamatory per se. Id. at § 573, cmt. f.

121 See, e.g., Coachmen Indus. v. Dunn, 719 N.E.2d 1271, 1275–76 (Ind. Ct. App. 1999) (noting that a claim of defamation per se requires no showing of special damages); Battista v. United Illuminating Co., 10 Conn.App. 486, 491, 523 A.2d 1356, 1359 (1987) (commenting that "[u]nder Connecticut law, when a party is the victim of libel *per se*, he is presumed to be injured and is entitled to general damages without proof of actual damages"); Ely v. National Super Mkts., Inc., 149 Ill.App.3d 752, 762, 500 N.E.2d 120, 127 (1986) (observing that "[w]here words are actionable *per se*, malice and special damages need not be proved").

122 Special damages are measurable economic losses such as loss of income, while general damages are for intangible losses such as pain and suffering or emotional distress.

123 See, e.g., Myers v. Mobile Press-Register, Inc., 266 Ala. 508, 511, 97 So.2d 819, 821 (1957) (stating that "[w]hen the language used is not actionable per se, it is incumbent upon the plaintiff to allege special damages").

124 See, e.g., Lynch v. Lyons, 303 Mass. 116, 118–19, 20 N.E.2d 953, 955 (1939) (noting that "it is well settled that words spoken orally are not actionable per se, unless they charge the plaintiff with a crime, or state that he is suffering from certain diseases, or prejudice him in his office, profession or business . . . ."); see generally Restatement (Second) of Torts § 573 ("One who publishes a slander that ascribes to another conduct, characteristics or a condition that would adversely affect his fitness for the proper conduct of his lawful business, trade, or profession . . . is subject to liability without proof of special harm.").

125 418 U.S. 323, 339–40 (1974).

was intended and that an expression of opinion may "imply an assertion of objective fact" that would be subject to a defamation claim[126] *Hoover v. Peerless Publications, Inc.*[127] provides an example of a job reference that gave rise to an action for defamation despite a defense argument that the statement was merely opinion. In *Hoover*, in response to a reference request, the defendant wrote a letter indicating that the plaintiff had mental problems while working for a prior employer, leading to his retirement, and implying that the mental problems continued with another employer, leading to a separation from that employment.[128] In response to a motion to dismiss, the court found these to be statements of fact rather than opinion, although they were not based on the defendant's personal knowledge.[129] In further support of its denial of the motion to dismiss, the court went on to say that even if they were statements of opinion, a jury could find that they implied defamatory facts and thus were actionable.[130] Similarly, in *Adler v. American Standard Corp.*, the court found that a statement that the employee was discharged for unsatisfactory performance carried with it the implication of undisclosed defamatory facts and could therefore state a claim for defamation.[131]

The First Amendment has also moved the Court to impose a high standard for liability in many defamation cases. In *New York Times v. Sullivan*, the Court held that to prevail on a defamation claim, a public figure must prove "actual malice."[132] Actual malice is established if the speaker either knew the statement was false or spoke with reckless disregard for the truth or falsity of the statement.[133] Along the same lines, in *Gertz*, the Court held that in actions by private individuals against media defendants, state defamation law cannot impose liability without fault, nor can it assess presumed or punitive damages without proof of actual malice as defined above.[134] The damages rule requiring actual malice was applied to a nonmedia defendant in *Dun & Bradstreet, Inc. v. Greenmoss Builders, Inc.*[135] but the Supreme Court has not ruled on the fault requirement in cases involving neither public figures nor

---

126 497 U.S. 1, 18 (1990).

127 461 F. Supp. 1206 (E.D. Pa. 1978).

128 Id. at 1208.

129 Id. at 1209.

130 Id. at 1209–10.

131 538 F. Supp. 572, 576 (D. Md. 1982).

132 376 U.S. 254, 279–80 (1964).

133 Id.

134 418 U.S. at 347–49.

135 472 U.S. 749 (1985).

media defendants, which describes most employment-related defamation claims.

Many lower courts in these cases continue to apply the rule that the truthfulness of the statement is a complete defense to defamation.[136] Courts treat the defense as an affirmative one and as such, the defendant has the burden of proving that the statement is true.[137]

Both prospective employees and employers have used creative methods of proving and avoiding defamation claims. Employees who suspect that a prior employer is providing negative information to prospective employers have used friends, relatives, and even private investigators to contact the employer seeking a reference. These strategies may defeat employee efforts to establish the publication element of the tort, however, which requires that the defamatory statement be communicated, intentionally or by a negligent act, to someone other than the person claiming defamation.[138] Some courts have found lack of publication where those receiving the information are agents of the employee.[139] In *Frank B. Hall & Co. v. Buck*, a Texas court found publication based on statements to an investigator hired by the employee although the speaker did not know the true identity of the person to whom the statement was published.[140] Subsequent cases in Texas have held, however, that if a plaintiff has reason to suspect that the employer will provide a negative reference, the plaintiff invites the defamation by employing an agent to contact the

---

136 See, e.g., Jones v. Palmer Communications, Inc., 440 N.W.2d 884, 891 (Iowa 1989); see also Restatement (Second) of Torts § 581A, cmt. a (observing that "[s]everal states have constitutional or statutory provisions to the effect that truth of a defamatory statement of fact is not a defense if the statement is published for 'malicious motives' ").

137 Restatement (Second) of Torts § 581A, cmt. a.

138 Restatement (Second) of Torts § 577(1).

139 See, e.g., Beck v. Tribert, 312 N.J. Super. 335, 350, 711 A.2d 951, 959 (1998) (statements to friends pretending to be prospective employers were not published); Chambers v. American Trans Air, Inc., 577 N.E.2d 612, 615 (Ind. Ct. App. 1991) (describing lower court's decision holding that statements to mother and boyfriend posing as employers were not published). Other courts have used different rationales to find that employees have no claim of defamation based on statements made to agents of the employee posing as employers. See Oliphint v. Richards, 167 S.W.3d 513, 516 (Tex. App. 2005) (finding employee who hired investigator to check references after learning that his prior employer was providing information about his termination that he believed was defamatory invited the defamation and therefore could not recover); Martinez v. New England Med. Ctr. Hosp., 307 F. Supp. 2d 257, 269 (D. Mass. 2004) (finding statement to friend of employee who pretended to be a prospective employer was invited and thus privileged).

140 678 S.W.2d 612, 618 (Tex. App. 1984).

employer for a reference, and therefore cannot sue based on the statement.[141]

Another avenue for proving publication of the defamatory statement is the doctrine of compelled self-publication. In general, if the defendant communicates the statement only to the plaintiff and the plaintiff then communicates the statement to a third party, there is no publication and consequently, no defamation.[142] Compelled self-publication is, however, an exception to this general rule. Under this doctrine, if the defamed individual was forced to communicate the defamatory statement to a third person, such as a prospective employer, and such communication was foreseeable to the defendant, the publication requirement is met.[143] *McKinney v. County of Santa Clara*[144] illustrates this narrow exception. The plaintiff, a former probationary deputy sheriff employed by the County of Santa Clara, was discharged for reasons the plaintiff claimed were defamatory. In his defamation claim, the plaintiff indicated that he had republished the alleged defamatory statements when he divulged their substance to police departments in the course of seeking a position as a police officer. He further stated that his re-publication of the statements was involuntary as he was required to do so by the police departments to which he applied for a new job. The Court of Appeals of California reversed the lower court's rulings against the employee on certain of his actions for libel and slander. The court explained its decision by observing that it was reasonably foreseeable to the defendant that the plaintiff would be compelled to disclose the alleged defamatory statement to third parties.

Many courts have been unreceptive to this doctrine in the employment context,[145] and the legislatures of both Minnesota and

---

[141] See Oliphint v. Richards, 167 S.W.3d at 516–517 and cases cited therein. The court distinguished *Frank B. Hall & Co. v. Buck* because the employee there had no reason to expect that the employer would defame him when he hired the investigator to check his references. Id.

[142] Restatement (Second) of Torts § 577, cmt. m.

[143] See, e.g., Churchey v. Adolph Coors Co., 759 P.2d 1336, 1343–44 (Colo. 1988); Lewis v. Equitable Life Assurance Society, 389 N.W.2d 876, 886 (Minn. 1986); see also Donato v. Plainview-Old Bethpage Cent. Sch. Dist., 96 F.3d 623, 631–32 (2d Cir. 1996) (finding that the requirement that there be public disclosure of stigmatizing statements about an employee that implicate the liberty interest in future employment in her field is met when they are likely to be disclosed because they are included in a personnel file that future employers will almost certainly request).

[144] 110 Cal.App.3d 787, 797–98, 168 Cal.Rptr. 89, 93–4 (1980).

[145] See, e.g., Cweklinsky v. Mobil Chem. Co., 267 Conn. 210, 212–13 837 A.2d 759, 761 (2004) (rejecting the theory of compelled self-publication in employee defamation); White v. Blue Cross & Blue Shield of Mass., Inc., 442 Mass. 64, 68, 809 N.E.2d 1034, 1037 (2004) (same); Austin v. Howard Univ., 267 F. Supp. 2d 22, 29 (D.D.C. 2003) (holding that the District of Columbia would not accept the theory of compelled self-publication); Olivieri v. Rodriguez, 122 F.3d 406, 408 (7th Cir. 1997) (rejecting the

Colorado reacted to decisions in their states. Colorado eliminated the self-publication doctrine altogether.[146] Minnesota law now allows employees to request employers to provide a truthful written reason for termination, which cannot be the basis for a defamation claim.[147] A likely reason for the quick legislative response is that it will almost always be foreseeable that a discharged employee will be asked to provide a prospective employer with the reason for a previous termination. Accordingly, the doctrine of compelled self-publication makes it easy to satisfy the publication element of the defamation claim, even if the employer provides no reference. To avoid a defamation claim, the employer would be encouraged to provide no reason for an employee's termination. The only alternative would be to rely on the claim of qualified privilege.[148]

The 2015 Restatement of Employment Law adopts the doctrine of self-publication, but its formulation is more limited.[149] Under the Restatement approach, the doctrine would apply if the employer knows the employee will have to repeat the defamatory statement.[150] In addition, the employer must either indicate that it will repeat the statement to third parties or refuse the employee's request not to do so.[151]

Courts that do not allow defamation based on compelled self-publication require that publication be made to a third party. The employment context poses two specific concerns for determining who qualifies as a third party for purposes of establishing publication.[152] First, courts tend to follow the Restatement of Torts and hold that dictation of defamatory statements to a third party such as a stenographer qualifies as publication.[153] Second, courts are split over the question of whether communications by an employer to an agent such as a supervisor qualifies as publication. Some courts adhere to the Restatement position and hold that there is publication, although

---

theory in constitutional case based on claim of deprivation of liberty of occupation as a result of defamatory statements of employer).

[146] Colo. Rev. Stat. Ann. § 13–25–125.5.

[147] Minn. Stat. Ann. § 181.933.

[148] See infra text accompanying notes 157–162 for discussion of qualified privilege.

[149] Restatement of Employment Law § 6.01(b)(3) (2015).

[150] Id. § 6.01, comment d.

[151] Id.

[152] See generally Mark A. Rothstein, et al., 1 Employment Law § 1.9, at 14–15 (2015).

[153] Restatement (Second) of Torts § 577, cmt. m. See generally Rothstein, et al., supra note 152, at 14–15.

it may be privileged,[154] while others take the position that communications between officers, agents, and employees of a company in the regular course of business do not constitute publication. From the perspective of these courts, such "intra-office communications" do not involve a third party because the corporation is simply talking to itself.[155] The Restatement of Employment Law includes as publication communications to individuals in the employer's organization, noting it is the majority rule.[156]

Many employment-related defamation claims turn on the issue of privilege. In the reference context, it is clear that a prior employer has a qualified privilege to communicate information about an employee to a prospective employer, for the parties have a mutual interest in the information which is furthered by sharing.[157] According to the Restatement of Torts, the qualified privilege can be lost by the following actions: (1) actual malice; (2) publication for a purpose other than the privileged purpose; (3) excessive publication to persons not reasonably believed necessary to accomplish the purpose of the privilege; (4) publishing defamatory matter not reasonably believed necessary to achieve the privileged purpose; or (5) publishing unprivileged as well as privileged material.[158] Most reference cases involve the issue of actual malice. The plaintiff must prove that the speaker acted with knowledge of the falsity or reckless disregard for the truth or falsity of the statement. Most courts hold that it is not sufficient to show that the speaker bore some hostility to the plaintiff during employment, without establishing that such animosity motivated the alleged defamation.[159] Nor does the fact that the referee gave a positive recommendation before providing the

[154] See, e.g., Dube v. Likins, 216 Ariz. 406, 417–18, 167 P.3d 93, 104–05 (Ct. App. 2007) (collecting cases); Wallulis v. Dymowski, 323 Or. 337, 347, 918 P.2d 755, 760 (1996).

[155] See Taggart v. Drake Univ., 549 N.W.2d 796, 802–03 (Iowa Sup. 1996) (listing cases).

[156] Restatement of Employment Law § 6.01(b)(2), comment b (2015).

[157] The Restatement of Employment Law also so specifies and in addition, finds a privilege to communicate to "regulatory or licensing authorities" and the employees and agents of the employer. § 6.02(a).

[158] Restatement (Second) of Torts §§ 599–605A. The Restatement of Employment Law states that the privilege is lost if the employer knows the statement is false or acts with reckless disregard of the truth or falsity or knows or should know that there is no legitimate interest in publishing the statement to the recipient. § 6.02(b).

[159] See, e.g., Chambers v. American Trans Air, Inc., 577 N.E.2d at 616 (showing of hostile and rude treatment during employment insufficient to establish that allegedly defamatory statements motivated by malice); Murray v. Holnam, Inc., 344 S.C. 129, 143–44, 542 S.E.2d 743, 750–51 (Ct. App. 2001) (stating actual malice must motivate the publication). But see Butler v. Town of Argo, 871 So. 2d 1, 26–27 (Ala. 2003) (stating that a showing of previous ill will can establish actual malice).

negative recommendation, without more, establish malice.[160] In one case, however, an employer was found liable for defamation where the supervisor made critical statements about the employee in reliance on general rumor while failing to disclose to the prospective employer that he had no firsthand knowledge about the work of the employee.[161] Because the supervisor misled the prospective employer about the source of his information even after learning that the employer wanted to speak with someone who had worked directly with the plaintiff, and could not identify any specific information on which he based his assessment, the court found that the supervisor acted with reckless disregard for the truth or falsity of the information he provided.[162]

Employers have responded to the increasing fear of defamation claims in several ways. One is to limit reference information as discussed above. Another is to require prospective employees to waive any claims against prior employers providing references in order to improve the chances of getting truthful references. Such waivers have received a mixed response in the courts, with some upholding them as consent to defamation[163] or as a conferral of absolute privilege on the prior employer,[164] and others finding that employers cannot contract out of intentional torts.[165] Employers have also lobbied for legislative relief, an effort that has caused a number of states to enact legislation that confers qualified immunity on employers providing references. Most statutes do little more than codify the common law,[166] although some add provisions protecting employees by requiring that they receive copies of references,[167] and

---

160 Zerr v. Johnson, 894 F.Supp. 372, 377 (D. Colo. 1995) (finding that a positive written recommendation followed by a more critical oral recommendation does not establish malice, noting that earlier kindness does not establish that later criticism is made with malice).

161 Sigal Construction Corp. v. Stanbury, 586 A.2d 1204 (D.C. 1991).

162 Id. at 1214–15.

163 See Hirschfeld v. Institutional Inv., Inc., 260 A.D.2d 171, 172, 688 N.Y.S.2d 31, 32 (1999) (finding that employee who requested that oral explanation of the reason for her termination be placed in writing consented to publication, which barred her defamation claim); Eitler v. St. Joseph Reg'l Med. Ctr. S. Bend Campus, Inc., 789 N.E.2d 497, 501 (Ind. Ct. App. 2003) (finding signed release consent that barred defamation claim).

164 Cox v. Nasche, 70 F.3d 1030, 1031 (9th Cir. 1995) (applying Alaska law and holding an absolute privilege applies to statements made by employer within the scope of release signed by the employee).

165 McQuirk v. Donnelley, 189 F.3d 793, 796 (9th Cir. 1999) (applying Cal Civ. Code § 1668 and finding a release that exempts a person from future liability for intentional wrongs is against public policy); Tudor v. Charleston Area Med. Ctr., 203 W.Va. 111, 126–27, 506 S.E.2d 554, 569–70 (1997) (finding that release could not absolve prior employer from liability for stating, falsely and with intent to injure, that employee would not be rehired because of an absenteeism problem).

166 See, e.g., Mich. Comp. Laws § 423. 452; R.I. Gen. Laws §§ 28–6.4–1 to 28–6.4–2.

167 See, e.g., Colo. Rev. Stat. § 8–2–114(5); Ind. Code § 22–5–3–1(c).

others provide greater immunity than exists at common law.[168] The laws that provide for employees to receive copies of references may encourage more lawsuits since a significant barrier to suit, as noted above, is the employee's inability to ascertain what information is provided in a reference. On the other hand, such laws may also discourage truthful negative references or provision of references at all.

The fear of defamation claims has led some employers to refuse to disclose all relevant job history information. This in turn has resulted in a different type of liability. In a few cases, third parties have sued employers who provided misleading references that led an employer to hire someone who later injured the third party. The cases are typically based on a theory of fraud or negligent misrepresentation and involve an employer who gives a reference that fails to disclose negative information where future harm is foreseeable. If the employee is then hired and harms the plaintiff through an action similar to that which would have been disclosed with a fully informative reference, the referencing employer may be liable.[169] For example, the California Supreme Court upheld a claim by a student who was sexually assaulted by a school district administrator.[170] The student successfully sued the administrator's former employer, which had provided a good reference to the hiring district even though the administrator had been forced to resign because of sexual misconduct. Such cases have helped fuel the claims of employers that they are between a rock and a hard place when it comes to references, and have encouraged legislatures to pass the immunizing legislation discussed above.

3.2.1.2 Credit Investigation

In recent years, employers have increasingly conducted credit checks as a part of the investigation of employees. Although enacted to protect consumers from abuse, the Fair Credit Reporting Act[171] provides some protection to prospective employees subject to credit investigations. Among its requirements, the employer must provide

---

168 See Va. Code Ann. § 8.01–46.1 (providing employer immunity from liability for providing reference information unless plaintiff can overcome presumption of employer good faith by clear and convincing evidence); Ind. Code § 22–5–3–1(b) (imposing liability on the employer only if the information was known to be false).

169 See, e.g., Kadlec Medical Center v. Lakeview Anesthesia Associates, 527 F.3d 412 (5th Cir. 2008) (upholding liability for doctors whose positive recommendation letters for anesthesiologist failed to mention his termination for narcotics addiction and his impairment during new employment caused patient's permanent vegetative state).

170 Randi W. v. Muroc Joint Unified Sch. Dist., 14 Cal.4th 1066, 929 P.2d 582 (1997).

171 15 U.S.C. §§ 1681–1681x.

notice to, and get authorization from, the applicant or employee in order to procure a credit report from a reporting agency for employment purposes.[172] The employer also must notify the individual prior to taking adverse action based on the report and provide the employee or prospective employee with a copy of the report and a statement of statutory rights.[173] A negligent violation of the statute triggers a remedy of actual damages, as well as attorneys' fees and costs, while a willful violation can subject the violator to damages of between $100 and $1000 as an alternative to actual damages, and punitive damages at the discretion of the court.[174] An employee or applicant may have a claim against the employer or a reporting agency for violation of the statute.[175]

The protections of the statute are limited, however, because the agency need only follow reasonable procedures to determine the accuracy of information, and the employee who feels that information is inaccurate can require reinvestigation but not correction if the agency is satisfied with the accuracy after reinvestigation.[176] Instead of correction, the employee can file an objection that must be included with the report.[177]

Several states also have laws limiting the use of credit checks by employers. Illinois, for example, prohibits obtaining credit reports or making employment decisions on the basis of credit history or credit reports, with exceptions for certain defined jobs where credit history is a bona fide occupational requirement.[178]

3.2.1.3 Criminal Background Checks

The use of criminal background checks for employment is increasingly common.[179] At the same time, because of the high incarceration rate in the United States, concern over the number of

---

172 15 U.S.C. § 1681b(b)(2).

173 15 U.S.C. § 1681b(b)(3); Woodell v. United Way, 357 F.Supp.2d 761, 774 (S.D.N.Y. 2005).

174 See 15 U.S.C. §§ 1681n, 1681*o*.

175 See Haley v. Talentwise, Inc., 9 F.Supp. 3d 1188 (W.D. Wash. 2014) (finding employee stated a claim against a credit reporting agency based on allegations that agency sent inaccurate report, reported information that was prohibited by the law, and failed to notify her about the report, which caused her to lose her job).

176 15 U.S.C. § 1681e(b); 15 U.S.C. § 1681i.

177 Id.

178 820 Ill. Comp. Stat. 70/10. See also Cal. Lab. Code § 1024.5; Colo. Rev. Stat. § 8–2–126; Or. Rev. Stat. § 659A.320.

179 EEOC, Enforcement Guidance: Consideration of Arrest and Conviction Records in Employment Decisions Under Title VII of the Civil Rights Act of 1964, April 12, 2015, available at https://www.eeoc.gov/laws/guidance/arrest_conviction.cfm#sdendnote49anc (citing survey indicating that 92% of employers use criminal background checks for some employees).

individuals unable to access employment after serving time in prison is also increasing.

In 2012, the EEOC issued guidance regarding the use of criminal background checks because of concern over their impact on employment of particular racial and ethnic groups, notably African-Americans and Hispanics.[180] The guidance cautions against using arrest records, since they do not establish guilt, unless the conduct underlying the arrest makes the person unfit for the position.[181] Conviction records do establish guilt, but if their use has a disparate impact on protected groups, disqualifications based on convictions must be job-related.[182] Among the factors that should be considered are the type and seriousness of the offense, the amount of time that has passed since the offense, and the job at issue.[183] While the guidance is not law, it indicates the type of cases in which the EEOC is likely to find cause to believe the law was violated and also will likely be considered by courts interpreting the statute.

Cases under Title VII have considered what justifies the use of criminal background disqualifications that have a disparate impact. In *El v. Southeastern Pennsylvania Transportation Authority (SEPTA)*,[184] the court found that the defendant adequately established that barring employees with convictions of felonies, misdemeanors of moral turpitude, or violence from positions as paratransit drivers was necessary because of the vulnerability of those transported and the risk of recidivism. On the other hand, a railroad could not justify a ban on any employee convicted of anything other than a minor traffic violation.[185]

A number of states also have laws limiting the use of criminal records in employment decisions.[186] A recent movement, known as "Ban the Box", has resulted in the enactment of statutes and local ordinances that prohibit employers from requiring applicants to reveal criminal backgrounds on employment applications, moving consideration of criminal history to later in the process.[187] Some

---

[180] Id.

[181] Id.

[182] Id.

[183] Id.

[184] 479 F.3d 232 (3d Cir. 2007).

[185] Green v. Missouri Pac. R. Co., 523 F.2d 1290 (8th Cir. 1975).

[186] See, e.g., Ark. Code Ann. § 12–12–1009(c); Cal. Lab. Code § 432.7(a); Mass. Gen. Laws ch. 151B, § 4 (9).

[187] See Amanda Y. Agan, & Starr, Sonja B. Starr, Ban the Box, Criminal Records, and Statistical Discrimination: A Field Experiment 1 (June 14, 2016). U of Michigan Law & Econ Research Paper No. 16–012. available at https://ssrn.com/abstract=2795795 (noting over 100 jurisdictions and twenty-three states have passed ban the box policies, most applying to public entities but some also applying to private employers).

evidence suggests that ban the box legislation results in discrimination against African-American men in the hiring process, however.[188] Employers unable to screen for criminal records call back many more white applicants than black applicants for further consideration.[189]

Like federal law, state laws allow the use of criminal convictions where related to the job. For example, the Hawaii Supreme Court considered the case of an applicant with a drug conviction denied a job as a radiology technician.[190] The court remanded the case for trial, finding a genuine issue of material fact as to whether there was sufficient access to controlled substances or vulnerable patients in the job to establish a rational relationship between the criminal conviction and the employee's job duties.

The Fair Credit Reporting Act also provides some protection for employees with criminal backgrounds. The statute prohibits consumer reports from including arrest records, though not convictions, more than seven years old.[191] Additionally it may be used to challenge inaccurate information regarding criminal records, other than convictions, in consumer reports.[192]

3.2.1.4 Constitutional Limitations

Background investigations have also been challenged on constitutional grounds. In *NASA v. Nelson*, employees of a government contractor challenged NASA's background check as violative of their right to privacy.[193] The Constitution applied because the investigation was required by the government for contractor employees. The government required information about educational and work background, honesty, drug and alcohol abuse, financial stability, emotional and mental stability, counseling and treatment received, and legal problems. The Court declined to decide whether a right to informational privacy exists. Assuming such a right, however, the investigation was justified by the government's interest in ensuring that individuals with access to government facilities and information are trustworthy and reliable.

---

[188] Id. at 4.

[189] Id.

[190] Shimose v. Hawaii Health Sys. Corp., 134 Haw. 479, 345 P.3d 145 (2015).

[191] 15 U.S.C. §§ 1681c(a)(2), (5).

[192] See Haley, 9 F.Supp. 3d at 1192–93 (finding plaintiff stated a claim under the FCRA against agency that reported a criminal charge that was dismissed as both a dismissal and a conviction).

[193] 562 U.S. 134 (2011).

3.2.2 Interrogation

In the private sector, employers have wide latitude to interrogate employees. The National Labor Relations Act imposes some limits, discussed below. In addition, there are restrictions on testing and medical inquiries discussed infra at Section 3.2.5. Some public employees have statutory protections similar to the National Labor Relations Act, as well as some constitutional protection.

3.2.2.1 Statutory Restrictions

In order to protect the right of employees under to engage in union activity, the NLRB has interpreted the NLRA's § 8(a)(1) prohibition on interference, restraint and coercion in the exercise of § 7 rights to bar some interrogation of employees about union activity.[194] Whether such interrogation is lawful depends on whether the NLRB finds that it is coercive based on all of the circumstances. Among the factors considered are the time and place of the interrogation, the identity of the interrogator, the known sympathies of the employee regarding the union, the information sought, the known preferences of the employer regarding the union, and other surrounding circumstances, including any other unlawful employer actions. Consider the following example. The employees of Employer X are organizing a union because of dissatisfaction with their working conditions and supervision. The morning after the first union meeting, Supervisor A asks Employee B, who attended the meeting, "What's up with this union thing? Why would anyone here want a union?"[195] The NLRB has held that such interrogation is coercive because it carries with it the implication of intended retaliation for union support, interfering with the employees' rights. Now suppose that Employee B arrived at work that morning wearing a "Union Yes" button and was met with the same question from Supervisor A. The NLRB would not find coercion because Employee B is a known union supporter, unlikely to be coerced by questioning regarding her union sympathies.[196] If Supervisor A added the question "Who else is involved in this thing anyway?," a finding of coercion is more likely, however, even if the employee herself is a known union supporter.[197]

---

[194] See 29 U.S.C. § 158(a)(1); Rossmore House Hotel, 269 N.L.R.B. 1176 (1984).

[195] See Acme Bus. Corp., 320 N.L.R.B. 458 (1995).

[196] See Gossen Co., Div. of U.S. Gypsum Co. v. NLRB, 719 F.2d 1354, 1358 (7th Cir. 1983).

[197] See DynCorp, Inc. v. NLRB, 233 F. App'x. 419, 429 (6th Cir. 2007) (unpublished) (finding interrogation of known union supporter coercive where it required employee to reveal level of campaign activity); Hanover Concrete Co., 241 N.L.R.B. 936, 936 (1979) (finding coercive interrogation about union sympathies and activities of other employees).

Suppose the questioning was more formal. The union has requested that the employer recognize it as the representative of its employees because, the union asserts, a majority of the employees support the union. The employer wants to ascertain the truth of this assertion so it conducts a formal poll of its employees, asking them to indicate in writing whether they support the union. The legality of this poll depends on whether the employer conducts it in accordance with the specified standards set by the NLRB. The employer has a legitimate interest in determining whether its employees support the union because it has a legal obligation to bargain with the union if a majority so desire. The employer can insist that majority status be determined by an NLRB election, but also can poll the employees prior to the filing of any petition for election, and recognize the union based on the poll. The safeguards that the NLRB requires for a legal poll are the following: (1) the purpose of the poll must be to determine the truth of a union's claim of majority; (2) this purpose must be communicated to the employees; (3) the employees must be assured that there will be no reprisal based on their choice; (4) the employees must be polled by secret ballot; and (5) the employer cannot have engaged in unfair labor practices or otherwise created a coercive atmosphere.[198] A poll that complies with these requirements is lawful and binds the employer to recognize the union if a majority of the employees so desire.

An alternative rule applies if the union already represents the employees of the employer and the employer seeks to poll the employees to determine whether there is a continuing obligation to recognize and bargain with the union. The employer must comply with the polling standards set forth above, but the poll cannot be taken unless the employer has a reasonable, good faith uncertainty as to whether the union continues to represent a majority of the employees.[199] This doubt must be based on evidence such as antiunion petitions from employees, employee statements regarding their own or other employees' opposition to the union, and employee statements of dissatisfaction with the union.[200]

Another NLRA interrogation limit was articulated by the Supreme Court in *NLRB v. J. Weingarten, Inc.*[201] There the Court held that § 8(a)(1) entitles unionized employees to a union representative when an employer conducts an investigatory interview that may lead to discipline. To exercise this right, the employee must request the representative. After receiving the

---

[198] Struksnes Constr. Co., 165 N.L.R.B. 1062, 1063 (1967).

[199] See Allentown Mack Sales & Serv. v. NLRB, 522 U.S. 359 (1998).

[200] See Levitz Furniture Co., 333 N.L.R.B. 717, 728–29 (2001).

[201] 420 U.S. 251 (1975).

request, the employer can choose not to conduct the interview with a representative present, but cannot force the employee to proceed without representation or discipline the employee for requesting representation and refusing to proceed without it. This right has at times been extended by the NLRB to employees in nonunion workplaces, allowing them to request that a fellow employee accompany them to an investigatory interview.[202] The current NLRB interpretation of the law, however, is that nonunion employees have no such right.[203] The agency held in its most recent decision on this issue that nonunion employees would not benefit substantially from the attendance of fellow employees and allowing their attendance could impair the employer's ability to conduct effective and necessary investigations of employee misconduct.

Similar interrogation rules apply under many public sector bargaining statutes that are based on the NLRA.[204] Some state bargaining statutes provide the right to union representation in investigatory interviews, while others do not.[205]

3.2.2.2 Constitutional Restrictions

Public employees and government contractors retain their constitutional right against self-incrimination. If employees or independent contractors are threatened with discharge or contract termination for asserting a privilege against self-incrimination, their coerced statements cannot be used against them in a criminal proceeding.[206] Nor can employees or contractors be terminated solely for invoking or refusing to waive the privilege.[207] Employees can, however, be fired for failing to answer questions directly related to their jobs.[208] Further, if there is no threat of criminal prosecution, for

---

[202] See Epilepsy Foundation, 331 N.L.R.B. 676 (2000), aff'd in relevant part, Epilepsy Foundation v. NLRB, 268 F.3d 1095 (D.C. Cir. 2001); Materials Research, 262 N.L.R.B. 1010 (1982), overruled by Prudential Ins. Co., 275 N.L.R.B. 208 (1985).

[203] IBM Corp., 341 N.L.R.B. 1288, 1308 (2004), overruling Epilepsy Foundation, 331 N.L.R.B. 676.

[204] See, e.g., Hardin Cty. Cmty. Unit Sch. Dist. No. 1 v. IELRB, 174 Ill.App.3d 168, 189–90, 528 N.E.2d 737, 750 (1988); Town of Clay v. Helsby, 51 A.D.2d 200, 206, 379 N.Y.S.2d 896, 901–02 (1976).

[205] See, e.g., City of Round Rock v. Rodriguez, 399 S.W. 3d 130 (Tex. 2014) (no right to union representation); N.Y. Civ. Serv. Law § 209–a(1)(g) (McKinney) (providing a right to union representation).

[206] Lefkowitz v. Turley, 414 U.S. 70, 84 (1973) (contractors); Garrity v. New Jersey, 385 U.S. 493, 498 (1967) (employees).

[207] Lefkowitz, 414 U.S. at 82–83 (contractors); Gardner v. Broderick, 392 U.S. 273, 279 (1968) (employees).

[208] See O'Brien v. DiGrazia, 544 F.2d 543, 546 (1st Cir. 1976) (finding that the privilege against self-incrimination was not violated when employees were suspended for refusing to answer questionnaire about personal finances because the importance of ensuring integrity of the police force established that this information was "specifically, directly, and narrowly relat[ed] to the performance of their official

example where immunity has been granted to the interrogated employee, the employer can compel the employee to answer questions on pain of termination.[209]

3.2.3 Searches

3.2.3.1 Constitutional Limitations

The leading case on workplace searches is *O'Connor v. Ortega,*[210] which involved a search of the office of a public employee. The search was conducted pursuant to an employer investigation for potential disciplinary purposes. The employee whose office was searched filed suit alleging that the search violated the Fourth Amendment's prohibition on unreasonable searches. The Court recognized that employees may have reasonable expectations of privacy in the workplace. Nevertheless, the Court indicated that while an employee may expect privacy protection against police searches, a different rule must apply in the context of searches by the employer, since one's office is seldom secure against entry by others in the workplace. According to the plurality in *O'Connor,* the determination of whether there is a reasonable expectation of privacy is made on a case by case basis and depends on factors such as the extent of access by others, whether the employee keeps personal items in the area searched, and whether there is any workplace policy regarding personal use of work space.

Once an expectation of privacy is established, it must be balanced against the government employer's need to supervise the employee and operate efficiently. The Court held that based on these interests, no warrant is required for workplace searches, nor must the employer establish probable cause for a search of an employee's work space.[211] The Court thus created a special needs exception from the warrant and probable cause requirements for workplace searches. Instead of these requirements, the plurality's test analyzes whether the search is reasonable in its inception and its scope.[212] It will be reasonable in the former if either the search is necessary for a work-related purpose such as retrieving a file or there is a reasonable basis to believe that the search will provide evidence of work-related misconduct. The reasonableness of the scope will be decided based on whether the search is reasonably related to its

---

duties. . . ." quoting Uniformed Sanitation Men Ass'n, Inc. v. Comm'r of Sanitation, 392 U.S. 280, 284 (1968)).

209 Lefkowitz, 414 U.S. at 84.

210 480 U.S. 709 (1987).

211 480 U.S. at 721–25.

212 While Justice Scalia agreed that the special needs exception applies in the workplace, he did not agree with the test for reasonableness applied by the plurality. Id. at 732.

objectives and not unnecessarily intrusive, a standard that clearly depends on the facts of the particular case.

Justice Scalia, concurring, would have applied a different and simpler test. He would find a reasonable expectation of privacy in employee offices in most situations without the need for a case by case analysis, unless the office was open to the public generally, not just to other employees.[213] Rather than a balancing test at the next step he "would hold that government searches to retrieve work-related materials or to investigate violations of workplace rules—searches of the sort that are regarded as reasonable and normal in the private-employer context—do not violate the Fourth Amendment."[214]

In subsequent cases, the Supreme Court has not settled the question of whether the plurality's test or Justice Scalia's applies. The *O'Connor* standards have formed the basis of analysis of other constitutional workplace privacy issues, however, such as drug testing, discussed in Section 3.2.5.6.

A growing number of cases involve searches of electronic equipment. In *City of Ontario v. Quon*,[215] the Supreme Court addressed the constitutionality of a search of the messages on a pager provided to a SWAT team police officer. The Court declined to decide whether the employee had a reasonable expectation of privacy. The reluctance was based on the lack of a majority approach to deciding workplace privacy expectations in *O'Connor* and the unsettled nature of the role of technology in society and the workplace.[216] The Court held, however, that the employer's review of pager transcripts was justified at inception because the employer was trying to determine why the pagers exceeded the monthly message limit, requiring the employee to pay for overages. The review was reasonable in scope because it was an effective way to determine whether the excess pages were work-related or personal. The Court noted that the employer redacted off-duty messages, minimizing the intrusion. Finally, the Court noted that the search would also satisfy Justice Scalia's test as it would be "reasonable and normal" in the private sector.[217]

Two other aspects of the decision are notable. First, the Court emphasized that Officer Quon's expectation of privacy was limited, because a law enforcement officer should know that his pager might

---

213 Id. at 731.

214 Id. at 732.

215 560 U.S. 746 (2010).

216 Id. at 758–59.

217 Id. at 764–65.

be audited for legal reasons. Second, while the court of appeals found that supervisory assurances that the messages would not be audited so long as employees paid for the overages created a reasonable expectation of privacy, the Supreme Court did not decide whether the supervisor's statements superseded earlier notice that pager messages were not private.

Both before and after *Quon*, the key to cases involving searches of electronic equipment in the workplace is usually the employer's policy. The employer can, and usually does, defeat any reasonable expectation of privacy. If the employer notifies employees that their computer use may be monitored by the employer and that they should not expect any privacy, any employer search will likely survive constitutional challenge.[218] Some courts also analyze whether the employer actually implemented the policy of computer monitoring or searches.[219] The employer can also support its arguments for authorized searches based on its ownership of the computers and policies that prohibit personal use or limit the employees' freedom to use the computer in other ways.[220]

What happens when an employer search reveals evidence of criminal misconduct? Can the employer provide the authorities with evidence seized in a warrantless search? Can the government then use it in a criminal prosecution? Several cases have addressed this issue, generally resolving it against the employee. One court found that the employer has a right to continue its investigation of workplace misconduct so long as it meets the requisite standards, even if it reveals criminal conduct and leads ultimately to criminal prosecution.[221] In another case, the employee's motion to suppress

---

[218] See, e.g., Biby v. Bd. of Regents of the University of Nebraska, 419 F.3d 845, 850–51 (8th Cir. 2005) (finding search reasonable where computer policy told users that there was no expectation of privacy if the university had a legitimate reason to search the computer and the search at issue was conducted pursuant to one of the specified legitimate reasons, a discovery request in litigation); U. S. v. Angevine, 281 F.3d 1130, 1134 (10th Cir. 2002) (finding university professor had no expectation of privacy in computer where employer reserved the right to monitor computer use, informed employees that information on the university network was not confidential, specified penalties for computer misuse, and reserved ownership of computers and data).

[219] See, e.g., Dombrowski v. Governor Mifflin Sch. Dist., No. CIV.A. 11–1278, 2012 WL 2501017, at *6 (E.D. Pa. June 29, 2012) (setting forth four factor test including whether employer actually monitored employee computer use or e-mail).

[220] See U.S. v. Thorn, 375 F.3d 679, 684 (8th Cir. 2004), cert. granted, 543 U.S. 1112 (2005), on remand, 413 F.3d 820 (8th Cir. 2005), cert. denied, 546 U.S. 1009 (2005) (upholding warrantless search of government employee's computer based on employer policy barring personal use of computer, specifically prohibiting e-mails, pictures or documents that were pornographic, sexual, inappropriate or harassing, and acknowledging the employer's right to audit use to insure compliance with the policy); U.S. v. Angevine, 281 F.3d at 1134.

[221] See U.S. v. Simons, 206 F.3d 392 (4th Cir. 2000). In this case, the FBI obtained a warrant to search the employee's computer and office after being alerted by the

the evidence of an employer search that led to criminal prosecution was denied on the basis that the employer had the authority to consent to the law enforcement search of the employee's computer.[222] Thus, the evidence could be used to prosecute the employee on child pornography charges. In other criminal cases, courts have found that the employee had no reasonable expectation of privacy because the employer's computer policy defeated any expectation of privacy in the workplace computer use.[223]

Under some circumstances, even when the employee uses his or her own computer in the workplace, a reasonable expectation of privacy may be lacking. In *United States v. Barrows*,[224] the court denied a suppression motion in a child pornography prosecution, where the employee's personal computer was connected to the employer's network, lacked password protection for the files, and was used in a place accessible to the public. Where an employee used her home computers for work with the permission of the employer, however, the court found that she had a reasonable expectation of privacy.[225] The employer's investigators violated the Fourth Amendment by searching her home and seizing the computers without a warrant, unless a recognized exception to the warrant requirement applied.[226] The court refused to apply the special needs exception to the warrant requirement for employer searches, but found a genuine issue of material fact as to whether the employee consented to the search.[227]

The absence of a policy informing employees that the employer may engage in computer monitoring or searches will support a finding that an employee has a reasonable expectation of privacy. For example, in *United States v. Slanina*,[228] the court found a reasonable expectation of privacy. The employer had no computer policy giving notice of monitoring, the employer did not regularly access the employee's computer, which was located in a private office and not

---

employer that it found child pornography on his computer. The employee argued unsuccessfully that the employer should have stopped its investigation once it found unauthorized internet use and since it did not, the investigation became criminal and required a warrant.

222 See U.S. v. Ziegler, 474 F.3d 1184, 1192 (9th Cir. 2007) (finding that because the company routinely monitored employee computer use and barred personal use, the employer could consent to a government search of the employee's computer). This case involved a private, rather than a public employer, so the employer's search was not limited by the constitution.

223 See, e.g., U.S. v. Thorn, 375 F.3d at 684; U.S. v. Angevine, 281 F.3d at 1134.

224 481 F.3d 1246, 1248 (10th Cir. 2007).

225 Sabin v. Miller, 423 F. Supp. 2d 943 (S.D. Iowa 2006)

226 Id. at 948.

227 Id. at 949–52.

228 283 F.3d 670 (5th Cir. 2002), vacated on other grounds, 537 U.S. 802 (2003).

connected to the city's computer network, and the employee had installed password protection software without the employer's knowledge. Slanina's expectation of privacy did not save him, however, as the court found the search to be a reasonably-based investigation of workplace misconduct. Similarly, the absence of a policy or practice of monitoring, combined with the computer's location in a private office, created a privacy expectation for the employee in *Leventhal v. Knapek*.[229] Like Slanina, the employee lost his case because the court found that the state's search was pursuant to an investigation into workplace misconduct.

Additionally, the employer's policy may provide some expectation of privacy. In *Brown-Criscuolo v. Wolfe*, the court found that a teacher had a reasonable expectation of privacy based on the employer's policy, which provided only limited exceptions for maintenance and misconduct investigations.[230] The school superintendent who accessed her computer during her absence, reading an e-mail and letter to her private attorney and then forwarding it to his own account, violated her Fourth Amendment rights.

3.2.3.2 Invasion of Privacy and Other Tort Claims

In the private sector, of course, constitutional search limitations do not apply. Private employers have substantial latitude to search the workplaces of their employees. Many states have a cause of action for invasion of privacy sounding in tort, however. There are several different claims that come under the rubric of invasion of privacy. The one most commonly used in search and monitoring cases is intrusion upon seclusion, and the elements of the cause of action bear a resemblance to the constitutional claim.[231] The three elements are as follows. First, the employee must have some reasonable expectation of privacy in the place searched.[232] Second, the employee must not have consented to the search, and finally, the invasion of privacy must be highly offensive to a reasonable person.[233]

As in the constitutional context, the employer can defeat the privacy expectation in work spaces and equipment by providing notice to employees that their offices, desks, file cabinets, lockers, computers and other devices are subject to search. Similarly, some courts have concluded that the employer can search the personal

229 266 F.3d 64, 73–74 (2d Cir. 2001).

230 601 F. Supp.2d 441, 449–50 (D. Conn. 2009).

231 See Restatement (Second) of Torts § 652(B); Restatement of Employment Law §§ 7.01–06.

232 Id. at cmt. c.

233 Id. at cmt. d.

belongings of employees, particularly if notice is provided, but not all courts agree.[234] Even in the absence of notice, the employer's ownership and control of the work space or equipment may defeat any expectation of privacy. Some courts have held that, contrary to communications sent through regular mail, employees who communicate using an employer computer system have no reasonable expectation of privacy, even where the employer has no policy, because the employer's ownership of the computer and network negate any such expectation.[235] In *Smyth v. Pillsbury*,[236] the court found no reasonable expectation of privacy despite employer assurances of confidentiality of e-mail communications. Further the court went on to hold that even if there were a reasonable expectation of privacy, no reasonable person would find an employer's review of the e-mail to be a highly offensive invasion of privacy.

On the other hand, the employee's personal use and control of the space with the employer's knowledge may establish an expectation of privacy.[237] For example, in *K-Mart Corp. v. Trotti*,[238] the court found that the employee had a reasonable expectation of privacy in her work locker and the contents within where she had purchased a lock at her own expense and installed it on the locker with the knowledge of the employer. Similarly, in *Stengart v. Loving*

---

[234] Compare Simpson v. Commonwealth, Unemployment Compensation Bd. of Review, 69 Pa.Commw. 120, 450 A.2d 305 (1982) (upholding denial of unemployment compensation benefits based on employee's discharge for misconduct where he refused to allow search of his lunch bucket on leaving the premises, finding employer's policy of random inspection of parcels leaving the premises in employees' possession was reasonable where there was a posted policy notifying employees of the employer's reservation of the right to search any bag leaving the premises) and Leedham v. State Unemployment Appeals Comm'n, 950 So. 2d 475 (Fla. Dist. Ct. App. 2007) (same regarding refusal to allow briefcase search where employer had a policy that notified employees of right to search) with People v. Desnoyers, 183 Misc. 2d 871, 705 N.Y.S.2d 851 (Sup. Ct. 2000) (stating in dicta that hospital's policy of randomly searching bags of employees was unauthorized because there was no strong justification for the policy) and Aker v. New York & Co., 364 F. Supp. 2d 661, 668 (N.D. Ohio 2005) (finding plaintiff stated cause of action for invasion of privacy based on employer's search of her purse, coat, bag and person as she left the premises). See also United States v. Gonzalez, 300 F.3d 1048, 1054 (9th Cir. 2002) (rejecting Fourth Amendment challenge to search of government employee's backpack as he was leaving work because he had notice of search policy and prevention of theft justified the policy).

[235] See, e.g., Smyth v. Pillsbury Co., 914 F.Supp. 97 (E.D. Pa. 1996). See also Thygeson v. U.S. Bancorp, No. CV–03–467–ST, 2004 WL 2066746 (D. Or. Sept. 15, 2004) (finding no reasonable expectation of privacy where the employee saved some e-mails in a personal folder, because he used the employer's computer and network and thus the employer could access the folder).

[236] 914 F.Supp. at 101.

[237] The Restatement of Employment Law recognizes that employer actions that treat a location as private, accompanied by employee efforts to retain privacy, can establish a reasonable expectation of privacy. § 7.03(b)(2).

[238] 677 S.W.2d 632 (Tex. App. 1984).

Care Agency[239], the court found that the employee had a reasonable expectation of privacy in her password-protected web-based e-mail account, although she used the employer's computer to access it. The e-mails at issue were communications with her lawyer about her discrimination case. Other courts have disagreed with the *Stengart* analysis, however, finding no reasonable expectation of privacy in e-mails on a company-issued computer even when they involve attorney-client communications on a private e-mail account.[240]

Employers are increasingly using social media and internet searches to investigate employees. A 2016 survey revealed that 41% of employers had used social media to research current employees, while 32% used internet search engines for that purpose.[241] One quarter of employers surveyed found information that caused them to discipline or fire an employee.[242] Unless the employer improperly evades privacy protections set up by an employee, however, a claim for invasion of privacy is unlikely to succeed since no reasonable expectation of privacy would attach to material posted on the internet.[243] For example, the Restatement of Employment Law indicates that an employer who creates a false social media account and uses it to obtain permission from the employee to access her account invades the employee's privacy.[244]

Where employer equipment or workspace is not involved, the employee is more likely to prevail on a privacy claim. In *Lawlor v. North American Corporation of Illinois*,[245] the court upheld a jury verdict in favor of an employee where, in the course of an investigation of the employee, the employer's agents pretended to be her and obtained information about telephone calls made on her home and cell phones.

Employee resistance to a search may be protected if the search would constitute an invasion of privacy. In *Borse v. Piece Goods Shop, Inc.*,[246] the court found that the plaintiff stated a claim for wrongful discharge in violation of public policy where she was terminated for

---

239 201 N.J. 300, 990 A.2d 650 (2010).

240 See, e.g., Aventa Learning, Inc. v. K12, Inc., 830 F. Supp. 2d 1083, 1110 (W.D. Wash. 2011).

241 Career Builder, supra note 111.

242 Id.

243 See Palmieri v. United States, 72 F. Supp. 3d 191, 209-10 (D.D.C. 2014) (finding that government contractor had no reasonable expectation of privacy in his social media account because he shared it with friends and one of those friends gave information to the government, which, among other information, led to revocation of his security clearance).

244 § 7.04, comment d.

245 2012 IL 112530, 983 N.E.2d 414.

246 963 F.2d 611 (3d Cir. 1992).

refusing to consent to a drug test and a search of her personal belongings, a new policy instituted after fifteen years of employment.[247] On remand, the plaintiff was required to show that the testing and searches would unlawfully invade her privacy in order to prevail.[248] Not all courts have agreed with this analysis, however.[249]

Occasionally a search may be the subject of a different tort claim, such as false imprisonment or intentional infliction of emotional distress. For example in *Bodewig v. K-Mart*,[250] the employee sued the employer for intentional infliction of emotional distress based on the employer's strip search of the employee after a customer complaint of missing money. The court allowed the claim to go to a jury, holding that because of the special relationship between employer and employee the jury could find liability even without the intent to cause emotional distress if the conduct was sufficiently egregious.[251]

3.2.3.3 Statutory Restrictions

The Stored Communications Act, which is contained in Title II of the federal Electronic Communications Privacy Act,[252] limits searches of communications stored electronically. There is a broad exception for employers, however, if they provide notice to employees that their computers and electronic communications are subject to search. Accordingly, employers who establish computer use policies that provide such notification may defeat any potential claim under the statute, as well as constitutional and common law claims.[253] Additionally, the provider of the electronic communications service is exempted from liability under the statute and that is often the employer, providing another basis for defeating employee claims.[254] Where an outside company is the provider of the electronic communications service to the employer, however, its release to the employer of the content of stored messages sent by employees

---

[247] The Restatement of Employment Law has recognized such a claim. § 7.07.

[248] For further discussion of wrongful discharge in violation of public policy, see Section 2.5.1.

[249] See Jennings v. Minco Technology Labs, Inc., 765 S.W.2d 497 (Tex. App. 1989), discussed infra in Section 3.2.5.6.3, Drug Testing.

[250] 54 Or.App. 480, 635 P.2d 657 (1981).

[251] The Oregon Supreme Court later clarified that the relationship of the parties was relevant to the determination of the outrageousness of the conduct, not the separate question of intent. On the question of intent, the employer need not intend to cause severe emotional distress, but must intend the act and know that the act would cause such distress. McGanty v. Staudenraus, 321 Or. 532, 546–51, 901 P.2d 841, 850–53 (1995).

[252] 18 U.S.C. §§ 2701–12.

[253] See discussion of constitutional and common law claims at Sections 3.2.3.1 and 3.2.3.2.

[254] See Bohach v. City of Reno, 932 F.Supp. 1232 (D. Nev. 1996).

violates the statute.[255] Similarly, an employer that accessed the employee's personal e-mail stored on an outside provider's server, but viewed occasionally on the employer's computer, violated the law as the employer's access was not authorized.[256] The Act also has potential to limit employers' unauthorized access to employees' social media postings. In *Pietrylo v. Hillstone Restaurant Group*, the court found the employer violated the statute by accessing a private chat group on My Space through coercively obtaining an employee's password.[257] Where a friend of the employee voluntarily provided screenshots to management, however, the access was not unauthorized and the statute was not violated.[258] As in the case of tort and constitutional claims, where an employer makes extensive efforts to access personal communications of the employee, courts are more likely to find a violation.

As a result of adverse publicity about employers who demand access to employees' social media accounts as a condition of employment, a number of states have enacted statutes prohibiting employers from requiring employees and applicants for employment to provide access to their social media postings.[259] The statutes typically provide protection from retaliation for refusal to provide access.[260] After a few statutes initially failed to contain exceptions for employer-issued electronic devices as well as accounts created or used for employment purposes, most now have such exceptions.[261] Exceptions for publicly available accounts and for certain types of employer misconduct investigations are also common.[262] These statutes relate to searches, but would also prevent demanding access

---

[255] See Quon v. Arch Wireless Operating Co., Inc., 529 F.3d 892, 903 (9th Cir. 2008), rev'd on other grounds sub. nom. City of Ontario v. Quon, 560 U.S. 746 (2010) (finding wireless company to be an electronic communications service under the statute and therefore liable for the release of personal text messages of police officer to the police department).

[256] Pure Power Boot Camp v. Warrior Fitness Boot Camp, 587 F.Supp.2d 548, 560–61 (S.D.N.Y. 2008). See also Owen v. Cigna, 188 F. Supp. 3d 790 (N.D. Ill. 2016) (finding employee stated a claim where employer accessed personal e-mail stored on a different server using the employee's company-issued computer); Lazette v. Kulmatycki, 949 F.Supp.2d 748 (N.D. Ohio 2013) (denying motion to dismiss where supervisor used former employee's returned company blackberry to access her personal e-mail on a provider's server).

[257] 2009 WL 3128420 (D.N.J. 2009).

[258] Ehling v. Monmouth-Ocean Hosp. Serv. Corp., 961 F. Supp. 2d 659 (D.N.J. 2013).

[259] See, e.g., Cal. Lab. Code §§ 908(b), (c); Del. Code Ann. tit. 19, § 709A(b); 820 Ill. Comp. Stat. 55/10 (b)(1).

[260] See, e.g., Cal. Lab. Code §§ 908(e); Del. Code Ann. tit. 19, § 709A(h); 820 Ill. Comp. Stat. 55/10 (b)(1).

[261] See, e.g., Cal. Lab. Code § 908(d); Del. Code Ann. tit. 19, §§ 709A(d)(i), (ii); 820 Ill. Comp. Stat. 55/10 (b)(2), (5).

[262] See, e.g., Cal. Lab. Code § 908(c); Del. Code Ann. tit. 19, §§ 709A(d), (g); 820 Ill. Comp. Stat. 55/10 (b)(2), (3).

for the purpose of surveillance and monitoring, discussed in Section 3.2.4 infra.

For unionized employees, the NLRA requires bargaining with the union about computer use policies.[263] This may provide some protection for employees represented by a union, which can negotiate limits on employer searches.

3.2.4 Surveillance and Monitoring

Surveillance and monitoring are closely related to searches and generally undertaken by employers for the same or similar purposes. Technological advances have substantially enhanced the employer's ability to monitor the activities of employees. The law has not developed at the same pace.

Several newer forms of employee monitoring have evolved in recent years. Employers are using global positioning systems (GPS) to determine the location of employees, particularly those who work outside the employer's premises. Some employers are also using radio frequency identification (RFID) for the same purposes. GPS transmitters are often placed on vehicles, but can also be implanted in electronic devices such as cell phones used by employees.[264] RFID chips may be implanted in cards or electronic devices or even under the skin of individuals.[265] GPS uses satellites to pinpoint location, speed, and direction, while RFID chips communicate information by radio frequency to a compatible reader.[266] RFID chips can transmit much more data, but require proximity to a reader to obtain the information.[267]

3.2.4.1 Constitutional Restrictions

Like searches, surveillance and monitoring have been challenged on Fourth Amendment grounds in the public sector employment context. The test from *O'Connor v. Ortega* has been used

---

[263] See California Newspapers Partnership d/b/a ANG Newspapers, 350 N.L.R.B. 1175 (2007).

[264] Corey A. Ciocchetti, The Eavesdropping Employer: A Twenty-First Century Framework for Employee Monitoring, 48 Am. Bus. L.J. 285, 310 (2011).

[265] In 2017, Three Square Market, a Wisconsin company, was apparently the first U.S. employer to offer voluntary insertion of chips to its employees to be used for vending machine payments, opening secure doors, and operating equipment such as computers and copy machines. Megan Trimble, Tech Company to Implant Microchips in Employees, U. S. News & World Rep., July 24, 2017, available at https://www.usnews.com/news/national-news/articles/2017-07-24/wisconsin-tech-company-to-implant-microchips-in-employees.

[266] Anthony P. Gatto, Under the Human Skin: Will Human Microchipping Prove to Be A Survivor in the Courtroom Just As DNA Evidence Did?, 16 J. High Tech. L. 409, 438 (2016)

[267] See id.

in monitoring cases also. As in the case of searches, many cases founder for lack of a reasonable expectation of privacy. In *Vega-Rodriguez v. Puerto Rico Telephone Co.*,[268] for example, the court concluded that the employees who worked in an open area had no reasonable expectation of privacy, finding no difference in this regard between continual video monitoring and personal monitoring by supervisors. The court in *Nelson v. Salem State College*[269] reached a similar conclusion where many people had access to the employee's office, even when it was locked, because keys were widely available. Even in a locker area, which employees used to store belongings and change clothes, a court found no reasonable expectation of privacy since other employees had access to the area because it contained heating and air conditioning equipment.[270]

Where video monitoring is part of a criminal investigation, however, some courts have applied probable cause and warrant requirements from the criminal context, even if the investigation originated as a workplace investigation.[271] In such a case, the Ninth Circuit required a warrant for videotaping in an employee's private office, even though it upheld an earlier warrantless search of the same office as part of a workplace investigation.[272]

Computer monitoring claims are usually defeated on the same grounds as those based on searches. If the employer has a policy notifying employees of the potential for monitoring or if the computer is owned by the employer or connected to the employer's network, courts frequently find no reasonable expectation of privacy as against monitoring exists.[273] And even if a reasonable expectation of privacy exists, they may find monitoring justified based on employer interests.

There have been few workplace claims based on GPS monitoring. The Supreme Court, in a criminal case, found that the government's warrantless installation of a GPS tracking device on a suspect's car was a search because it physically intruded on the suspect's property.[274] A New York court subsequently rejected a constitutional challenge to the New York City Taxi and Limousine Commission's warrantless installation of a GPS tracker on a taxi,

---

268 110 F.3d 174 (1st Cir. 1997).

269 446 Mass. 525, 845 N.E.2d 338 (2006).

270 Thompson v. Johnson County Community College, 930 F.Supp. 501 (D. Kan. 1996).

271 See U.S. v. Taketa, 923 F.2d 665 (9th Cir. 1991).

272 Id. at 675.

273 See Sections 3.2.3.1 and 3.2.3.2 for discussion of the reasonable expectation of privacy in cases involving employer searches.

274 U.S. v. Jones, 132 S. Ct. 945 (2012).

citing the exception to the warrant requirement for workplace searches.[275] Where the employer installed a GPS device on an employee's personal vehicle and tracked his location at all times, including evenings, weekends and vacations, however, the New York Court of Appeals found the search unreasonable, suppressing the evidence from the GPS tracker in the employee's disciplinary proceeding.[276]

3.2.4.2 Invasion of Privacy and Other Tort Claims

Common law or statutory invasion of privacy claims may be based on employer monitoring and surveillance. Like the constitutional claims, most will fail based on either the lack of a reasonable expectation of privacy or a legitimate employer purpose for the monitoring.[277] Plaintiffs have succeeded in establishing an invasion of privacy where the area of monitoring is in no way public and the purpose of the monitoring is not a legitimate one, however. For example in *Benitez v. KFC National Management Co.*,[278] female employees prevailed on claims of both invasion of privacy and intentional infliction of emotional distress where supervisors and employees poked a hole in the wall and observed them in the restroom.[279] In an unusual case, the Illinois Appellate Court reversed summary judgment in favor of the employer where the employer used an undercover agent to investigate employee drug use and theft.[280] The court found that a genuine issue of material fact existed as to whether there was an invasion of privacy, noting that although the information was provided voluntarily to the investigators, that fact

---

[275] Carniol v. New York City Taxi and Limousine Commission, 126 A.D.3d 409, 2 N.Y.S.3d 337 (2015). See also State v. Meredith, 337 Or. 299, 306–07, 96 P.3d 342, 345 (Or. 2004) (holding that the employer's use of an electronic tracking device on a vehicle used by an employee to perform her job in a national forest did not require a warrant because she had no privacy interest in concealing her location and work-related activities).

[276] Cunningham v. N.Y. State Dep't of Labor, 21 N.Y.3d 515, 997 N.E.2d 468 (2013).

[277] See, e.g., Hernandez v. Hillsides, Inc., 47 Cal. 4th 272, 294–301, 211 P.3d 1063, 1078–1083 (2009) (finding a reasonable expectation of privacy in the employees' private office but concluding that video surveillance was not highly offensive because the employer had a legitimate reason for the monitoring and made efforts to limit the surveillance to that necessary to identify the employee suspected of improper conduct).

[278] 305 Ill.App.3d 1027, 714 N.E.2d 1002 (1999).

[279] For reasons that are not clear in the case, the employees were only able to recover against the individuals, and not against the employer. 305 Ill.App.3d at 1031–32, 714 N.E.2d at 1005. See also Koeppel v. Speirs, 808 N.W.2d 177, 184–85 (Iowa 2011) (reversing summary judgment for employer who installed video camera in employee bathroom finding genuine issue of material fact as to intrusion where it was not clear whether the camera actually could have functioned to observe the plaintiff but finding all other elements of the cause of action met).

[280] Johnson v. K Mart, 311 Ill.App.3d 573, 723 N.E.2d 1192 (2000).

was not dispositive because deception was involved.[281] The court also reversed summary judgment for the employer on the claim of public disclosure of private facts, another invasion of privacy claim, based on the investigators' reports to the employer of private information such as employees' family problems and romantic relationships.[282] The claim of intentional infliction of emotional distress failed because the plaintiffs did not establish severe emotional distress as a result of the employer's conduct.[283]

The few challenges to GPS monitoring on privacy grounds have been largely unsuccessful, particularly because the information revealed, an employee's presence in a particular location, is generally publicly available by observation and not unduly invasive of privacy.[284] Several states have enacted legislation which bars individuals or businesses from requiring implantation of RFID chips into an individual's body,[285] but the laws do not prohibit employers from requiring employees to carry cards or use equipment containing RFID devices.

3.2.4.3 Statutory Restrictions

The NLRA almost certainly contains the oldest prohibition on surveillance. The NLRB has long held that employers who engage in surveillance of the protected activities of employees, such as union meetings or strikes and picketing, violate employee rights.[286] The employer may be able to justify such monitoring in some circumstances, however. For example, if there has been violence on a picket line, the employer may be justified in installing cameras to record activities on the line.[287] The NLRA also requires bargaining with unions representing employees prior to initiating employee surveillance systems.[288]

---

[281] Id. at 578–79, 723 N.E.2d at 1196.

[282] Id. at 579, 723 N.E.2d at 1197.

[283] Id., 723 N.E.2d at 1198.

[284] See, e.g., Elgin v. Coca-Cola Bottling Co., No. 4:05CV970–DJS, 2005 WL 3050633 (E.D. Mo. Nov. 14, 2005) (finding that use of GPS tracking device on company truck to investigate loss of money from vending machines serviced by employee did not invade privacy because it provided no more information than could be obtained by visual observation of public streets).

[285] See N.D. Cent. Code § 12.1–15–06 (imposing criminal liability on persons requiring chip implantation); Wis. Stat. Ann. § 146.25 (imposing civil liability on individuals requiring implantation); Cal. Civ. Code § 52.7 (barring individuals and businesses from requiring implantation, including a prohibition on conditioning employment on implantation and providing for both civil penalties and a private right of action for damages); Mo. Rev. Stat. § 285.035 (making it a misdemeanor for employers to require employees to have chip implanted).

[286] See Tennessee Packers, Inc., 124 N.L.R.B. 1117, 1123 (1959).

[287] See Larand Leisurelies, Inc. v. NLRB, 523 F.2d 814, 819 (6th Cir. 1975).

[288] See Colgate-Palmolive Co., 323 N.L.R.B. 515 (1997).

Title III of the Omnibus Crime Control and Safe Streets Act of 1968,[289] also known as the Wiretap Act, has been used by some employees to challenge employer monitoring. The Act limits electronic surveillance, but contains two exceptions that often defeat employee claims. If one party to the conversation consents, either expressly or impliedly, to the monitoring or if the interception of the communication occurs in the ordinary course of business, the action does not violate the law.[290] Whether the monitoring is in the ordinary course of business typically will depend on the employer's purpose. The Second Circuit upheld recording of all telephone calls at an alarm company because of the sensitive security information involved in the business.[291] When an employer becomes aware that a monitored telephone call is personal, it can avoid liability by terminating the monitoring.[292] While the employer may have an interest in knowing that an employee is making personal calls on company time or using company phones, it does not have an interest in the substance of the conversation.

The Electronic Communications Privacy Act amended the Wiretap Act to include electronic communications.[293] It bars interception of electronic communications, but because of the narrow definition of interception and the speed of most electronic communication, it is unlikely to apply to e-mail, which is far more often searched after it is in storage.[294]

Two states require both public and private employers to provide notice of computer monitoring to employees.[295] Delaware mandates either daily notice or a signed acknowledgement from the employee of receipt of the employer's computer policy. Connecticut requires notice also, but has exceptions if the employer reasonably believes the employee is violating the law or creating a hostile work environment.[296]

---

289 18 U.S.C. §§ 2510–2522.

290 While the federal law requires only one party to consent to recording, some states require all parties to consent. See, e.g., Cal. Penal Code §§ 631–32.7.

291 Arias v. Mutual Central Alarm Serv., 202 F.3d 553, 559 (2d Cir. 2000).

292 See Fischer v. Mt. Olive Lutheran Church, 207 F.Supp.2d 914, 932 (W.D. Wis. 2002)

293 Pub. L. 99–508, 18 U.S.C. §§ 2510–22.

294 See Owen v. Cigna, 188 F. Supp. 3d 790 (N.D. Ill. 2016) (finding employee failed to state a claim where the employer accessed e-mails after transmission); Fraser v. Nationwide Mutual Ins. Co., 352 F.3d 107 (3d Cir. 2003). See the discussion of computer searches at Section 3.2.3.

295 See Del. Code Ann. tit. 19, § 705; Conn. Gen. Stat. § 31–48d. The Connecticut law does not create a private right of action, however. Gerardi v. City of Bridgeport, 294 Conn. 461, 472–73,985 A.2d 328, 334–35 (2010).

296 Conn. Gen. Stat. § 31–48d(b)(2).

3.2.4.4 A Duty to Monitor?

Employers frequently monitor for the purpose of avoiding liability. This raises the question of whether an employer that discovers that an employee is engaging in activities that may cause harm to another has any resulting duty to take action to avoid harm. In *Doe v. XYC Corp.*,[297] the New Jersey Superior Court found such a duty where the employer was aware that an employee was viewing child pornography, but neither terminated him nor advised the police. The employee had used his workplace computer to transmit photographs of his wife's ten year old daughter in the nude. The wife filed a negligence claim, and the court found a duty to act, remanding the case for a determination of whether the employer's breach of duty proximately caused harm to the daughter. Similarly, in *Doe v. Lafayette School Corp.*,[298] the court found that a school district owed a duty of care to a student who was subjected to sexual conduct by a teacher, remanding for a jury determination of whether the duty was breached where the school had learned of potentially inappropriate e-mail exchanges between a student and the teacher and failed to investigate further. These recent cases suggest that courts may find a duty to act on the part of employers who become aware of behavior that may foreseeably injure third parties.[299] Imposition of such a duty may discourage employer monitoring or alternatively prompt more intensive monitoring.

3.2.5 Pre-Employment and Employment Testing

3.2.5.1 Polygraph Examinations

The first, and until the enactment of the Genetic Information Nondiscrimination Act (GINA) in 2008[300] the only, employer investigatory practice to provoke a specific response from Congress was the polygraph examination. In 1988 Congress passed the Employee Polygraph Protection Act,[301] which limits employer use of polygraph exams. Congress was motivated by concerns about the reliability of polygraph exams and testimony about abusive practices in their use. As a result of the Act, most employers are prohibited from requesting or requiring that employees or applicants take polygraph exams, and from using the results of such exams.[302]

---

[297] 382 N.J. Super. 122, 887 A.2d 1156 (2005).

[298] 846 N.E.2d 691 (Ind. Ct. App. 2006).

[299] Professor Finkin criticizes the decisions in his treatise, calling them "questionable" because the string of causation seemed "attenuated at best." Matthew Finkin, Privacy in Employment Law 390, n.289 (4th ed. 2013).

[300] For a discussion of GINA, see Section 3.2.5.5.

[301] 29 U.S.C. §§ 2001–2009.

[302] 29 U.S.C. § 2002.

Additionally, the statute prohibits discrimination for refusal to take a test or for asserting rights under the Act.[303]

Congress established several exemptions from the Act's prohibitions, first and perhaps foremost, for federal, state and local governments.[304] The government is not only allowed to polygraph its own employees, but also employees of federal contractors and consultants involved in national defense, national security, or counterintelligence.[305]

Another exemption, known as the investigation exemption, applies to all employers and allows them to request an employee polygraph in connection with an investigation into economic loss or injury to the employer's business, such as theft, embezzlement or sabotage.[306] Certain conditions must be met to use the exemption. The employee must have had access to the property that is the subject of the investigation and the employer must have a reasonable suspicion that the employee was involved based on evidence other than the polygraph.[307]

Additionally, prior to the exam, the employer must give the employee a statement signed by an employer representative (not the examiner), setting forth the details of the incident being investigated and the basis for testing the employee, including information about employee access and the basis for reasonable suspicion.[308] No employee can be fired or disciplined solely on the basis of a polygraph exam given under this exception.[309] The reliability of the exam improves when the population being tested by an exam has been narrowed by previous investigation to include more individuals likely to possess the trait tested for, providing empirical support for this exception.

Employers can test applicants for security jobs with companies that provide security to power plants, public water supplies, toxic waste materials, public transportation, currency, precious commodities and similar operations that significantly impact health, safety, or national security.[310] Similarly applicants for jobs involving access to controlled substances are subject to testing, as are employees in connection with an investigation of misconduct

---

303 29 U.S.C. § 2002(4).

304 29 U.S.C. § 2006(a).

305 29 U.S.C. § 2006(b), (c).

306 29 U.S.C. § 2006(d)(1).

307 29 U.S.C. § 2006(d)(2), (3).

308 29 U.S.C. § 2006(d)(4).

309 29 U.S.C. § 2007(a).

310 29 U.S.C. § 2006(e).

involving controlled substances to which the employee had access.[311] The latter exemption, unlike the general investigation exemption, does not require reasonable suspicion prior to testing.

The Polygraph Act is enforced by the Secretary of Labor, but private actions for enforcement are available to employees and applicants as well.[312] Legal actions based on the Polygraph Act are not common, however, perhaps because many employers began to use other tests after the enactment of the statute.

3.2.5.2 Honesty Tests

The severe restrictions on polygraph testing led employers to seek other methods to determine employee honesty prior to hiring. Paper and pencil honesty tests are not covered by the federal Polygraph Act or most state laws, although a few states restrict the use of honesty tests. For example, Rhode Island law allows employers to give written honesty tests, but precludes their use as the "primary basis for an employment decision."[313] Massachusetts bars employers from requiring any lie detector test, including a written honesty test, as a condition of either initial or continuing employment.[314]

There is much debate and little independent evidence about the reliability of these tests. The most significant public policy concern is false positives, which occur when the test results label honest employees as dishonest.[315] Like the polygraph, if there are few dishonest employees or applicants in the test pool, the rate of false positives will be higher, even if the test is relatively accurate.

3.2.5.3 Psychological and Personality Tests

Some employers use personality or psychological tests to screen prospective employees.[316] One of the few legal challenges to such tests arose in California in *Soroka v. Dayton Hudson Corp.*[317] The lower court denied a request to enjoin Target's use of a psychological screening test for security officer applicants. The California Court of Appeals reversed the denial of the preliminary injunction. The plaintiffs' suit was based on the privacy provision of the California Constitution, which applies to private as well as public employers,

---

311 29 U.S.C. § 2006(f).

312 29 U.S.C. §§ 2004, 2005.

313 See R.I. Stat. §§ 28–6.1–1, 28–6.1–4.

314 See Mass. Gen. Laws Ch. 149, § 19B.

315 See Office of Technology Assessment, U.S. Congress, The Use of Integrity Tests for Pre-employment Screening 54–58 (1990), available at http://www.theblackvault.com/documents/ota/Ota_2/DATA/1990/9042.PDF.

316 See Susan J. Stabile, The Use of Personality Tests as a Hiring Tool: Is the Benefit Worth the Cost?, 4 U. Pa. J. Lab. & Emp. L. 279 (2002).

317 1 Cal.Rptr.2d 77 (1991).

and the California Fair Employment and Housing Act. The employer conceded that the test invaded the privacy of the applicants, requiring the court to consider whether Target had a compelling interest to support the invasion and whether there was a sufficient nexus between the interest and the means chosen to achieve it. The court focused on the test's questions about religious beliefs and sexual orientation and concluded that, based on these questions, the test did not have a sufficient connection to Target's legitimate interest in emotionally stable security officers. Thus, the court held that the plaintiffs were likely to succeed on the merits of their constitutional claim. Similarly, since the discrimination law barred religious and sexual orientation discrimination, the plaintiffs were likely to succeed on those claims as well. A petition for review was granted, but then dismissed after the case settled.[318]

The *Soroka* case offers little hope to employees and applicants with privacy claims based on testing for several reasons. First, the California Constitution is relatively unique in applying to private entities. And second, even in *Soroka*, the court did not broadly strike a blow for privacy, but instead focused on particular intrusive questions on the test. Finally, subsequent decisions by the California Supreme Court have eroded several elements of the *Soroka* decision. In *Hill v. NCAA*,[319] the court held that a balancing test, rather than a compelling interest test, applies to constitutional privacy claims where the defendant is a private entity. And in *Loder v. City of Glendale*,[320] the court allowed a public employer to drug test applicants, but not employees, finding a lesser invasion of privacy and stronger employer need to test job applicants.

Common law invasion of privacy claims are unlikely to provide much assistance to employees or applicants subjected to employment tests. If the individual refuses to answer the questions, privacy is not invaded.[321] Answering questions may waive a privacy claim unless the answer was compelled by a threat not to hire or to terminate. Under the federal Constitution, challenges to such tests have often failed either because the tests are not considered searches[322] or

---

318 Soroka v. Dayton Hudson Corp., 862 P.2d 148 (Cal. 1993).

319 7 Cal.4th 1, 865 P.2d 633 (1994).

320 14 Cal.4th 846, 927 P.2d 1200 (1997).

321 See Cort v. Bristol Meyers, 385 Mass. 300, 302, 431 N.E.2d 908, 910 (1982) (finding no invasion of privacy where employees refused to answer intrusive questions on employer questionnaire).

322 See Greenawalt v. Ind. Dep't of Corr., 397 F.3d 587, 590–91 (7th Cir. 2005) (finding questioning is not a search).

because the employer's interests in hiring fit and stable employees have been deemed to outweigh the privacy interests of employees.[323]

3.2.5.4 Medical Tests

Where a test is psychological, rather than a personality test, the Americans with Disabilities Act (ADA) might provide an avenue for relief. The ADA bars employers with 15 or more employees from requiring pre-employment medical tests unless the person has been given an offer of employment conditioned on passing the test, the test is given to all applicants for the job, and any disqualification based on the test is job-related.[324] Thus, an applicant with a back impairment could be disqualified for a job loading trucks, but not an office clerical position that involved no physical requirements. The ADA also permits only job-related medical tests for employees.[325] The Minnesota Multiphasic Personality Inventory (MMPI), is a commonly used clinical test which was created to diagnose mental illness, but evolved into a classification system for personality types and psychopathology. The test is used by some employers, has been held to be a medical test under the ADA by one Court of Appeals, even where the employer used it to identify personality traits rather than mental illness.[326] The line between personality tests and medical tests can be elusive, however. Other courts have permitted the use of tests to make decisions based on personality traits, even where the test might be used for medical purposes.[327] The Equal

---

[323] See, e.g., McKenna v. Fargo, 451 F.Supp. 1355, 1381 (D.N.J. 1978), aff'd, 601 F.2d 575 (3d Cir. 1979) (approving the use of personality tests in hiring firefighters because the city's interest in screening out unfit candidates outweighed the privacy interests of the applicants); Down v. Ann Arbor Pub. Sch., 29 F.Supp. 3d 1030, 1038–39 (E.D. Mich. 2014) (finding teacher unlikely to succeed on the merits of her claim that psychological test violated the Fourth Amendment since the search would not be unreasonable in light of her diminished expectation of privacy), See also Matter of Vey, 135 N.J. 306, 639 A.2d 718 (1994) (upholding decision by Merit System Board to remove plaintiff's eligibility for police officer position based on results on psychological tests).

[324] 42 U.S.C. § 12112(d); 29 C.F.R. § 1630.14(b).

[325] 42 U.S.C. § 12112(d)(4); 29 C.F.R. § 1630.14(c). See, e.g., Kroll v. White Lake Ambulance Auth., 763 F.3d 619, 623–25 (6th Cir. 2014) (finding genuine issues of material regarding whether required counseling was a medical exam and whether employer had reasonable belief that employee's behavior was a serious problem for the business, justifying required counseling).

[326] See Karraker v. Rent-A-Center, Inc., 411 F.3d 831 (7th Cir. 2005).

[327] In *Thompson v. Borg-Warner Protective Services Corp.*, a district court in California refused to find that the use of the PASS-III D.A.T.A Survey to screen applicants for security guard positions violated the ADA. No. C–94–4015 MHP, 1996 WL 162990, at *6 (N.D. Cal. Mar. 11, 1996). The court stressed the importance of allowing employers to consider personality traits in hiring decisions. The court also decided that the test, which provided scores on alienation, trustworthiness and drug attitudes of the test takers, was not a medical exam under the ADA because it was neither given nor interpreted by a medical professional, it was not physically invasive, and no medical equipment was used in the test's administration. The Eighth Circuit, in *Miller v. City of Springfield*, did not reach the issue of the distinction between

Employment Opportunity Commission (EEOC), the administrative enforcement agency for the ADA, considers the following factors to determine whether a test is medical: whether it is either designed or utilized to discover an impairment; whether it is given and interpreted by medical personnel; and whether the test is regularly used in a medical setting.[328]

While employers may be interested in medical screening to reduce costs, the ADA limits their ability to screen out employees with medical problems unless they are clearly job-related. The ADA outlaws discrimination against qualified individuals with disabilities unless they cannot perform the essential functions of the job, with or without reasonable accommodation.[329] Further, the law prohibits inquiries about disabilities unless they are a part of an authorized medical examination or for a current employee, job-related.[330] Additionally, the law bars discrimination against individuals who are perceived to have a disability or have a history of a disability.[331] Employers may be limited by this provision in their ability to avoid hiring individuals who are likely to have high health care costs or high absenteeism rates. Of course, the fact that someone has (or previously had) a disability does not necessarily mean that medical costs or absenteeism will be higher than those of other employees. Indeed, one reason for the ADA was to end discrimination which was often based on myths, fears and stereotypes about individuals with disabilities.

3.2.5.5 Genetic Testing and Use of Genetic and Biometric Information

With the rapid growth in both the scientific knowledge about the importance of genes and the ability to test for genetic disorders, fears about genetic screening and discrimination have multiplied. The

---

medical and personality testing, instead dismissing the plaintiff's claim because she failed to establish that she was disabled or regarded as disabled under the ADA. 146 F.3d 612 (8th Cir. 1998). Since she was not disabled, she could not prevail on her claim that the MMPI unlawfully screened out her application for a police officer's position. The court did state that "appropriate psychological screening is job-related and consistent with business necessity where the selection of individuals to train for the position of police officer is concerned." 146 F.3d at 615. But see Boston Police Dep't v. Kavaleski, No. SUCV200904978C, 2014 WL 5422562 (Mass. Super. Aug. 15, 2014) (finding psychological screening of police officer candidate unlawful because it was not used solely to determine whether she could do the job with reasonable accommodations as required by Massachusetts statute).

[328] U.S. Equal Employment Opportunity Commission, ADA Enforcement Guidance: Preemployment Disability-Related Questions and Medical Examinations 14 (1995).

[329] 42 U.S.C. § 12112(b)(5); 29 C.F.R. § 1630.14(a).

[330] 42 U.S.C. § 12112(d); Harrison v. Benchmark Electronics Huntsville, Inc., 593 F.3d 1206 (11th Cir. 2010).

[331] 42 U.S.C. § 12102(2).

public concern led Congress to pass the Genetic Information Nondiscrimination Act (GINA) in 2008.[332] GINA bars discrimination by employers, unions, employment agencies, and health insurers based on genetic information. The coverage of the statute is very broad, including employers and employees[333] covered by various other nondiscrimination statutes such as Title VII of the Civil Rights Act,[334] the Congressional Accountability Act,[335] and the Government Employee Rights Act.[336] Employees and their families cannot be denied insurance coverage, charged higher premiums, or barred from employment based on genetic information.[337] The law also prohibits discriminatory discharge, discriminatory compensation, and discrimination in other terms and conditions of employment, including training programs and apprenticeships.[338] Further GINA prohibits covered entities from requiring, requesting or buying genetic information about employees and their families, with limited exceptions.[339] Among the exceptions are information needed to comply with certification requirements for family medical leave under the FMLA and information needed to monitor the impact of exposure to toxic substances in the workplace.[340]

If genetic information is obtained, it must be treated as a confidential medical record[341] and it is subject to the privacy regulations of the Health Insurance Portability and Accountability Act (HIPAA).[342] There are civil penalties for insurers who violate the statute and the remedies against employers, unions and employment agencies are the same as those in the underlying discrimination

---

332 Pub. L. No. 110–233, 122 Stat. 881 (2008).

333 42 U.S.C. § 2000ff (2)(A), (B).

334 See 42 U.S.C. §§ 2000e(b), (f), 2000e–1 and 2000e–16.

335 See 2 U.S.C. § 1301.

336 See 42 U.S.C. §§ 2000e–16a to 2000e–16c.

337 42 U.S.C. § 2000ff–1.

338 42 U.S.C. §§ 2000ff–1(a), 2000ff–2(a); 2000ff–3(a) 2000ff–4(a).

339 42 U.S.C. §§ 2000ff–1(b); 2000ff–2(b); 2000ff–3(b) 2000ff–4(b). See Equal Employment Opportunity Comm'n v. Grisham Farm Prod., Inc., No. 6:16–CV–03105–MDH, 2016 WL 3221161, at *4 (W.D. Mo. June 8, 2016) (finding employer violated GINA by requiring completion of health history form by applicants for employment).

340 42 U.S.C. §§ 2000ff–1(b)(3), (5).

341 42 U.S.C. § 2000ff–5.

342 HIPAA, Pub. L.,104–191,110 Stat. 1936, was enacted in 1996 to limit the ability of employers and insurers to exclude employees' preexisting medical conditions from coverage under health insurance plans. Once employees have been covered by insurance for twelve months, preexisting conditions cannot be excluded by the plan or future plans when the employee changes insurance so long as the employee does not have a 63 day break in coverage. 42 U.S.C. § 300gg–3. HIPAA also bars discrimination by group health plans based on health status. 42 U.S.C. §§ 300gg–1; 300gg–4. HIPAA directed issuance of privacy regulations for medical information by the Department of Health and Human Services. 42 U.S.C. §§ 1320d–1320d–8. GINA applied these regulations to genetic information. 42 U.S.C. § 1320d–9.

statutes from which employee coverage is derived such as Title VII, the Congressional Accountability Act and the Government Employee Rights Act.[343] These remedies typically include reinstatement and back pay with benefits, and in some cases compensatory and punitive damages.

Prior to GINA, genetic discrimination was addressed by both state and federal governments. A number of state laws bar discrimination based on genetic tests or genetic information by employers, insurance companies or both, although not all prohibit employers from obtaining such information.[344] A federal executive order, E.O. 13145, bars such discrimination by federal employers.[345] Additionally, the EEOC has taken the position that genetic discrimination is prohibited by the ADA, although the ADA's application is less important in light of GINA.[346] The EEOC did file an action for injunctive relief against Burlington Northern Santa Fe Railroad to challenge the company's practice of conducting genetic testing of employees who filed claims for work-related injuries based on carpal tunnel syndrome.[347] The case settled quickly, with the company ending the testing. HIPAA also bars health insurers from requiring genetic testing and from using genetic information to exclude individuals from coverage or charge higher premiums.[348]

Several states have enacted legislation limiting the use of biometric information such as eye, hand and facial scans and fingerprints. The laws require notice and consent for collection of such information, limit disclosure of the information, and mandate policies for retention and destruction.[349] As employers increasingly use biometric information for access and time tracking, they are subject to these limitations.

---

[343] 42 U.S.C. § 2000ff–6.

[344] See Finkin, supra note at 299, at 40–44 (describing various state laws on genetic testing and information); id at 50–69 (describing the variety of state limitations on the use of medical information by employers).

[345] Exec. Order No. 13,145, 2000 WL 142053 (Pres. Exec. Order), 65 Fed. Reg. 6877; EEOC: Policy Guidance on Executive Order 13145: To Prohibit Discrimination in Federal Employment Based on Genetic Information; Notice Number EEOC 915.002 (July 26, 2000).

[346] See EEOC: Compliance Manual, Volume 2, EEOC Order 915.002, § 902 (March 14, 1995).

[347] See EEOC's First Genetic Testing Challenge Settled for $2.2 Million, Parties Announce, Daily Lab. Rep. (BNA) No. 90, at A–1 (May 9, 2002).

[348] 42 U.S.C. §§ 300gg–4(a)(6), (b)(3) and (c).

[349] See, e.g., 740 Ill Comp. Stat. 14/1–14/99; Rev. Code Wash. § 40.26.010–020 (applying to state agencies only); Tex. Bus. & Com. Code Ann. § 503.001 pplying to information obtained for a commercial purpose).

3.2.5.6 Drug Testing

Since the Reagan-initiated "War on Drugs" in the 1980s, employer drug testing has been commonly used by many employers[350] and required by the federal government for some employees. For example, the Omnibus Transportation Employee Testing Act requires alcohol and drug testing of many employees in the transportation industry.[351] Employers continue drug testing because they believe in its effectiveness.[352]

3.2.5.6.1 Constitutional Restrictions

Two leading cases decided on the same day analyzed the constitutionality of employer drug testing. *Skinner v. Railway Labor Executives' Association*[353] involved a challenge to Federal Railroad Administration regulations requiring that railroads test crews after accidents. *National Treasury Employees Union v. Von Raab*[354] dealt with a challenge to Customs Service testing of applicants for promotion to jobs that involved carrying firearms, drug interdiction, or access to classified information. The Court upheld the testing in both cases, but remanded with regard to testing of employees with access to classified information in *Von Raab*. In both cases, the Court found the testing to be a Fourth Amendment search, and then applied a balancing test to determine whether the government's need for testing outweighed the employees' expectations of privacy. Although there was no evidence of a drug problem in the Customs Service, the *Von Raab* Court found no need for individualized suspicion to support testing. The public safety risk created by employees with firearms and the need to ensure that employees engaged in drug interdiction are fit, honest, and not subject to the temptation of drugs won out. A particularly pointed dissent by Justice Scalia accused the majority of accepting the government rationale of symbolism to justify a "search

---

[350] See American Management Association, AMA 2004 Workplace Testing Survey: Medical Testing 3 (2004), available at http://www.amanet.org/research/pdfs/Medical_testing_04.pdf (finding 63% of companies tested either newly hired or existing employees, a reduction from prior years); Roy Mauer, Nearly 8 in 10 Employers Screen for Alcohol, Drugs, Society for Human Resource Management, May 21, 2013 (citing 2013 survey showing that 78% of companies tested applicants, current employees or both); HireRight Annual Employment Screening Benchmark Report, 2015 edition, at 25, http://hosteddocs.ittoolbox.com/2015-employment-screening-benchmark-report_final.pdf (finding 66% of employers surveyed engage in drug or alcohol screening).

[351] See 49 U.S.C. § 45102 (testing of air carrier employees); 49 U.S.C. § 31306 (testing of operators of commercial motor vehicles); 49 U.S.C § 5331 (testing of public transportation employees).

[352] Kathy Gurchiek, Employer Testing Credited for Drop in Worker Drug Use, Society for Human Resource Management (2007), available at https://www.shrm.org/hr-today/news/hr-news/pages/cms_021232.aspx.

[353] 489 U.S. 602 (1989).

[354] 489 U.S. 656 (1989).

particularly destructive of privacy and offensive to personal dignity."[355]

Following these two decisions, many categories of government employees have been lawfully subjected to suspicionless drug testing, not only those who carry firearms or work with drugs but other categories of employees where the court perceives that an impaired employee poses a risk by virtue of the nature of the job.[356] Courts upholding testing frequently rely on risks to the public,[357] although they need not be direct,[358] but also cite risks to other employees and others present in the workplace.[359] Courts do not always agree, however, as to which employees may pose such a risk.[360]

In addition to the federal Constitution, state constitutions may provide a basis for challenging drug testing. Even where the state constitution protects privacy rights relating to drug testing, however, employer interests may outweigh employee interests. For example in *Loder v. City of Glendale*,[361] the court upheld drug screening for all applicants for employment based on the employer's legitimate interest in learning whether an applicant uses drugs. State

---

[355] Id. at 680.

[356] See, e.g., National Treasury Employees Union v. United States Customs Serv., 27 F.3d 623 (D.C. Cir. 1994) (sustaining drug testing of employees with access to certain computer data bases); Taylor v. O'Grady, 888 F.2d 1189 (7th Cir. 1989) (upholding urinalysis for prison guards); Harmon v. Thornburgh, 878 F.2d 484 (D.C. Cir. 1989) (allowing urinalysis for Justice Department employees with top security clearance); Krieg v. Seybold, 427 F.Supp. 2d 842 (N.D. Ind. 2006), aff'd, 481 F.3d 512 (7th Cir. 2007) (allowing random drug testing to deter drug use where employee was the operator of heavy equipment, even when the job did not require the possession of a commercial operator's license); Crager v. Bd. of Educ. of Knott County, 313 F.Supp.2d 690 (E.D. Ky. 2004) (permitting random, suspicionless testing of teachers in public schools); New Jersey Transit PBA Local 304 v. New Jersey Transit Corp., 384 N.J. Super. 512, 895 A.2d 472 (2006) (upholding testing as part of an annual medical examination required of all transit police officers); Aguilera v. City of East Chicago Fire Civil Serv. Comm'n, 768 N.E.2d 978 (Ind. Ct. App. 2002) (authorizing random drug testing of firefighters).

[357] See, e.g., New Jersey Transit PBA Local 304, 384 N.J. Super. at 522, 895 A.2d at 478 (citing risk to public safety from impaired transit police officers); Krieg v. Seybold, 427 F.Supp.2d at 857 (citing risk to public safety from impaired operators of heavy equipment in areas where public travels).

[358] See, e.g., NTEU v. U. S. Customs Serv., 27 F.3d at 628–29 (citing risk that employees with computer access could provide drug smugglers with information that would enable them to avoid detection, noting serious drug problem in the country that affects the health and welfare of citizens); Harmon v. Thornburgh, 878 F.2d at 491–92 (upholding random testing of employees with high level national security clearance because of the risk of disclosure of important security information).

[359] See, e.g., Taylor v. O'Grady, 888 F.2d at 1197 (indicating that prisoner access to drugs poses a risk to prison employees, visitors, prisoners and the public).

[360] Compare Hatley v. Dep't of the Navy, 164 F.3d 602 (Fed. Cir. 1998) (allowing random drug testing of firefighters) with Petersen v. City of Mesa, 207 Ariz. 35, 83 P.3d 35 (2004) (striking down as unconstitutional random drug testing of firefighters).

[361] 14 Cal.4th 846, 927 P.2d 1200 (1997).

constitutions, with the exception of California,[362] do not typically apply their privacy protections to private sector employees.[363]

3.2.5.6.2 Statutory Restrictions

There is no federal statute limiting drug testing. Indeed, the ADA exempts drug testing from its prohibition on medical testing.[364] A number of states have laws regulating drug testing, but none bar testing outright.[365] For example, Connecticut law allows employers to drug test employees based on reasonable suspicion of drug or alcohol use.[366] North Carolina imposes qualitative requirements for drug testing, including insuring the chain of custody of samples and confirming positive results with a second test.[367] And Minnesota requires that an employee who tests positive for drugs for the first time be given an opportunity for rehabilitation.[368] For private sector unionized employees, drug testing is a mandatory subject of bargaining, which means that employers cannot impose it unilaterally but must bargain with the union over the terms of testing.[369]

3.2.5.6.3 Common Law Claims

Private sector employees may rely on the state statutes mentioned above, but have limited ability to challenge employer drug testing. Some employees have sought to challenge drug testing using common law tort claims, primarily wrongful discharge in violation of public policy or invasion of privacy. Some cases have been successful under each theory, though many have failed. In *Twigg v. Hercules Corp.*,[370] the West Virginia Supreme Court found that a discharge for refusal to submit to a drug test violates public policy unless the employer has a reasonable good faith suspicion that the employee is

---

[362] See Luck v. Southern Pacific Transp. Co., 218 Cal.App.3d 1, 19, 267 Cal.Rptr. 618, 628 (1990). For a discussion of the story of Luck and its impact, see Pauline T. Kim, The Story of Luck v. Southern Pacific Transportation Co.: The Struggle to Protect Employee Privacy in Employment Law Stories 85 (Samuel Estreicher & Gillian Lester, eds., 2007).

[363] See., e.g., Luedtke v. Nabors Alaska Drilling, Inc., 768 P.2d 1123, 1130 (Alaska 1989) (holding state constitutional right to privacy did not apply to private action).

[364] See 42 U.S.C. § 12114(d).

[365] See Finkin, supra note 299, at 123–62 (detailing various state laws regarding drug testing). For a compilation of state drug and alcohol testing statutes, see id. at 781–936.

[366] Conn. Gen. Stat. § 31–51x.

[367] N.C. Gen. Stat. § 95–232.

[368] Minn. Gen. Stat. §§ 181.953.10.

[369] See Johnson-Bateman Co., 295 N.L.R.B. 180 (1989).

[370] 185 W.Va. 155, 406 S.E.2d 52 (1990). The protection of *Twigg* applies only to employees not applicants, who can be subjected to drug tests. Baughman v. Wal-Mart Stores, Inc. 215 W. Va. 45, 592 S.E.2d 824 (2003).

using drugs or the job involves public safety or the safety of other employees. Thus, while the court recognized a possible cause of action, it is limited. The Restatement of Employment Law agrees with the *Twigg* court, indicating that an employer violates the law if it discharges the employee for refusing to consent to a violation of the right to privacy.[371] The employee must be correct, however, in assessing the resisted intrusion as wrongful.[372] An honest and reasonable belief that the employer's action is unlawful is insufficient.[373]

Other courts have disagreed with *Twigg*. In *Jennings v. Minco Technology Labs, Inc*,[374] challenging the employer's newly instituted drug testing program on privacy grounds, the Texas Court of Appeals stated:

> Jennings may consent or not to any future requirement that she give a urine sample or participate in a rehabilitation program, should either be asked of her; or she may reject further employment on the modified terms proposed by the company. She may not, however, determine unilaterally what the terms of her employment shall be and compel the company to contract with her on that basis against its will. In any case, her privacy interest will not be invaded without her consent, which is to say it will not be invaded by the company unlawfully so as to require and justify the injunctive relief she requested.[375]

Under this view, the value of the privacy interest is a matter between the employee and the employer, not a matter for intervention of the courts based on public policy. Alternatively, the court may be valuing competing public policies, elevating the policy preserving at-will employment over the policy protecting employee privacy.

The court in *Kelley v. Schlumberger*[376] upheld a jury verdict in favor of an employee who challenged the drug testing procedure of collecting a urine specimen while under direct observation as an invasion of privacy and negligent infliction of emotional distress. A few employees have also succeeded on negligence claims against drug

---

371 § 7.07.

372 Id., comment c.

373 Id.

374 765 S.W.2d 497 (Tex. App. 1989).

375 765 S.W.2d at 502.

376 849 F.2d 41 (1st Cir. 1988) (applying Louisiana law).

testing laboratories for failing to use sufficient care in testing procedures.[377]

The increasing number of state medical marijuana laws have led to claims from employees who have been terminated or denied employment based on lawful use of medical marijuana. Employees alleging wrongful termination based on public policy reflected in medical marijuana statutes have been unsuccessful in several states, as courts have found the law was not intended to regulate employment.[378] Employees alleging violation of disability discrimination statutes[379] and statutes protecting lawful off-duty conduct have been similarly unsuccessful.[380] The fact that federal law continues to prohibit use of medical marijuana has influenced courts considering these cases to rule for employers.[381]

Critics of workplace drug testing raise a number of arguments.[382] First, they point out that many drugs stay in the system for hours or days, so that testing for the presence of a substance does not indicate impairment. Additionally, testing requires disclosure of legal drugs taken, invading the privacy of employees beyond the test for illegal drugs. If employers are not required to use accurate tests and qualified labs, individuals may be falsely accused of drug use. Widespread drug testing is expensive and there is little evidence that it results in either more productive or safer workplaces or reductions in drug use. Add that to the embarrassing nature of the procedure and the fact that any safety and productivity issues can be equally caused by legal drugs, and critics claim that testing is counterproductive and wasteful.

---

377 See, e.g., Stinson v. Physicians Immediate Care, Ltd., 269 Ill.App.3d 659, 646 N.E.2d 930 (1995) (finding lab owed duty of reasonable care to individuals whose specimens it tested for employment purposes). See also Sharpe v. St. Luke's Hosp., 573 Pa. 90, 821 A.2d 1215 (2003) (finding hospital which tested urine samples of employees pursuant to a contract with their employer owed employees a duty of reasonable care and remanding for a determination of whether the duty was breached).

378 See, e.g., Ross v. RagingWire Telecommunications, Inc., 42 Cal. 4th 920, 70 Cal. Rptr. 3d 382, 174 P.3d 200 (2008); Roe v. TeleTech Customer Care Mgmt. (Colorado) LLC, 171 Wash. 2d 736, 257 P.3d 586 (2011).

379 See, e.g., Emerald Steel Fabricators, Inc. v. Bureau of Labor & Indus., 348 Or. 159, 230 P.3d 518 (2010) (finding employer need not accommodate the use of medical marijuana under disability discrimination law and finding federal Controlled Substances Act would preempt any interpretation of state law that required employer accommodation); Garcia v. Tractor Supply Co., 154 F. Supp. 3d 1225 (D.N.M. 2016) (same); Ross v. RagingWire, 42 Cal. 4th at 926–30, 70 Cal. Rptr. at 386–90, 230 P.2d at 204–07 (finding disability discrimination law did not require accommodation of medical marijuana use).

380 See Coats v. Dish Network, LLC, 2015 CO 44, 350 P.3d 849 (Colo. 2015).

381 See, e.g., Garcia, 154 F. Supp. 3d at 530; Emerald Steel Fabricators, 348 Or. at 190, 230 P.3d at 536.

382 For a critical discussion of drug testing in the workplace, see Adam D. Moore, Drug Testing and Privacy in the Workplace, 29 J. Marshall J. Computer & Info. L. 463 (2012).

Nevertheless, drug testing has gained widespread acceptance among employers, the general public, and even some unions.

3.2.6 Regulation of Off-Work Activity

An employee's activities away from work raise the most serious questions about the justification for employer regulation. Employees believe that the employer has little or no legitimate interest in either knowing about or controlling off-duty activities. Employers, on the contrary, contend that off-work activities can adversely affect the workplace and when they do, employer regulation of those actions is warranted.

3.2.6.1 Constitutional Protections

Constitutional privacy protections, as well as the First Amendment, may provide public employees with some protection from employer sanctions based on their non-work activities. In *Barrow v. Greenville Independent School District*,[383] the court ruled that a school district violated a teacher's constitutionally protected privacy right to direct her children's education by refusing to hire her because her children were enrolled in private school. Similarly, in *Peterson v. Minidoka County School District No. 331*,[384] a school violated the Free Exercise Clause of the First Amendment when it reassigned an elementary school principal because he decided to educate his children at home in order to emphasize religious aspects of their education.

The First Amendment protects the rights of employees to engage in political and religious activity on their own time. Even on the employee's own time, however, activity may be sufficiently connected with work to justify employer action against the employee. For example, in *Hudson v. Craven*,[385] the court held that a college did not violate speech and associational rights of a teacher by refusing to renew her contract because of her attendance at a WTO (World Trade Organization) protest rally on her own time with some of her students. Balancing her interests against those of the college, the court concluded that the college's interests in the safety of students and limiting the mixing of the teacher's politics with her professional responsibility in the classroom outweighed the teacher's rights. She remained free to attend the rally without her students and to discuss the issues with students in or out of the classroom.

---

[383] 332 F.3d 844 (5th Cir. 2003).

[384] 118 F.3d 1351 (9th Cir. 1997), amended, 132 F.3d 1258 (9th Cir. 1997).

[385] 403 F.3d 691 (9th Cir. 2005). The court in *Hudson* applied the *Pickering* balancing test in the context of this hybrid speech/association claim. See discussion of the application of the test in associational cases in Section 3.1.2.

The First Amendment speech and associational claims discussed in Sections 3.1.1 and 3.1.2 above also implicate the concern about regulation of off-work activities. In another example of such a case, the court held that the allegation that a public employee was discharged due to his father's political activity stated a claim for impermissible infringement on the constitutional right of intimate association.[386] In *Kipps v. Caillier*,[387] however, the court found that the dismissal of an assistant football coach at a public university violated no constitutional right where the dismissal resulted from the decision of his son, a highly recruited athlete, to enroll at a different college. While the coach's relationship with his son was protected as a right of association, the claim was still barred because of qualified immunity since the university acted to mitigate damage to alumni relations. This is another example of a case where the strong interests of the employer outweigh the employee's clear constitutional interests.

3.2.6.2 Common Law Claims

Some employees have alleged wrongful discharge in violation of public policy to challenge employer terminations based on off-work activity. Such claims can succeed only where the employee can establish that the discharge implicated a public policy recognized by the state. For example, Texas rejected a claim where the employee alleged that she was fired because of her volunteer work with AIDS patients, finding that no public policy protected her right to engage in such activity.[388] As noted in Section 3.1.1, a few courts have recognized that constitutional rights of speech and association might form a public policy sufficient to sustain a wrongful discharge claim, but many courts have rejected such arguments. In another example of such a case, *Graebel v. American Dynatec Corp.*,[389] the court upheld the termination of an employee fired because a local newspaper printed his comments about Asian immigration, which included the use of several racial epithets, refusing to find that the admittedly important free speech right could form the basis of a public policy exception to the doctrine of employment at will.

Despite the Supreme Court's recognition of constitutional privacy claims relating to marital relationships, courts have rejected wrongful discharge claims based on employer interference with romantic and marital relationships. In *Delmonte v. Laidlaw Environmental Services, Inc.*,[390] for example, the court found no

---

386 Sutton v. Village of Valley Stream, 96 F.Supp.2d 189 (E.D.N.Y. 2000).

387 197 F.3d 765, reh'g en banc denied, 205 F.3d 203 (5th Cir. 1999).

388 Brunner v. Al Attar, 786 S.W.2d 784 (Tex. App. 1990).

389 230 Wis. 2d 748, 604 N.W.2d 35 (Ct. App. 1999) (unpublished).

390 46 F.Supp.2d 89 (D. Mass. 1999).

public policy implicated by the employer's termination of an employee who refused to resign his job or have his fiancé resign hers. The fiancé had been laid off by Laidlaw and accepted another job. The resignation demand was made immediately upon the announcement of the engagement, but the reason for the demand was unclear. The court found that constitutional rights did not apply as this was a private employer and nothing in Massachusetts law created a well-defined public policy that would be violated by the employer's action. The court also rejected an invasion of privacy claim, suggesting that Massachusetts privacy law was limited to tangible invasions of bodily privacy. Wrongful discharge cases are further discussed in Section 2.5.1.

Recently employee concerns have surfaced about employer terminations based on the employee's participation in blogging, posting on Facebook, or similar off-duty conduct. A public employee may have a First Amendment claim, but private sector employees are unlikely to find a cause of action in most circumstances. As noted above, most courts do not find wrongful discharge in violation of public policy based on constitutional speech rights. If the substance of Facebook discussions is working conditions, however, such discussions are protected by the NLRA, like those in other venues, as concerted activity.[391] Another alternative is that facebooking and blogging might be considered lawful off-duty activity protected by the broadest of lifestyle statutes discussed in Section 3.2.6.3 below. Finally, if the social media participation relates to another statutorily protected activity, such as religion or political activity in those states that protect it, the employee might have a statutory claim.

Common law invasion of privacy claims may have limited success when related to off-duty conduct because of the likely circumstances of the employer's discovery. If the employer becomes aware of employee's off-duty conduct, it is probable that the employee engaged in the behavior in a context in which there was no reasonable expectation of privacy—in a place where he or she could be easily observed or using a computer that belonged to the employer or was connected to an employer network. A California court held that a supervisor had no reasonable expectation of privacy in his relationship with a subordinate since company policy required notice

---

[391] See Hispanics United of Buffalo, 359 NLRB 368, 368 (2012). Blogging about working conditions may also be protected if it meets the test for concerted activity under the NLRA. See Rafael Gely & Leonard Bierman, Social Isolation and American Workers: Employee Blogging and Legal Reform, 20 Harv. J.L. & Tech. 287, 303–14 (2007).

of, and discouraged, such relationships.[392] If the employer questions employees about off-duty conduct, failure to reply means that there is no invasion while providing information may be deemed consensual unless it was offered in response to a threat of adverse action. Egregious conduct by the employer may lead to recovery, however. An employee prevailed on a privacy claim in Louisiana where the employer terminated the employee after the employer went to the employee's home when he failed to report to work and broke in when he did not answer the door, finding him passed out surrounded by whiskey bottles.[393]

3.2.6.3 Statutory Claims

Many states have statutes, often denominated as "lifestyle statutes," which protect the rights of employees to engage in lawful activities outside of the workplace.[394] The original motivation for many of these laws, and the probable explanation for their widespread adoption, was the desire of the tobacco companies to protect employees' rights to smoke. Smoking raises health care and absenteeism costs for employers, prompting their interest in restricting the practice. Employee privacy concerns, supported by the tobacco companies' interest in continuing to sell their product, led a number of legislatures to adopt protective statutes. Most of the laws protect the right to smoke off duty and some protect the right to drink alcohol as well. A few extend to other lawful activities in general or specify particular lawful activities that are permissible. For example, New York law protects against discrimination based on political activities and recreational activities, defined as any "lawful, leisure-time activity, for which the employee receives no compensation and which is generally engaged in for recreational purposes, including but not limited to sports, games, hobbies, exercise, reading and the viewing of television, movies and similar material."[395] Employees have used the law to challenge discrimination based on political affiliation,[396] but New York courts have declined to find that romantic relationships constitute recreational activity under the statute.[397] Nevada law prohibits discrimination by the employer for

---

[392] Barbee v. Household Auto. Fin. Corp., 113 Cal.App.4th 525, 6 Cal.Rptr.3d 406 (2003).

[393] Love v. Southern Bell Tel. & Tel. Co., 263 So.2d 460 (La. Ct. App. 1972).

[394] See Finkin, supra note 299, at 113–14, 691–716.

[395] New York Lab. Law § 201–d.

[396] See, e.g., Cavanaugh v. Doherty, 243 A.D.2d 92, 675 N.Y.S.2d 143 (1998) (finding employee stated claim for unlawful termination under statute where she alleged that she was fired because she had a political argument with a high level executive after work hours in restaurant).

[397] See, e.g., Hudson v. Goldman Sachs & Co., 283 A.D.2d 246, 725 N.Y.S.2d 318 (2001) (finding romantic relationship with coworker not recreational activity protected by the statute); Bilquin v. Roman Catholic Church, 286 A.D.2d 409, 729 N.Y.S.2d 519

lawful use of any product outside the premises of the employer.[398] A Colorado statute makes it an unfair employment practice for an employer to discharge an employee for engaging in any lawful activity off the premises of the employer during nonworking hours.[399] The protection does not extend to medical marijuana use, however, because although legal in Colorado, it still violates federal law.[400]

Each statute provides exceptions which allow employers to take action to vindicate legitimate employer interests. The Nevada law allows employers to take action based on the lawful use of a product off duty if it adversely affects job performance or the safety of other employees. North Dakota forbids discrimination for participation in lawful activity off the employer's premises during nonworking hours only if the employee's activity is not in direct conflict with the essential business-related interests of the employer.[401] New York does not protect activity that creates a conflict with the employer's interest, or violates a legal or contractual obligation of the employee.

In applying these laws and determining the applicability of the exceptions to statutory protection, the courts must balance the interests of the employees and the employers. In a Colorado case, the court decided that although an employee was fired for the protected activity of writing a letter to the editor of a local newspaper critical of his employer, the employer could lawfully terminate him because the letter violated an implied duty of loyalty to his employer, which fit under the statutory exception permitting employers to restrict employees' lawful off-duty activities pursuant to bona fide occupational requirements.[402] Had the employee been a whistleblower raising an issue relating to public safety, the court suggested, the outcome would have been different, but the employee's criticism was based on the employer's use of cheaper contract workers.

Discrimination laws also may protect employees from interference with off-work activity. Title VII of the Civil Rights Act of 1964 and many similar state statutes prohibit discrimination on the basis of religion or pregnancy, the most common categories under federal law that might provide a basis for challenge to regulation of

(2001) (finding plaintiff's cohabitation with married man not recreational activity protected by the statute).

[398] Nev. Rev. Stat. Ann. § 613.333.

[399] Colo. Rev. Stat. Ann. § 24–34–402.5.

[400] Coats v. Dish Network, LLC, 350 P.3d 849, 852–53 (Colo. 2015).

[401] N.D. Cent. Code § 14–02.4–03.

[402] Marsh v. Delta Air Lines, 952 F.Supp. 1458 (D. Colo. 1997). See also Ruiz v. Hope for Children, Inc., 2013 COA 91, 352 P.3d 983 (upholding termination of employee for romantic relationship with former client of employer that created conflict of interest, another defense under the statute).

off-duty conduct. Some state statutes also protect against discrimination on the basis of political activity and marital status.[403] Laws against marital status discrimination are of limited utility in challenging the most common forms of differential treatment in many states, however. Some states have found that they do not apply to rules relating to working relationships of spouses or to actions taken on the basis of marriage to a particular person.[404] Other states have held that the prohibition does not apply to cohabiting couples, but instead to those married, single, widowed or divorced.[405]

The Polygraph Act also provides protection for employees from employer questioning about off-duty conduct. Even where the polygraph is permissible, the employer cannot ask about political beliefs or affiliations, beliefs or opinions regarding racial matters, religious beliefs or affiliations, sexual behavior, or union activity or beliefs.[406]

3.2.6.4 Contractual Claims

Labor arbitrators, interpreting collective bargaining agreements that require just cause for termination, have frequently addressed the question of whether off-work activity constitutes just cause. Arbitrators in these cases look for a nexus between the conduct and work.[407] In the absence of such a nexus, the discharge will be overturned. Consider this example. An employee is arrested for simple possession of marijuana. She misses no time from work, pleads guilty to a reduced charge, and is given probation. Despite the criminal conviction, many arbitrators would find an insufficient connection with work to warrant termination. Suppose that the employee is a drug counselor, however. In that case, the termination would likely be upheld, for the employer's interest in having drug

---

[403] See, e.g., Mich. Comp. Laws Ann. § 37.2102; Or. Rev. Stat. § 659A.030; Wis. Stat. Ann. § 230.01(2); Cal. Lab. Code. § 1101.

[404] See, e.g., Boaden v. Dep't of Law Enf't, 171 Ill. 2d 230, 238 664 N.E.2d 61, 65 (1996); Muller v. BP Expl. (Alaska) Inc., 923 P.2d 783, 791–92 (Alaska 1996). But see Aase v. Wapiti Meadows Cmty. Techs. & Servs., Inc., 832 N.W.2d 852, 854 (Minn. Ct. App. 2013) (finding that discharging employee because her husband took a position with a competitor was a violation of the marital status prohibition and therefore not a legitimate nondiscriminatory reason for termination). The decision was based on the specific language of the Minnesota statute, which bans discrimination "based on the identity, situation, actions, or beliefs of a spouse". Minn. Stat. Ann. § 363A.03, Subd. 24.

[405] See Waggoner v. Ace Hardware Corp., 134 Wash.2d 748, 953 P.2d 88 (1998) (finding employer did not violate the statute by terminating a cohabiting couple for violation of a no fraternization policy, where they did not marry until four months after termination).

[406] 29 U.S.C. § 2007(b)(1)(C)(i)–(v).

[407] See Elkouri & Elkouri, How Arbitration Works 15–12 to 15–18 (Kenneth May, ed., 6th ed. 2016).

counselors who are not actively or recently involved in drug activity would provide a sufficient nexus to the job to justify termination.

3.2.7 Grooming and Dress Restrictions

Employers frequently seek to control employee appearance in the workplace, primarily for reasons of image and customer preference. At the same time, employees desire to control their own appearance for reasons of self-expression. With some aspects of appearance, such as hair length, beard and weight, it is difficult, if not impossible, to differentiate between work and non-work appearance. For others, such as dress or make-up, employer control easily can be limited to the workplace. Legal challenges to appearance restrictions have primarily relied on the Constitution and discrimination statutes.

3.2.7.1 Constitutional Claims

The Supreme Court addressed a constitutional challenge to a police department's regulation of the hair length and facial hair of male employees in *Kelley v. Johnson*.[408] The employee's challenge was based on the First Amendment right of free expression, as well as his Fourteenth Amendment liberty and equal protection rights. The Court assumed a liberty interest in personal appearance but gave great weight to the employer's interest in regulating employees, recognizing a presumption of legislative validity for the regulation of organization, dress and equipment for law enforcement officers. The test applied by the court was whether there was any rational connection between the regulation and the employer's promotion of public safety. A constitutional infringement exists only if the regulation is so irrational that it is arbitrary. In assessing the regulation, the court found that similarity in appearance of police officers based on either a desire that they be recognizable by the public, or a preference for creating esprit de corps, was a sufficiently rational connection to survive the challenge. The court did not address the gender-specific nature of the requirements, instead focusing on the liberty interest.

Although the *Kelley* Court focused on the particular needs of law enforcement, its holding has not been so limited by lower courts. The interests that justified the restriction in *Kelley* were used to support similar restrictions for a park naturalist in *Lowman v. Davies*.[409] Dress and grooming restrictions for teachers below the college level

---

[408] 425 U.S. 238 (1976).

[409] 704 F.2d 1044 (8th Cir. 1983).

have generally been upheld.[410] A few cases have found grooming restrictions irrational, however, including a beard restriction for college faculty.[411]

The free exercise clause of the First Amendment[412] also has been a source of protection for employees with religious reasons for contesting employer grooming requirements. Where an employer made accommodations for employees with medical reasons for maintaining beards in violation of the employer's rule, the refusal to allow an exception for employees with religious objections to shaving led the court, applying heightened scrutiny, to find a free exercise violation.[413] Had the employer not provided an exemption for secular reasons, however, the court would not have applied heightened scrutiny to the neutral policy, which only incidentally burdened religion.[414]

Employees have challenged restrictions on tattoos as violative of the free speech clause.[415] One court found a hospital employee's "HIV Positive" tattoo to be a protected expression on a matter of public concern, but found the employer's interests outweighed those of the employee.[416] Other courts, however, have found tattoos to be unprotected personal expressions.[417] Courts have also found that police department policies requiring covering of tattoos have a rational basis and do not violate equal protection.[418]

---

[410] See, e.g., Domico v. Rapides Parish Sch. Bd., 675 F.2d 100 (5th Cir. 1982) (finding prohibition on beards for school employees not irrational).

[411] See Hander v. San Jacinto Junior College, 519 F.2d 273 (5th Cir. 1975).

[412] "Congress shall make no law respecting an establishment of religion, or prohibiting the free exercise thereof; or abridging the freedom of speech, or of the press; or the right of the people peaceably to assemble, and to petition the Government for a redress of grievances." U.S. Const. Amend. I.

[413] Fraternal Order of Police, Newark Lodge No. 12 v. City of Newark, 170 F.3d 359 (3d Cir. 1999).

[414] A student succeeded in enjoining application of a grooming policy requiring him to wear his long hair in a bun or a braid in A.A. ex rel. Betenbaugh v. Needville Indep. Sch. Dist., 611 F.3d 248 (5th Cir. 2010). The court found a substantial burden on his free exercise rights and determined that the school's interests in discipline, uniformity, safety and hygiene were not compelling. The court avoided the constitutional claim, deciding the case under the Texas Religious Freedom Restoration Act.

[415] For a thorough discussion of tattoos and employment, see Stephen Allred, Rejecting the Tattooed Applicant, Disciplining the Tattooed Employee: What Are the Risks, 67 Lab. L. J. 475 (2016).

[416] Baldetta v. Harborview Medical Center, 116 F.3d 481 (9th Cir. 1997).

[417] See, e.g., Medici v. City of Chicago, 144 F. Supp. 3d 984, 988 (N.D. Ill. 2015); Riggs v. City of Ft. Worth, 229 F. Supp. 2d 572, 580–81 (N.D. Tex. 2002).

[418] See Inturri v. City of Hartford, 165 F. App'x 66, 69 (2d Cir. 2006); Riggs, 229 F. Supp.2d at 580–81. The *Inturri* court also found no liberty interest at issue. 165 F. App'x at 69.

3.2.7.2 Statutory Causes of Action

Because of the high standard applied to overcome grooming restrictions challenged on a constitutional basis and the fact that such claims are limited to public employees, most challenges to dress and grooming policies have utilized anti-discrimination statutes. The predominant bases for such challenges have been gender and religious discrimination. Occasionally race, ethnic and disability discrimination claims have also been filed. Except in the few states where other statutory claims are available, employers who do not discriminate on one of the above bases have wide latitude to impose grooming and dress requirements on employees.

Many gender discrimination cases have focused on disparate grooming requirements for men and women. In the 1970s males argued that allowing long hair for women and not men constituted sex discrimination. Most claims were rejected, with the essence of the rationale grounded in the different social norms for men and women. Among the justifications were the following, with some courts relying on several of these arguments. Some courts found that men and women were not discriminated against by employers when each was required to comply with prevailing social norms on grooming and dress.[419] Others ruled that only discrimination based on immutable characteristics was prohibited.[420] Still others concluded that restrictions on hair length did not create barriers to employment opportunity.[421] At bottom, the courts decided that the purpose of Title VII was to provide men and women with equal access to jobs and not to govern employer decisions about dress and grooming, giving great deference to employer control over image. Similar arguments were later applied to differential requirements for dress (pants for men and dresses for women)[422] and ornamentation such as jewelry (no earrings for men).[423]

---

[419] See, e.g., Boyce v. Safeway Stores, Inc., 351 F.Supp. 402 (D.D.C. 1972).

[420] See, e.g., Fagan v. Nat'l Cash Register Co., 481 F.2d 1115 (D.C. Cir. 1973) (finding employer requirement that men wear short hair does not constitute discrimination based on immutable characteristic and therefore does not violate Title VII).

[421] See, e.g., Dodge v. Giant Food, Inc., 488 F.2d 1333 (D.C. Cir. 1973) (allowing women to have long hair but not men does not unlawfully deprive men of employment opportunities based on sex).

[422] See Lanigan v. Bartlett & Co. Grain, 466 F.Supp. 1388 (W.D. Mo. 1979) (finding no prima facie case of sex discrimination based on rule barring women from wearing pants, because such policies are decisions about how to operate the business and do not implicate equal employment opportunities).

[423] See Lockhart v. Louisiana Pacific Corp., 102 Or.App. 593, 795 P.2d 602 (1990) (finding employer did not discriminate on the basis of sex by allowing females but not males to wear facial jewelry, as reasonable grooming and dress rules do not violate the law even where differentially applied).

These early cases were decided prior to the Supreme Court's determination that employer decisions based on sex stereotyping violate Title VII.[424] In a highly publicized 2006 case, *Jespersen v. Harrah's Operating Co.*,[425] the Ninth Circuit rejected the argument that a makeup requirement for female bartenders (while makeup for male bartenders was prohibited) violated Title VII because it stereotyped women. The court found that the requirement was a small part of an overall grooming policy which would not affect a woman's ability to do the job. The court also found no evidence of a stereotypical motivation on the part of the employer and distinguished the case from the Supreme Court's decision in *Price Waterhouse v. Hopkins*.[426] In *Price-Waterhouse*, the Court concluded that the plaintiff was placed in a Catch-22, or double bind, penalized for her perceived lack of femininity based on her aggressive behavior, which was prized in men and necessary for success in the competitive consulting business. To be promoted, she had to abandon the behavior that had made her a top producer and therefore a strong candidate for promotion. In addition to distinguishing the case from *Price-Waterhouse* because there was no Catch-22 for the female employees, the *Jesperson* court rejected the argument that the make-up requirement imposed an unequal burden on women. The rationale of earlier decisions on hair and grooming pervaded this more recent opinion as well.[427]

Although unsuccessful in *Jesperson,* the unequal burdens analysis has been applied to invalidate some employer grooming requirements. Where an employer applied medium frame weight maximums to female flight attendants but large frame weight maximums to male flight attendants, the court found unlawful discrimination.[428] A few courts have agreed that requiring women but not men to wear uniforms constitutes sex discrimination,[429] but

---

[424] Price Waterhouse v. Hopkins, 490 U.S. 228 (1989).

[425] 444 F.3d 1104 (9th Cir. 2006).

[426] 444 F.3d at 1112.

[427] For thorough discussion and criticism of the *Jesperson* case, see Symposium, Makeup, Identity Performance & Discrimination, 14 Duke J. Gender L. & Pol'y 1 (2007).

[428] Frank v. United Airlines, 216 F.3d 845 (9th Cir. 2000).

[429] See, e.g., Carroll v. Talman Fed. Sav. & Loan Ass'n, 604 F.2d 1028 (7th Cir. 1979) (relying on both the unequal burden on women and the demeaning implication of the difference); O'Donnell v. Burlington Coat Factory Warehouse, Inc., 656 F.Supp. 263 (S.D. Ohio 1987) (finding a requirement that female sales clerks wear smocks while men were allowed to wear shirts and ties constituted sex discrimination, as it suggested that women were of lower status); Dep't of Civil Rights v. Edward W. Sparrow Hosp. Ass'n, 423 Mich. 548, 377 N.W.2d 755 (1985) (requiring women lab technicians to wear uniforms and special shoes while allowing male technicians to wear white lab coats so the women would look more like nurses and the men like doctors was discriminatory because it was burdensome and demeaning).

courts have been less receptive to the argument that requiring different uniforms based on sex is unlawful.[430] Requiring women to wear contact lenses rather than eyeglasses with no similar requirement for men was also found to be an unequal burden, and thereby unlawful.[431] In both the eyeglasses case and the uniform case, the court found a financial burden on women as a result of the requirement.

Immutability has been a factor in cases alleging that grooming requirements discriminate on racial grounds. In *EEOC v. Catastrophe Management Solutions*, the court found that a refusal to hire because an applicant wore dreadlocks did not constitute race discrimination because hairstyle was not immutable.[432] The court rejected the EEOC's argument that dreadlocks are a part of racial identity, as well as a "natural outgrowth of the immutable trait of black hair texture . . . ."[433] The court distinguished the case from another, *Jenkins v. Blue Cross Mutual Hospital Insurance, Inc.*,[434] indicating that the discrimination in *Jenkins* was based on hair texture, an immutable characteristic.[435]

Legal challenges to grooming and dress requirements on religious grounds have frequently turned on the duty to accommodate religious beliefs and practices. Where the employer's appearance rules conflict with the employee's religious obligations, the court must decide whether there is a reasonable accommodation that does not impose undue hardship on the employer. The religious accommodation requirement in Title VII[436] is limited, however, because of concerns about the establishment of religion.[437] The employer need not offer the accommodation desired by the employee,[438] nor must the employer violate a collective bargaining agreement or incur more than de minimis cost.[439] Applying these requirements, in *Webb v. City of Philadelphia*, the court found that allowing police officers to wear religious garb with their uniforms would cause undue hardship as the police force needed to be

---

430 See Frank v. United Airlines, Inc., 216 F.3d at 855 (requiring different but equally burdensome uniforms for men and women was not unlawful).

431 Laffey v. Northwest Airlines, 366 F.Supp. 763 (D.D.C. 1973).

432 Equal Employment Opportunity Comm'n v. Catastrophe Mgmt. Sols., 837 F.3d 1156, 1167–68 (11th Cir. 2016).

433 Id. at 1161.

434 538 F.2d 164, 168 (7th Cir. 1976).

435 837 F.3d at 1167–68.

436 42 U.S.C. § 2000e(j).

437 See Trans World Airlines v. Hardison, 432 U.S. 63 (1977).

438 Ansonia Bd. of Ed. v. Philbrook, 479 U.S. 60, 68 (1986).

439 Trans World Airlines v. Hardison, 432 U.S. at 81.

identifiable and deemed impartial by residents.[440] In *EEOC v. Abercrombie & Fitch*, however, the court concluded that Abercrombie did not establish by mere testimony that hiring a sales clerk with a hijab would cause undue hardship by negatively impacting the brand.[441]

In the context of appearance requirements, several cases have found that requiring an employer to violate a state statute to accommodate an employee is an undue hardship. In *Bhatia v. Chevron U.S.A., Inc.*[442] the court found that the employer did not have to risk violation of state safety standards, which required the use of respirators in jobs requiring exposure to toxic fumes, in order to accommodate an employee whose religious beliefs prohibited shaving. Facial hair often prevents a respirator from sealing properly and thus renders it ineffective at protecting the employee. The court found that other accommodations would unduly burden either coworkers, who would have to accept the plaintiff's assignments to jobs with such exposure risks, or the employer, by requiring it to revise its method of job assignments. Similarly, in *United States v. Board of Education for the School District of Philadelphia*,[443] the court found that the employer need not violate the state statute that barred teachers from wearing religious garb in the classroom to accommodate a Muslim teacher whose religious convictions required her to wear a head scarf.

A few states have enacted specific statutory requirements relating to grooming and dress. The District of Columbia prohibits appearance discrimination, which includes grooming, dress, hair style, and beards.[444] The D.C. appearance law has been read broadly to protect an employee allegedly terminated for being a

---

[440] 562 F.3d 256, 261–62 (3d Cir. 2009). See also Cloutier v. Costco Wholesale Corp., 390 F.3d 126, 136 (1st Cir. 2004) (same result regarding facial piercings as employer wanted professional image). Cf. E.E.O.C. v. Red Robin Gourmet Burgers, Inc., No. C04–1291JLR, 2005 WL 2090677 (W.D. Wash. Aug. 29, 2005) (finding employer did not establish that allowing employee to display uncovered tattoo would cause undue hardship).

[441] 798 F. Supp.2d 1272, 1287 (N.D.Okla. 2011). The Tenth Circuit reversed the district court finding that there was no proof that the employer knew the applicant wore the hijab for religious reasons and therefore there was no proof of religious discrimination. 731 F.3d 1106 (2013). The Supreme Court then reversed the Tenth Circuit finding that the employer's motive, rather than its knowledge was determinative of whether there was a violation, remanding the case. 135 S.Ct. 2028 (2015).

[442] 734 F.2d 1382 (9th Cir. 1984).

[443] 911 F.2d 882 (3d Cir. 1990).

[444] D.C. Code §§ 2–1401.01 to 1402.13.

transsexual.[445] California has a law which prohibits employers from denying employees the right to wear pants because of their gender.[446]

The NLRA protects the right of employees to wear clothing or insignia expressing the support of unions.[447] Where special circumstances exist, however, the employer can restrict the right. For example, in *George J. London Memorial Hospital,*[448] the NLRB found that a psychiatric hospital's rule barring wearing of union insignia in patient care areas was presumptively valid because of the potential adverse effect on patients in a locked area where the most seriously ill patients were treated. However, because the rule was not limited to patient care areas, it was overly broad and violated the Act. Where the union insignia pose a safety concern, the employer may ban them also.[449]

§ 3.3 Negligent Hiring, Supervision and Retention

As noted above, one reason for employer investigation, monitoring, and testing is to avoid liability for employee actions. In recent years, the development of causes of action for negligent hiring and supervision has prompted greater employer attention to these practices. These common law tort claims are doctrines of primary liability, subjecting employers to punitive damages where appropriate, and precluding reliance on intervening unlawful conduct by employees outside the scope of employment to avoid liability. The most egregious cases involve employers who fail to conduct criminal background checks which would have revealed previous conduct by an employee that puts third parties at risk. The analysis in these cases is a traditional negligence analysis and should be familiar from tort law.

To make a claim for negligent hiring a plaintiff must show that the employer had a duty to investigate the employee prior to hiring which it negligently performed, thereby causing the plaintiff's injury. *Malorney v. B & L Freight*[450] is a typical case, at least on the facts. In *Malorney*, the employer hired an over-the-road truck driver who falsely denied any prior criminal convictions, a denial that the

---

445 Underwood v. Archer Mgmt. Serv., 857 F.Supp. 96 (D.D.C. 1994).

446 Cal. Gov. Code § 12947.5.

447 See Republic Aviation Corp. v. NLRB, 324 U.S. 793 (1945) (finding statutory right to wear union buttons at work); De Vilbiss Co., 102 N.L.R.B. 1317 (1953) (finding employer violated the statute by requiring employees to remove union buttons and T-shirts).

448 238 N.L.R.B. 704 (1978).

449 See, e.g., Albis Plastics, 335 NLRB 923 (2001) (finding employer prohibition of union stickers on safety helmets was a reasonable safety measure to insure visibility).

450 146 Ill.App.3d 265, 496 N.E.2d 1086 (1986).

employer failed to verify, although it verified his denial of prior vehicular convictions. Subsequently, the driver picked up a minor female hitchhiker, raping and beating her in his truck's sleeping compartment. Contrary to his denial, he had been convicted of violent sex-related crimes and arrested for sodomizing teenage hitchhikers while driving a truck for a previous employer. The court upheld the lower court's denial of summary judgment for the employer, holding that the employer had a duty to insure that the driver was fit and competent. The court indicated that the particular injury need not be foreseeable, noting that the employer gave the driver a vehicle with a sleeping compartment and knew or should have known that truckers frequently pick up hitchhikers, despite employer rules prohibiting the practice.

In a similar case out of Utah, the court found no liability for negligent hiring.[451] Like the plaintiff in *Malorney*, the plaintiff in *C.C. v. Roadrunner Trucking* was a minor hitchhiker, picked up and raped by the truck driver.[452] Unlike the driver in *Malorney*, however, the driver in the Utah case had no criminal convictions that would have been revealed by a further investigation.[453] The Utah court found that the employer owed no duty to the hitchhiker because it was not foreseeable that the driver posed a risk of sexually assaulting hitchhikers.[454] Even if such a duty existed, however, the court found that there was no breach of the duty and no proximate causation because there was no evidence that a more extensive background investigation would have revealed anything that would have made the plaintiff's injury foreseeable.[455] In contrast to the Illinois court in *Malorney*, the court went so far as to suggest that criminal background checks were expensive and difficult in Utah and not required for truck driving positions.[456]

The Virginia Supreme Court has utilized a narrower interpretation of foreseeability than the Illinois court in negligent hiring cases. In *Interim Personnel of Central Virginia v. Messer*,[457] the plaintiff was injured by an intoxicated driver. The driver, a temporary employee from the staffing agency, had stolen a pick-up truck from the university alumni association to which he was assigned. Although the job involved driving, neither the staffing agency nor the alumni association verified the employee's claim that

---

451 C.C. v. Roadrunner Trucking Inc., 823 F. Supp. 913 (D. Utah 1993).

452 Id. at 913.

453 Id. at 923.

454 Id.

455 Id. at 923–24.

456 Id. at 923–34.

457 263 Va. 435, 559 S.E.2d 704 (2002).

he was a licensed driver. Had either done so, they would have learned that the employee had no license. He had twice been convicted of DUI, failed to pay the fines or attend counseling, and been declared a habitual offender, Nevertheless, the court denied the plaintiff's negligent hiring claim. The court found that knowledge of these facts would not have made foreseeable the employee's actions of stealing the truck and driving it while intoxicated during non-business hours away from his workplace. As in *Malorney* the employee had engaged in similar behavior in the past and the employer probably would have learned about the previous behavior had it investigated whether he was a licensed driver. However, the court emphasized that none of the prior behavior was on the job. The court also observed that the employee had been a model employee prior to this incident. Accordingly, the court did not find it foreseeable that the employee would steal the employer's truck and drive it while intoxicated, injuring another driver.

The key to the existence of a duty to investigate in these cases is foreseeability. If the employer had conducted a reasonable investigation into the employee's background, would the investigation have revealed facts that made it foreseeable that the employee would engage in the behavior that injured the plaintiff?

Review of the cases finding employer liability reveals that many involve situations where the employee has access to either vulnerable populations or individuals in vulnerable situations, and the employer failed to do a careful background check of the employees. Employees who work with children or those, like apartment managers or maintenance personnel, who have access to people's homes, have often been the subject of negligent hiring claims.[458] Employers who employ such workers would be wise to engage in reasonable background investigations to avoid liability. In some circumstances, courts have even found negligent hiring of independent contractors as well as employees, utilizing similar standards.[459]

---

[458] See, e.g., J. v. Victory Tabernacle Baptist Church, 236 Va. 206, 372 S.E.2d 391 (1988) (finding plaintiff stated a claim for negligent hiring of church employee previously convicted of sexual assault of young girl, where employee was entrusted with duties that brought him into contact with children, one of whom he sexually assaulted); Pittard v. Four Seasons Motor Inn, 101 N.M. 723, 688 P.2d 333 (1984) (denying summary judgment in claim against hotel that hired employee as a steward after earlier firing him from a dishwashing job for drinking, where employee had access to alcohol, contact with customers, and limited supervision, sexually assaulting the plaintiff's son while on duty); Ponticas v. K.M.S. Invs., 331 N.W.2d 907 (Minn. 1983) (finding owner of apartment complex liable for negligent hiring of a caretaker with a criminal background after minimal investigation, where caretaker raped the plaintiff in her apartment).

[459] See, e.g., Jones v. C.H. Robinson Worldwide, Inc., 558 F.Supp.2d 630 (W.D. Va. 2008) (applying Virginia law and finding that injured truck driver had cause of action against motor carrier broker for negligent hiring of independent contractor whose

The causes of action for negligent supervision and retention are similar to those for negligent hiring. In negligent supervision and retention cases, the employer has notice of an employee's propensity to cause harm yet fails to take action needed to avoid it. The test is similar to that applied in negligent hiring cases: Did the employer have information that would have led a reasonable employer to take action against an employee, such as termination, discipline or closer supervision, which would have avoided a foreseeable injury to the plaintiff?

---

truck collided with his truck, causing injuries); Puckrein v. ATI Transport, Inc., 186 N.J. 563, 897 A.2d 1034 (2006) (reversing summary judgment for company that hired independent contractor to haul waste, holding that principal could be liable for negligent hiring of contractor driving truck with faulty brakes which ran a traffic light and hit a car, killing and injuring its occupants).

Chapter 4

EMPLOYEE OBLIGATIONS TO EMPLOYERS

The employment relationship imposes obligations on both employers and employees. As evidenced by the coverage of this book, the vast majority of disputes in the context of the employment relationship involve employees' claims against employers. The employment relationship, however, also creates a number of obligations on employees. As discussed in Chapter 2, supra, an employee who enters a contract for a specific duration can sue the employer if the contract is terminated prematurely. However, the employee can also be sued if the employee decides to leave prior to that time.[1] In addition to contractually agreed obligations, employees might be subject to other duties towards their employers which are created by law, and thus implied in all employment contracts.

Whether implied or voluntary, the obligations discussed in this chapter are intended to protect employer interests. Employers, for example, might seek to restrict disclosure of business information that has been provided to employees in the course of employment, which could be of benefit to competitors. Employers might also want to limit the ability of a departing employee to solicit their customers or to entice other employees to leave the organization. Sometimes, employers might want to "recover" the investments they have made in training employees, by limiting the ability of employees to change jobs until the employer has had the opportunity to benefit from that training.

Protecting the interests of employers raises two complications, however. First, there are countervailing interests. For instance, one way in which employers can protect their investment in the training of employees is by limiting the ability of employees to obtain employment after their termination by means of a covenant not to compete.[2] By making it more difficult for employees to work following their current jobs, employers increase the costs to the employee of moving and thus, reduce the chance of departure. The enforcement of non-competition agreements, however, results in costs to employees, and potentially the public at large. Such agreements, by definition, limit the ability of employees to earn a living and thus

---

[1] See supra Section 2.4.1.2. Like employment contracts for a definite term, such suits are uncommon.

[2] See infra Section 4.4.

appear to be contrary to the fundamental principle that individuals should be free to sell their labor to whomever they please. Covenants not to compete, colloquially known as non-competes, also limit the currency of the information employees might have learned in their jobs, by delaying the time at which employees can begin to use that information in future jobs. In addition, non-competes deprive society of the benefit of the employee's labor and of the increased competition and potential innovation that results from the unconstrained movement of labor.

Second, employers can abuse the various legal devices available for protecting their interests, inflicting significant costs on employees. Consider again the case of agreements not to compete. Employers clearly have an interest in protecting their investments in employee training. There is, however, no legitimate interest in limiting the ability of employees to use skills and training that they might have gained throughout their careers. Blanket enforcement of non-compete agreements, however, will have the effect of allowing employers to deprive employees of the value of their own human capital. Non-competes, enforceable or not, can also discourage employees from leaving to start new businesses, which may deprive society of the innovation derived from business creation.

Courts and legislatures have attempted to balance these competing interests by creating rules that protect not only the business interests of employers, but also the countervailing interests of employees and the public.[3] These various rules and the competing interests they seek to balance are discussed in this chapter.

§ 4.1 Implied Duty of Loyalty

Under the common law of agency, agents have a duty of loyalty towards their principals.[4] This duty requires the agent "to refrain

---

[3] There is a voluminous literature regarding the theoretical underpinnings of the rules pertaining to employees' obligations. See, e.g., Norman D. Bishara & Michelle Westermann-Behaylo, The Law and Ethics of Restrictions on an Employee's Post-Employment Mobility, 49 Am. Bus. L.J. 1 (2012); Harlan M. Blake, Employee Agreements Not to Compete, 73 Harv. L. Rev. 625 (1960); Catherine Fisk, Removing the 'Fuel of Interest' from the 'Fire of Genius': Law and the Employee-Inventor, 1830–1930, 65 U. Chi. L. Rev. 1127 (1998); Ronald Gilson, The Legal Infrastructure of High Technology Industrial Districts: Silicon Valley, Route 128, and Covenants Not to Compete, 74 N.Y.U.L. Rev. 575 (1999); Alan Hyde, Working in Silicon Valley: Economic and Legal Analysis of a High-Velocity Labor Market (2003); Gillian Lester, Restrictive Covenants, Employee Training, and the Limits of Transaction-Cost Analysis, 76 Ind. L.J. 49 (2001); Orly Lobel, Talent Wants to Be Free (Yale University Press 2013); Robert P. Merges, The Law and Economics of Employee Inventions, 13 Harv. J.L. & Tech. 1 (1999); Paul Rubin & Peter Shed, Human Capital and Covenants Not to Compete, 10 J. Leg. Studies 93 (1981).

[4] According to the Restatement (Third) of Agency, "An agent has a fiduciary duty to act loyally for the benefit of the principal in all matters connected with the agency relationship." Restatement (Third) of Agency § 8.01.

from competing with the principal and from taking action on behalf of or otherwise assisting the principal's competitors."[5] This duty has been incorporated into the employment relationship by many courts.[6] Not all courts have been willing to impose a duty of loyalty on employees who do not have a fiduciary relationship with the employer, however.[7] A fiduciary relationship may not exist in cases where an at-will employee is only entrusted to perform a specific job competently. Without greater agency, some courts conclude that such employees owe no duty of loyalty.

The duty of loyalty overlaps with trade secret law, discussed in Section 4.2, where the employee is accused of misappropriation of trade secrets.[8] Other duty of loyalty cases tend to involve two types of scenarios. First, prior to departure, an employee might contact customers in an attempt to solicit their business, or contact co-workers to offer them future job opportunities. Second, employees planning to leave their jobs might attempt to provide assistance to competing firms.

4.1.1 Soliciting Customers or Co-Workers

Perhaps the most common application of the duty of loyalty involves situations where employees who anticipate leaving their present jobs and either starting or joining a competing business discuss their plans with customers or co-workers. *Jet Courier Service, Inc. v. Mulei,*[9] is illustrative. Following disagreements with the plaintiff over various work-related issues, the defendant (plaintiff's company regional manager) decided to start his own business, directly competing with the plaintiff. During the next several months and before departing his job with the plaintiff, the defendant talked to several of plaintiff's customers, making a variety of statements regarding the type of service he would be able to provide them in his new company.[10] The defendant also discussed with various co-workers the possibility of joining him in his new company. The plaintiff brought action claiming that the defendant's pre-

5 Restatement (Third) of Agency, § 8.04.

6 Restatement of Employment Law, § 8.01.

7 See, e.g. Dalton v. Camp, 353 N.C. 647, 548 S.E.2d 704 (2001) (finding no cause of action for breach of the duty of loyalty in the absence of a fiduciary relationship which did not exist for manager who was employee at will); Physician Specialists in Anesthesia v. Wildmon, 238 Ga. App. 730, 521 S.E.2d 358 (1999) (same).

8 See, e.g., Lamorte Burns & Co. v. Walters, 770 A.2d 1158, 1169–70 (N.J. 2001) (finding employees violated the duty of loyalty by collecting protected customer information from their employer during their employment to use in starting a competing business, even though they did not actually solicit those customers until after resignation).

9 771 P.2d 486 (Colo. 1989).

10 For example, the defendant told one customer that he "would try to give them the same service" they were receiving from the plaintiff. Id. at 490.

termination meetings with its customers and employees to discuss future operations constituted violations of the defendant's duty of loyalty.

The court began by discussing the competing interests it had to balance in the case. On one hand, noted the court, "[u]nderlying the duty of loyalty arising out of the employment relationship is the policy consideration that commercial competition must be conducted through honesty and fair dealing."[11] On the other hand the court recognized that "[a] limiting consideration in delineating the scope of an agent's duty not to compete is society's interest in fostering free and vigorous economic competition."[12]

In attempting to reconcile these competing considerations, the court distinguished between active competition and permissible preparations[13] with regard to communications between the departing employee and both customers and coworkers. Regarding communications with customers, the court noted that an employee will not violate the duty of loyalty by advising current customers of the impending departure. However, "solicitation" of customers before departure would violate the duty of loyalty.[14]

With regard to communications with co-workers, the court in *Jet Courier*, considered three factors in determining whether the employee's actions amounted to impermissible solicitation: the nature of the employment relationship; the actual or potential impact of the employee's action on the employer's operations; and the extent of any benefits promised or inducements made to co-workers to obtain their services.[15] The court also noted that as in the case of customer solicitation, the employee's solicitation of co-workers did not need to be successful to violate the duty of loyalty.[16] Finally, the court made clear that the fact that a defendant continues otherwise to perform her obligations does not preclude a finding that there was a violation of the duty of loyalty.[17]

---

[11] Id. at 492.

[12] Id. at 493.

[13] This distinction is found in § 8.04 of the Restatement (Third) of Agency. According to the Restatement "an agent may take action, not otherwise wrongful, to prepare for competition following termination of the agency relationship."

[14] The line between advising customers and solicitation has been hard to draw in practice. For example, in Nilan's Alley, Inc. v. Ginsburg, 208 Ga.App. 145, 430 S.E.2d 368 (1993), the court classified as preparations conversations between the defendant and his customers, even where the defendant inquired whether the customers would consider continuing to place orders through him if he was to change jobs.

[15] 771 P.2d at 497.

[16] Id.

[17] Id. at 498.

Some employees have argued that solicitation of an at-will co-worker should not be the basis for a breach of the duty of loyalty claim. That is, it should not be a violation of the duty of loyalty for a departing employee to solicit at-will co-workers, who otherwise have the right to leave their jobs at any time and for any reason.[18] Some courts have held that a violation of the duty of loyalty can be established even when the co-worker solicited was an at-will employee.[19] Other courts have refused to extend the duty to solicitation of employees terminable at will.[20]

4.1.2 Assisting a Competitor

The duty of loyalty may not only prohibit customer and co-worker solicitation, but can also be violated by taking other actions contrary to the employer's interests. For example, in *Scanwell Freight Express STL, Inc. v. Chan*,[21] the court found that the defendant violated her duty of loyalty by failing to take the necessary actions to secure the renewal of the lease of the premises occupied by the plaintiff, where the employee's actions were intended to facilitate the acquisition of such premises by a competitor. Similarly, in *Platinum Mgmt., Inc. v. Dahms*,[22] the court found a violation of the duty of loyalty where the defendant deliberately delayed making appointments with various clients until he began his new job.

4.1.3 Remedies

Employees found to have violated their duty of loyalty may have to repay any compensation received during the period when they engaged in activities constituting a breach. For example, the court found that the defendant in *Jet Courier Services* was not entitled to receive any compensation for any period during which he was engaged in acts amounting to a breach of his duty of loyalty.[23] Some courts, however, do not require forfeit of full compensation if the breach is minor and the employee still provides substantial services

---

[18] See, e.g., Headquarters Buick-Nissan, Inc. v. Michael Oldsmobile, 539 N.Y.S.2d 355, 357, 149 A.D.2d 302, 304 (1989); Spring Steel Inc. v. Molloy, 400 Pa. 354, 364, 162 A.2d 370, 375 (1960).

[19] See, e.g., Augat, Inc. v. Aegis, Inc., 409 Mass. 165, 174, 565 N.E.2d 415, 421 (1991); Barden Cream & Milk Co. v. Mooney, 305 Mass. 545, 546, 26 N.E.2d 324 (1940).

[20] See, e.g., Headquarters Buick-Nissan, Inc., 539 N.Y.S.2d at 356–57, 149 A.D.2d at 303–04.

[21] 162 S.W.3d 477 (Mo. 2005).

[22] 285 N.J. Super. 274, 666 A.2d 1028 (1995).

[23] Jet Courier Services, 771 P.2d at 500. See also Design Strategies v. Davis, 384 F.Supp.2d 649 (S.D.N.Y. 2005), where the court found that the defendants were required to pay damages equal to the salary they received during the period in which they engaged in activities violating their duty of loyalty.

to the employer.[24] Employers might also be able to recover other damages caused by the departing employee, to the extent that the employer can establish that the losses were attributable to the employee's breach of the duty of loyalty.[25]

§ 4.2 Trade Secrets

The duty of loyalty described above protects the interests of the employer against detrimental employee actions arising during the course of employment. Employers might also desire to protect their interests following the departure of particular employees. As discussed in Section 4.4 infra, employers can contractually protect their post-termination interests via non-compete agreements. In addition, employers enjoy the protection of the common law duty not to disclose trade secrets, which has been codified in most states and in 2016 in federal law as well.[26] This duty does not require an agreement between the employer and the employee and is enforced by means of the tort of trade secret misappropriation.

4.2.1 Definition of Trade Secrets

Most states have adopted the Uniform Trade Secrets Act (UTSA).[27] Consistent with the definition developed under common law, the UTSA defines trade secrets as: "information, including a formula, pattern, compilation, program, device, method, technique, or process, that: (1) Derives independent economic value . . . from not being generally known to the public . . . and (2) Is the subject of efforts that are reasonable under the circumstances to maintain its secrecy."[28] This rather broad definition covers, for example, information related to the ingredients used in manufacturing a particular product (e.g., a secret formula). The definition goes much farther than the secret formula case, however, and has been applied in cases involving disputes over production and process manuals,[29] confidential business information contained in the employer's product and vendor files,[30] pricing information and marketing

---

24 See Cameco, Inc. v. Gedicke, 157 N.J. 504, 520–21, 724 A.2d 783, 791–92 (1999).

25 See, e.g., Keystone Fruit Marketing, Inc. v. Brownfield, No. CV 05 5087 RHW, 2008 WL 1971412 (E.D. Wash. May 5, 2008) (awarding one year of lost profits), aff'd, 352 Fed. App'x 169 (9th Cir 2009).

26 Defend Trade Secrets Act, Pub. L. 114–153 (2016). See Section 4.2.3 infra for further discussion of this federal statute, which supplements state law protection.

27 Uniform Trade Secrets Act (amended 1985), available at http://www.uniformlaws.org/Act.aspx?title=Trade+Secrets+Act.

28 Id. § 1(4).

29 See, e.g., 3M v. Pribyl, 259 F.3d 587 (7th Cir. 2001).

30 See, e.g., Sigma Chemical Co. v. Harris, 794 F.2d 371 (8th Cir. 1986).

strategies,[31] and customer lists.[32] The protection afforded by trade secret law in these cases is significant, since none of that information can be protected under patent or copyright law.

Employers have attempted to expand the reach of trade secrets to include information that, while not completely unknown to the general public, has been costly to collect and thus valuable to the employer. Most of the litigation regarding trade secrets appears to have centered on the issue of whether the information is generally known to the public and thus incapable of qualifying as a trade secret. Consider, for example, disputes over information contained in customer lists. On one hand, one can easily identify the interests employers seek to protect when guarding customer lists. Compiling a customer list, and the information likely to be included therein (e.g., the customer's preferences, prior sales records) could have taken the employer years. Departing employees could easily transfer the customer data to their new employer, reducing or destroying the value of such information. Thus, some kind of protection appears to be proper. On the other hand, some of that information might be public knowledge, in the sense that anyone could have collected the names of the customers from various public sources. Protecting employers by limiting the ability of employees to use information that is publicly available is unwarranted.

Ikon Office Solutions, Inc. v. American Office Products, Inc.[33] illustrates how courts decide these types of cases. The plaintiff, a supplier of copy machines, brought action against several ex-employees, arguing that they had misappropriated the defendant's customer list. The plaintiff argued that the identity of the customers, the names of the contact persons at these companies, and information regarding each account (such as the type of copy machine used, the volume of copies, the customer's needs and preferences) were trade secrets. The court acknowledged that where the employer has expended considerable time and money to pinpoint a narrow segment of the population as a potential market, a customer list could qualify as a trade secret.[34] The court, however, rejected plaintiff's contention that the identity of the customers, the contact person for each customer, and the information about each customer were trade secrets. Regarding the names of customers, the court noted that "a person with a rudimentary knowledge of the industry, the Yellow pages and business data publicly available from sources such as the

---

[31] See, e.g., LeJeune v. Coin Acceptors, Inc. 381 Md. 288, 849 A.2d 451 (2004).

[32] See, e.g., Morlife, Inc. v. Perry, 56 Cal.App.4th 1514, 66 Cal.Rptr.2d 731 (1997).

[33] 178 F.Supp.2d 1154 (D. Or. 2001), aff'd, 61 Fed. App'x. 378 (9th Cir. 2003) (unpublished).

[34] Id. at 1167.

Chamber of Commerce, can quickly identify the principal consumers of copying equipment in the region."[35] Regarding the names of the contact persons for each customer, the court noted that competitors could obtain the name of the contact person "simply by calling the company and inquiring."[36] Similarly, the court noted that the information regarding customers' accounts could easily be obtained by way of a few inquiries, and thus was generally available to the public.

Some other courts have been more protective of the employers' interests in customer lists, particularly where the list includes information that took "substantial time effort, and expense" to compile.[37] For example, in *Courtesy Temporary Service v. Camacho*, the court found that a customer list qualified as a trade secret where the employer had made significant investments in advertising, entertainment expenses, promotional gifts, and personnel in creating the list,[38] The court noted in particular that the information about the clients' interests in using the employer's services was not otherwise publicly available.[39] Finally, the court also noted that in addition to names, the list contained information about customer needs, pay rates, billing rates, important contacts, and profit margins.[40]

The first prong of the trade secret definition also requires the employer to establish that the trade secret has independent economic value. Thus, for example, where the information employers try to protect is found to be outdated, courts are likely to find that the independent economic value is lacking.[41]

The second prong of the UTSA's trade secret definition requires a showing that the employer engaged in reasonable efforts to maintain the information's secrecy. In determining the reasonableness of employer efforts to keep the information secret courts have considered several factors, including: whether the parties have entered a written agreement requiring confidentiality;[42]

---

[35] Id. at 1168.

[36] Id.

[37] Courtesy Temp. Serv., Inc. v. Camacho, 222 Cal. App. 3d 1278, 1287, 272 Cal. Rptr. 352, 357 (1990).

[38] Id. at 1282, 1291, 272 Cal. Rptr. at 354, 360.

[39] Id. at 1282, 272 Cal. Rptr. at 354.

[40] Id.

[41] See, e.g., Applied Indus. Materials Corp. v. Brantjes, 891 F.Supp. 432 (N.D. Ill. 1994).

[42] See, e.g., Zoecon Industries v. American Stockman Tag Co., 713 F.2d 1174 (5th Cir. 1983).

whether knowledge was confined to a limited group of employees;[43] and the extent of other measures to guard access to the information.[44] For example, in *Hexacomb Corp. v. GTW Enterprises*,[45] a case involving the manufacturer of paper making machines, the court found that reasonable efforts were established because the former employee had entered a confidentiality agreement with the predecessor manufacturer.[46] Employers also can satisfy this prong by showing that efforts were taken to limit the disclosure of information to those employees in need of the information.[47] However, where a customer list was posted on a bulletin board where all employees and visitors could see it, one court found the employer had failed to establish that reasonable efforts were undertaken to keep the information secret.[48]

4.2.2 Misappropriation of Trade Secrets

Once the existence of a trade secret is established, the employer also has to show that the trade secret was misappropriated.[49] The UTSA defines misappropriation as:

> (1) Acquisition of a trade secret of another by a person who knows or has reason to know that the trade secret was acquired by improper means; or
>
> (2) Disclosure or use of a trade secret of another without express or implied consent by a person who:
>
> (A) Used improper means to acquire knowledge of the trade secret; or
>
> (B) At the time of disclosure or use, knew or had reason to know that his or her knowledge of the trade secret was:
>
> (i) Derived from or through a person who had utilized improper means to acquire it;
>
> (ii) Acquired under circumstances giving rise to a duty to maintain its secrecy or limit its use; or

---

43 See, e.g., Jet Spray Cooler, Inc. v. Crampton, 361 Mass. 835, 282 N.E.2d 921 (1972).

44 See, e.g., Hexacomb Corp. v. GTW Enterprises, 875 F. Supp. 457, 467 (N.D. Ill. 1993) (employer wrote memo regarding need for confidentiality and reminded employees in their exit interview).

45 Id.

46 Id. at 464.

47 See, e.g., Enterprise Leasing Co. of Phoenix v. Ehmke, 197 Ariz. 144, 151, 3 P.3d 1064, 1071 (App. Div. 1 1999).

48 Dicks v. Jensen, 172 Vt. 43, 50, 768 A.2d 1279, 1285 (2001).

49 Uniform Trade Secrets Act § 1(2) (amended 1985).

(iii) Derived from or through a person who owed a duty to the person seeking relief to maintain its secrecy or limit its use; or

(C) Before a material change of his or her position knew or had reason to know that it was a trade secret and that knowledge of it had been acquired by accident or by mistake.[50]

Establishing misappropriation frequently requires use of circumstantial evidence. For example, in *Sunbelt Rentals, Inc. v. Head & Engquist Equipment*,[51] where the ex-employee's new business went from having no customers to acquiring several customers of the former employer and enjoying substantial profits in the first year of operation, the court found that there had been misappropriation even in the absence of any direct evidence that the employee had ever taken or copied the customer list. Similarly, although ex-employees are permitted to announce their new employment affiliation to customers of the prior employer, misappropriation will be found if the ex-employee engages in solicitation.[52]

In addition to protecting against "actual" misappropriation, the UTSA provides for the issuance of injunctions in cases of "threatened" misappropriation.[53] Threatened misappropriation has been found in cases where the employees' actions before departure raise the likelihood of disclosure. For example, in *Ackerman v. Kimball International*,[54] the court found that the former employer was entitled to a preliminary injunction preventing a former employee's employment with competitors and threatened disclosure, use or misappropriation of trade secrets in "in light of [the employee's] pre-departure harvesting of [the employer's] proprietary information. . . ."[55]

Employers have sought to expand the reach of the tort of trade secrets misappropriation through the "inevitable disclosure" doctrine. Under the inevitable disclosure doctrine a court will issue an injunction preventing the employee from working for a competitor and from disclosing certain information where the employer can demonstrate a real and present danger of disclosure.[56] In the

---

50 Id.

51 174 N.C.App. 49, 57–58, 620 S.E.2d 222, 229 (2005).

52 See, e.g., Mai Systems Corp. v. Peak Computer, Inc., 991 F.2d 511, 521 (9th Cir. 1993)..

53 Uniform Trade Secrets Act § 2(a) (amended 1985).

54 652 N.E.2d 507 (Ind. 1995).

55 Id. at 501–11.

56 See, e.g., Merck & Co., Inc. v. Lyon, 941 F.Supp. 1443 (M.D. N.C. 1996).

principal case of *PepsiCo., Inc. v. Redmond*,[57] PepsiCo sought to enjoin its former employee from working for its competitor, the Quaker Oats Company, in a position comparable to the one he held at PepsiCo. During his employment, the employee had acquired a number of trade secrets such as knowledge of the company's plans for specific markets. PepsiCo argued that the employee would "inevitably disclose" the trade secrets acquired at PepsiCo to Quaker because his new position gave him substantial input on Quaker's marketing and other business practices. The court agreed with PepsiCo, finding the injunction, which limited employment for less than six months, was appropriate. According to the court, "unless [the employee] possessed an uncanny ability to compartmentalize information, he would necessarily be making decisions" that would result in the disclosure of trade secrets.[58]

While several courts have adopted some form of the inevitable disclosure doctrine,[59] other courts have refused to apply it.[60] Courts taking this latter position note that adopting the doctrine will permit employers to enjoin former employees based only upon an inference that the departing employee will use knowledge of trade secrets in the new job. This arguably will turn an injunction against the use of trade secrets, into "an injunction restricting employment."[61] Effectively, the doctrine allows the employer to obtain a covenant not to compete without negotiation or consideration.[62] Critics argue that a large and well-funded employer may be able to discourage competition, to the detriment of society at large, using misappropriation actions or threats of misappropriation actions. These actions will be costly to defend and may prevent the success of new, and perhaps more effective, businesses.

4.2.3 Defend Trade Secrets Act of 2016

In 2016 Congress created a federal cause of action for trade secret misappropriation if the product or service involved is in

---

[57] 54 F.3d 1262 (7th Cir. 1995).

[58] Id. at 1269.

[59] See, e.g., Bimbo v. Botticella, 613 F.3d 102 (3d Cir. 2010) (enjoining employment of one of the few individuals who knew the secret formula for Thomas english muffins by a competitor); RKI, Inc. v. Grimes, 177 F.Supp.2d 859 (N.D. Ill. 2001); H & R Block Eastern Tax Services, Inc. v. Enchura 122 F.Supp.2d 1067 (W.D. Mo. 2000) (recognizing the doctrine but finding that the facts did not support its application in the particular case).

[60] See, e.g., Del Monte Fresh Produce Co. v. Dole Food Co., Inc., 148 F.Supp.2d 1326 (S.D. Fla. 2001); Danjaq LLC v. Sony Corp., 1999 WL 317629 at n. 1 (C.D. Cal.); EarthWeb v. Schlack, 71 F.Supp.2d 299 (S.D.N.Y. 1999) (criticizing the doctrine and refusing to apply it but not rejecting altogether).

[61] Whyte v. Schlage Lock Co., 101 Cal.App.4th 1443, 1463, 125 Cal.Rptr.2d 277, 292 (2002).

[62] Id. at 1463, 125 Cal. Rptr. at 293.

interstate commerce.[63] The federal law is similar to the Uniform Trade Secrets Act in many ways and does not displace state law.[64] Among the differences, however, is the federal provision for civil seizure of property in extraordinary circumstances to prevent use of a trade secret.[65] The statute also authorizes injunctive relief and compensatory damages, including double damages for willful misappropriation.[66] Injunctive relief is available only in cases of actual or threatened misappropriation and not on the theory of inevitable disclosure,[67] which is permitted by some state laws. In addition, the statute protects employees and contractors who disclose trade secrets to the government in reporting a violation of law, to their attorneys for filing a lawsuit alleging retaliation for whistleblowing, and in court filings made under seal.[68] The employer must notify employees of this exception for whistleblowers.[69] Failure to do so bars the employer from recovering double damages and attorneys' fees in a trade secret case.[70]

§ 4.3 Employee Inventions

When employees develop inventions or other creative work in connection with or as a result of their employment, employers may desire to obtain rights to such employee works. The assignment of ownership rights over inventions and creative works raises some of the same policy concerns as the duty of loyalty and the protection of trade secrets. Failure to provide some rights over the ownership and use of such work might deprive employers of a return on their investment, with a resulting disincentive to invest in research and development. On the other hand, to the extent that the employee is the creator of the invention, and given the long legal tradition in the U.S. of protecting private property, a regime that deprives employees of any rights over their inventions might have also have a disincentive effect. Thus, as in the case of the duty of loyalty and the protection of trade secrets, the rules that have developed in this area seek to strike a proper balance in protecting the interests of both employers and employees.

The fact that an employee conceptualized or developed an invention while employed is insufficient to give the employer any

---

63 18 U.S.C. § 1836(b).

64 See 18 U.S.C. § 1838.

65 18 U.S.C. § 1836(b)(2).

66 18 U.S.C. § 1836(3).

67 18 U.S.C. § 1836(3)(A)(i).

68 18 U.S.C. § 1833(b).

69 18 U.S.C. § 1833(b)(3)(A), (B).

70 18 U.S.C. § 1833(b)(3)(C).

right to the invention.[71] The employer must establish that it hired the individual to exercise her inventive abilities for the benefit of the employer.[72] Where an employee is hired to invent, the employer will have ownership rights over the invention.[73]

4.3.1 The Shop Right Doctrine

The rules for employees who were not hired specifically to invent, but who create an invention during their job tenure are more complicated. In such a case, where no contract specifies otherwise, ownership rights are divided, with the right to the patent going to the employee and a "shop right" to the employer.[74]

A shop right allows employers to use the employee's invention without liability for infringement, but without obtaining ownership of it.[75] A shop right will be found to exist in two types of scenarios. First, a shop right will be created "where an inventor or owner of an invention acquiesces in the use of the invention by another, particularly where he induces and assists in such use without demand for compensation. . . ."[76] So, for example, in *Francklyn v. Guildford Packing Co.*,[77] where the employee-inventor gave permission to his employer to use his invention (an improved clam harvester) in a different boat from the one used by the employee, the court found that a shop right was created.

Second, a shop right will also be found where the invention was developed by an employee during the employer's time or with the employer's assistance, as for example where the employee uses tools provided by the employer or otherwise uses the employer's property.[78] So, where the employee-inventor used the employer's equipment and the employer tested and assisted in perfecting the invention, adapting its operations to use the invention, the court found that the employer had acquired a shop right.[79] Further supporting the shop right, the employee allowed the employer to use

---

71 Under copyright laws, however, "works made for hire" are considered the property of the employer. See infra Section 4.3.1.

72 See, e.g., Wommack v. Durham Pecan Co., 715 F.2d 962, 965 (5th Cir. 1983) Restatement of Employment Law § 8.09.

73 See, e.g., United States v. Dubilier Condenser Corp., 289 U.S. 178, 187 (1933).

74 See, e.g., Scott System, Inc. v. Scott, 996 P.2d 775, 778 (Colo. App. 2000); Restatement of Employment Law § 8.09. See also Bd. of Trustees of Leland Stanford Junior Univ. v. Roche Molecular Sys., Inc., 563 U.S. 776, 786 (2011).

75 See Pittsburg State Univ. v. Kansas Bd. of Regents, 280 Kan. 408, 425, 122 P.3d 336, 347 (2005).

76 Kierulff v. Metropolitan Stevedore Co., 315 F.2d 839, 841 (9th Cir. 1963) (quoting Gate-Way, Inc. v. Hillgren, 82 F.Supp. 546, 555 (S.D. Cal. 1949)).

77 695 F.2d 1158 (9th Cir. 1983).

78 See, e.g., Wommack, 715 F.2d at 965.

79 Id. at 969.

the invention for a year and relied on that experience to support his patent application.[80]

The rights the employer acquires by means of a shop right are limited, however. The holder of a shop right cannot sell or assign the right to others, nor prevent others from using it.[81]

The various cases so far discussed in this subsection involve disputes between *employees and employers* regarding ownership over inventions. It should be noted that a shop right could also be found to arise where an *independent contractor's* work results in an invention. As with the case of employees, where the employer can show acquiescence or use of the employer's time or property, a shop right will be found, regardless of the independent contractor status.[82] Where the relevant conditions are met, both employees and independent contractors are subject to the shop right doctrine.

Whether an individual is an employee or an independent contractor, however, turns out to be highly significant in the context of disputes over *creative work or work subject to copyright laws*.[83] The Copyright Act of 1976 protects "works of authorship,"[84] which in turn are defined to include: literary works; musical works, including any accompanying words; dramatic works, including any accompanying music; pantomimes and choreographic works; pictorial, graphic, and sculptural works; motion pictures and other audiovisual works; sound recordings; and, architectural works.[85] While in general copyright ownership "vests initially in the author or authors of the work,"[86] when an employee produces copyrightable "works made for hire," unless the parties expressly agree otherwise, the employer is considered the author.[87] Works made for hire are defined as "work prepared by an employee within the scope of his or her employment."[88] Thus, employers are likely to have copyrights over all the creative work of employees. The rule, however, does not extend to independent contractors. The copyrights over work of independent

---

[80] Id.

[81] Id. at 965.

[82] See, e.g., Crowe v. M&M/Mars, Div. of Mars Inc., 242 N.J. Super. 592, 577 A.2d 1278 (1990) (holding that the "shop right" rule defeated plaintiff's action even though plaintiff was not an employee).

[83] See Restatement of the Law, Employment Law § 8.09, comment b.

[84] 17 U.S.C. § 102.

[85] Id.

[86] 17 U.S.C. § 201(a).

[87] Id. § 201(b).

[88] Id. § 101.

contractors remain with the individual contractor, unless otherwise agreed by the parties.[89]

4.3.2 "Holdover" Provisions

As discussed above, the shop right doctrine applies where the conception and perfection of the invention occurs during the course of the inventor's employment.[90] Sometimes, however, the point in time of conception and perfection is unclear. An invention begins with an idea that might take years to come to fruition. While most of the work on it might have been done while the individual was employed by an employer, the invention might not be completed until later. To protect their interests in this type of situation, employers might require employees to agree to a "holdover" provision. "Holdover" or "trailer" provisions are a response to employers' concerns that employees will wait until after departing their jobs to complete an invention, so as to circumvent any contractual or common law duty (e.g., shop right doctrine) which otherwise provides some ownership interests to the employer. Holdover provisions raise some of the same policy concerns as some of the other legal doctrines allocating rights between employer and employees—a balancing of the need to protect the employer's investment while protecting and encouraging the employee's creativity.

Ingersoll-Rand v. Ciavatta,[91] is illustrative of cases examining the enforceability of holdover provisions. In *Ingersoll-Rand*, the defendant, after leaving his job, completed an improved model of a product sold by the plaintiff. Although the defendant had performed a variety of functions during his employment, he had not worked on research and development. The defendant, however, had signed a holdover provision wherein he agreed to assign to the employer all invention rights that arose during the period of employment or "within one year after termination of such employment."[92] The question presented to the court was the enforceability of this provision.

In evaluating the enforceability of the holdover provision, the court in *Ingersoll-Rand* adopted a reasonableness test. A holdover provision will be found to be unreasonable if it: "(1) extends beyond any apparent protection that the employer reasonably requires; (2) prevents the inventor from seeking other employment; or (3) adversely impacts on the public."[93]

---

89 See Restatement of Employment Law, supra note 83, at § 8.09, comment b.

90 See, e.g., Dubilier, 289 U.S. at 188 (1933).

91 110 N.J. 609, 542 A.2d 879 (1988).

92 Id. at 615, 542 A.2d at 882.

93 Id. at 627, 542 A.2d at 888.

In applying the reasonableness test to the facts of the case the court found that the employer's interests were "weak" because the employee did not rely on any trade secrets in developing his invention; rather the information needed for development of the invention was publicly available. The court also found that the employee developed the idea after he left his employment, which did not involve inventive work.[94] Accordingly, the agreement was unreasonable and unenforceable.[95]

4.3.3 Statutory Protections

Recognizing the importance of the allocation of property rights in employee inventions, a number of states have adopted legislation that regulates assignment of invention rights between employees and employers. For example, in Minnesota:

> Any provision in an employment agreement which provides that an employee shall assign or offer to assign any of the employee's rights in an invention to the employer shall not apply to an invention for which no equipment, supplies, facility or trade secret information of the employer was used and which was developed entirely on the employee's own time, and (1) which does not relate (a) directly to the business of the employer or (b) to the employer's actual or demonstrably anticipated research or development, or (2) which does not result from any work performed by the employee for the employer. Any provision which purports to apply to such an invention is to that extent against the public policy of this state and is to that extent void and unenforceable.[96]

Similar provisions have been adopted in California,[97] Delaware,[98] Illinois,[99] Kansas,[100] North Carolina,[101] and Washington.[102]

§ 4.4 Noncompetition Covenants

Noncompetition covenants, also known as covenants not to compete, are contractual agreements between employers and

94 Id., 542 A.2d at 888.

95 Id. at 640–42, 542 A.2d at 895–96.

96 Minn. Stat. § 181.78.

97 Cal. Labor Code § 2870.

98 19 Del. Code Ann. § 805.

99 765 Ill. Comp. Stat. 1060/2.

100 Kan. Stat. Ann. § 44–130.

101 N.C. Gen. Stat. Ann. § 66–57.1.

102 Wash. Rev. Code Ann. § 49.44.140.

employees that bar the employee from engaging in employment that competes with the employer after termination. As the United States has transitioned from a manufacturing-based economy to a knowledge-based economy, the use of noncompetition agreements has increased. Research indicates about thirty million U.S. workers have noncompete agreements.[103] While some professional and executive employees may negotiate these agreements, many other employees sign employer-proffered agreements as a condition of employment. Some employers have also used narrower agreements to restrict employees' post-employment activities without directly limiting the type of jobs they could do. For example, the employee might sign a nondisclosure or confidentiality agreement, which limits disclosure of confidential information, or a non-solicitation agreement, which prevents solicitation of the employer's customers and/or employees. Most states treat these narrower restrictions like noncompete agreements,[104] although a few treat them differently.[105]

4.4.1 Enforceability

Historically, courts have been reluctant to enforce noncompetition agreements both because they restrain trade and because they bar employees from using their skills to support themselves. Also, during the period of enforcement, society is deprived of the employee's talents. But employers have an interest in preventing employees from using the employer's trade secrets, training, customer information and good will to help competing businesses or to start their own. Barred from preventing such defections, employers might limit investments in research, development and training.[106] While the law barring misappropriation of trade secrets may protect substantially the same employer interests as a covenant not to compete, the covenant offers the employer some advantages over trade secret protection.[107] If an employee is permitted to work in the same industry, the employee may use or disclose confidential or trade secret information, intentionally or unintentionally. It may be difficult, however, for an employer to prove or even to know whether the employee is violating

---

[103] See U.S. Dep't of Treasury, Non-compete Contracts: Economic Effects and Employment Implications 3 (March 2016), available at https://www.treasury.gov/resource-center/economic-policy/Documents/UST%20Non-competes%20Report.pdf.

[104] See Restatement of Employment Law, § 8.06, comment b.

[105] See, e.g., Loral Corp. v. Moyes, 174 Cal.App.3d 268, 219 Cal.Rptr. 836 (1985) (enforcing agreement not to solicit employee of employer despite statutory prohibition on enforcing noncompetition agreements).

[106] Skeptics of this rationale, however, point to the success of Silicon Valley and other California businesses despite the state's prohibition on enforcement of noncompetition agreements.

[107] Gilson, supra note 3, at 605.

the obligation not to disclose trade secrets, in part because there is often a fine line between confidential information and the employee's knowledge and skills.[108] As a result, the covenant not to compete or a nondisclosure agreement may provide more effective protection for the employer's interests.[109]

As in the case of the other issues discussed in this chapter, courts have developed a test for the enforcement of such covenants that attempts to accommodate the interests of employers, employees and society. Covenants not to compete must be ancillary to "an otherwise valid transaction or relationship."[110] Like any contract, the covenant must be supported by consideration. In most states, a covenant will be enforced if the employer can establish a legitimate interest in protecting information within the knowledge of the employee, and can demonstrate that the covenant is reasonable in duration, geographic limitation, and the scope of prohibited employment.[111]

Some states, however, refuse to enforce such covenants except when they are connected to the sale of a business or the dissolution of a partnership, or restrict only the use of trade secrets.[112] These states reason that those negotiating covenants in connection with business sales or partnership dissolutions have the power to protect themselves and, in all likelihood, the income to sustain themselves during the period of unemployment. Moreover, sales of businesses might be hampered if buyers could not be assured that the former owner would not immediately set up a competing business and destroy the value of the purchase. Some commentators have argued that limiting the enforceability of noncompetition agreements encourages employee mobility and innovation, citing the success of Silicon Valley, in a state where most noncompetes are unenforceable, as an example.[113]

In states where the agreements are enforceable, they may be governed by statute or, more often, by common law. The first question a court will address when evaluating a noncompetition agreement is whether consideration was provided in exchange for that promise. Many courts will find an agreement entered at the time of hire to be

---

108 Id.

109 Id.

110 Restatement (Second) of Contracts § 187. Typically they will accompany an employment agreement, a partnership agreement, or a contract for sale of a business.

111 See, e.g., Simmons v. Miller, 261 Va. 561, 581, 544 S.E.2d 666, 678 (2001) (stating that the function, geographic scope and duration of the covenant must be considered together to determine the reasonableness of the restriction); Gelder Medical Group v. Webber, 41 N.Y.2d 680, 683, 363 N.E.2d 573, 576 (1977).

112 See, e.g., N.D. Cent. Code § 9–8–6; Cal. Bus. & Prof. Code §§ 16600–16602; Mont. Code Ann. §§ 28–2–703 to 28–2–705.

113 See, e.g., Gilson, supra note 3, at 607–08.

supported by the consideration of employment itself, even when the employment is at-will, with no guarantee that the job will last.[114] Some courts also apply the same rule to covenants adopted during employment, accepting continued work as consideration.[115] Courts in other states require additional consideration for these agreements to be valid, such as a pay raise or change in employment status.[116] Finally, some courts consider the duration of employment in evaluating whether a noncompete agreement is enforceable.[117]

In almost every state, the ultimate test for enforceability is reasonableness.[118] A covenant is reasonable if it is no greater than necessary to protect the interests of the employer and does not impose undue hardship on the employee or injury to the public.[119] Accordingly, initially the court explores whether the agreement reasonably protects a legitimate interest of the employer. Does the employee have knowledge obtained as a result of employment that would aid a competing business? If the employee has knowledge of a trade secret, an action under trade secret law might be combined

---

114 See, e.g., Riedman Corporation v. Jarosh, 290 S.C. 252, 349 S.E.2d 404 (1986); Wilmar, Inc. v. Corsillo, 24 N.C. App. 271, 273 210 S.E.2d 427, 430 (1974) (finding consideration though employment was terminable at will on fifteen days notice).

115 See Runzheimer Int'l, Ltd. v. Friedlen, 2015 WI 45, 362 Wis. 2d 100, 122, 862 N.W.2d 879, 890–91 (finding forbearance from the right to discharge at will to be consideration); Int'l Paper Co. v. Suwyn, 951 F.Supp. 445, 448 (S.D.N.Y. 1997); Runzheimer Int'l, Ltd. v. Friedlen, 2015 WI 45, 362 Wis. 2d 100, 122, 862 N.W.2d 879, 890–91 (same).

116 See, e.g., Charles T. Creech, Inc. v. Brown, 433 S.W.3d 345, 352 (Ky. 2014) (refusing to enforce covenant signed after 16 years of employment with no change in the employment relationship because no consideration was provided); Poole v. Incentives Unlimited, Inc., 345 S.C. 378, 548 S.E.2d 207 (2001) (finding continued at will employment insufficient consideration for covenant entered into during employment with no change in duties or pay); Socko v. Mid-Atl. Sys. of CPA, Inc., 126 A.3d 1266, 1278 (Pa. 2015) (finding that at will employment can be consideration for covenant entered into at hiring but not during employment; additional consideration is required such as a beneficial change in employment status or compensation); Standard Register Co. v. Kerrigan, 238 S.C. 54, 119 S.E.2d 533 (1961) (finding covenant enforceable where it was accompanied by an increase in pay and change in duties).

117 See, e.g., Brown & Brown, Inc. v. Mudron, 379 Ill. App. 3d 724, 728–29, 887 N.E.2d 437, 440 (2008) (stating that two years of post-signature employment is typically sufficient under Illinois law to constitute consideration); Fifield v. Premier Dealer Servs., Inc., 2013 IL App (1st) 120327, 993 N.E.2d 938, 943 (applying two-year employment rule even though the employee voluntarily quit after a few months, finding it to be bright line rule). The Illinois Supreme Court has twice declined to hear appeals on the issue of whether the two-year rule is a bright line rule.

118 An exception is South Dakota, which permits enforcement of covenants of less than two years duration in a specified geographic area without a specific inquiry into reasonableness, unless the employee was terminated without good cause. See S.D. Codified Laws § 53–9–11; Central Monitoring Serv. v. Zakinski, 553 N.W.2d 513, 520 (S.D. 1996).

119 Restatement (Second) of Contracts § 188.

with an action for enforcement of a covenant.[120] In addition to employee knowledge of trade secrets or other confidential information, enforcement of a covenant may be justified on grounds that the employer has an investment in good will that the employee may take upon departure.[121] Training costs also may be protected by a covenant, but only if the training is sufficiently specialized and provided to an employee who does not already have expertise in the field.[122] In lieu of noncompetition agreements, some employers have adopted a practice of requiring an employee who leaves before the employer has recouped its investment in training to repay the employer for training costs. Courts have generally reviewed these agreements on similar grounds of reasonableness, considering whether the length of the departure restriction and the amount of repayment are reasonably related to the investment in training, and thus no greater than needed to protect the employer's interest.[123]

Consider, for example, an employee who sells cell phones. If the employee is an outside sales person who sells phones to business customers and has information about the particular packages available, the customers to whom they were sold, and the needs of those customers that the packages were designed to address, the court might find an interest worthy of protection. On the other hand, if the employee sells phones to walk-in customers in a retail store, the employer interest is unlikely to warrant protection unless the employee has information or specialized training about the

---

[120] See, e.g., Comprehensive Technologies Int'l v. Software Artisans, 3 F.3d 730 (4th Cir. 1993), vacated and dismissed pursuant to settlement. See Section 4.2 for further discussion of trade secrets.

[121] Weber v. Tillman, 259 Kan. 457, 913 P.2d 84, 92(1996). See also Buffkin v. Glacier Group, 997 N.E.2d 1, 11 (Ind. App. 2013) (finding the "competitive advantage gained for an employer through personal contacts between employee and customer when the products offered by competitors are similar" to be a protectable interest).

[122] Compare Aero Kool Corp. v. Oosthuizen, 736 So.2d 25 (Fla. App.1999) (upholding covenant where employee with no prior experience received 185 hours of training in aviation repair, along with FAA certification) with Austin v. Mid State Fire Equipment of Central Florida, 727 So.2d 1097 (Fla. App. 1999) (finding that a service technician who had worked in the industry before employment with the employer received no specialized training that warranted enforcement of broad noncompetition agreement). See also Buffkin v. Glacier Group, 997 N.E.2d at 12 (finding that "accumulated training, knowledge, and skills acquired by Buffkin are not, in themselves, legitimate interests to be protected"); Nat'l Emp. Serv. Corp. v Olsten Staffing Serv., Inc., 145 N.H. 158, 161, 761 A.2d 401, 405 (2000) (finding unreasonable covenant where employer's only interest is cost of recruiting and hiring employees).

[123] See, e.g., American Consulting Environmental Safety Services, Inc. v. Schuck, No. 71A–05–0707–CV–409, 2008 WL 2346154 (Ind. App. June 10, 2008) (unpublished) (refusing to enforce contract for repayment of training costs which had no reasonable relationship to actual damages to employer and thus was an unenforceable penalty on termination); Med+Plus Neck and Back Pain Ctr. v. Noffsinger, 311 Ill.App.3d 853, 726 N.E.2d 687 (2000); City of Pembroke v. Hagin, 194 Ga.App. 642, 391 S.E.2d 465 (1990).

customers, phones, pricing or packages that would be unknown to or undiscoverable by others.[124]

If there is a legitimate employer interest to protect, the reasonableness test is applied to the three aspects of the agreement's scope—the time limitation, the geographic limitation, and the employment limitation. As noted above, a covenant is reasonable if it is no greater in scope than is necessary to protect the employer's interest, does not unduly prevent the employee from earning a living, and is in accordance with public policy. Courts have recognized that the public has an interest in business competition to ensure the availability of a wide range of products and services in the marketplace at reasonable prices. Because the test is reasonableness, the determination will vary based on the facts of the particular case.

Applying these factors to the time limitation leads to the conclusion that an agreement will be enforced if it is limited to the time necessary to protect the employer's interest, does not prevent the employee from earning a living for too long, and does not unduly restrict the availability of products and services to the public. Some states impose a statutory maximum on the length of noncompetes.[125] In rapidly changing industries, the length of the covenant should be shorter, as the employer's interest in restraint should not exceed the utility of the employee's knowledge. For example, in the well-publicized case of *EarthWeb v. Schlack*,[126] the court stated that a one-year covenant not to compete was unreasonably long in the dynamic internet industry. If the employer compensates the employee for the period of unemployment, the covenant may be more likely to be enforced, as the employee is not deprived of livelihood. If the employee will be kept out of the labor market long enough to impair the ability to continue to work in that field of employment, however, even compensation may not render the agreement reasonable.[127] In *EarthWeb*, the court indicated that even if the one-year covenant were reasonable, the adverse effect on Schlack's career created by a one-year absence from the industry, which the court called "several generations, if not an eternity" would outweigh any harm to the

---

[124] See Follmer, Rudzewicz & Co., P.C. v. Kosco, 420 Mich. 394, 402, 362 N.W.2d 676, 680 (1984) ("an employee is entitled to the unrestricted use of general information acquired during the course of his employment or information generally known in the trade or readily ascertainable").

[125] See, e.g., Ore. Rev. Stat. § 653.295(2) (limiting post-employment restriction to eighteen months).

[126] 71 F.Supp.2d 299 (S.D.N.Y. 1999), aff'd, 2000 WL 1093320 (2d Cir.).

[127] See, e.g., Estate of Schroeder v. Gateway Transp. Co., 53 Wis.2d 59, 69–70, 191 N.W.2d 860, 865–66 (1971) (invalidating as unreasonable a pension agreement requiring forfeiture if employee worked anywhere in the industry). Note that pension forfeiture might today violate ERISA, enacted in 1974.

company caused by denial of enforcement.[128] Thus the court in *EarthWeb* found a number of reasons to deny preliminary injunctive relief.

The same factors apply to the analysis of geographic limitations. For example, in many states a territorial salesperson legitimately may be prevented from competing in the same territory in which he or she worked because of the knowledge of the customers and their particular needs, but restriction in other geographic areas is unlikely to be upheld.[129] And the employer certainly cannot restrict the employee from working in geographic areas where it does not compete.[130] An interesting current issue is how widely the restriction can be applied if the employer engages in web-based sales, potentially allowing a worldwide restriction.[131]

The reasonableness of the scope of employment restriction commonly turns on whether the restriction is limited to the type of work that the employee did for the employer. If so, the employee is more likely to be able to use the confidential information, trade secrets, and training obtained from the employer in a new job, and enforcement of the covenant is warranted. However, if the new job duties are different, the restriction likely will be found unreasonable.[132] If the employee will be working in a different industry, even in the same job, a finding of reasonableness is less likely. For example, a restriction that would prevent an employee selling cell phones for a wireless company from selling audio systems for vehicles in the same geographic area would be unreasonable.

---

[128] 71 F.Supp.2d at 316.

[129] See Welcome Wagon Int'l v. Hostesses, 199 Neb. 27, 28, 255 N.W.2d 865, 866 (1977) (declining to enforce agreement prohibiting competition anywhere in the U.S where the employer was operating or intending to operate, stating it must be restricted to the area where the employee worked); All Stainless, Inc. v. Colby, 364 Mass. 773, 780, 308 N.E.2d 481, 486 (1974) (refusing to enforce noncompetition agreement as to new territory not formerly covered by employee).

[130] See Taylor Freezer Sales Co. v. Sweden Freezer Eastern Corp., 224 Ga. 160, 163, 160 S.E.2d 356, 359 (1968) (refusing to enforce agreement prohibiting engagement in manufacture or distribution of products competitive with those of the employer in any area in which the employer's products might be distributed or sold).

[131] See National Bus. Servs. v. Wright, 2 F.Supp.2d 701, 708 (E.D. Pa. 1998) (upholding a national restriction on competition because "[t]ransactions involving the Internet, unlike traditional 'sales territory' cases, are not limited by state boundaries"); PrecisionIR Inc. v. Clepper, 693 F. Supp. 2d 286, 294 (S.D.N.Y. 2010) (interpreting Virginia law to find restriction on competition in U.S. and Canada reasonable for internet webcasting company, in light of limited six-month time restraint).

[132] See, e.g., Assured Partners, Inc. v. Schmitt, 2015 IL App (1st) 141863, 44 N.E.3d 463, 472 (finding unreasonable restriction that barred employee from working with all types of professional liability insurance in the entire U.S. when he only specialized in one type of insurance in his work with the employer).

The three prongs may be considered together in determining reasonableness. Thus, for example, an agreement that is broad in geographic scope may be considered reasonable if it is shorter in duration and/or limited in the activities barred.[133] The greater the breadth and the less moderated by narrower restrictions on other prongs, the more likely the agreement will be found unenforceable.[134]

When an employee with a restrictive covenant is terminated rather than voluntarily quitting, some courts factor that into the enforcement decision. In Pennsylvania, for example, termination of the employee is not conclusive but very strong evidence that the covenant is unenforceable since "the need to protect itself from the former employee is diminished by the fact that the employee's worth to the corporation is presumably insignificant."[135] Other states' courts, however, enforce covenants without regard to whether the employee was terminated or quit.[136] Still others will enforce only if the termination was in good faith.[137]

When the agreement applies to certain professional employees (application to lawyers is discussed infra in Section 4.4.3), the public interest in insuring that communities have access to professional services plays an important role.[138] Some states have addressed this by outlawing noncompetition agreements for individuals in certain occupations.[139] Others closely scrutinize agreements that have the potential to limit access to services.[140] Where public access is not

---

[133] See, e.g., PrecisionIR, 693 F. Supp.2d at 294; Oce N. Am., Inc. v. Brazeau, No. 09C2381, 2010 WL 5033310, at *9 (N.D. Ill. Mar. 18, 2010) (distinguishing cases finding covenants enforceable where "the breadth of one restriction was tempered by the limitations of another").

[134] See, e.g., id. (finding agreement barring any employment with a competitor nationwide for twelve months unreasonable).

[135] Insulation Corp. of Am. v. Brobston, 446 Pa. Super. 520, 532, 667 A.2d 729, 735 (1995). See also Wrigg v. Junkermier, Clark, Campanella, Stevens, P.C., 362 Mont. 496, 505, 265 P.3d 646, 653 (2011) (finding "employer normally lacks a legitimate business interest in a covenant when it chooses to end the employment relationship").

[136] See, e.g., Weiss v. Wiederlight, 208 Conn. 525, 532 546 A.2d 216, 221 (Conn. 1988).

[137] See, e.g., Hopper v. All Pet Animal Clinic, Inc., 861 P.2d 531, 541–42 (Wyoming 1993).

[138] See, e.g., Emerick v. Cardiac Study Ctr., Inc., P.S., 170 Wash. App. 248, 257–58 286 P.3d 689, 694 (2012), as amended (Aug. 8, 2012).

[139] See, e.g., Colo. Rev. Stat. Ann. § 8–2–113(3) (invalidating noncompetition agreements for physicians but allowing agreements providing for payment of damages on termination of employment or partnership agreements); Del. Code Ann. tit. 6, § 2707 (same).

[140] See, e.g., Valley Med. Specialists v. Farber, 194 Ariz. 363, 368 982 P.2d 1277, 1282 (1999).

substantially harmed, however, many courts will enforce agreements that limit professional services.[141]

Where an agreement is not reasonable in one or more respects, states take different approaches to enforceability. Some states will not enforce an agreement that is unreasonable in any part, in order to discourage overreach by employers.[142] Other states allow judicial modification of the agreement to make it enforceable.[143] Of the latter, some states use the "blue pencil rule" to determine enforceability. Under this rule, an invalid covenant provision may be changed or deleted if the contract terms are easily divisible.[144] If the provision is not easily severable, however, the entire agreement is unenforceable. Courts that do not follow this rule may modify the agreement even where the problematic provision is not easily separable.[145]

In the digital age, several courts have grappled with the question of whether social media postings constitute solicitations. While a specific solicitation of customers or employees on social media is treated no differently than any other solicitation,[146] posting of a new position on LinkedIn, inviting former coworkers or customers to connect, and even posting a job listing at the new company there have been found not to violate noncompete or non-solicitation agreements.[147]

---

[141] See, e.g., Mohanty v. St. John Heart Clinic, S.C., 225 Ill. 2d 52, 79, 866 N.E.2d 85, 100 (2006) (enforcing restrictions on competition where there were "a sufficient number of cardiologists *in the area* to meet patient needs"); Hopper v. All Pet Animal Clinic, 861 P.2d at 544 (enforcing agreement where the services provided by the employee were available from other vets and thus the public would not be harmed by the restriction).

[142] See, e.g., Wis. Stat. § 103.465; Uni-Worth Enterprises, Inc. v. Wilson, 244 Ga. 636, 640, 261 S.E.2d 572, 575 (1979) (finding one sub-paragraph of the agreement unenforceable as overbroad and therefore refusing to enforce any part of the agreement).

[143] See, e.g., Ferrofluidics Corp. v. Advanced Vacuum Components, Inc., 968 F.2d 1463, 1470 (1st Cir. 1992) (holding that either Massachusetts or New Hampshire law applied and both led to the same result, modifying the contract by reducing the term of five year covenant not to compete since contract was reasonable except for length of the term); Data Mgmt., Inc. v. Greene, 757 P.2d 62, 64 (Alaska 1988) (allowing reasonable modification of agreement for enforceability unless it appears that the agreement was not drafted in good faith).

[144] See, e.g., Smart Corp. v. Grider, 650 N.E.2d 80, 83 (Ind. Ct. App. 1995) (applying blue pencil rule to strike out unreasonable geographic restrictions).

[145] See, e.g., Data Mgmt., Inc. v. Greene, 757 P.2d at 64.

[146] See, e.g., Amway Global v. Woodward, 744 F.Supp.2d 657, 674 (E.D. Mich. 2010) (stating that "communications qualifying as solicitations do not lose this character simply by virtue of being posted on the Internet.").

[147] See, e.g., Bankers Life & Cas. Co. v. Am. Senior Benefits LLC, 83 N.E.3d 1085, 1091 (Ill. App. Ct. 2017) (finding generic e-mail invitations to connect on LinkedIn and subsequent posting of job opening at new employer on LinkedIn did not violate non-solicitation agreement); BTS, USA, Inc. v. Executive Perspectives, LLC, No. X10CV116010685, 2014 WL 6804545, at *12 (Conn. Super. Ct. Oct. 16, 2014)

4.4.2 Remedies

Much of the litigation involving noncompetition contracts focuses on preliminary injunctive relief, as the former employer seeks to bar the employee from working for a new employer, arguing that any violation of the agreement would cause irreparable harm to the former employer. Thus, many cases involve both an assessment of likelihood of success on the merits and a determination of the probability of irreparable harm, traditional tests for preliminary injunctive relief.[148] Another factor in the determination is balancing the harm to the employee from enjoining the competition and the harm to the employer from declining to do so.[149] In addition to, or in lieu of, injunctive relief, the court may award damages resulting from the breach of the agreement.[150]

Some employers impose these agreements on employees for deterrent effect, well aware of the unlikelihood of actual enforcement. The mere threat of enforcement may prevent an employee from leaving to work for a competitor, given the cost of defending a lawsuit and the potential for losing subsequent employment. If an employee does accept employment with a competitor, in addition to suing the departing employee for violating the agreement, an employer may sue the new employer for interference with contract or similar claims.[151]

4.4.3 Noncompetition Agreements and Lawyers

Rule 5.6 of the ABA Model Rules of Professional Conduct bars lawyers from entering into agreements restricting the right to practice. Thus, in many states, entering into such an agreement will subject lawyers to discipline by the bar. The rationale of the rule is that such an agreement harms clients by preventing them from using the lawyer of their choice. Some states will enforce agreements that assess reasonable financial penalties to attorneys who leave their

---

(unpublished order) (posting new job on LinkedIn and inviting those linked to visit new employer's web site did not violate noncompete agreement).

148 See, e.g., EarthWeb v. Schlack, 71 F.Supp.2d at 308.

149 Id. at 316.

150 See, e.g., Mercer Mgmt. Consulting Inc. v. Wilde, 920 F.Supp. 219, 238–39 (D.D.C. 1996) (awarding a percentage of the revenues of the competing company set up by former employees to Mercer as damages).

151 See Ecolab Inc. v. Paolo, 753 F.Supp. 1100, 1114–15 (E.D. N.Y. 1991) (finding subsequent employer liable for tortious interference with employee covenant not to compete); Gorman Publ'g Co. v. Stillman, 516 F.Supp. 98, 106 (N.D. Ill. 1980) (finding prior employer stated claim against subsequent employer for tortious interference with contract); Microsoft Corp. v. Lee, No. 05–2–23561–6 SEA (Wash. Super. Ct. Sept. 13, 2005) (Microsoft sued former employee for breach of noncompete agreement and Google for tortious interference); Louis Altman, 1A Callmann on Unfair Competition, Trademarks, and Monopolies § 9:2, at 9–15–16 (4th ed. 2007).

firms to practice elsewhere, however, finding that such agreements do not restrict the right to practice.[152] Many other states have disagreed with this rationale and invalidated such agreements as against public policy, viewing them in the same light as noncompetition covenants.[153]

4.4.4 Public Policy Implications

Critics of noncompete agreements argue that they impede innovation and competition.[154] Empirical studies indicate that jurisdictions that enforce the covenants tend to have lower employee mobility.[155] Evidence regarding the effects on investment in employees is mixed.[156] Opponents also decry employers who use unenforceable or questionable agreements to deter employees from leaving their employment.[157] This concern has grown as more employers have begun requiring lower-paid workers to sign such agreements, which substantially reduces their bargaining power. Sandwich makers, delivery drivers, warehouse workers and pet sitters have been required by their employers to sign noncompete agreements.[158] Research indicates that greater enforcement of noncompetes lowers wages.[159] In response, several states have recently limited enforcement of covenants signed by low-wage employees.[160] Other states have tried to limit abuse of noncompetes

---

[152] See, e.g., Pettingell v. Morrison, Mahoney & Miller, 426 Mass. 253, 258, 687 N.E.2d 1237, 1240 (1997) (suggesting that in some cases a reasonable payment might be enforceable, but declining to enforce the provision in the particular case); Howard v. Babcock, 6 Cal.4th 409, 25 Cal.Rptr.2d 80, 863 P.2d 150 (1993).

[153] See, e.g., Dowd & Dowd, Ltd. v. Gleason, 181 Ill.2d 460, 693 N.E.2d 358 (1998); Jacob v. Norris, McLaughlin & Marcus, 128 N.J. 10, 607 A.2d 142 (1992).

[154] See supra note 113 and accompanying text.

[155] See U.S. Dep't of Treasury, supra note 103, at 18; Bishara & Westermann-Behaylo, supra note 3, at 20 & n.81.

[156] See U.S. Dep't of Treasury, supra note 103, at 12 (finding some workers receive more training with more enforcement and that training increases with consideration for the noncompete); Bishara & Westermann-Behaylo, supra note 3,. at 20 & n.81 (citing studies showing reduced investment with greater enforcement).

[157] See U.S. Dep't of Treasury, supra note 103, at 12 (noting that almost 19 percent of employees in California have noncompete agreements although they are unenforceable).

[158] See Dave Jamieson, Jimmy John's 'Oppressive' Noncompete Survives Court Challenge, The Huffington Post, April 10, 2015, http://www.huffingtonpost.com/2015/04/10/jimmy-johns-noncompete-agreement_n_7042112.html (describing noncompete agreements used by Jimmy John's to restrict employment of sandwich makers and delivery drivers at other sandwich shops for two years, as well as those used by a pet sitting service to restrict pet sitters from similar employment and Amazon to restrict subsequent employment of warehouse workers).

[159] See U.S. Dep't of Treasury, supra note 103, at 18–21; Bishara & Westermann-Behaylo, supra note 3, at 20 & n.81 (2012).

[160] Effective in 2017, Illinois outlawed covenants not to compete for low-wage workers only, defined as employees making thirteen dollars per hour or less. 820 Ill. Comp. Stat. 90/10. Oregon limits enforcement to situations where the worker makes

by requiring employers who attempt to enforce unenforceable agreements to pay damages and attorneys' fees to the departing employee.[161]

Other states have imposed additional requirements designed to protect employees from overreaching employers. For example, New Hampshire requires employers who force employees to sign a noncompete agreement as a condition of employment to provide them a copy before they accept the job offer.[162] Failure to do so makes the agreement unenforceable.[163] This legislation responds to the concerns about transparency, since evidence indicates that many employees are unaware of the significance of these agreements and also not advised of the requirement to sign until after accepting employment.[164]

On the other hand, some proponents of the agreements have argued that noncompete agreements should not be viewed with disfavor, but instead enforced like any other contracts regardless of reasonableness.[165] These critics are skeptical that the covenants are harmful and enthusiastic about their benefits.[166]

§ 4.5 Computer Fraud and Abuse Act

Some employers have used the federal Computer Fraud and Abuse Act[167] against their employees who have used the employer's computer information for their own business or that of a competitor. The law, which has both civil and criminal provisions, prohibits accessing a computer without authorization and exceeding authorized access. This statute was originally enacted to target hackers, subjecting them to criminal penalties, but the inclusion of civil liability and a private right of action, along with broad statutory language, have created a tool for employers to target employees.[168]

---

more than the median family income for a family of four. Ore. Rev. Stat. § 653.295(1)(d).

161 See Utah Code § 34–51–301. The same legislation limits all post-employment restrictions to one year from termination. Utah Code § 34–51–201 (effective for agreements entered into after May 10, 2016).

162 N. H. Rev. Stat. § 275:70. See also Ore. Rev. Stat. § 653.295(1)(a)(A), (B) (requiring notice of noncompete two weeks before first day of employment or alternatively, the noncompete is required in connection with a promotion.)

163 N. H. Rev. Stat. § 275:70.

164 See U.S. Dep't of Treasury, supra note 103, at 12–13.

165 See Outsource Int'l, Inc. v. Barton & Barton Staffing Solutions, 192 F.3d 662, 670–71 (7th Cir. 1999) (Posner, J., dissenting).

166 See id.

167 18 U.S.C. § 1030.

168 Stephanie M. Greene & Christine Neylon O'Brien, Exceeding Authorized Access in the Workplace: Prosecuting Disloyal Conduct under the Computer Fraud and Abuse Act (50 American Business Law Journal 281, 286–87 (2013).

The most common factual scenario involves employees who have authorization to access the computer but improperly use information obtained through such access. For example, employees may use an employer's confidential information to assist a competitor or to start and operate a competing business. Employees have faced both civil suits by their employers and criminal prosecution under the statute. In both civil and criminal cases, courts have split on whether an employee who has authorization to access information, but uses it improperly, violates the law.[169] It is also not clear that an employer can obtain damages caused by misuse of information accessed.[170]

---

[169] Compare WEC Carolina Energy Solutions LLC v. Miller, 687 F.3d 199 (4th Cir. 2012) (finding no violation in civil action because access was authorized) and U.S. v. Nosal, 676 F.3d 854 (9th Cir. 2012) (en banc) (finding in criminal case that employee who violated employer's confidentiality and computer use policies by using information accessed to set up a competing business did not violate the law because it does not prohibit unauthorized use of information) with Int'l Airport Ctrs., LLC v. Citrin, 440 F.3d 418 (7th Cir. 2006) (finding in civil claim that where employee accesses for a purpose adverse to the employer, the employee loses authority to access and thus violates the law) and U.S. v. Rodriguez, 628 F.3d 1258 (11th Cir. 2010) (upholding criminal conviction of employee who accessed data for nonbusiness reason in violation of employer policy although he was authorized to access the data for business reasons).

[170] Am. Family Mut. Ins. Co. v. Rickman, 554 F. Supp. 2d 766 (N.D. Ohio 2008) (finding no cause of action under the CFAA because the employer's only damage was from misuse of the information obtained from the computer and not from misuse of the computer).

Chapter 5

MANDATED TERMS AND CONDITIONS OF EMPLOYMENT

The U.S. Congress and legislatures across many states have been actively engaged in the regulation of various aspects of the employment relationship, requiring employers to provide certain terms and conditions of employment to employees, and directly regulating the provision of certain types of employment benefits. This chapter discusses these legislative efforts. We begin with a discussion of various statutes regulating wages and hours of employment. We then turn our attention to the regulation of employee benefits, discussing mandates regarding employee leave for family and medical reasons, and issues pertaining to the regulation of pensions and other welfare plans. We conclude the chapter with a discussion of issues pertaining to separation of employment, specifically obligations that employers may owe to their current or former employees.

§ 5.1 Wages and Hours

5.1.1 Introduction

Legislative efforts regarding wages and hours are perhaps one of the oldest forms of workplace regulation in the United States. Long before there were any laws protecting the right of employees to form unions or protecting their pension rights, or mandating leave time for family or medical reasons, there were regulations limiting the number of hours certain employees could work.[1] Since the early 1800s, workers' groups have exerted pressure on employers to limit the number of hours employees were required to work.[2] In response to this pressure, both federal and state governments have a long history of experimentation with various forms of regulation of hours. The intent was to protect both vulnerable workers, and the well-being of the population in general.[3] The constitutionality of these efforts, which was in doubt during the *Lochner* era of the early 20th

---

1 See Scott D. Miller, Revitalizing the FLSA, 19 Hofstra Lab. & Emp. L. J. 1,7 (2001).

2 Id. at 8.

3 Id. at 11–17.

century,[4] was finally resolved in 1937 *West Coast Hotel Co. v. Parrish*,[5] with the approval by the U.S. Supreme Court of Washington's minimum wage statute.[6] Shortly thereafter, Congress enacted the Fair Labor Standards Act of 1938.[7]

Legislative attempts to regulate wages and hours, whether in the form of a minimum wage, overtime pay, or living wage ordinances, are not without critics. A longstanding academic debate exists regarding the effect of minimum wage and overtime laws, for example. Critics argue that the laws are nothing more than an attempt by organized labor to increase the cost of substitute labor, thereby increasing the job security of their members.[8] Other critics argue that minimum wage laws tend to hurt the most vulnerable workers by reducing the demand for unskilled and young workers. These critics note that establishing a minimum wage increases the price of labor, resulting in a corresponding reduction in demand for unskilled and inexperienced labor.[9] Supporters of minimum wage laws, on the other hand, point to data indicating that the minimum wage has a minimal effect on employment,[10] and that minimum wage increases are accompanied by increases in workers' productivity.[11] This debate remains largely unresolved, resurfacing every time there are calls in Congress to increase minimum wage levels. In more recent years, the debate has moved from the federal to the state and local levels, as several cities and municipalities have enacted ordinances raising the minimum wage within their jurisdictions.[12]

---

[4] The *Lochner* era is named after the Supreme Court decision in *Lochner v. New York*, 198 U.S. 45 (1905), where the Court invalidated a state law limiting the number of hours bakers could work each week.

[5] 300 U.S. 370 (1937).

[6] The state law at issue authorized the fixing of minimum wages for women and minors. Id. at 379.

[7] 29 U.S.C. §§ 201–219.

[8] See Harry Hutchinson, Toward a Critical Race Reformist Conception of Minimum Wage Regimes: Exploding the Power of Myth, Fantasy, and Hierarchy, 34 Harv. J. Legis. 93, 118–119 (1997).

[9] See David Neumark & William Wascher, Employment Effects of Minimum and Subminimum Wages: Panel Data on State Minimum Wage Laws, 46 Indus. & Lab. Rel. Rev. 55 (1992).

[10] See David Card & Alan B. Krueger, Myth and Measurement: The New Economics of the Minimum Wage (1995).

[11] See Richard A. Ippolito, The Impact of the Minimum Wage if Workers Can Adjust Effort, 46 J. Law & Econ. 207 (2003).

[12] For example, in 2017 two studies published within weeks from each other reached conflicting results regarding the employment effects of Seattle's law increasing the minimum wage. Compare, Michael Reich, Sylvia Allegretto, & Anna Godoey, Seattle's Minimum Wage Experience 2015–16, Center for Wage and Employment Dynamics, Institute for Labor and Employment University of California, Berkeley (June 2017), with Ekaterina Jardim, Mark C. Long, Robert Plotnick, Emma van Inwegen, Jacob Vigdor, & Hilary Wething, Minimum Wage Increases, Wages, and

Section 5.1 discusses various statutes dealing with the regulation of wages and hours. The Fair Labor Standards Act is the centerpiece wage and hour legislation at the federal level. Next follows a brief discussion of recent attempts to use "living wage" legislation to fill what some see as gaps in the federal law. Finally, state wage payment laws regulating the form and timing of wages paid to employees are considered. The section concludes with a discussion of the Equal Pay Act.

5.1.2 Fair Labor Standards Act

5.1.2.1 Overview

The Fair Labor Standards Act (FLSA),[13] establishes a minimum wage,[14] overtime pay for work over 40 hours per week at a rate of one and one half times the regular rate of pay,[15] and child labor standards.[16] Originally, the minimum wage was 25 cents an hour, and over the years it has been increased to its current level of $7.25. The FLSA affects full-time and part-time workers in the private sector and in Federal, state, and local governments.[17]

The FLSA has been amended several times. In 1947 the FLSA was amended by the Portal to Portal Act, to clarify the definition of compensable time.[18] Subsequent amendments to the FLSA have extended the law's coverage to additional employees and raised the level of the minimum wage. For example, the 1961 amendments greatly expanded the FLSA's scope in the retail trade sector by incorporating the definition of enterprise coverage.[19] Later amendments extended coverage to public schools, nursing homes, laundries, the entire construction industry, and farms.

In response to the Supreme Court's 1985 decision in *Garcia v. San Antonio Metropolitan Transit Authority et.al.*,[20] Congress amended the FLSA regarding its application to public sector employees. Following these amendments, state and local governments were permitted to compensate their employees for overtime hours worked with compensatory time off in lieu of overtime pay, at a rate of one and one half hours of compensatory time for each

---

Low-Wage Employment: Evidence from Seattle, NBER Working Paper No. 23532 (June 2017).

13 29 U.S.C. §§ 201–219.

14 Id. § 206(1).

15 Id. § 207(a)(1).

16 Id. § 212.

17 Id. § 203(d).

18 Id. §§ 251–262.

19 See infra Section 5.1.2.3.2.

20 469 U.S. 528 (1985).

hour of overtime worked.[21] More recent amendments have focused on specific concerns raised in particular industries. For example, in 1990 Congress enacted legislation requiring regulations to be issued providing a special overtime exemption for certain highly skilled professionals in the computer field.

Enforcement duties rest primarily with the Secretary of Labor and the Administrator of the Wage and Hour Division of the Department of Labor. The FLSA authorizes a variety of enforcement actions including actions by the Secretary of Labor, the Department of Justice, and private plaintiffs.

5.1.2.2 Substantive Obligations

The FLSA provides three main mandates. First, the Act requires that a minimum wage be paid to all covered employees. Second, the Act requires that overtime pay be paid for work in excess of 40 hours per week. Third, the Act significantly limits the employment of children.

5.1.2.2.1 Minimum Wage

Under the FLSA, covered nonexempt workers are entitled to a minimum wage. Currently the minimum wage rate is $7.25 per hour, with much public discussion of raising it as high as $15.00 per hour. The FLSA allows states to establish their own minimum wage rates in excess of the federal minimum wage and the majority of states have done so. In Washington, for example, the minimum wage is set at $11.00 and is scheduled to be raised in each of the next three years to the amount of $13.50. After that, the statute provides that the rate will be adjusted annually for inflation using the consumer price index for urban wage earners and clerical workers for the prior year.[22] Some local governments have also raised the minimum wage above the state level.[23] At the same time, some states have enacted laws forbidding local governments to raise the minimum wage above the state level.[24]

---

[21] 29 U.S.C. § 207(*o*).

[22] Wash. Rev. Code Ann. § 49.46.020. For a useful summary of the various state minimum wage laws see Minimum Wage Laws in the States, July 1, 2017, available at https://www.dol.gov/whd/minwage/america.htm.

[23] For example, as of July 1, 2017, the minimum wage in Illinois is $8.25 per hour, but in Chicago it is $11.00 per hour. See Economic Policy Institute, Minimum Wage Tracker, July 10, 2017, http://www.epi.org/minimum-wage-tracker/#/min_wage/Illinois. Forty localities have minimum wages above their state's minimum wage as of July 1, 2017. Id.

[24] See, National Employment Law Project, Fighting Preemption: The Movement for Higher Wages Must Oppose State Efforts to Block Local Minimum Wage Laws 2–3, July 2017, http://www.nelp.org/content/uploads/Fighting-Preemption-Local-Minimum-

For purposes of establishing compliance with the minimum wage requirement, the workweek is the appropriate measurement unit.[25] Thus, to determine whether the employer has complied with the minimum wage requirement, one would take the total compensation received by the employee during a workweek and divide it by the number of hours worked in that week. The result of this calculation, which is referred to as the "regular rate of pay" must satisfy the established minimum wage. In general, the Act requires that payments to employees be made in cash or a negotiable instrument.[26]

As discussed earlier, the minimum wage requirement has been criticized as likely to result in employment losses for individuals whose wages are at or near the minimum wage. Recognizing that imposing a minimum wage might have some employment dislocation effects for young and low skill workers, the FLSA provides special rules for workers in these groups. For example, the Act provides that newly hired young employees (individuals under 20 years of age) may be paid a lower wage for the first ninety days of employment.[27] A similar type of provision is made for "tipped employees."[28] Employees that customarily and regularly receive more than $30 a month in tips, can be paid a subminimum wage ($2.13 per hour) if, when adding the tips, they will earn the federal minimum wage rate.[29] As in the case of the regular minimum wage, some states and localities have raised the minimum wage for tipped employees.[30]

5.1.2.2.2 Overtime Pay

Although the FLSA does not restrict the total number of hours employees may be required to work, it requires employers to pay a premium at a rate of not less than one and one-half times employees' regular rate (i.e., the overtime rate) for work in excess of 40 hours in a workweek ("time-and-a-half" in common workplace parlance). The overtime provisions of the FLSA were intended to protect employees by providing extra compensation for longer workweeks. Perhaps more importantly, the overtime provisions were also intended to

---

Wage-Laws.pdf (indicating that 25 states have enacted legislation preventing localities from enacting their own minimum wage laws).

25 29 U.S.C. § 206(a).

26 Where the employee receives other compensation in addition to the hourly rate or salary, as for example room and board, that additional amount should be added to the earnings for the particular workweek and the regular rate must then be calculated accordingly. See infra Section 5.1.2.4.2.

27 29 U.S.C. § 206(g)(1).

28 Id. § 203(t).

29 Id. at § 203(m).

30 See Economic Policy Institute, supra note 23 (showing Illinois's tipped minimum wage as $4.95 and Chicago's as $6.10 in July 2017).

spread work opportunities around and to reduce unemployment. The rationale was that employers would be likely to hire more employees and pay them the regular rate, instead of having to pay existing employees the overtime premium.[31] However, costs associated with hiring and training, as well as the costs associated with providing benefits to new employees, mitigate against this rationale.

As in the case of the minimum wage, the unit of measurement is the single workweek. Calculations regarding overtime pay compliance are made in terms of a workweek and employers are not allowed to average two or more weeks to determine compliance. Thus, an employee who works twenty-five hours in one week and fifty-five hours the following week is entitled to receive overtime pay for the extra fifteen hours worked in the second week, even though the average number of hours worked in the two weeks does not exceed forty hours.[32]

The overtime rate is calculated on the basis of the employee's regular rate of pay (i.e., the total pay received in one workweek divided by the total number of hours worked).[33] As discussed above, the regular rate of pay at which the employee is employed cannot be lower than the statutory minimum wage. If the employee's regular rate of pay exceeds the minimum wage, the overtime compensation must be computed at a rate not less than one and one-half times such higher rate.[34]

5.1.2.2.3 Child Labor Restrictions

The FLSA prohibits the use of "oppressive child labor."[35] Whether the employment of children is considered to be oppressive depends on the age of the child. In particular:

- Youths age 18 or older are not subject to restrictions on jobs or hours.[36]
- Youths age 16 and 17 may perform any job not declared hazardous by the Secretary, and have no restrictions on hours.[37]

---

[31] See Overnight Motor Transp. Co. v. Missel, 316 U.S. 572, 577 (1942). See also, Ronald G. Ehrenberg & Paul L. Schumann, Longer Hours or More Jobs? 3–4 (Cornell Studies in Indus. and Labor Relations No. 22, Cornell Univ. 1982)

[32] 29 C.F.R. § 778.104. The regulations also provide a definition of a workweek as any fixed and regularly reoccurring period of 168 hours. 29 C.F.R. § 778.105.

[33] Issues regarding the calculation of the rate of pay for overtime pay purposes are discussed in Section 5.1.2.4.2 infra.

[34] 29 C.F.R. § 778.107.

[35] 29 U.S.C. § 212.

[36] 29 C.F.R. § 570.2(a).

[37] Id. § 570.50.

- Youths age 14 and 15 may work outside school hours in various nonmanufacturing, nonmining, nonhazardous jobs with some restrictions.[38]

Employers are required to keep records of the dates of birth of employees under age 19, as well as detailed records of their employment history (e.g., starting and quitting times, their daily and weekly hours of work, and their occupations). Employers may protect themselves from unintentionally violating the child labor provisions by keeping on file an employment or age certificate for each young worker to show that the youth is the minimum age for the job.

Violations of the child labor provisions are subject to civil monetary penalties (of up to $11,000) for each employee who was subject to such violation.[39] Violations resulting in death or serious injury are punishable with a fine of up to $50,000, and such penalties may be doubled, up to $100,000, if the violations are found to be willful or repeated.[40] Criminal fines and imprisonment are allowed for willful and repeated violations.[41] The Secretary may also enjoin persons from violating the Act.[42]

5.1.2.3 Coverage

In determining whether a particular dispute is covered under the FLSA, one needs to address three separate inquiries: (1) Whether there exists an employer-employee relationship; (2) Whether the employee is covered individually (that is, whether the employee is engaged in commerce or in the production of goods for commerce) or whether the employee works for an "enterprise" that is engaged in commerce; and (3) Whether the employee is exempt from the statutory requirements.

5.1.2.3.1 The Employer-Employee Relationship

The FLSA only covers "employees." The Act defines an employee broadly as "any individual employed by an employer,"[43] and it defines "employ" as "to suffer or permit to work."[44] As discussed in Chapter 1, a particularly difficult situation has been that of distinguishing between employees and independent contractors. Guided by the amplitude of the statutory definition, the Supreme Court has applied the "economic reality" test to determine whether an individual is an

---

38 Id. § 570.31.

39 Id. § 579.1(a)(1)(i)(A).

40 Id. § 579.1(a)(1)(i)(B).

41 29 U.S.C.A. § 216(a).

42 Id.

43 29 U.S.C. § 203(e).

44 Id. § 203(g).

employee under the FLSA. Under the economic reality test, the key question is whether the individuals are economically dependent on their jobs for their continued employment.[45]

Not only have courts struggled with the employee/independent contractor distinction, but they also have struggled with the treatment of trainees. Although the statutory language is broad, the Supreme Court has made clear that the FLSA does not make all persons employees, particularly where individuals work for their own advantage on the premises of another.[46] Trainees and individuals participating in internship programs are an example. The discussion about the status of trainees and interns has acquired added significance given the central role that training and internship programs play in today's labor market. Internships have become an important component of the transition from school to the labor force. Educational institutions, from high school to college, rely on internships as a way of providing students an entry into the workforce. Internships have also become a recruiting avenue for private employers.[47]

Whether trainees are employees of an employer under the FLSA will depend upon all of the circumstances surrounding their activities on the premises of the employer. Trainees and interns will not be considered employees if: (1) the program is similar to that which would be given in a vocational school (even if it takes place at the actual workplace); (2) the experience is intended for the benefit of the trainees/interns; (3) the trainees/interns work under close supervision and do not displace regular employees; (4) the employer receives no immediate advantage from the activities of the trainees/interns; (5) the trainees/interns are not necessarily entitled to a job at the conclusion of the training period; and (6) the parties agree that the trainees/interns are not entitled to wages for the time spent in training.[48] The U.S. Court of Appeals for the Second Circuit has held, however, that the main focus of the inquiry should be on whether the intern or the employer is the primary beneficiary of the relationship.[49]

---

[45] For a detailed discussion of the application of the economic reality test, see supra Section 1.1.1.2.2.

[46] See, e.g., Walling v. Portland Terminal Co., 330 U.S. 148 (1947).

[47] Robert J. Tepper & Matthew P. Holt, Unpaid Internships: Free Labor or Valuable Learning Experience?, 2015 B.Y.U. Educ. & L. J. 323 (2015).

[48] See Reich v. Parker Fire Protection Dist., 992 F.2d 1023, 1024 (10th Cir. 1993) (quoting the Wage and Hour Manual (BNA) 91:416 (1975)).

[49] See Glatt v. Fox Searchlight Pictures, Inc., 811 F.3d 528 (2nd Cir. 2016).

5.1.2.3.2 Individual or Enterprise Coverage

For an employee to be covered under the FLSA, that employee must be "engaged in commerce or in the production of goods for commerce."[50] The term "commerce" is defined broadly and it covers "employees doing work involving or related to the movement of persons or things (whether tangibles or intangibles, and including information and intelligence) 'among the several States or between any State and any place outside thereof. . . .' "[51] The statute is intended to cover those individuals whose work is fairly related and essential to the production process. Thus, employees may be "engaged in production of goods for commerce" even if they are not engaged in the actual physical work of producing the product itself. Employees will be considered to be within the general coverage of the FLSA if they work in a place of employment where goods sold or shipped in interstate commerce or foreign commerce are being produced.[52] The U.S. Supreme Court has noted that the FLSA is to be "construed liberally to apply to the furthest reaches consistent with congressional direction."[53]

In determining whether employees are covered, the workweek is the appropriate standard.[54] Thus, if in any workweek an employee is engaged in both covered and non-covered work he is entitled to both the wage and hours benefits of the FLSA for all the time worked in that week. Because the coverage determination is made on a weekly unit basis, an employee may be subject to the Act in one workweek and not in the next.[55]

As noted earlier, in 1961 Congress amended the FLSA by adopting the concept of enterprise coverage. Enterprise coverage focuses on the activities of the employer, as opposed to those of individual employees. The amendment had the effect of expanding the coverage of the FLSA to every business which met the required income threshold.

Under enterprise coverage all employees of an enterprise will be covered if: (1) the enterprise,[56] is (2) "engaged in commerce or in the

---

50 29 U.S.C. §§ 206(a), 207(a)(1).

51 29 C.F.R. § 776.9.

52 Id. § 776.15(b).

53 See Mitchell v. Lublin, McGaughy & Associates, 358 U.S. 207 (1959).

54 Id.

55 Id. § 776.4(a), (b).

56 29 U.S.C. § 203(r)(1).

production of goods for commerce,"[57] and, (3) a minimum dollar volume threshold is satisfied.[58]

An "enterprise" is defined as "the *related activities* performed (either through *unified operation or common control*) by any person or persons for a *common business purpose*."[59] It includes all such activities performed in one or more establishments or by one or more corporate or other organizational units.[60]

Activities performed by a particular entity are considered "related activities" for the purposes of the FLSA if they are the same or similar, they are auxiliary and service activities, they are part of an integrated structure, or they "serve a business purpose common to all the activities of the enterprise. . . ."[61] For example, where an insurance company owned and maintained an office building which facilitated the internal operation of its insurance business and established a favorable public image, the court found that the activities of the home office and office building were performed for a common business purpose, and thus custodial employees working in the office building were covered under minimum wage provisions.[62]

The "unified operation" or "common control" requirements are likely to be satisfied where more than one entity operates under common ownership or under contractual arrangements which have the effect of aligning or integrating the activities of one company with the activities of others.[63]

Finally, the regulations define a common business purpose to include activities "which are directed to the same business objective or to similar objectives. . . ."[64] Thus, in *Brennan v. Arnheim & Neely, Inc.*,[65] the United States Supreme Court found that a real estate company which operated several buildings had the common business purpose of "managing commercial properties for profit."[66]

For an enterprise to be covered it must also be "engaged in commerce or in the production of goods for commerce" and satisfy a dollar volume test. Section 203(s) defines "engaged in commerce or in the production of goods for commerce" to include any enterprise

---

[57] Id. § 203(s)(1)(A)(i).

[58] Id. § 203(s)(1)(A)(ii).

[59] Id. § 203(r)(1) (emphasis added).

[60] Id.

[61] 29 C.F.R. § 779.206(b).

[62] See Wirtz v. Columbian Mut. Life Ins., 380 F.2d 903 (6th Cir. 1967).

[63] 29 C.F.R. § 779.218.

[64] Id. § 779.213.

[65] 410 U.S. 512 (1973).

[66] Id. at 518.

"which has employees engaged in commerce or in the production of goods for commerce, including employees handling, selling or otherwise working on goods that have been moved in or produced for commerce by any person."[67] Employees are considered to be "engaged in production of goods for commerce," if their work relate to the movement of both tangible or intangible things, to any place outside the state.[68] For example, employees involved in the communication industry (e.g., radio, television) are considered to be engaged in commerce.[69]

Unlike the case with regard to individual coverage, which uses a weekly unit basis, § 203(s) envisions a yearly unit basis. Thus, an enterprise will be considered to have employees engaged in commerce or in the production of goods for commerce, if during the relevant annual period, "it regularly and recurrently has at least two or more employees engaged in such activities."[70]

Finally, the Act imposes a relatively low minimum jurisdictional threshold of $500,000 in annual gross volume of sales or business done,[71] resulting in the exclusion from coverage of only fairly small businesses.[72] Small employers who might not meet this jurisdictional threshold might still be covered under state minimum wage laws.

5.1.2.3.3 Exempt and Nonexempt Employees

The FLSA exempts from coverage various groups of employees.[73] Thus, individual workers could be considered "employees" and "covered" (either on an individual basis or by means of enterprise coverage) and still not be entitled to either the minimum wage or overtime protections if they fall in one of the many exemptions available under the Act. The terms "exempt" and "non-exempt" are commonly used in U.S. workplaces, often but mistakenly correlated to "white collar" vs. "blue collar" or "salaried" vs. "hourly." In fact,

[67] 29 U.S.C. § 203(s)(1).

[68] See Les A. Schneider & J. Larry Stine, 1 Wage & Hour Law § 4.3 (2017).

[69] Id. at § 4.6.

[70] 29 C.F.R. § 779.238.

[71] 29 U.S.C. § 203(s)(1)(A)(ii).

[72] Under § 203(s)(1)(b), "hospitals; institutions primarily engaged in the care of the sick, aged, mentally ill, or disabled who reside on the premises; schools for children who are mentally, or physically disabled or gifted; preschools, elementary, and secondary schools and institutions of higher education; and federal, state, and local government agencies" are covered regardless of the dollar volume of sales.

[73] Some employees are exempted from both the minimum wage and overtime provisions (e.g., employees of certain seasonal amusement or recreational establishments; employees of certain small newspapers; casual babysitters; and persons employed as companions to the elderly or infirm). 29 U.S.C. § 213(a). Other employees are exempted from the overtime pay requirements only (e.g., certain retail employees; taxi drivers; announcers; news editors; and chief engineers of certain non-metropolitan broadcasting stations). 29 U.S.C. § 213(b).

white collar or salaried employees can be and often are non-exempt, and blue collar or hourly employees can be exempt, though less commonly. It always depends on what they do, not what they are called by job title or colloquially.

The burden of showing that an exemption applies falls on the employer.[74] The exemptions cover a wide range of jobs in varying industries and at all wage levels. For example, at the low end of the wage spectrum are employees at certain amusement and recreational establishments,[75] certain agricultural workers,[76] and certain domestic service workers.[77] At the high end of the wage spectrum are likely to be those employees covered by the "white collar" exemptions such as individuals employed in an executive, administrative, or professional capacity.[78]

As a matter of illustration, consider two of the exceptions which have generated significant commentary: the exemption for certain domestic service workers, and the white collar exemption.

Domestic service employment is defined as "services of a household nature performed by an employee in or about a private home (permanent or temporary) of the person by whom he or she is employed."[79] Although a variety of domestic service workers are included under the Act (e.g., cooks, butlers, maids, housekeepers, nurses, janitors, handymen, gardeners, and chauffeurs of automobiles for family use),[80] three specific types of domestic workers are excluded. Casual babysitters and employees who provide "companionship services for individuals who (because of age or infirmity) are unable to care for themselves" are excluded from both the minimum wage and overtime provisions.[81] In addition, a worker who "is employed in domestic service in a household and who resides in such a household" is exempted from the overtime provisions only.[82]

The domestic service workers' exemptions have gained added importance as the demand for homecare workers caused by the aging of the U.S. population has increased. The issue has become more contentious due to the increase in domestic service workers who are employed by third-party agencies (e.g., temporary worker agencies). Department of Labor regulations have extended the FLSA's domestic

---

74 See Walling v. General Industries Co., 330 U.S. 545 (1947).

75 29 U.S.C. § 213(a)(3).

76 Id. § 213(a)(6)(A), (B) and (C).

77 Id. § 213(a)(15).

78 Id. § 213(a)(1), (17).

79 29 C.F.R. § 552.3.

80 Id.

81 29 U.S.C. § 213(a)(15).

82 Id. § 213(b)(21).

service workers' exemption to homecare workers employed by third-party agencies.[83] Various domestic service workers advocacy groups argue that the exemption should not apply to domestic workers' employed by third-party agencies. These groups note that the Department of Labor's regulation regarding domestic workers define domestic service employment as services performed "in or about a private home . . . of person by whom [the employee] is employed."[84] Since domestic service workers employed by third-party agencies do not work "in or about" the home of their employer, but instead are assigned to private homes to provide their services, they should not be covered by the exemption, but should receive overtime compensation. In 2007, in *Long Island Care at Home, Ltd. v. Coke*,[85] the Supreme Court rejected similar arguments, upholding instead application of the exemption to domestic workers employed by third-party agencies. In response to these developments, in 2015 the Department of Labor amended the domestic workers regulations. The amended regulations clarify and narrow the scope of duties that fall within the definition of companionship services. The regulations limit the exemption to those direct care workers who are performing "elder sitting" rather than the professionalized workforce for whom home care is a vocation.[86] The regulation also prohibits employers of direct care workers other than the individual receiving services or his or her family or household from claiming the companionship services or live-in domestic service employment exemptions.[87]

The "white collar" exemption also has been fairly controversial. Section 13(a)(1) exempts individuals employed "in a bona fide executive, administrative, or professional capacity" from both the minimum wage and overtime requirements of the FLSA.[88] The exemption was premised on the rationale that the jobs of individuals performing white collar functions were significantly different from those of other covered employees, and thus difficult to fit into the 40 hours a week framework which is used to calculate the overtime provisions of the FLSA.[89] It also was believed that white collar employees enjoyed wages and other benefits significantly over the minimum wage and thus such employees were likely not to need the

---

83 29 C.F.R. § 552.109(a).

84 Id. § 552.3.

85 551 U.S. 188 (2007).

86 29 C.F.R. § 552.6.

87 29 C.F.R. § 552.109(a). In Home Care Association of America v. Weil, 799 F.3d 1084 (DC Cir. 2015), the Court of Appeals for the District of Columbia Circuit, rejected a challenge to the regulations finding that they were grounded on a reasonable interpretation of the FLSA and was neither arbitrary nor capricious.

88 29 U.S.C. § 213(a)(1).

89 See Timothy Glynn et. al., Employment Law: Private Ordering and Its Limitations 695 (2007).

minimum wage protections. Finally, to the extent that such workers were interested in the type of protections afforded under the FLSA, it was believed that they were in a position to negotiate such protections. While likely relevant when the FLSA was enacted, the reasons advanced in favor of excluding white collar workers appear to be less relevant today, as organizational hierarchies have flattened, and the standardization of job duties has reached many of the traditional white collar functions.

In deciding whether an employee qualifies for the white collar exemption, the following tests must be satisfied. First, the employee must be paid a predetermined and fixed salary that is not subject to reduction because of variations in the quality or quantity of work performed ("salary basis test").[90] Second, the amount of salary paid must meet a minimum specified amount ("salary level test").[91] Finally, the employee's job duties must primarily involve executive, administrative, or professional duties as defined by the regulations ("duties test").[92]

To meet the salary basis test the employee must regularly receive in each pay period a predetermined amount constituting all or part of the employee's compensation."[93] The regulations allow for some salary deductions (e.g., because of absence due to personal reasons) without affecting the employee salary status. However, an employer who makes improper salary deductions, risks losing the exemption "if the facts demonstrate that the employer did not intend to pay employees on a salary basis."[94] The exemption could be lost where, for example, the employer makes a large number of improper deductions over a long period of time and fails to adopt a clear policy prohibiting improper deductions.[95]

The salary level test, requires that the employee be paid a minimum specified amount. In 2004 the Department of Labor set the salary threshold that the employee needed to meet the salary level test at a rate no less than $455 per week ($23,660 annually) exclusive of board, lodging or other facilities."[96]

---

[90] 29 C.F.R. § 541.602(a).

[91] 29 C.F.R. § 541.601.

[92] 29 C.F.R. § 541.100.

[93] 29 C.F.R. § 541.602.

[94] 29 C.F.R. § 541.603(a).

[95] Id.

[96] See 29 C.F.R. § 541.100(a)(1) (covering executives); § 541.200(a)(1) (covering administrative employees); and, § 541.300(a)(1) (covering professional employees). To be paid on a salary basis requires that the employee regularly "receives each pay period on a weekly, or less frequent basis, a predetermined amount constituting all or part of the employee's compensation, which amount is not subject to reduction because

Finally, to qualify for the white collar exemption employees also need to satisfy a duties test. As the name implies, the focus of this prong is on the substantive duties of the employee's job, in particular on what constitutes the employee's "primary duty." Primary duty is defined as "the principal, main, major or most important duty that the employee performs."[97] The determination of an employee's primary duty must be based on all the facts in light of factors such as: "the relative importance of the exempt duties as compared with other types of duties; the amount of time spent performing exempt work; the employee's relative freedom from direct supervision; and the relationship between the employee's salary and the wages paid to other employees for the kind of nonexempt work performed by the employee."[98]

The specific requirements of the duties test for executive, administrative and professional employees are as follows. An executive employee will be exempted from the FLSA: where the individual's "primary duty is management of the enterprise in which the employee is employed or of a customarily recognized department or subdivision thereof"; where the individual "customarily and regularly directs the work of two or more other employees"; and, where the individual "has the authority to hire or fire other employees or . . . [make] suggestions and recommendations as to the hiring, firing, advancement, promotion or any other change of status of other employees [which] are given particular weight."[99]

Administrative employees are exempt if their primary duty "is the performance of office or non-manual work directly related to the management or general business operations of the employer or the employer's customers".[100] Additionally their primary duty must include the exercise of discretion and independent judgment with respect to matters of significance.[101]

To qualify as an exempt professional employee, the employee's primary duties must include "the performance of work: (i) Requiring knowledge of an advanced type in a field of science or learning customarily acquired by a prolonged course of specialized intellectual instruction; or (ii) Requiring invention, imagination, originality or talent in a recognized field of artistic or creative endeavor."[102]

---

of variations in the quality or quantity of the work performed" or without regard to the number of days of hours worked. 29 C.F.R. § 541.602(a).

97 Id. § 541.700(a).

98 Id.

99 Id. § 541.100.

100 Id. § 541.200.

101 Id.

102 Id. § 541.300 (describing creative professionals).

The 2004 regulations added a new type of worker to the white collar exemption: "highly compensated individuals." Such employees are be considered exempt if their total annual compensation is at least $100,000 and the employee customarily and regularly performs any one or more of the exempt duties or responsibilities of an executive, administrative or professional employee.[103]

In 2016, the Department of Labor issued a new set of regulations seeking to narrow the scope of the exemption and consequently, make more workers eligible to receive overtime pay. The 2016 regulations made three key changes. First, the regulations increased the threshold salary level to $913 per week or $47,476 annually. Second, the regulations also increased the total annual compensation requirement for highly compensated employees subject to the minimal duties test to $134, 004. Finally, the regulations established a mechanism for automatically updating the salary and compensation levers every three years, in order to ensure that the thresholds provide effective levels for the application of the exemption. The 2016 regulations might be proven to be short lived. In November 2016, the U.S. District Court for the Eastern District of Texas granted an emergency injunction request halting the regulations and in August 2017, the same court granted a motion filed by the plaintiffs for expedited summary judgment striking down the rule.[104]

5.1.2.4 Implementation Problems

Determining compliance with the minimum wage and overtime pay provisions of the FLSA requires information about wages and about hours. As discussed above, to determine compliance with the minimum wage requirement, one needs to calculate the regular rate of pay (the total compensation received in a week divided by the number of hours worked in that week). The regular rate of pay must equal or exceed the minimum wage. To calculate the overtime provisions, one first determines whether the employee worked more than forty hours in a workweek. The overtime pay is then calculated by multiplying the excess number of hours (i.e., hours over forty) by one and a half times the regular rate of pay. While this is likely to involve a fairly simple calculation for employees who are paid a pre-set wage amount, who earn no in-kind compensation such as lodging, and whose working time is easily identifiable, the calculation can get much more complex for employees who, for example, work on commissions, receive compensation in forms other than wages, or for

103 Id. § 541.601(a).

104 State of Nevada v. U.S. Dept. of Lab., 218 F.Supp. 3d 520 (E.D. Texas 2016). See also, State of Nevada v. U.S. Dept. of Lab., 2017 WL 3780085 (E.D. Texas 2017).

whom it is not clear when a workday starts and ends. In this section we discuss some of these possible complications.

5.1.2.4.1 *Defining Compensable Time*

As originally enacted, the FLSA did not include a definition of compensable time. Early Supreme Court decisions interpreted the statute broadly, by holding that time spent by employees walking from time clocks to their workstations was compensable.[105] In response, Congress enacted the 1947 amendments, known as The Portal to Portal Act.[106] The 1947 amendments made non-compensable "walking, riding, or traveling" to and from the place where the employee's principal activities are performed, as well as similar "preliminary" and "postliminary" activities performed "prior" or "subsequent" to the principal activity.[107]

Following the enactment of the 1947 amendments, the Supreme Court confronted the question of whether the time incident to changing clothes at the beginning of a shift, and showering at the end, in a work environment where employees had to handle dangerous and toxic materials, was compensable time.[108] In describing the work environment, the Court noted that some of the chemicals were spilled or dropped, had become "a part of the dust in the air," and that abnormal concentrations of the chemicals had been discovered in the bodies of some of the plaintiffs.[109] In *Steiner v. Mitchell*, the Court noted that, as used in § 254(a), the term principal activity or activities included "all activities which are an 'integral and indispensable part of the principal activities.' "[110] Accordingly, the Court held that the "donning and doffing of specialized protective gear" was compensable.[111]

In *IBP Inc. v. Alvarez*,[112] the Supreme Court reaffirmed the holding in *Steiner*, to the extent that any "integral and indispensable" activity is considered a principal activity. Alvarez involved a large producer of fresh beef, pork, and related products. All production-line workers were required to wear hardhats, hairnets, earplugs, gloves,

---

105 See Tennessee Coal, Iron & R. Co. v. Muscoda Local No. 123, 321 U.S. 590 (1944) (finding that time spent by iron ore miners in traveling underground in mines to and from place of work was compensable, where the travel occurred under employer's strict control and involved continuous physical and mental exertion as well as hazards to life and limb).

106 29 U.S.C. §§ 251–262.

107 Id. § 254.

108 See Steiner v. Mitchell, 350 U.S. 247, 248 (1956).

109 Id. at 249–50.

110 Id. at 253.

111 Id. at 256.

112 546 U.S. 21 (2005).

sleeves, aprons, leggings, boots, and those who use knives in performing their duties also had to wear a variety of protective equipment for their hands, arms, torsos, and legs. Plaintiffs sued to recover compensation for this preproduction and postproduction activities, including the time spent donning and doffing protective gear and walking between the locker rooms and the production floor. The Court held that compensable time starts when employees engage in any activity that is "integral and indispensable" to the principal activity. Accordingly, the Court held that the time spent walking from the place where employees put on unique protective gear to the production floor is compensable time, although the time waiting to don the protective gear is not.

Disputes regarding the issue of what activities are "integral and indispensable" continue to arise despite the Court's pronouncement in *Alvarez*. If the time waiting to don protective gear is not compensable, what about the time spent waiting to undergo security screenings? In *Integrity Staffing Solutions v. Busk*,[113] the Court concluded that it was not compensable. The case involved warehouse employees whose job duties involved retrieving products from a storage area and packing them for shipment to Amazon.com customers. The employees alleged that they were entitled to compensation for the time spent waiting to undergo the screening as well as the time of the screening itself, given that the screenings were conducted as a theft prevention measure and thus were done solely for the benefit of the employer. The Court found that because the employer "could have eliminated the screenings altogether without impairing the employees' ability to complete the work" the screenings were not an intrinsic element of the employees' principal activities (i.e., retrieving products from warehouse shelves or packaging them for shipment.)[114] The fact that the screenings were for the benefit of the employer was not controlling.

Not only has there been litigation regarding which of the activities that occur immediately before or after the beginning of work are compensable, but also a number of questions have been raised over the years with respect to other types of activities that occur during the workday. Such is the case with what is referred to as "on-call" time. Is the time that employees are on-call (i.e., available to return to work on short notice) compensable time? Soon after the enactment of the FLSA, the Supreme Court in *Skidmore v. Swift & Co.*,[115] indicated that under certain circumstances, on-call time could be considered working time for purposes of the overtime provisions

113 135 S. Ct. 513 (2014).

114 Id. at 518.

115 323 U.S. 134 (1944).

of the FLSA. The Department of Labor regulations provide that an employee who "is required to remain on call on the employer's premises or so close thereto that he cannot use the time effectively for his own purposes is working while on call."[116] On the other hand, employees who do not have to stay on the premises, and are only required to notify the employer where they can be reached, are not considered to be working.[117]

The key question in those cases is whether the on-call employees can effectively use the on-call time for their own purposes. *Bright v. Houston*[118] is illustrative. The plaintiff, a medical equipment repair technician, was required to wear an electronic paging device during off-duty hours and to be on-call to come to the hospital to make emergency repairs.[119] The plaintiff was free to go anywhere and do whatever he wanted subject to three constraints: he was not allowed to be intoxicated; he was required to be reachable by beeper; and, he was required to arrive at the hospital within 20 minutes after the call.[120] The plaintiff received no compensation for the on-call time and brought an action claiming that the on-call time was working time and thus compensable, when appropriate, at the overtime pay rate. The court found that plaintiff's on-call time was not compensable since the plaintiff could use the on-call time for his own personal purposes.[121] According to the court, the plaintiff was not restricted to any given location, and could do anything he wanted with very few restrictions.

Other courts have reached different results in cases involving similar types of restrictions, as for example, where the frequency of the calls from the employer during the on-call period substantially limited the ability of employees to use the on-call time for their own purposes.[122]

The Department of Labor has also issued regulations dealing with the compensability of other specific time periods such as rest periods,[123] meal periods,[124] sleep time,[125] and training time.[126]

---

116 29 C.F.R. § 785.17.

117 Id.

118 934 F.2d 671 (5th Cir. 1991).

119 Id. at 672.

120 Id. at 673.

121 Id. at 676.

122 See, e.g., Renfro v. City of Emporia, 948 F.2d 1529 (10th Cir. 1991), cert. dismissed, 503 U.S. 915 (1992).

123 29 C.F.R. § 785.18.

124 Id. § 785.19.

125 Id. § 785.20.

126 Id. § 785.27.

5.1.2.4.2 Determining the Base Rate

The general overtime pay standard in § 7(a) requires that overtime must be compensated at a rate not less than one and one-half times the *regular rate* at which the employee is actually employed.[127] Although the Act does not require employers to compensate employees on an hourly basis, the regular rate under the Act is a rate per hour. Thus, where employees are paid on a salary basis, or where they are compensated on commission, their remuneration has to be recalculated on an hourly basis.

In general, the regular hourly rate of pay is determined by dividing the total compensation received by the employee (except statutory exclusions) in any workweek by the total number of hours actually worked in that workweek for which such compensation was paid. So for example, assume an employee is paid a salary of $400 for a 40 hour week. The employee's regular rate is $10 ($400 divided by 40 hours). If in a given week the employee works 46 hours, the employee will be entitled to a total compensation of $490 (40 hours at $10 plus 6 hours at $15).

Where the employee receives other compensation in addition to the hourly rate or salary, that additional amount should be added to the earnings for the particular workweek and the regular rate calculated accordingly. Thus, if the employer furnishes lodging to his employees in addition to cash wages, the reasonable cost or the fair value of the lodging (per week) must be added to the cash wages before the regular rate is determined.[128]

Similarly, commissions must be included in the regular rate, regardless of whether the commission is the sole source of the employee's compensation or is paid in addition to a guaranteed salary or hourly rate.[129] Commissions will be added to the employee's remuneration for the week in which they are earned. So, if the commission is paid on a weekly basis, it is added to the employee's other earnings for that workweek and the total is divided by the total number of hours worked in the workweek to obtain the employee's regular hourly rate.[130]

For example, assume that the employee described above, in addition to the set salary receives a commission of $80 at the end of the week. The employee's total compensation is now $480. The regular rate is accordingly increased to $12 ($480 divided by 40

---

[127] 29 U.S.C. § 207(a). The Act provides limited exceptions to the general standard of subsection (a).

[128] 29 C.F.R. § 778.116.

[129] Id. § 778.117.

[130] Id. §§ 778.118, 119.

hours). If the employee works 46 hours in the week in which the commission was earned, the employee will be entitled to $588 (40 hours at $12 plus 6 hours at $18).[131]

Not all remuneration is included in the calculation of the regular rate, however. Section 207(e) excludes, for example, sums of money paid as gifts (e.g., Christmas gifts or gifts for other special occasions), vacation and holiday pay, payments for insurance benefits and overtime premiums already paid, among others. Notice that by excluding these types of compensation from the kind of payments that are used to calculate the employee's total weekly remuneration, the effect of § 207(e) is to reduce the potential employer's overtime liability since the overtime rate depends on the regular rate, which in turn depends on the total weekly remuneration.

Of the various forms of remuneration that the employer can exclude from the regular rate calculation under § 207(e), only the overtime premiums already paid can be used to reduce any potential overtime pay liability.[132] Thus, the Act prohibits employers from satisfying their overtime pay liability by arguing that they have in effect paid those amounts to employees in the form of vacation pay, or insurance premiums for example. One exception to this rule however, involves public sector employers and the use of compensatory time. Under some specific conditions, § 207(*o*) of the Act allows public employers to provide compensatory time off instead of overtime pay. Private sector employers each year pursue congressional legislation allowing them also to give "comp time" instead of overtime, as in the public sector. They also each year seek legislation allowing longer calculation periods for averaging 40-hour weeks, such as two weeks or a calendar quarter, to avoid overtime pay liability. For example, using a 2-week calculation, an employee who works 50 hours one week and 30 hours the next week would not get time-and-a-half for 10 hours in the 50-hour week).

5.1.2.5 Enforcement Issues

The FLSA authorizes a variety of enforcement actions including actions by the Secretary of Labor, the Department of Justice, and private plaintiffs. Section 216(b) allows employees to bring an action for unpaid minimum wages and overtime compensation in state or federal court. The section also allows employees to recover liquidated damages in an amount equal to the unpaid compensation.

---

[131] Commissions not paid on a weekly basis involve a more difficult computation, requiring apportioning the commission to the workweek in which it was earned. Id. at §§ 778.119–122.

[132] 29 U.S.C. § 207(h).

Section 216(b) also provides for a collective action procedure. A collective action is an action to recover unpaid minimum wages or overtime compensation "by any one or more employees for and in behalf of himself or themselves and other employees similarly situated."[133] The collective action procedure makes it possible to pursue actions that might not be economically viable if pursued by a single individual. A § 216(b) collective action requires each participant to affirmatively give consent in writing to join the action and only the opt-in plaintiffs are bound by the results of the litigation.[134]

Private actions in general, and collective actions in particular have become increasingly common in FLSA-related litigation.[135] Accordingly, a variety of issues involving collective actions have received increased attention in recent years. One such issue involves the definition of "similarly situated" under Section 216(b). In deciding whether potential members of the class are similarly situated, courts usually follow a two-step approach. At the first step (the "notice stage") the court seeks to determine if certification is proper for purposes of sending notice of the action to potential collective action members.[136] In making this determination, courts apply a fairly lenient standard requiring only a showing that the "putative class members were together the victims of a single decision, policy or plan."[137]

If the court decides in favor of certification for notice purposes, discovery follows. After discovery, and usually prompted by a motion to decertify, the court revisits the certification issue. At this step, courts follow a stricter standard, and consider a number of factors such as: the difference in treatment and employment settings among the putative class members; whether different defenses are available to the defendant for different employees; and fairness and procedural considerations.[138] The use of these factors indicates that at this stage "the similarities necessary to maintain a collective action . . . must extend beyond the mere facts of job duties and pay provisions."[139] More recently, and in light of the U.S. Supreme Court decision in *Wal-Mart Stores, Inc. v. Dukes*,[140] some courts have heightened the standard applicable in the second step of the certification process by

---

133 Id. § 216(b).

134 Id.

135 Les A, Schneider & Larry Stine, Wage and Hour Law: Compliance and Practice § 20:1 (2016).

136 Thiessen v. Ge. Elec. Capital Corp., 267 F.3d 1095 (10th Cir. 2001).

137 Id. at 1102–05.

138 Id. at 1103.

139 Anderson v. Cagle's Inc., 488 F.3d 945 (11th Cir. 2007).

140 564 U.S. 338 (2011).

requiring a showing of more than "all potential class members work for the same company, are eligible for the same remedies, or even suffered a violation of the same provision of law . . . ."[141]

Although as described earlier, the FLSA applies to public employees, the Supreme Court has ruled that the Eleventh Amendment to the United States Constitution, bars FLSA actions for damages by state employees against the state.[142] Actions for damages by employees of state political subdivisions (e.g., school districts) are not barred by the Eleventh Amendment.[143] Similarly, although states may not be sued by employees for alleged FLSA violations, they may be sued on behalf of employees by the Secretary of Labor.[144]

Section 215(a)(3) includes an anti-retaliation provision protecting employees against retaliation where the employee has commenced or cause to commence a proceeding under the Act or where the employee has testified in such a proceeding. In *Kasten v. St. Gobain Performance Plastics Corporation*, the Supreme Court held that oral complaints are protected by the provision.[145] The Court did not address the question of whether a complaint to the employer is sufficient to trigger anti-retaliation protection,[146] The appellate courts that have considered the issue are in agreement such complaints are protected.[147] To be protected, the complaint must be sufficient to put a reasonable employer on notice that the employee is asserting a violation of FLSA rights.[148]

The Secretary of Labor is permitted to bring three different types of actions. First, under § 216(c), the Secretary may sue on behalf of affected employees. As in the case of actions brought by individual employees, damages may include unpaid minimum wage and overtime pay, as well as an equal amount in liquidated damages. Second, the Secretary may pursue injunctive relief for minimum wage, overtime and child labor violations under § 217. Recordkeeping violations are also brought under this latter section.[149] Third, under § 216(e), the Secretary is allowed to pursue civil penalties of up to $1,000 for repeated and willful violations of the minimum wage and overtime provisions, and up to $11,000 for child labor violations. An

[141] Ealy v. Pinkerton Government Services, Inc., 514 Fed. Appx. 299 (4th Cir. 2013). See also Schneider & Stine, supra note 135, at § 20:10.

[142] See Alden v. Maine, 527 U.S. 706, 712 (1999).

[143] Id. at 756.

[144] Id.

[145] 563 U.S. 1, 17 (2011).

[146] Id. at 16–17.

[147] Greathouse v. JHS Sec. Inc., 784 F.3d 105, 110 n.8 (2d Cir. 2015).

[148] 563 U.S. at 14.

[149] Record keeping violations can be prosecuted only in conjunction with other violations.

employee may not bring suit if he or she has accepted back wages under the supervision of the Wage and Hour Division of the Department of Labor or if the Secretary of Labor has already filed suit to recover the wages.

Section 216(a) allows the Department of Justice to prosecute willful violations. Sanctions under § 216(a) include a maximum fine of $11,000 and/or imprisonment for up to six months (the latter only in the case of repeated violations).

The Portal to Portal Act (the 1947 amendments to the FLSA) provides employers with various defenses to FLSA violations. First, the amendments establish a two-year statute of limitations for non-willful violations and a three-year period for willful violations.[150] Because FLSA violations normally involve continuing violations, the major effect of the statute of limitations is to limit the amount of damages. Thus, establishing the presence of a willful violation is of great importance for it will increase the amount of recovery. An FLSA violation will be considered willful where "the employer either knew or showed reckless disregard for the matter of whether its conduct was prohibited by the statute."[151]

The Portal to Portal Act also provides for a complete defense for a violation by the employer where the employer can show that the violation was "in good faith in conformity with and in reliance of any written administrative regulation, order, ruling, approval, or interpretation" of FLSA's enforcing body.[152] Under § 260, where the employer shows that the violation "was in good faith and that he had reasonable grounds for believing that his act or omission was not a violation", the court may reduce or eliminate liquidated damages.[153]

5.1.3 Living Wage Ordinances

Despite the various amendments Congress has enacted over the years increasing the minimum wage, the real value of the minimum wage, when adjusted for inflation, has actually dropped since the 1970s. To counter this continuing decline in value, workers' advocacy groups have exerted pressure on cities and municipalities to enact so-called "living wage" ordinances.[154]

---

[150] 29 U.S.C. § 255(a).

[151] See McLaughlin v. Richland Shoe Co., 486 U.S. 128, 133 (1988).

[152] 29 U.S.C. § 259(a).

[153] Id. § 260.

[154] Mark Brenner and Stephanie Luce, Living Wage Laws in Practice: The Boston, New Haven, and Hartford Experiences, Amherst MA: Political Economy Research Institute (2005).

A living wage ordinance requires employers to pay wages that are above federal or state minimum wage levels.[155] The ordinances usually apply only to workers employed by businesses that have a contract with a city or county government or that receive economic development subsidies from the local governmental unit. Usually, the ordinance will require the enacting body to pay a living wage to its employees also. Some living wage ordinances are not limited to employers contracting with or receiving aid from the local government entity, but require compliance with the living wage by all private employers within the municipality limits. For example, the city of Santa Fe's living wage ordinance applies to any private business which is required to have a business license or business registration.[156]

Although the ordinances vary significantly, most living wage ordinances set the wage at the level required for a full-time worker to support a family above the federal poverty line. Some ordinances also require the covered employers to provide certain benefits, such as health insurance and paid vacation.[157]

Proponents of living wage ordinances argue that their efforts are necessary to address the failure of Congress to reverse the loss in value of the national minimum wage. They also argue that city and county governments should not contract with or subsidize employers who pay poverty-level wages. Further, by enacting living wage legislation, local governments prevent the race to the bottom, which results from business shopping around for the cheapest labor across different municipalities.

Opponents argue that as with the minimum wage, living wage laws are likely to hurt those living at or near poverty through resulting job losses and the shifting of entry-level jobs from lower-skilled workers to higher-skilled workers. They also argue that municipalities adopting living wage ordinances risk the loss of business, as employers might decide to relocate to avoid the increased labor costs.

---

[155] See Scott L. Cummings, Law in the Labor Movement's Challenge to Wal-Mart: A Case Study of the Inglewood Site Fight, 95 Cal. L. Rev. 1927 (2007); Clayton P. Gillette, Local Redistribution, Living Wage Ordinances and Judicial Intervention, 101 N.W. U. L. Rev. 1057 (2007).

[156] Santa Fe, N.M., Wage Requirements: Minimum Wage Payment Requirements, ch. XXVIII, 1.5.

[157] To the extent that living wage ordinances require employers to provide benefits, such as health insurance, they might be preempted by the Employee Retirement and Income Security Act of 1971 (ERISA). For a detailed discussion of ERISA, see infra Section 5.3.

Living wage ordinances have been challenged on a variety of grounds. For example, in *RUI One Corporation v. City of Berkeley*,[158] the Ninth Circuit U.S. Court of Appeals considered and rejected a variety of constitutional challenges raised against the City of Berkeley's living wage ordinance.[159] The court found that the ordinance did not violate the Contract Clause of the United States Constitution.[160] The plaintiff had argued that the ordinance interfered with the contract (a lease agreement) it had with the city of Berkeley. The court found that since the lease agreement did not involve the payment of wages or provision of employment benefits, the ordinance (which dealt with those terms) did not interfere with the lease agreement.[161] The court also rejected an equal protection challenge on the basis that the city had identified a rational basis for its decision to expand coverage to only a handful of employers.[162] Finally, the court rejected the federal and constitutional due process challenges raised by the plaintiff. The plaintiff argued that by allowing employees in bona fide collective bargaining agreements to opt out of the ordinance, the city had unconstitutionally delegated its legislative power to the labor unions involved in the negotiation of these contracts. In rejecting this argument, the court noted that the provision allowing employees bargaining collectively to opt out of the provisions of the ordinance was not a delegation of legislative power at all.[163]

5.1.4 State Wage Payments Laws

In addition to minimum wage laws at the state level and the more recent efforts by local governments to enact living wage ordinances, most states have enacted laws regulating the manner and timing of the distribution of wages, as well as laws protecting employees against the garnishment of wages.

Most wage laws regulate both the form and timing of wage payments, by requiring employers to pay wages in cash or negotiable instrument,[164] and by requiring that payments be made on a regular basis (e.g., monthly).[165]

---

158 371 F.3d 1137 (9th Cir. 2004).

159 Berkeley Ordinance No. 6548–N.S.

160 United States Const. art. I, 10, cl.1.

161 RUI One Corporation, 371 F.3d at 1148.

162 Id. at 1156.

163 Id. at 1156–57.

164 See e.g., Mich. Comp. Laws Ann. 408.476 (requiring that wages be paid in one of the following: "(1) Payment in United States currency; (2) Payment by a negotiable check or draft payable on presentation . . .; (3) Direct deposit or electronic transfer . . .; (4) Issuance of a payroll debit card to the employee . . .").

165 See, e.g., Mass. Gen. Laws Ann. Ch. 149, 148.

Some states also restrict the type of deductions and withholdings that the employer can excise on the employees' pay, limiting such deductions and withholdings to those permitted by law or deductions to which the employee has agreed. Some states, however, prevent certain deductions even where the employee has agreed to them. For example, Maine's wage law prohibits agreements between employers and employees deducting amounts intended to pay for damages caused by the employee to the employer's property.[166]

Finally, most state wage payments laws provide protections regarding the distribution of wages following separation from employment. While the requirements vary significantly from state to state, the general intent of these laws is to assure that employees will receive the wages to which they are entitled soon after the termination of the employment relationship.

One issue that has generated some litigation in this area is that of deciding whether forms of compensation other than wages, as for example vacation pay, constitute wages within the statutory definition. In general, wage payment laws tend to broadly define wages, allowing most courts to include vacation pay in the definition of wages. For example, in *Hartman v. Freedman*,[167] the state statute defined wages as including all amounts for labor or service performed by an employee, but excluded deferred compensation, such as profit-sharing plans.[168] In an action by an ex-employee to recover vacation pay under the state wage payment law, the court found that vacation pay fell under the definition of wages and thus was recoverable. The court noted that vacation pay is considered taxable income and also considered compensation in calculating unemployment benefits.

Employees have been unable to recover vacation pay, however, where their employment contracts require them to provide notice of their intent to quit their jobs, and they have failed to do so. In those cases, courts have held that the employee's failure to give proper notice prevents the employee from recovering unused vacation time as unpaid wages.[169]

5.1.5 Equal Pay Act

The Equal Pay Act of 1963 (EPA) was enacted by Congress as an amendment to the FLSA.[170] Although involving many of the same

---

[166] 26 Me. Rev. Stat. Ann. 626.

[167] 197 Colo. 275, 591 P.2d 1318 (1979).

[168] Id. at 279, 591 P.2d at 1321.

[169] See, e.g., Sweet v. Stormont Vail Regional Medical Center, 231 Kan. 604, 647 P.2d 1274 (1982).

[170] 29 U.S.C. § 206(d).

issues normally discussed in the context of employment discrimination law—a subject beyond the scope of this book—the provisions of the EPA are relevant to the discussion on wage protections.

5.1.5.1 Overview

Since the Equal Pay Act is a part of the FLSA, it has the same basic coverage as the FLSA with two principal exceptions. First, the EPA applies to executive, administrative, and professional employees who are normally exempted from the FLSA. Second, unlike the FLSA, which makes certain allowances for state and local employees with regard to overtime compensation, the EPA treats state and local governments as any other employer. The enforcement and remedial features of the EPA are the same as those of the FLSA, except that since 1979 the Equal Employment Opportunity Commission (EEOC), rather than the Department of Labor, has been in charge of the administration and enforcement of the law.

Section 206(d)(1) requires that men and women working in the same establishment receive equal pay for "equal work," unless different wages are justified on the basis of a seniority system, a merit system, a system which measures earnings by quantity or quality of production, or any factor other than sex. Specifically, the section provides that:

> No employer having employees subject to any provisions of this section shall discriminate, within any establishment in which such employees are employed, between employees on the basis of sex by paying wages to employees in such establishment at a rate less than the rate at which he pays wages to employees of the opposite sex in such establishment for equal work on jobs the performance of which requires equal skill, effort, and responsibility, and which are performed under similar working conditions, except where such payment is made pursuant to (i) a seniority system; (ii) a merit system; (iii) a system which measures earnings by quantity or quality of production; or (iv) a differential based on any other factor other than sex.[171]

The mandate of the EPA is fairly narrow in that it only deals with disparities in pay and it requires that the jobs being compared are equal (as defined below, infra). Other forms of sex discrimination, as for example, segregated job assignments or discrimination against women in unequal jobs, are not covered by the EPA, although they

---

[171] Id.

may be actionable under other anti-discrimination laws. In fact, to a large extent, claims regarding pay discrimination are commonly raised in the context of Title VII claims.

5.1.5.2 Elements of a Violation

To establish a prima facie case under the EPA the plaintiff must demonstrate that she and a member of the opposite sex: (1) worked in the same establishment; (2) received unequal wages; (3) for work that was equal in terms of skill, effort, and responsibility; and (4) that was performed under similar working conditions. The plaintiff has the burden of persuasion in all of these elements. The first two elements are fairly simple to establish, while the last two have generated most of the existing litigation.

First, the EPA only prohibits wage differentials between men and women who work in the same establishment. The term establishment "refers to a distinct physical place of business rather than to an entire business or 'enterprise' which may include several separate places of business."[172] Thus, to establish an EPA violation, it must be established that a wage differential exists between a man and a woman located in the same physical place of employment, not only that they are employed by the same employer.[173]

Second, the plaintiff must establish that the wages paid to employees of one sex are less than the wages paid to the employees of the opposite sex. For purposes of the EPA, wages are defined broadly as including "all payments made to [or on behalf of] an employee as remuneration for employment."[174] Thus, contrary to the way the regular rate is calculated for minimum wage purposes, no deductions are made for items like vacation and holiday pay.

The third element requires the plaintiff to prove that the jobs for which different wages are being paid are "equal." In particular, the EPA prohibits discrimination by employers on the basis of sex in the wages paid for jobs that require "equal skill, effort and responsibility. . . ."[175] Courts interpreting this section have interpreted the "equal work" language to require the jobs to be "substantially equal" not necessarily identical.[176] "Substantially

---

[172] 29 C.F.R. § 1620.9.

[173] Two or more physical locations might be treated as a single establishment where they share a central administration that makes the relevant employment decisions, and where the employees frequently interchange work and perform similar duties. Id. See e.g., Collins v. Dollar Tree Stores, 788 F. Supp. 2d 1328 (N.D. Alabama 2011).

[174] 29 C.F.R. § 1620.10.

[175] 29 U.S.C. § 206(d).

[176] See, e.g., Shultz v. Wheaton Glass Co., 421 F.2d 259 (3d Cir. 1970); Riser v. QEP Energy, 776 F.3d 1191 (10th Cir. 2015).

equal" jobs are those which share some basic elements, even if they are different at the margins.[177]

The determination of whether jobs are substantially equal depends on the actual content of the job—not mere job descriptions or titles.[178] Instead, substantial equality is evaluated in terms of the statutory criteria of skill, effort, and responsibility. In determining whether the two jobs required equal skill, factors such as "experience, training, education, and ability" are to be considered.[179] "Effort" relates to "the measurement of the physical or mental exertion needed for the performance of a job" and it "encompasses the total requirements of a job."[180] Finally, "responsibility" focuses on the degree of accountability associated with the job, particularly the level of obligation.[181]

The last element requires the plaintiff to establish that the jobs were being performed under similar conditions. According to the EEOC regulations, in determining whether the jobs involved similar working conditions, the surroundings (e.g., the work environment) and hazards (e.g., physical dangers) of the two jobs are relevant considerations.[182]

5.1.5.3 Employer's Defenses

Once the plaintiff establishes the elements of the violation, the burden then shifts to the employer to demonstrate the applicability of one of four affirmative defenses. To avoid liability, the employer must show that the unequal pay resulted from one of the following: a seniority system; a merit system; a system that measures earnings by quantity or quality of production (i.e., an incentive system); or from any other factor other than sex.

A seniority system seeks to reward employees on the basis of the length of their employment. A merit system rewards exceptional job

---

177 See, e.g., Brobst v. Columbus Services Intern., 761 F.2d 148, 150 (3d Cir. 1985). It is important to distinguish the "equal work" requirement under the EPA from the "comparable worth" argument that has been raised in the context of sex discrimination claims under Title VII. The basic idea behind the comparable worth argument is that it should be discriminatory to pay different wages to individuals performing jobs which are "comparable" or similar in value to the employer. The Equal Employment Opportunity Commission has rejected the comparable worth argument. Several circuits have also rejected sex discrimination in pay claims based on the comparable worth concept. See, e.g., AFSCME v. State of Washington, 770 F.2d 1401 (9th Cir. 1985).

178 EEOC v. Cent. Kan. Med. Ctr., 705 F.2d 1270, 1273 (10th Cir.1983), overruled on other grounds by McLaughlin v. Richland Shoe Co., 486 U.S. 128, 133 n. 10, 108 S.Ct. 1677, 100 L.Ed.2d 115 (1988).

179 29 C.F.R. § 1620.15(a).

180 Id. § 1620.16(a).

181 Id. § 1620.17(a).

182 Id. § 1620.18(a).

performance. An incentive system bases compensation decisions on the quality or quantity of production.[183]

To be considered a bona fide system, the specific system must not have been adopted with discriminatory intent; it must be based on predetermined criteria; it must have been communicated to employees; and it must have been applied consistently and even-handedly to employees of both sexes. A bona fide merit system must involve a structured procedure, including evaluations at regular intervals according to predetermined criteria.[184] The criteria used in evaluating performance in a merit system can be objective (e.g., a test) or subjective (e.g., a supervisory rating). Where the latter is used, the employer must show that the system was consistently applied.[185]

In addition to the three defenses involving the existence of a system, the EPA permits a compensation differential based on a factor other than sex. The statutory language indicates that the employer must establish that any compensation disparity is explained by a consistently applied sex-neutral factor. While the EEOC and several courts of appeals take the position that the "factor other than sex" must be related to job requirements,[186] some courts have read the provision literally, permitting the employer to raise *any* factor even if not job related.[187]

Over the years, employers have raised as a defense a wide variety of factors other than sex including the education, training, ability and skill of the individuals;[188] the need for a shift differential;[189] and the fact that the individuals work in departments that differ in the amount of revenue they generate.[190] In general the courts have been skeptical of many of these factors, since they might tend to mask the very gender bias that the EPA seeks to eliminate.

---

183 EEOC Compliance Manual Section 10.IV.F.1.

184 See e.g., Cooke v. U.S. 85 Fed. Cl. 325 (Ct. Fed. Claims 2008).

185 Id.

186 For example, the Second, Sixth, Ninth, and Eleventh Circuits have taken a position consistent with that of the EEOC. See Aldrich v. Randolph Cent. Sch. Dist., 963 F.2d 520, 528 (2d Cir.1992); EEOC v. J.C. Penney Co., 843 F.2d 249, 252 (6th Cir. 1988); Kouba v. Allstate Ins. Co., 691 F.2d 873, 876 (9th Cir. 1982); Glenn v. General Motors Corp., 841 F.2d 1567, 1571 (11th Cir. 1988).

187 See Fallon v. State of Ill., 882 F.2d 1206, 1211 (7th Cir. 1989).

188 See, e.g., Tomka v. Seiler Corp., 66 F.3d 1295, 1312 (2d Cir. 1995).

189 See, e.g., Corning Glass Works v. Brennan, 417 U.S. 188 (1974).

190 See, e.g., Ryduchowski v. Port Authority of New York & New Jersey, 203 F. 3d 135 (2nd Cir. 2000).

5.1.5.4 Remedies

The EPA shares the same enforcement provisions as the FLSA. Wages withheld in violation of the EPA "have the status of unpaid minimum wages or unpaid overtime compensation under the FLSA."[191] Accordingly, either the EEOC or the affected individual may bring suit for back pay and an equal amount as liquidated damages. The EEOC may also seek a court injunction to restrain any person from violating the law, including the unlawful withholding by an employer of proper compensation. A two-year statute of limitations applies to the recovery of unpaid wages, except for willful violations, which are subject to a three-year period. Willful violations of the Act may also be prosecuted criminally and the violator fined up to $10,000, with additional violations subject to imprisonment.

The EPA provides specifically that where a violation has been found, an employer can come into compliance only by raising the wage rate of the lower paid sex.[192] Transferring employees to eliminate the disparity without a wage adjustment is not permitted.

§ 5.2 Family and Medical Leave Act

5.2.1 Overview

There are several federal statutes that grant leave time to employees under various circumstances. Arguably the most important is the Family and Medical Leave Act of 1993 ("FMLA"), which was enacted by Congress to "promote the stability and economic security of families" and to preserve family integrity.[193] It accomplishes these goals by allowing employees to take unpaid, job-protected leave from work in the event of certain circumstances and by prohibiting employers from interfering with the ability of employees to take such leave.

The FMLA applies to all employers employing fifty or more employees during twenty weeks of the current or preceding calendar year, along with public agencies and schools, which are covered regardless of the number of employees.[194] It secures for "eligible" employees of such employers the right to take up to twelve weeks of unpaid leave from work per twelve-month year,[195] with the exception of those caring for military service members with active duty injuries

---

[191] 29 C.F.R. § 1620.33.

[192] 29 U.S.C. § 206(d)(1).

[193] 29 U.S.C. § 2601(b)(1).

[194] 29 C.F.R. § 825.104(a).

[195] The regulations provide several alternative methods for determining the "12-month period" in which the 12 weeks of leave entitlement occurs. 29 C.F.R. § 825.200(e).

or illnesses who get twenty-six weeks of leave.[196] To be eligible, an employee must have worked for the employer at least twelve months (which need not be consecutive), and must have worked for the employer for at least 1250 hours during the preceding twelve-month period.[197] Eligible employees may take FMLA leave in the event of:

(1) the employee's own serious health condition,

(2) the need to care for a spouse, child or parent suffering from a serious health condition,

(3) birth of the employee's child,

(4) adoption of a child or the placement of a child with the employee for foster care or

(5) because of exigencies required by a family member's call to active duty military service.[198]

Employers are permitted to require that a request for FMLA leave related to a serious health condition be "supported by a certification issued by the health care provider."[199] Exigency leaves and leaves to care for service members must also be supported by appropriate documentation.[200]

Several things minimize any potential hardship to the employer for having to provide employees with such leave (in addition to the obvious fact that the leave is unpaid, meaning that employees are unlikely to abuse the ability to take leave). First, if the employee's need for leave is "foreseeable," the employee must provide the employer with at least 30-days notice before the date the leave is to begin.[201] This requirement applies to both leave for childbirth and adoption and leaves resulting from serious health conditions. If, as is likely in the case of leave for serious health conditions, exigencies mandate that the employee needs to leave work with less than 30-days notice, the employee must provide notice as soon as

---

[196] 29 U.S.C. § 2612(a)(4).

[197] 29 C.F.R. § 825.110(a)(2). The regulations provide that the principles established under the Fair Labor Standards Act (FLSA) determine whether an employee has had at least 1250 hours of service during the preceding 12-month period. "The determining factor is the number of hours an employee has worked for the employer within the meaning of the FLSA." 29 C.F.R. § 825–110(c). The employer bears the burden of proving that the employee has not worked the required hours for eligibility for leave. Id.

[198] 29 U.S.C. § 2612(a)(1). Exigencies are defined by regulation and include non-medical needs such as military events, childcare and school activities and financial and legal arrangements. 29 C.F.R. § 825.126.

[199] 29 U.S.C. § 2912(a)(1)(D).

[200] 29 C.F.R. §§ 825.309, 825.310.

[201] 29 C.F.R. § 825.302(a).

practicable.[202] The employee is also bound to make "reasonable effort" to schedule medical treatment so as not to "unduly disrupt" the operations of the workplace.[203]

Second, although the FMLA permits "intermittent leave" in the case of serious health conditions, leave for childbirth or adoption must be taken in a single continuous period, unless the employer agrees otherwise.[204]

Third, where spouses work for the same employer, they are entitled to a single 12-week leave for childbirth, adoption or childcare.[205]

Fourth, although the FMLA generally requires that employees leaving for medical reasons will be restored to their pre-leave job or a job equivalent in responsibility, pay and benefits, the requirement does not operate with respect to certain highly paid employees if denying reinstatement "is necessary to prevent substantial and grievous economic injury to the operations of the employer."[206]

Further, in regards to intermittent leave, employers are offered greater flexibility in terms of placing employees.[207] The regulations issued by the Department of Labor (DOL) provide, for example, that an employer may temporarily transfer an employee taking intermittent leave "to a part-time job with the same hourly rate of pay and benefits, provided the employee is not required to take more leave than is medically necessary."[208] However, the regulations specifically state that such alternative placements may not be intended "to discourage the employee from taking leave or otherwise work a hardship on the employee."[209] Thus, for example, the regulations make clear that it would not be permissible to assign a white collar employee to perform the work of a laborer or to reassign a day shift worker to work the graveyard shift.[210] When the leave is no longer needed the employee must be returned to the previous job or an equivalent position.[211]

---

[202] Id.

[203] 29 C.F.R. § 825.302(e).

[204] 29 C.F.R. § 825.203(b).

[205] 29 U.S.C. § 2612(f).

[206] 29 C.F.R § 825.216(3)(b). The exception applies in the case of an employee who is among the highest paid ten percent of employees working at the same site as the employee. 29 C.F.R. § 825.217(c).

[207] 29 C.F.R. § 825.204(c).

[208] Id.

[209] 29 C.F.R. § 825.204(d).

[210] Id.

[211] 29 C.F.R. § 825.204(e).

Finally, the FMLA allows an employer to require that employees substitute any accrued paid leave that the employer provides for FMLA unpaid leave.[212] The employee can also choose to substitute paid leave.[213] The employer can require that the employee comply with any normal requirements applicable to the paid leave, however, such as notice periods, limitations to full days of leave, or restricting sick leave to the employee's own illness.[214]

One of the most frequent employer complaints regarding the FMLA relates to intermittent leave. Among other things, employers complain that employees often give notice of the need for intermittent leave no more than 24 hours in advance. In 2008, the DOL adopted changes to the FMLA, clarifying that employees must make a "reasonable effort" (not merely an "attempt") to schedule their leave so that it does not unduly disrupt an employer's operation.[215]

Although FMLA leave is unpaid, employers must continue to provide group health benefits to employees while they are on leave.[216] This creates a practical issue regarding collection of employee contributions toward health care, which are typically deducted from employees' paychecks. The regulations provide a variety of methods through which the employer may collect employee payments, but prohibit the employer from requiring prepayment before leave or charging higher premiums.[217] The FMLA allows an employer to recoup its payments for such insurance coverage from employees who do not return to work after leave, unless the employee is unable to do so for reasons beyond her control.[218]

The FMLA authorizes actions by the Secretary of Labor to enforce the statute.[219] It also permits employees to bring civil actions to enforce their rights under the statute, although an individual may not sue for the same relief sought by the Secretary of Labor.[220] In the case of private suits, the statute allows employees to recover damages for lost wages and benefits and other monetary loss suffered as a direct result of the FMLA violation (such as, for example, the cost of providing care[221]), as well as equitable remedies, including

212 29 C.F.R. § 825.207(a).

213 Id.

214 Id.

215 29 C.F.R. § 825.203.

216 29 C.F.R § 825.209(a).

217 29 C.F.R. § 825.210.

218 29 U.S.C. § 2614(c)(2).

219 29 U.S.C. § 2617(b).

220 29 U.S.C. § 2617(a).

221 The maximum limit on the recovery of monetary losses is the "amount equal to 12 weeks of wages or salary for the employee." 29 U.S.C. § 2617(a)(1)(A)(II).

reinstatement. The FMLA allows for an equal amount in liquidated damages unless it can be shown that "the act or omission which violated [the Act] was in good faith and that the employer had reasonable grounds for believing that the act or omission was not a violation."[222] The statute of limitations for actions brought under the FMLA is two years in the case of non-willful violations and three years in the case of willful violations.[223] Jury trials are permitted in FMLA actions except for claims seeking reinstatement or promotion, which must be heard by a judge.[224]

While the FMLA applies to public agencies, private suits for damages against the states have been challenged as barred by Eleventh Amendment immunity. In *Nevada Department of Human Resources v. Hibbs*, the Supreme Court found that in enacting the caregiving provisions of the statute, Congress constitutionally abrogated the states' immunity pursuant to Section 5 of the Fourteenth Amendment.[225] The Court found that Congress relied on evidence of gender discrimination by the states in providing leave benefits.[226] With respect to the self-care provisions of the statute, however, the Court held that Congress did not validly abrogate state immunity because there was no Congressional finding of unconstitutional conduct by the states motivating the provision of leave for the employee's own illness.[227]

A number of states have adopted statutes that provide more generous leave than the FMLA, expanding either the amount of unpaid leave, the coverage of the statute, or the circumstances under which leave may be taken.[228] In addition, some states provide for paid leave.[229] Five states have public temporary disability benefit

---

222 29 U.S.C. § 2617(a)(1)(A)(iii).

223 29 U.S.C. § 2617(c)(1)(2). In the context of the FLSA, the Supreme Court has said that "willful" requires more than mere negligence; conduct is willful if "the employer either knew or showed reckless disregard for the matter of whether its conduct was prohibited by the statute." McLaughlin v. Richland Shoe Co., 486 U.S. 128, 133 (1988).

224 Id.

225 538 U.S. 721 (2003).

226 Id. at 730–35.

227 Coleman v. Court of Appeals of Maryland, 132 S. Ct. 1327 (2012).

228 See, e.g., Or. Rev. Stat. Ann. § 659A.153 (covering employees of employers with 25 or more employees); R.I. Gen. Laws §§ 28–48–2; 28–28–12 (13 weeks leave for FMLA purposes in a two-year period and additional leave for school conferences or other school activities of children); Tennessee § 4–21–408 (4 months unpaid leave for birth or adoption of a child if employer has 100 or more employees); Wash. Rev. Code Ann. § 49.78.020(7) (defining family member to include domestic partner).

229 Cal. Unemp. Ins. Code § 3301 (providing up to six weeks paid leave to care for an ill family member or a child after birth or adoption); Oh. Stat. § 124.136(B) (up to four weeks paid parental leave for full-time workers and a prorated amount of paid leave for part-time workers).

programs for employees[230] and states and localities are increasingly enacting requirements for paid sick leave which cover even minor illnesses not included in the FMLA.[231] The FMLA specifically states that it does not supersede any state or local law providing "greater family or medical leave rights."[232] In addition to state and local paid leave requirements, Executive Order 13706, issued in 2015 and effective in 2017 provides that federal agencies should require federal contractors to provide at least one hour of paid sick leave for every thirty hours worked.[233]

5.2.2 Typically Litigated Issues

To bring a successful claim under the FMLA, an employee must show that: (1) she engaged in conduct protected by the FMLA; (2) the employer was aware of this exercise; (3) the employer took an employment action adverse to the employee; and (4) there was a causal connection between the protected activity and the adverse employment action. In terms of the third element, an employee bringing suit under the FMLA is typically alleging either that the employer interfered with the employee's rights under the statute or that the employer retaliated against the employee for exercising her rights under the statute. Demonstrating retaliation requires a showing that either the employee was treated less favorably than an employee who had not requested FMLA leave or that the adverse decision was made because of the requested leave. An employer's subjective intent is not relevant to a claim of interference, but is very much relevant when the claim is retaliation. An employee may claim both interference and retaliation based on the same conduct.[234]

Most cases arising under the FMLA have revolved around three general areas. First, disputes arise as to whether the health condition which gives raise to the FMLA claim meets the standard of "serious." Second, parties dispute the adequacy of an employer's notice of FMLA rights, or notice provided by an employee in an attempt to invoke FMLA coverage. Finally, employees who return to work often

---

230 John G. Kilgour, California's State Disability and Paid Family Leave Program With a Review of Other State Actions, 43 Comp. & Benefits Rev. 282, 282 (2011) (describing programs of California, Hawaii, New Jersey, New York, and Rhode Island).

231 National Partnership for Women and Families, Interactive Map: Paid Sick Days Campaigns, Statistics and Stories, http://paidsickdays.org/?referrer=http://www.nationalpartnership.org/issues/work-family/paid-sick-days.html?referrer=http://www.nationalpartnership.org/issues/work-family/family-friendly-america/oregon.html.

232 29 U.S.C. § 2651(b).

233 See Executive Order 13706; 29 C.F.R. §§ 13.1–13.58 (implementing regulations).

234 See Goelzer v. Sheboygan County, 604 F.3d 987 (7th Cir. 2010) (alleging termination was to interfere with the right to reinstatement after leave and retaliation for taking leave).

file claims stating that they did not return to the same or an equivalent position or that the employer took some other form of retaliatory action. The DOL has provided specific guidelines for most areas of dispute and the federal courts have offered some further examination of these three areas.

5.2.2.1 What Is a Serious Health Condition?

As interpreted by the Department of Labor, a "serious health condition" for purposes of the FMLA involves inpatient care or continuing treatment by a health care provider.[235] Continuing care must include incapacity (defined as an "inability to work, attend school or perform other regular daily activities") of more than three full consecutive days and subsequent treatment for the same condition.[236] While seemingly straightforward, the plain language of the text has been examined by courts on a number of occasions.

Of the challenges brought based on statutory language, issues dealing with "continuing treatment" have proved particularly irksome. The FMLA was not designed to cover non-serious ailments. However, courts have found that employees who have sought the aid of a physician twice in a short period of time meet the Act's plain language and DOL guidelines.[237] This is the case even if the ailment in question would not commonly constitute a serious condition. For example, In *Miller v. AT & T*,[238] a federal district court held that an employee with the flu qualified for FMLA leave because the employee met the statute's definitional requirements. The existence of a physician's certification stating that the condition in question is chronic will greatly assist a determination that the condition qualifies as a serious health condition.

There are, however, limits to how far the term "serious" can be stretched. The regulations state that ailments such as the common cold, flu, upset stomach, and routine dental problems do not typically qualify as serious health conditions, absent complications.[239] By and large, courts have followed the regulations, denying FMLA coverage for conditions such as routine dental care and regular chiropractic adjustments.[240] Courts have also held that acute conditions such as

---

235 29 C.F.R. § 825.113(a).

236 29 C.F.R. §§ 825.113(b); 825.115(a).

237 See, e.g., Thorson v. Gemini, Inc., 205 F.3d 370 (8th Cir. 2000); Municipality of Anchorage v. Gregg, 101 P.3d 181, 190–91 (Alaska 2004).

238 60 F.Supp.2d 574 (S.D. W.Va. 1999).

239 29 C.F.R. § 825.113(d).

240 See, e.g., Godwin v. Rheem Mfg. Co., 15 F.Supp.2d 1197 (M.D. Ala. 1998); Bond v. Abbott Labs., 7 F.Supp.2d 967 (N.D. Ohio 1998).

poison ivy[241] and hematochezia (passage of bloody stool)[242] do not qualify as serious medical conditions under the Act. Pregnancy itself is not per se a serious health condition, although the DOL regulations make clear that it may become so if it produces a period of incapacity or otherwise requires care.[243] Courts have found pregnancy to constitute a serious health condition where work would present "an unacceptable risk to the pregnancy."[244]

Where the employee does not satisfy the requirements of the regulations, courts have denied coverage. For example, in *Johnson v. Wheeling Mach. Prod.*, the court found that high blood pressure was not a serious health condition because it did not require two physician's visits within a thirty day period nor did any physician supervise or require supervision of his use of the prescribed medication.[245]

When considering whether an absence is due to a serious health condition, a physician's certification often provides decisive evidence. As already noted, employers may require that a request for FMLA leave be supported by a health care provider's certification.[246] The physician's certification may establish that a condition is serious.[247] If an employee's physician fails to classify a condition as one that necessitates missing work, or if an employee takes leave for a period exceeding the amount of time delineated by her physician, then FMLA coverage may be denied by the court.[248]

The foregoing suggests that when assessing whether a medical condition satisfies the FMLA's seriousness prong there will be a three-stage evaluative process. As a rule of thumb, DOL determinations are good guideposts. In the eyes of the courts, the plain language of the statute is even better. For employers evaluating an employee's condition, however, relying on the certification provided by a medical doctor is often the best way to determine whether the FMLA provisions apply.

---

241 Godwin v. Rheem Mfg. Co., 15 F.Supp.2d 1197 (M.D. Ala. 1998).

242 Bauer v. Varity Dayton-Walther Corp., 118 F.3d 1109 (6th Cir. 1997).

243 29 C.R.F. § 825.120(4).

244 See, e.g., Whitaker v. Bosch Braking Systems Division, 180 F.Supp.2d 922, 927 (W.D. Mich. 2001).

245 779 F.3d 514 (8th Cir. 2015).

246 29 U.S.C. § 2912(a)(1)(D).

247 See Kauffman v. Fed. Exp. Corp., 426 F.3d 880 (7th Cir. 2005) (finding physician's certificate contained sufficient information that employee's bronchitis met the requirements of a serious health condition).

248 See, e.g., Culpepper v. BlueCross BlueShield of Tennessee, Inc., 321 F. App'x 491 (6th Cir. 2009) (unpublished); Harville v. Texas A & M Univ., 833 F. Supp. 2d 645, 658 (S.D. Tex. 2011) (finding "the plaintiff could have been terminated for repeatedly missing work in excess of her medical certification").

5.2.2.2 Notice Questions

The FMLA has notice requirements for both employers and employees. Employers are required to post FMLA information in the worksite and in any existing employee handbook.[249] Once aware of the employee's need for leave, the employer must provide notice of eligibility or ineligibility to the employee within five business days.[250] The employer must notify the employee in writing of rights and responsibilities relating to the FMLA, such as any need for certification and any requirement to make premium payments for continuing health insurance.[251] Finally, the employer must give the employee notice of designation of leave as FMLA leave.[252]

The Supreme Court invalidated a regulation that provided that if the leave was not designated as FMLA leave, it did not count against the employee's entitlement.[253] The Court found the regulation improperly imposed a penalty regardless of whether the employee suffered any prejudice from the failure to designate.[254] In response, the Department of Labor amended the regulations to provide that the employer may be liable for harm the employee suffers from the employer's failure to comply with the notice requirements.[255]

Like employers, employees have statutory notice obligations. The employee must notify the employer that he or she is seeking FMLA leave. An employee must provide notice of a "foreseeable" leave (i.e. pregnancy, adoption or planned surgery) thirty days in advance.[256] Where the need for leave is not foreseeable, the regulations dictate that the employee shall provide such notice as soon as practicable under the circumstances, generally within two days.[257] The employee need not mention the FMLA but is obligated to provide notice that is sufficient to let the employer know that a medical condition is potentially FMLA qualified.[258] The employee

249 29 U.S.C. § 2619(a); 29 C.F.R. 29 § 825.300(a).

250 29 C.F.R. § 825.300(b).

251 29 C.F.R. § 825.300(c).

252 29 C.F.R. § 825.300(d).

253 Ragsdale v. Wolverine World Wide, Inc., 535 U.S. 81 (2002).

254 Id. at 88.

255 29 C.F.R. § 825.300(e).

256 29 U.S.C. § 2612(e).

257 29 C.F.R. § 825.302(a).

258 29 C.F.R. § 825.302(c).

may be required to comply with any employer requirements for leave requests, unless special circumstances justify the failure.[259]

Litigation dealing with notice requirements often hinges on issues of specificity of the employee's notice. If the information offered to an employer about an employee's condition is vague or misleading, an employer's denial of FMLA leave will generally be upheld even if the medical condition in question would otherwise have qualified.[260]

5.2.2.3 Employee's Reinstatement to the Same or Equivalent Position

The FMLA mandates that an employee returning from qualified leave must be reinstated to the same or an equivalent position.[261] However, if the returning employee cannot perform the essential job functions of her former position, then she has no right to restoration to another position.[262]

Reinstatement suits often take the form of retaliation or discrimination claims. When a claim alleges discrimination or retaliation against an employee for exercising FMLA rights, rather than substantive denials of FMLA benefits,[263] courts have applied the *McDonnell Douglas*[264] burden-shifting framework in analyzing the matter. Under the *McDonnell Douglas* framework, an employee carries the initial burden of coming forward with sufficient evidence to establish a prima facie case of discrimination or retaliation. If the employee does so, the burden then shifts to the employer to "articulate some legitimate, nondiscriminatory reason" for its action. If the employer can meet that burden, the burden shifts back to the employee to demonstrate that the reason given by the employer was a pretext for discrimination or retaliation.[265] The prima facie case is based on an employer's negative actions stemming from an

---

259 29 C.F.R. § 302(d). See Srouder v. Dana Light Axle Mfg., 725 F.3d 608 (6th Cir. 2013) (finding termination of employee who failed to call in each day of absence to a specific number as required by employer policy did not violate FMLA).

260 See, e.g., Crux v. Publix Super Markets, Inc., 428 F.3d 1379 (11th Cir. 2005); Satterfield v. Wal-Mart Stores, Inc., 135 F.3d 973 (5th Cir. 1998); Gay v. Gillman Paper Co., 125 F.3d 1432 (11th Cir. 1997).

261 29 C.F.R. § 825.214.

262 29 C.F.R. § 825.216(c).

263 Where the employee's claim is that the employer failed to comply with the substantive leave provisions and not discrimination, courts have suggested that the *McDonnell Douglas* approach is not called for. See Hodgens v. General Dynamics Corp., 144 F.3d 151, 159 (1st Cir. 1998); Diaz v. Fort Wayne Foundry Corp., 131 F.3d 711, 712–713 (7th Cir. 1997).

264 McDonnell Douglas Corporation v. Green, 411 U.S. 792 (1973).

265 See, e.g., Hodgens, 144 F.3d at 160–61; Peters v. Community Action Comm., Inc., 977 F.Supp. 1428 (M.D. Ala. 1997).

employee's accessing or attempting to access rights under the FMLA.[266]

The Supreme Court in *University of Texas Southwestern Medical Center v. Nassar* held that retaliation claims under Title VII require proof that the protected conduct was the but-for cause of the adverse action against the plaintiff.[267] Courts have divided on whether this test applies to retaliation claims under the FMLA with most courts declining to decide the issue.[268]

5.2.3 Policy Considerations

While leave proponents laud the benefits provided by the FMLA, they decry the limitations on coverage and the lack of paid leave.[269] Employees in lower income brackets are less likely to have paid leave, making it difficult for those employees to take leave and continue to support themselves.[270] Reducing the number of employees required for employer coverage and the tenure and work hours requirements for employee coverage would expand the availability of leave.[271] Additionally the amount of leave may be insufficient for employees with some serious health conditions such as cancer. Proponents are advocating for these changes, as well as for state laws with these protections.[272]

From a different perspective, other critics argue that the definition of serious health condition needs to be restricted and the use of intermittent leave for chronic conditions needs to be limited.[273] The Department of Labor updated its regulations in 2008, making a few changes in response to employer concerns about these issues but leaving the regulations relating to serious health conditions and chronic conditions largely unchanged.[274]

---

266 Id.

267 133 S.Ct. 2517 (2013).

268 See Chase v. United States Postal Serv., 149 F. Supp. 3d 195, 207–09 (D. Mass. 2016) (discussing the positions of various courts).

269 See Abt Assocs., Family Medical Leave in 2012: Technical Report I, 21–22,97 (2013), available at http://www.dol.gov/asp/evaluation/fmla/FMLA-2012-Technical-Report.pdf (reporting on survey results indicating that 41% of employees are ineligible for FMLA leave and about one third of employees receive no pay for FMLA leave).

270 Id. at 99, 106.

271 Id. at 146.

272 See National Partnership for Women and Families, Work and Family, http://www.nationalpartnership.org/issues/work-family/.

273 Gerald Mayer, The Family Medical Leave Act: Policy Issues 17 (Congressional Research Service 2013).

274 Guide to the Final FMLA Revised Regulations 25–27 (Thompson 2008).

§ 5.3 Employee Retirement Income Security Act

5.3.1 Overview

People often speak of the "three-legged stool" of retirement income, an image derived from the fact that retirement income consists of three primary sources: employer-sponsored pension plans, Social Security, and private savings. Our focus here is on the regulation of the first of those three sources, employer-sponsored pension plans, which represent an important aspect of retirement security given the reality of low personal savings rates in the United States[275] and increasing uncertainty about the future of Social Security.

The federal Employee Retirement Income Security Act of 1974 (ERISA)[276] is the primary source of regulation of private pension plans in the United States, although it also provides for regulation of non-pension employee benefit plans, such as medical plans.

Pension plans fall into two broad categories: defined benefit plans and defined contribution plans. Defined benefit plans are plans that promise to pay to participants a specified amount each year from the date of retirement until death. Defined contribution plans are defined in terms of contributions rather than benefits. Each participant in a defined contribution plan has an individual account into which is a specified annual contribution is deposited. The most common form of defined contribution plan today is the 401(k) plan, sometimes referred to as a "cash-or-deferred arrangement."

The other category of plans covered by ERISA is employee welfare benefit plans. Welfare benefit plans include plans providing for health, accident, disability or unemployment insurance, as well as other benefits such as vacation, training programs, day-care benefits, scholarship funds, or legal services.

Importantly, the statute does not mandate that employers provide pensions or any other benefits to their employees. The decision whether or not to offer a plan remains a business decision on the part of the employer. Instead, the statute seeks to ensure that employees are not deprived of the benefit that has been promised to them. It does so by imposing on employers a set of minimum design

---

[275] The Employee Benefits Research Institute 2008 Retirement Confidence Survey reports that "[w]orkers are more likely to save in a tax-qualified retirement plan at work than they are on their own." Employee Benefits Research Institute, 2008 Retirement Confidence Survey, EBRI Issue Brief, Apr. 2008, at p.19.

[276] ERISA is codified at 29 U.S.C. § 1001 et seq. However, most people who work with ERISA refer to ERISA statutory sections, rather than using the U.S.C. section numbers. Thus, all footnote and text references in this section are to ERISA section numbers.

features that must be contained in pension plans, by mandating specified reporting and disclosure with respect to all plans covered by ERISA, and by subjecting those who deal with employee benefit plans and plan assets to high fiduciary standards. It also establishes a system of pension insurance for certain pension plans.

The decision to provide retirement security through a voluntary, employer-based system has consequences. First, it means that many Americans will have no plan coverage, either because they are not employed or because their employer does not sponsor a plan. The tax-driven nature of pension plans also means that those employers least likely to offer plans are those whose workers are less well-paid (making them less sensitive to tax implications) and therefore least likely to have adequate personal savings to provide for their retirement income needs. Second, the voluntary nature of the system inevitably affects discussions about proposals to amend ERISA in ways to make it more protective of plan participants. Always in the background is the argument that employers will cease providing plans if regulation becomes too restrictive.

5.3.1.1 Coverage of ERISA

As a general matter, ERISA regulates employee benefit plans provided by *private* employers for their employees. That is, it does not regulate plans established by the United States or by any state or local government. Employee benefit plans of state and local governmental entities are regulated by state and local law and sometimes by state constitutions, and the level of protection provided to employees covered by such plans varies tremendously from state to state. Plans established by churches or church associations for their employees are also exempt from ERISA coverage.[277]

Not all employee benefit plans of private employers are covered by ERISA. Title I of ERISA excludes so-called excess-benefit plans,[278] that is, plans designed to provide benefits to highly-compensated employees in excess of the benefits entitled to favorable tax treatment under the Internal Revenue Code. Additionally, so-called "top-hat" plans are exempt from certain of ERISA's requirements. Top-hat plans are plans that are "unfunded and maintained by an employer primarily for the purpose of providing deferred compensation for a select group of management or highly

---

[277] ERISA § 4(b)(2). In *Advocate Health Care Network v. Stapleton*, the Supreme Court held that a pension plan established by the benefits committee of a church-affiliated hospital and maintained by an organization whose principal purpose was to maintain a plan for employees of a church or church-affiliated organization, was exempt. 137 S.Ct. 1652 (2017).

[278] ERISA § 4(b)(5).

compensated employees."[279] The rationale for the exclusion of both excess benefits plans and top-hat plans is that participants of such plans do not need the protection afforded by ERISA.

Additionally, ERISA does not cover plans "maintained outside of the United States primarily for the benefit of persons substantially all of whom are nonresident aliens," or plans that are "maintained solely for the purpose of complying with applicable workmen's compensation laws or unemployment compensation laws or disability insurance laws."[280]

5.3.1.2 What Is a Plan?

ERISA regulates employee benefit *plans*, not employee benefits. Thus, central to understanding the coverage of the statute is to understand the meaning of "plan" for ERISA purposes. Lamentably, the definition section of the statute provides remarkably little help. It defines the term "plan," to mean an employee welfare benefit plan or an employee pension benefit plan,[281] the two basic categories of plans under ERISA. Then, the definitions of both employee pension benefit plan and employee welfare benefit plan begin by defining that plan as a "plan, fund, or program."[282] The statute provides no further explanation of what it means to be a "plan, fund, or program," causing the Supreme Court to complain that the term plan is "defined only tautologically."[283]

Over time, courts have fashioned useful tests for determining whether an employee benefit is provided pursuant to a plan and, therefore, subject to ERISA. The most frequently cited case regarding the definition of plan is the Eleventh Circuit's opinion in *Donovan v. Dillingham*.[284] In *Dillingham*, the Eleventh Circuit announced a four-part test for determining whether a plan under ERISA existed, finding that a plan exists if a reasonable person could ascertain from the surrounding circumstances: (1) the intended benefits; (2) a class of beneficiaries; (3) a source of financing of the benefits; and (4) a procedure for receiving the benefits. The *Dillingham* test has been adopted by all the circuits.

The most important factor in determining the existence of a plan is the fourth of the *Dillingham* factors, the existence of a procedure for receiving benefits. That is because in most cases where the question arises, it will be fairly easy to identify the intended benefits

279 ERISA § 201(2).

280 ERISA §§ 4(b)(3), (4).

281 ERISA § 3(3).

282 ERISA § 3(1), (2).

283 Fort Halifax Packing Co. v. Coyne, 482 U.S. 1, 8 (1987).

284 688 F.2d 1367 (11th Cir. 1982).

and the intended beneficiaries. Moreover, courts have generally not been demanding regarding a source of financing, presuming that if no specific source is stated financing will come from the employer's general revenues. Thus, the crucial factor for courts is that a plan must have "some minimal, on-going 'administrative' scheme or practice."[285]

Although the Supreme Court has articulated no clear guidance as to what constitutes a sufficient ongoing administrative scheme, several circuits have come up with a set of factors helpful in that determination. Illustrative is the approach taken by the Second Circuit, which looks to (1) whether the employer's promise "requires managerial discretion," such that it could not be fulfilled without "ongoing, particularized, administrative" analysis of each case;" (2) whether "a reasonable employee would perceive an ongoing commitment by the employer to provide some employee benefits;" and (3) whether "the employer was required to analyze the circumstances of each employee's [situation] separately in light of certain criteria."[286] Thus, courts refuse to find plans in the case of one-time payments made on the basis of mechanical determinations that require no discretion. Regarding the importance of the exercise of discretion, the First Circuit has explained that "[w]here subjective judgments would call upon the integrity of an employer's administration, the fiduciary duty imposed by ERISA is vital. But where benefit obligations are administered by a mechanical formula that contemplates no exercise of discretion, the need for ERISA's protection is diminished."[287]

Applying this last factor has proven to be particularly difficult in cases involving single, one-time payments. For example, in a case where an employer first announced and then cancelled an offer under which employees would be given 60 days of pay following their termination provided that they stayed at work until the termination date, the court found that the offer did not constitute a plan under ERISA.[288]

Much of the litigation concerning whether a particular benefit arrangement constitutes a plan arises in the context of ERISA preemption litigation, a subject explored in Section 5.3.5.3, infra.

---

285 District of Columbia v. Greater Washington Board of Trade, 506 U.S. 125, 134 n.2 (1992).

286 Kosakow v. New Rochelle Radiology Associates, 274 F.3d 706, 737 (2d Cir. 2001).

287 O'Connor v. Commonwealth Gas Co., 251 F.3d 262, 267 (1st Cir. 2001).

288 James v. Fleet/Norstar Financial Group, 992 F 2d. 463, 466 (2nd Cir. 1993).

5.3.1.3 Who Is an Employee?

Like many employment law statutes, ERISA's protection extends only to employees, and not to workers who are not employees. Again, the statute is of remarkably little assistance here; ERISA defines employee as "any individual employed by an employer."[289]

As already discussed in Section 1.1.1.2.1 of Chapter 1, in *Nationwide Mutual Ins. Co. v. Darden*,[290] the Supreme Court adopted a common law agency test to determine whether a worker is an employee for purposes of ERISA. In so doing, the Court rejected the approach of the Fourth Circuit, which had applied a test that focused on the employee's expectations. The Fourth Circuit had held that a person can be an employee for purposes of ERISA by demonstrating "(1) that he had a reasonable expectation that he would receive benefits, (2) that he relied on this expectation, and (3) that he lacked the economic power to contract out of [the plan's] forfeiture provisions."[291]

Some argue that the broad purposes of ERISA are better served by the reasonable expectation approach to determining employee status rather than by the common law agency approach.[292] Nonetheless, courts consistently apply the *Darden* analysis in determining employee status under ERISA.[293]

On occasion, courts have had to address the question whether an employer can also be an employee for purposes of ERISA. In *Yates v. Hendon*,[294] the Supreme Court held that a working owner of a business could be treated as an employee, so long as "the plan covers one or more employees other than the business owner and his or her spouse."[295] Courts have also held that partners in a partnership may be sufficiently lacking in rights of ownership and control so as to justify their treatment as employees of the partnership for purposes of ERISA.[296]

---

[289] ERISA § 3(6).

[290] 503 U.S. 318 (1992).

[291] Darden v. Nationwide Mutual Ins. Co., 922 F.2d 203, 205 (4th Cir. 1991), rev'd, Nationwide Mutual Ins. Co. v. Darden, 503 U.S. 318 (1992).

[292] For a defense of the Fourth Circuit approach, see Note, Insurance Agents Slip Through the "Good Hands" of ERISA, 28 Wake Forest L. Rev. 1099 (1993).

[293] For examples of cases using the *Darden* analysis to reject employee status for workers, see, e.g., Moore v. Lafayette Life Ins. Co., 458 F.3d 416 (6th Cir. 2006) (licensed insurance agent is not an employee); Resilient Floor Decorators Ins. Fund v. A & M Installations, Inc., 395 F.3d 244 (6th Cir. 2005) (carpet installers are not employees); Capital Cities/ABC, Inc. v. Ratcliff, 141 F.3d 1405 (10th Cir. 1998) (newspaper carriers not employees).

[294] 541 U.S. 1 (2004).

[295] Id. at 2.

[296] See, e.g., Simpson v. Ernst & Young, 100 F.3d 436 (6th Cir. 1996).

5.3.1.4 Reporting and Disclosure Obligations

All pension and welfare benefit plans subject to ERISA must meet the reporting and disclosure requirements set out in §§ 101–111 of the statute. Consistent with the theory underlying federal securities laws, the aim here is to subject plans to public scrutiny to ensure that they are being operated according to law and in the best interests of plan participants. ERISA thus requires that certain specified documents and reports be provided to participants and/or to the Department of Labor.

Most important among the required documents is the summary plan description ("SPD"). Since most participants never read an actual plan document, the SPD is the primary source of information about the plan for participants and beneficiaries. ERISA requires that the SPD contain basic information such as the name and type of the plan, participation requirements, explanation of benefits provided, and source of funding. The SPD must also set out a claims procedure and advise participants of their rights under ERISA.

ERISA requires that the SPD be "written in a manner calculated to be understood by the average plan participant," and that it be "sufficiently accurate and comprehensive to reasonably apprise such participants and beneficiaries of their rights and obligations under the plan,"[297] two requirements that sometimes are in tension. Department of Labor regulations direct plan administrators to "exercise considered judgment and discretion" in drafting an SPD, taking into account factors such as "the level of comprehension and education of typical participants," and to avoid "technical jargon" and "long, complex sentences."[298] Regulations also prohibit an SPD from being drafted in a manner that would have "the effect of misleading, misinforming or failing to inform participants and beneficiaries."[299]

In order to keep the SPD up to date, ERISA also requires that plan administrators prepare a summary of material modifications to reflect changes in plan terms or in any other information provided in the SPD. "Up to date" is something of a misnomer in this context, as the summary of material modifications must be provided within 210 days after the end of the plan year to which a change relates. However, where a change effects a "material reduction in covered services or benefits under a group health plan," notification must be provided within a shorter period of time.[300]

---

[297] ERISA § 102(a).

[298] 29 C.F.R. § 2520.102–2(a).

[299] 29 C.F.R. § 2520.102–2(b).

[300] ERISA § 104(b).

The SPD requirement gives rise to a frequently litigated issue: what happens when the terms of the SPD conflict with actual plan terms? Which document controls? In the words of the Second Circuit, ERISA "contemplates that the summary will be an employee's primary source of information regarding employee benefits, and employees are entitled to rely on the description contained in the summary."[301] Thus, where the description of plan terms contained in the SPD is more generous to participants than the terms of the actual plan, the SPD controls in the case of a conflict.[302] However, where the SPD is less generous to plan participants, courts tend to hold the employer to the terms of the actual plan.[303]

In 2011, the Supreme Court raised some doubts about the predominance that courts have given SPDs. In *CIGNA Corp. v. Amara,*[304] the employer decided to convert its traditional defined benefit plan to a cash-balance plan. The conversion negatively affected a group of employees whose benefits became "frozen" for a period of time following the conversion (the so-called "wear-away" effect). The participants received a newsletter and SPD about the new plan. None of the documents, however, mentioned the negative effects of the conversion. Various participants filed a class action challenging the conversion. The district court found that while the cash-balance plan was lawful, CIGNA, as the plan administrator had violated ERISA's notice and disclosure requirements, and that CIGNA had intentionally misled participants about the negative effects that the changes to the plan would have on their benefits. In deciding the appropriate remedy, the district court found that the SPD was part of the plan and thus the court ordered the plan reformed so as to prevent any of the negative effects of the conversion. The district court reasoned that ERISA Section 502(a)(1)(B) provided the authority to award participants the benefits to which they are entitled under the terms of the newly-reformed plan. Section 502(a)(1)(B) authorizes participants or beneficiaries to bring a civil action to recover benefits due under the terms of a plan, to enforce rights under the terms of a plan, or to clarify rights to future benefits under a plan.[305] The Second Circuit affirmed.

---

[301] Heidgerd v. Olin Corp., 906 F.2d 903, 907–08 (2d Cir. 1990).

[302] See, e.g., Burstein v. Retirement Account Plan for Employees of Allegheny Health Education & Research Foundation, 334 F.3d 365 (3d Cir. 2003); Heidgerd, 906 F.2d 903; Lutheran Medical Center of Omaha v. Contractors, Laborers, Teamsters & Engineers Health & Welfare Plan, 25 F.3d 616 (8th Cir. 1994); Flacche v. Sun Life Assurance Co. of Can., 958 F.2d 730 (6th Cir. 1992).

[303] See, e.g., Shaw v. Connecticut General Life Ins. Co., 353 F.3d 1276 (11th Cir. 2003).

[304] CIGNA Corp. v. Amara, 563 U.S. 421 (2011).

[305] See infra Section 5.3.5.1.

The Supreme Court remanded the case to the district court. While the Court ultimately held that the participants were entitled to a remedy of reformation, that remedy was available to the participants not under Section 501(a)(1)(B), but instead under Section 502(a)(3). That section authorizes participants, beneficiaries or fiduciaries to seek equitable remedies for any act or practice which violates ERISA or plan terms, or to seek other equitable relief to redress such violations or enforce any provisions of ERISA. The Court reasoned that Section 502(a)(1)(B) provides for the enforcement of the "terms of the plan," not the terms of the SPD. SPDs, the Court said, are not terms of the plan. The Court noted that ERISA's requirement that participants be furnished SPDs advising them of their rights and obligations under the plan, suggests that the summaries are not themselves part of the plan.[306] The Court also concluded that a finding that SPDs constitute terms of the plan would obfuscate the roles of plan sponsors (who set the terms of the plan) and plan administrators (who manages the plan) since it would allow plan administrators to set plan terms by including them in the SPDs.[307]

The Court decision regarding SPDs surprised many observers.[308] As noted above, prior to *Amara,* court steadily followed the "SPD prevails" rule.[309] That rule seems to be weakened by the *Amara*'s holding that there cannot be a claim under 502(a)(1)(B) based on terms provided in the SPDs. However, commentators have noted that the effect "might be more procedural than substantive," since "courts can reform a plan to comport with the terms of a contrary SPD as an equitable remedy under § 502(a)(3)," and thus "it appears that participants may continue to receive benefits consistent with their SPD, at least in certain circumstances."[310]

Another important required document is the plan's annual report, which must be filed with the Department of Labor. The annual report contains information with respect to the plan's assets and liabilities, information about transactions with parties in interest to the plan and other potential violations of ERISA and, in the case of plans subject to ERISA's funding requirements, an actuarial statement with information about the plan's actuarial assumptions.[311] Because the report is fairly lengthy and complex,

---

306 563 U.S. at 436.

307 Id. at 437.

308 Caroline Turner English & Nancy S. Heermans, The Supreme Court's Cigna v. Amara Decision: Surprises and Curiosities, Tax Management Compensation Planning Journal, available at https://www.arentfox.com/sites/default/files/English-Heerman-CignavAmara.pdf (2011).

309 Id. at 6.

310 Id. at 7.

311 ERISA § 103.

ERISA also requires that the plan administrator submit a summary annual report which "fairly summarizes the latest annual report."[312]

In the case of tax-qualified pension plans, an annual report must also be filed with the Secretary of the Treasury.[313] Additionally, defined benefit plans subject to Title IV of ERISA must do an annual filing with the Pension Benefit Guaranty Corporation.[314]

5.3.2 Pension Plans

A pension plan is a plan that "by its express terms or as a result of surrounding circumstances, . . . (i) provides retirement income to employees, or (ii) results in deferral of income by employees for periods extending to the termination of covered employment or beyond."[315] Courts have tended to construe the definition broadly. Indeed, the Ninth Circuit has suggested that the statutory definition is sufficiently broad that "virtually any contract that provides for some type of deferred compensation will also establish a de facto pension plan, whether or not the parties intended to do so."[316]

Pension plans typically specify a "normal retirement age," the age at which participants can retire and receive full benefits. The statute specifies age 65 as the presumptive retirement age in the absence of something different in the plan. At the time ERISA was enacted, it was commonly assumed that people would retire at age 65 and the Age Discrimination in Employment Act (ADEA) permitted employers to require that employees retire at that age. ADEA now bars mandatory retirement,[317] and there are some tensions between ADEA and the ERISA concept of normal retirement age. Those tensions are beyond the scope of this section.

5.3.2.1 Types of Pension Plans

Pension plans fall into two broad categories: defined benefit plans and defined contribution plans. Defined benefit plans are the traditional plans that dominated at the time ERISA was passed—plans that promise to pay to participants a specified amount each year from the date of retirement until death. Benefits under such a plan are typically based on a participant's compensation and years of service. For example, a plan might promise to pay participants an annual pension equal to 3% of the participant's final compensation times the participant's years of service with the employer. Cash

---

312 29 CFR § 2520.104(b)–10.

313 29 U.S.C. § 6058(a).

314 ERISA § 4065.

315 ERISA § 3(2).

316 Modzelewski v. Resolution Trust Corp., 14 F.3d 1374, 1377 (9th Cir. 1994).

317 29 U.S.C. §§ 623(a), 623(f)(2).

balance plans, discussed in Section 5.3.2.5, infra, are a form of defined benefit plan.

Defined contribution plans, in contrast, specify (define) a contribution rather than a benefit. Each participant in a defined contribution plan has an individual account into which is deposited the specified annual contribution. The benefit to which the participant is entitled at retirement is simply the value of the participant's individual account, that is, the value of contributions plus the earnings (or minus the losses) over time on those contributions.

The most common form of defined contribution plan today is the 401(k) plan, sometimes referred to as a "cash-or-deferred arrangement." The name refers to the fact that employees voluntarily elect to forego current receipt of a portion of their earnings in favor of the employer contributing those earnings on their behalf to the plan. Often, 401(k) plans include an employer match on employee contributions, often at a match rate of 50%, up to a ceiling. (Matching contributions are particularly useful as an inducement to participation by lower-paid employees.) Typically, although not inherently, employees direct the investments of their 401(k) plan contributions as well as any employer matching contributions, although some employers direct the investment of the matching contributions.

Like all defined contribution plans, 401(k) plans place investment risk on employees. Unlike the defined benefit plan, which promises a fixed benefit—with the result that poor investment returns require larger employer contributions to pay the promised benefit—a defined contribution plan does not promise employees any particular level of benefit.

Although defined benefit plans were the dominant form of pension plan at the time ERISA was enacted, there has been a marked trend toward the use of the 401(k) plan. In 2015, close to 80% of workers who participated in employer-sponsored plans in medium and large private establishments were enrolled in defined contribution plans.[318]

Thus, defined contribution plans, once viewed as supplemental plans, have become the primary retirement vehicle for a significant number of workers. Some have attributed this shift to the increasing mobility of workers, others to the change in the labor force from goods-producing to service-producing occupations, and still others to the extensive regulation of defined benefit plans that makes them

---

[318] Employee Benefit Research Institute (EBRI) Databook on Employee Benefits, chapter 5 (October 2015).

more costly to employers. It is also argued that Internal Revenue Code-imposed limits on the benefits that can be provided to highly compensated corporate executives under qualified plans also makes defined benefit plans less attractive to employers. A final possible explanation is employer self-interest; defined contribution plans involve lesser expense, and, importantly, more predictable expense to employers than do defined benefit plans. Doubtless all of these factors have played some part in the shift.

The impact of the shift from defined contribution plans to 401(k) plans as a primary retirement vehicle is enormous. The 401(k) plan puts the decision whether to participate and how much to contribute to the plan in the hands of employees, meaning many workers choose not to participate and many that do participate fail to contribute amounts sufficient to accumulate adequate retirement savings. Such plans also typically put investment decisions in the hands of often financially unsophisticated employees rather than professional asset managers. Despite efforts on the part of many employers to provide investment education to their employees, predictably, defined contribution plans tend to experience inferior investment returns to those of defined benefit plans.[319] This is particularly troublesome because, as already noted, defined contribution plans place investment risk on the employee.

5.3.2.2 Minimum Plan Design Features

As already noted, ERISA left the basic decision whether to offer a pension plan in the hands of employers. The statute also does not mandate that employers provide a particular level of pension benefit. What the law does do is impose a set of minimum plan design features relating to plan participation and vesting and, in the case of defined benefit plans, rules relating to benefit accrual and plan funding. Each of these rules is discussed in this section. That the statute mandates a set of *minimum* features deserves emphasis; an employer is always free to have more generous provisions in its plan (such as shorter vesting or faster benefit accrual) than those provided for in the statute.

One of the ways of depriving an employee of the ability to earn significant retirement income is to impose stringent age and service conditions on plan participation. Although employers may require some waiting period before allowing employees to participate in a plan, ERISA imposes limits on that waiting period. Specifically, a pension plan cannot require a period that extends beyond the later of the employee's attainment of age 21 or completion of one year of

[319] Alicia Munnell, et al., Pension Participation, Wealth and Income: 1992–2010, Center for Retirement Research Issue in Brief, July, 2016.

service.[320] What it means to complete a year of service for this purpose and for purposes of ERISA's vesting requirements is set out by statute; for most employees, a year of service will mean a 12-month period during which the employee has not less than 1000 hours of service.[321]

Allowing participants into a plan is not sufficient if benefits earned under the plan remain forfeitable for an extended period of time. The minimum vesting schedule imposed by ERISA represents an attempt to balance the desire to promote the nonforfeitability of pension benefits with an employer's legitimate desire to have some workforce stability.

ERISA provides employers with a choice between two alternative vesting schedules.[322] The first allows for so-called cliff vesting, under which an employer may provide that an employee's benefits are completely forfeitable if the employee does not complete five years of service; upon completion of five-years of service, the employee is 100% vested. (Hence the term cliff: the benefits go from completely forfeitable to completely nonforfeitable.) The second allows for so-called graded vesting, pursuant to which an employee's benefits partially vest over time and become fully vested no later than upon completion of seven years of service.

There are variations on these basic rules. For example, an employee's contributions to a plan, such as salary deductions contributed to a 401(k) plan, are always fully vested. Additionally, matching contributions made by an employer to a 401(k) plan vest pursuant to a faster schedule than the normal one. Plans must provide for immediate vesting of all participants upon plan termination. There are also special rules dealing with breaks in service.

Benefit accrual rules supplement vesting rules by imposing limits on the backloading of pension benefits. Participants are vested only in the amount of benefit they have accrued (i.e., earned). Thus, if a plan had a rapid vesting schedule but a slow rate of benefit accrual, a participant could be 100% vested in a very small benefit.

ERISA sets out three alternative rules, at least one of which must be satisfied by a plan in order to comply with the statute.[323] The first is the three-percent rule, which calculates the maximum annual retirement benefit possible under the plan (i.e., the benefit which would be received by a participant who entered the plan at the

---

[320] ERISA § 202(a)(1)(A).

[321] ERISA § 202(a)(3)(A).

[322] ERISA § 203(2)(A).

[323] ERISA § 204(b)(1).

earliest possible date and stayed in the plan until the earlier of age 65 and the plan's normal retirement age) and requires that at least 3% of that total benefit accrue each year. Thus, if the maximum possible benefit payable under a plan is 60% of a participant's compensation, the plan's benefit accrual formula must be such that a participant who works for 10 years accrues a benefit of at least 18% of compensation (10 times 3% of 60%).

The second alternative is the 133-1/3% rule, which, simply stated, requires that the rate of benefit accrual in any given year cannot be more than 133-1/3% of the rate of benefit accrual in any prior year. Thus, for example, a plan could not accrue benefits at a rate of 1% of final compensation in early years and 1.5% of compensation in later years (or indeed any amount greater than 1.33%) without violating the 133-1/3% rule.

The final alternative, the fractional rule, is best thought of as a variation on the three percent rule. The three-percent rule spreads the maximum possible benefit available under the plan over a hypothetical working life of 33-1/3 years. The fractional rule test asks what is the maximum benefit to which an individual employee would be entitled based on when that employee commenced employment and assuming the employee continues to work to normal retirement age. It then requires that the benefit accrue in equal amounts over the employee's actual working life. Thus, with the fractional rule test, employees who start working at different ages will accrue benefits at a different rate.

In the case of a defined contribution plan, there is no need to specify any formula for accrual of benefits. The participant's accrued benefit is always simply the balance of his account.

ERISA also contains rules relating to the funding of defined benefit plans. Plans must meet minimum funding standards designed to ensure that there are sufficient funds available to pay benefits when they become due.

It is easy to understand why funding standards are necessary. Unlike defined contribution plans, in which the participant is simply entitled to whatever amount is in the participant's individual account at retirement, defined benefit plans promise a particular benefit. So the question is: how much does the employer have to contribute to the plan each year to ensure that sufficient funds are available to pay the promised benefit?

Determining that required contribution amount is no easy task. The determination depends on a number of actuarial assumptions, such as salary at retirement, age at retirement, how many years the retiree will receive benefits, investment experience, forfeitures, etc.[324]

What ERISA does is to create permissible funding methods (savings patterns) that can be used by employers to determine their annual plan contributions.[325] In broad terms, the different funding methods authorized by the statute fall into one of two categories: benefit allocation cost methods and cost allocation cost methods. The benefit allocation cost methods focus on the benefit accrued by a participant in a given year and seek to determine how much money must be put aside in that year to provide enough to pay that accrued amount when it becomes due. In contrast, cost allocation methods focus on the anticipated total cost of a participant's pension and allocate that cost evenly between periods, regardless of the rate at which benefits are actually accrued. That means that with benefit allocation methods, the funding obligations for a participant increase the closer the participant is to retirement, whereas cost allocation methods are essentially straight-line funding throughout the participant's work life.

In addition to rules relating to age and service, vesting, benefit accrual and funding, ERISA contains a number of other protective requirements. Thus, it establishes a default rule of spousal protection. Although the right can be waived by the beneficiary spouse, in the absence of a waiver, defined benefit plan benefits must be paid in the form of a joint and survivor annuity.[326] In addition, all ERISA-governed pension plans must provide that benefits may not be assigned or alienated.[327]

5.3.2.3 Code Limitations and Nondiscrimination Rules

Although ERISA is the primary federal statute regulating pension plans of private employers, ERISA and the Internal Revenue Code may be viewed as intersecting universes. This is because tax-qualified pension plans are afforded beneficial tax treatment. In contrast to the matching principle that generally operates in tax law,

---

[324] As an historical aside, it was once not uncommon for plans and other annuity providers to use sex distinct mortality tables for purposes of making certain funding and benefit determinations for pension plans and for welfare benefit plans such as life insurance plans. As a result, in contributory plans women paid less for life insurance and more for annuities, because women as a class live longer then do men. In *City of Los Angeles v. Manhart*, 435 U.S. 702 (1978), the Supreme Court found the gender-based distinction to violate Title VII of the Civil Rights Act of 1964, saying that although women as a class live longer than men, individual women may not. As a result of *Manhart*, companies generally use unisex mortality tables for their benefit plans.

[325] ERISA § 303.

[326] ERISA § 205.

[327] ERISA § 206(d).

while employers receive an immediate tax deduction for contributions made to qualified plans, participants are not treated as receiving any currently taxable income with respect to contributions made on their behalf. In addition, earnings on those contributions accumulate tax-free. Thus, no tax is paid on qualified plan contributions or earnings until distributions are made to plan participants. In order to obtain such favorable tax treatment, plans must meet a number of requirements set out in § 401(a) of the Code.

Although many of the requirements for tax qualification mirror ERISA requirements, such as the participation and vesting rules, a number of the Code requirements have no ERISA counterpart. The two-fold aim of the additional Code requirements is to control the extent of the tax subsidy for tax-qualified plans and to ensure that plan benefits are not disproportionately provided to highly compensated employees.

The Code's nondiscrimination rules aim to ensure that employers do not provide contributions or benefits that disproportionately benefit "highly compensated employees," a term that, in general, includes employees who are 5% owners of the employer or who earn in excess of $120,000 in 2016.[328] (The income figure is adjusted for inflation.) Although § 401(a)(4) of the Code merely prohibits discriminating in favor of highly compensated employees with respect to contributions or benefits, the simple statutory requirement has been interpreted in staggeringly detailed and complex regulations. The coverage tests aim to ensure that a sufficient percentage of nonhighly compensated employees receive benefits under the plan. The benefits tests aim to ensure that benefits provided to nonhighly compensated employees are meaningful by limiting the amount of benefits that can be provided to highly compensated employees in relation to the benefits provided to nonhighly compensated employees. A consideration of the specifics of the rules is beyond the scope of this book.

Whereas the nondiscrimination rules limit the benefits that can be provided to highly compensated employees in relation to the benefits provided to nonhighly compensated employees, the Code's limits on contributions and benefits provide an absolute cap on benefits that can be provided by a qualified plan. Section 415 of the Code contains limits on the annual contributions that can be made under a defined contribution plan and the annual benefits that can be paid from a defined benefit plan. For example as of January 1, 2017, the limitation on the annual benefit under a defined benefit

[328] Code § 414(q).

plan under Section 415(b)(1)(A) $215,000. The limitation for defined contribution plans under Section 415(c)(1)(A) is $54,000.

5.3.2.4 Plan Termination and Insurance

One of the concerns animating the passage of ERISA was the termination of pension plans without sufficient assets to pay benefits due under the plan.[329] Accordingly, Title IV of ERISA establishes both procedures governing the termination of pension plans and a system of insurance designed to ensure that when plans terminate with insufficient assets, participants receive at least a guaranteed amount of benefits. To oversee both plan terminations and the termination insurance program, the statute established a new regulatory authority, the Pension Benefit Guaranty Corporation (the "PBGC").

Title IV governs only defined benefit pension plans and multiemployer pension plans.[330] The exclusion of defined contribution plans from Title IV coverage is understandable: since the only benefit to which a defined contribution plan participant is entitled is the amount in the participant's individual account, there is no promised benefit to insure.

In contrast, notwithstanding ERISA's funding rules, there will be circumstances where a defined benefit plan's assets will not cover its liabilities. As discussed in Section 5.3.2.2, supra, determinations of funding requirements depend on any number of actuarial assumptions. Actual investment returns lower than those projected for funding purposes, retirees living longer and therefore receiving benefits for longer periods than projected, or variations with respect to any of the other assumptions used can have a dramatic impact on funds available to pay benefits. Plan underfunding can also arise from granting past service credits to participants or the passage of amendments that increase plan benefits. For example, *PBGC v. Ouimet Corp.*,[331] involved a pension plan adopted by Avon Sole Company, subsequently acquired by Ouimet. Avon's plan gave credit

---

[329] One of the incidents prompting the enactment of ERISA, involved the loss of retirement benefits occurring in 1963 when Studebaker, an automobile manufacturer located in South Bend, Indiana, terminated its employee pension plan, causing over 4,000 auto workers to lose some or all of their promised pension plan benefits. See ERISA at 40: Four Decades of Protecting America's Employee Benefits (available at https://www.dol.gov/featured/erisa40/historical.)

[330] The rules governing termination of multiemployer plans were substantially revised by the Multiemployer Pension Plan Amendment Act of 1980, and again in 2014. Pub.L. No. 113–235, Div. O, 128 Stat. 2130, 2773–2822 (amending the PPA, 29 U.S.C. §§ 1084–1085 and 26 U.S.C. §§ 431–432, among other things). The 2014 amendments prior reforms in allowing certain plans in financial distress to reduce accrued benefits. The discussion in this section addresses the termination of single-employer plans.

[331] 630 F.2d 4 (1st Cir. 1980).

to its employees for their service with the company prior to the company's adoption of the pension plan, without requiring any immediate funding to cover the benefit liability created by the granting of such service credit. Subsequently, the plan was amended several times to increase benefits, again without the company making additional current contributions to fund the increased benefits. The result was significant underfunding of the plan when Avon subsequently went bankrupt.

A final factor that contributes to underfunding is the ability of plan sponsors to seek waivers from the IRS of their funding obligations when faced with a "temporary and substantial business hardship."[332] Indeed, waivers can have the effect of aggravating already existing plan underfunding.

An employer sponsoring a pension plan can voluntarily terminate the plan in either a standard termination or a distress termination. In a standard termination, the plan has sufficient assets to cover all of its liability for benefits. In a distress termination, assets are insufficient to pay liabilities.

When a plan terminates with insufficient assets, the PBGC takes over the plan and assures some payment. In 2016 the maximum payment for a covered participant retiring at the age of 65 was $60,136 per year).[333] The plan sponsor and all members of the plan sponsor's "controlled group"[334] are then liable to the PBGC for all unfunded benefits, and to the extent that the PBGC can collect that liability, it will pay nonguaranteed benefits as well.

In addition to the two types of voluntary termination permitted by Title IV, Title IV also gives the PBGC the ability to initiate a termination on its own (involuntary termination) if certain statutory criteria are met. Those criteria include failure of a plan sponsor to meet the minimum funding standard, the inability of a plan to pay benefits when due, and the occurrence of one of a number of statutory "reportable events," events designed to give early warning of a problem. Under certain circumstances, such as if a plan does not have assets to pay current benefits under the plan or has insufficient assets to pay guaranteed benefits, the PBGC *must* initiate an involuntary termination. Where the PBGC initiates involuntary termination, it generally asks for the court to appoint a trustee to administer the plan pending the issuance by the court of a termination decree.

---

332 Code § 412.

333 ERISA § 4022.

334 The term "controlled group" is defined by ERISA to mean a plan sponsor and "all other persons under common control" with the sponsor. ERISA § 4001(a)(14)(A).

The threat of termination by the PBGC is a strong weapon that the PBGC has not hesitated to use, particularly where the plan sponsor of an underfunded plan is contemplating some corporate transaction such as a merger or a spin-off that would have some effect on the identity of the controlled group. Since the PBGC's termination would mature the agency's claim against the controlled group for the amount a plan is underfunded, the threat can have a significant impact on a planned divestiture, spin-off, or other transaction. The PBGC actively monitors corporate transactions and has sometimes used the threat of termination to force parties negotiating a merger or other transaction that would affect the composition of a controlled group to provide plan participants with protection beyond that required by statute.

Title IV sets out elaborate procedures with respect to each of the three types of terminations.[335] The important thing to realize is that termination proceeds under the supervision of the PBGC. An employer cannot just decide it is terminating its plan and do so.

The termination of a pension plan raises a number of issues beyond the scope of the discussion here. Although those issues are different depending on whether or not the plan at the time of termination has assets sufficient to make all benefit payments due under the plan, in one sense they may be viewed as flip sides of fundamentally the same question: Who bears the loss when there are insufficient assets? Who gets the benefit when there are more than sufficient assets?

5.3.2.5 Amendment of Pension Plans

ERISA requires the plan document of every plan to "provide a procedure for amending such plan."[336] Although plan amendment is not subject to ERISA's fiduciary rules (discussed in Section 5.3.4, infra), there are some restrictions on an employer's ability to amend plans.

The most important limitation on the amendment of pension plans is the so called anti-reduction or anti-cutback rule contained in ERISA § 204(b), which prohibits an amendment to a plan that has the effect of reducing an already accrued benefit. There has been a significant amount of litigation concerning what type of amendments have the effect of reducing an already accrued benefit.[337]

---

[335] ERISA § 4021.

[336] ERISA § 402(b)(3).

[337] See, e.g., Thornton v. Graphic Communications Conference of the International Brotherhood of Teamsters Supplemental Retirement and Disability Fund, 566 F. 3d 597 (6th Cir. 2009) (finding post-retirement increase in pension benefits not to be an accrued benefit); Board of Trustees of the Sheet Metal Workers'

In recent years, a number of traditional defined benefit pension plans have been amended to convert the plan to a cash balance plan. A cash balance plan is a hybrid plan, in that it is a defined benefit plan that looks in many ways like a defined contribution plan. Each participant has a hypothetical account balance that is credited each year with an employer contribution and interest at a rate specified in the plan. Employer contributions are made monthly or annually and interest is typically credited monthly. At retirement, the participant is entitled to the value of the hypothetical account.

At one level, cash balance plans can be viewed as combining positive elements of both defined benefit and defined contributions. However, because most cash balance plans arise from conversions, litigation has arisen concerning the potential discriminatory effect of such conversions on older workers,[338] the failure by plan administrators to satisfy the notice requirements,[339] and that the conversion to a cash balance plan results in the reduction of an accrued benefit.[340]

5.3.3 Welfare Plans

The other category of plans covered by ERISA is employee welfare benefit plans. The statute defines employee welfare benefit plan as a plan that provides, "through the purchase of insurance or otherwise, . . . medical, surgical, or hospital care or benefits, or benefits in the event of sickness, accident, disability, death or unemployment, or vacation benefits, apprenticeship or other training programs, or day care centers, scholarship funds, or prepaid legal services."[341]

ERISA provides for very little regulation of welfare benefit plans. Unlike pension plans, as to which the statute imposes a minimum set of design features, welfare benefit plans are not subject to requirements such as vesting. With the exception of COBRA requirements and some specific provisions regarding health plans that have been added by amendment, which are discussed in Section

---

National Pension Fund v. Commissioner, 318 F.3d 599 (4th Cir. 2003) (elimination of a cost of living adjustment does not violate the anti-cutback rule); Pratt v. Petroleum Prod. Management, Inc. Employee Savings Plan & Trust, 920 F.2d 651 (10th Cir. 1990) (retroactive change in valuation date under a profit sharing plan violates the anti-cutback rule).

[338] See, e.g., Register v. PNC Financial Services Group, Inc., 477 F.3d 56 (3d Cir. 2007); Cooper v. IBM Personal Pension Plan, 274 F.Supp.2d 1010 (S.D. Ill. 2003); Tootle v. ARINC, Inc., 222 F.R.D. 88 (D. Md. 2004).

[339] See, e.g., Tomlison v. El Paso Corp., 653 F.3d 1281 (10th Cir. 2011); Jensen v. Sovay Chemicals, Inc., 721 F.3d 1180 (10th Cir. 2013).

[340] See, e.g., Walker v. Monsanto Co. Pension Plan, 614 F.3d 415 (7th Cir. 2010).

[341] ERISA § 3(1). The definition also includes benefits described in Section 302(c) of the Labor Management Relations Act.

5.3.3.2, infra, there is little substantive regulation of such plans, although ERISA's reporting and disclosure requirements, fiduciary standards, and enforcement provisions (including preemption) do apply to welfare plans.

5.3.3.1 Types of Welfare Benefit Plans

Employers may provide their employees with a number of welfare benefit plans. Perhaps the most important are health benefit plans, the regulation of which is discussed below. Other common welfare benefit plans include disability plans, plans providing benefits in the case of accidental death, and severance plans.

With respect to disability plans, many employers provide their employees with benefits in the event of short-term and/or long-term disability. As with all employee benefit plans, employers have the discretion to determine what constitutes a disability and what benefits will be provided in the event of disability (with no requirement that plans provide equal benefits for different disabilities). The issue of whether a particular condition qualifies as a disability entitling a participant to benefits under a plan is one that is litigated very frequently and is a very fact-specific determination.

Among the questions that repeatedly arise is the relationship between disability for purposes of receiving Social Security disability benefits and disability for the purpose of receiving benefits under an employer's plan. Although to a lay person the fact that one may be disabled for one purpose but not for another is a difficult concept to grasp, the fact that a plan's definition of disability may be different from the Social Security definition means that entitlement to Social Security benefits is no guarantee of entitlement to benefits under a plan and vice versa.[342] Nevertheless, the Supreme Court upheld a decision by the Sixth Circuit Court of Appeals finding an insurer abused its discretion in denying disability benefits to an employee who was awarded benefits under the Social Security Act.[343] The Court decided that the lower court properly considered the insurer's conflict of interest as a factor because the company encouraged the employee to apply for Social Security Disability benefits and when she was successful in obtaining retroactive payments, offset to its own payment obligation under the plan.[344] The insurer subsequently

---

[342] See, e.g., Anderson v. Plasterers' & Cement Masons' Local 12 Pension and Welfare Plans, 991 F.2d 356 (7th Cir. 1993). But see McLeod v. Hartford Life & Accident Ins. Co., No. Civ.A.01–4295, 2004 WL 2203711 (E.D. Pa. Sept. 27, 2004) (where a plan definition of disability is narrower than the Social Security definition, the conclusion that a participant is disabled for Social Security purposes will suggest that the participant is disabled for plan purposes).

[343] See Metropolitan Life Ins. Co. v. Glenn, 554 U.S. 105 (2008).

[344] Id. at 118.

determined that she was able to work, ignoring the agency's finding.[345] These facts, and others, justified finding an abuse of discretion.[346] In later cases, other courts have reached similar decisions, often where the insurer failed to address the determination under the Social Security Act.[347]

Like the disability determination, rules employed for purposes of determining Social Security eligibility, such as the "treating physician rule" that accords special deference to the opinion of the participant's treating physician, are not necessarily applicable in the context of ERISA disability.[348] The most that can be said is that while Social Security concepts are "instructive" in ERISA claims,[349] they are not dispositive.

5.3.3.2 Regulation of Health Plans

As originally enacted in 1974, ERISA contained no substantive regulation of health plans. Amendments over the years have changed that, however.

In 1985, ERISA was amended to require that a sponsor of a group health plan make continuation coverage (so-called COBRA coverage) available to employees who lose coverage following the occurrence of a "qualifying event."[350] Upon the occurrence of a "qualifying event," a participant in a group health plan must be given the opportunity to elect to continue to be covered under the group health plan for either 18 or 36 months, depending on the nature of the qualifying event. The principal qualifying event is termination of employment for reasons other than an employee's "gross misconduct" and the question of whether an employer's grounds for terminating an employee constitute gross misconduct is one that is heavily litigated.[351] Other qualifying events include the death or divorce of

---

[345] Id.

[346] Id.

[347] See, e.g., Brown v. Hartford Life Ins. Co., 301 F. App'x 772, 775–76 (10th Cir. 2008); Raybourne v. Cigna Life Ins. Co. of New York, 700 F.3d 1076 (7th Cir. 2012); Salomaa v. Honda Long Term Disability Plan, 642 F.3d 666, 679 (9th Cir. 2011); Schexnayder v. Hartford Life & Acc. Ins. Co., 600 F.3d 465, 471 (5th Cir. 2010).

[348] Black & Decker Disability Plan v. Nord, 538 U.S. 822, 825 (2003) (holding that ERISA "plan administrators are not obliged to accord special deference to the opinions of treating physicians").

[349] Halpin v. W.W. Grainger, Inc., 962 F.2d 685, 695 n.11 (7th Cir. 1992).

[350] ERISA §§ 602, 603.

[351] Contrast Lloynd v. Hanover Foods Corp., 72 F.Supp.2d 469 (D. Del. 1999) (ordinary negligence and incompetence is not gross misconduct) with Boudreaux v. Rice Palace, Inc., No. Civ.A.04–541 2006 WL 3345198, at *4 (W.D. La. Nov. 15, 2006) (repeated instances of improper use of controlled substances constitutes gross misconduct). In *Nero v. University Hospitals Management Services Organization*, No. 1:04CV1833, 2006 WL 2933957, 39 EB Cases (BNA) 2181 (N.D. Ohio Oct. 12, 2006), the district court concluded based on a review of available cases interpreting "gross

the participant resulting in loss of coverage to the spouse, or the loss of coverage of a dependent child who ceases to be dependent.

The COBRA provisions of ERISA allow an employer to require that a person electing continuation coverage pay a premium for that coverage in an amount not to "exceed 102 percent of the applicable premium" for active employees.[352] Nonetheless, because of self-selection, i.e., the people most likely to elect COBRA coverage are those who are older or sicker, COBRA coverage is costly to employers. Studies have shown that those electing COBRA coverage use more medical services than do active employees.[353]

To make the right to elect COBRA coverage meaningful, ERISA requires that employees and their spouses receive written notice of COBRA rights at the commencement of coverage under the group health plan and upon the occurrence of a qualifying event. A significant amount of COBRA litigation concerns whether an employer adequately complied with these notice provisions.

Following the attempt by President William Clinton in 1994 to achieve national health insurance, ERISA was again amended to include a number of special-purpose health benefit mandates. These mandates, adopted pursuant to several statutes passed between 1996 and 1998, are contained in Part 7 of Title I of ERISA. They include restrictions on the scope of preexisting condition clauses,[354] a requirement that plans cover a minimum of 48 hours of hospitalization for both mother and infant after birth,[355] restrictions on the ability of a health plan to apply limits on mental health care that are different from limits on physical health care,[356] and a requirement that plans cover post-mastectomy reconstructive surgery.[357] As the list suggests, these requirements do not represent an effort to determine in any systematic way what plans should cover so much as an ad hoc approach to regulation based on what issues have generated a lot of attention.

---

misconduct" that in the absence of "any evidence that the [employee's] action was intentional, wanton, willful or deliberate," mistakes due to "absentmindedness" did not constitute gross misconduct notwithstanding the fact that the mistakes could have had "serious consequences." Id. at *13–14.

[352] ERISA § 604.

[353] Congressional Research Service, CRS Report for Congress: Medicare Expansion: President Clinton's Proposals to Allow Coverage Before Age 65, Mar. 31, 1998 ("COBRA enrollees on average use more health care than active workers. Among people who are eligible, those who need care are more likely to elect coverage, while those in good health tend to purchase individual policies or forego insurance.").

[354] ERISA § 701.

[355] ERISA § 711.

[356] ERISA § 712.

[357] ERISA § 713.

In addition to regulation imposed by ERISA, a number of other laws may impact an employer's provision of health benefits to its employees. First, in 2010, President Obama signed into law the Patient Protection and Affordable Care Act,[358] and the Health Care and Education Reconciliation Act,[359] collectively referred to as the "Affordable Care Act" or "ACA." The ACA drastically changed the state of the delivery of health insurance coverage in the U.S., and thus, not surprisingly, it has been controversial, as evidenced by the frequent attempts by Republicans to repeal it and by the various challenges brought in court against it. A full discussion of the ACA is beyond the scope of this book. We note, however, that some of the mandatory provisions incorporated in the ACA apply to health care plans provided by employers. Most notable among these provisions is the "shared responsibility" provision, which imposes a penalty on employers with more than fifty employees. The penalty is triggered when an employer fails to provide employees a group health plan that qualifies as "minimum essential coverage" or if the coverage that the employer provides is inadequate or unaffordable under the terms of the statute.[360]

Second, because ERISA's preemption provision, discussed in Section 5.3.5.3, infra, contains an exception for state insurance laws, such laws have the effect of indirectly regulating employee benefit plans. Although a state law may not require an employer to provide a particular benefit, requirements of state insurance law can have an effect on the operation of an employer's plan. Thus, for example, a state statute requiring that all insurance policies in that state provide specified minimum mental healthcare benefits has the effect of requiring that an employer who provides healthcare benefits to his employees through the purchase of insurance in that state provide such benefits to his employees.[361]

Third, federal laws other than ERISA may also have an effect on health benefits provided by an employer. The Family and Medical Leave Act, discussed in Section 5.2 supra, prevents an employer from discontinuing medical coverage during the period an employee is taking leave provided for under that statute. The Americans with Disabilities Act may prevent a plan from discriminating in the provision of benefits on the basis of disability. Title VII prevents an employer from treating pregnancy differently than other disabilities.

---

[358] Pub. L. 111–148, 124 Stat. 119 (2010).

[359] Pub. L. 111–152, 124 Stat. 1029 (2010).

[360] Pub. L. 111–148, 124 Stat. 119 (2010). See generally, Michael J. Canan & William D. Mitchell, § 10A:5 Employee Fringe & Welfare Benefit Plans (2017).

[361] This was the statute at issue in the Supreme Court's decision in *Metropolitan Life Ins. Co. v. Massachusetts*, 471 U.S. 724 (1985).

5.3.3.3 Amendment of Welfare Plans

Because welfare benefit plans are not subject to ERISA's vesting and benefit accrual rules, an employer is "generally free under ERISA, for any reason at any time, to adopt, modify, or terminate welfare plans."[362] Thus, for example, in *McGann v. H & H Music Co.*,[363] a case that received tremendous attention at the time it was handed down, the Fifth Circuit upheld the ability of an employer to amend its plan to impose a lifetime maximum of $5000 for AIDs-related claims. The plan had previously provided for lifetime medical benefits of up to $1,000,000 to all employees. Learning that one of its employees had AIDS, the company reduced the lifetime maximum for only AIDS-related claims, without imposing any limit on benefits for other catastrophic illnesses. Although the court assumed for purposes of its analysis that the company's knowledge of the plaintiff's illness "was a motivating factor in their decision to reduce coverage for AIDs-related expenses,"[364] the court found no violation of ERISA in the plan amendment since the employer had never promised it would not amend the $1,000,000 limit.[365]

The amendment of plans to reduce or eliminate retiree medical coverage has been the subject of a tremendous amount of litigation. Because there is no vesting of welfare benefits and courts have rejected efforts to find implied vesting upon retirement,[366] the issue in such cases is typically whether the employer has contractually promised that it would not amend such benefits. The issue is thus largely dependent upon the language of plan documents. Ordinary principles of contract law apply to the interpretation of the documents and the Supreme Court has stated that courts should not infer an intent to create lifetime benefits from contractual silence or ambiguous language regarding benefit duration.[367] These are not easy cases for plaintiffs to win. Even if a plan promises the benefits will be provided "for life," if the plan also reserves the employer's right to "amend, alter or terminate the plan," a court is not likely to disallow an amendment eliminating retiree benefits.[368]

---

[362] Curtiss-Wright Corp. v. Schoonejongen, 514 U.S. 73, 78 (1995).

[363] 946 F.2d 401 (5th Cir. 1991), cert. denied, 506 U.S. 981 (1992).

[364] Id. at 404 n.4.

[365] *McGann* was decided before the effective date of the Americans with Disabilities Act, so the court did not address whether the plan amendment violated the ADA.

[366] See, e.g., Hansen v. White Motor Corp., 788 F.2d 1186 (6th Cir. 1986).

[367] M & G Polymers USA, LLC v. Tackett, 135 S. Ct. 926, 936–37 (2015).

[368] Sprague v. General Motors Corp., 133 F.3d 388, 401 (6th Cir. 1998) (en banc) (emphasizing that "the promise made to retirees was a qualified one: the promise was that retiree medical benefits were for life provided the company chose not to terminate the plans, pursuant to clauses that preserved the company's right to [terminate]").

5.3.4 Fiduciary Regulation

A central part of the protection provided by ERISA involves placing control over plan assets, and plan management and administration, in the hand of fiduciaries and then imposing on those fiduciaries stringent standards of behavior with respect to the performance of their duties. ERISA both establishes affirmative obligations on fiduciaries and prohibits particular transactions with respect to a plan and its assets.

Liability for failing to live up to the affirmative standards imposed by § 404 or for violating the prohibitions set out in § 406 is established by § 409(a) of ERISA, which provides that fiduciaries have personal liability for losses to a plan resulting from their breach and are subject to "such other equitable or remedial relief as the court may deem appropriate."[369] In addition to the liability imposed by § 409, § 405 of ERISA provides for liability on the part of a fiduciary for breaches by co-fiduciaries. If a fiduciary knowingly participates in a breach by another fiduciary, enables another fiduciary to commit a fiduciary breach by his own failure to live up to his fiduciary responsibilities, or fails to make reasonable efforts to remedy a breach by another fiduciary of which he has knowledge, the fiduciary has liability under § 405.[370]

5.3.4.1 Who Is a Fiduciary?

ERISA adopts a functional approach to the definition of fiduciary. A person is a fiduciary to the extent that (1) "he exercises any discretionary authority or discretionary control" in the management of a plan "or exercises any authority or control respecting management or disposition of [plan] assets;" (2) renders investment advice for a fee; or (3) "has any discretionary authority [in] the administration" of the plan.[371] The idea of defining fiduciary in such broad terms is to "allow plan designers to have considerable flexibility in allocating plan functions, while still preserving the protective principle that persons exercising material discretion must be responsible as fiduciaries for their conduct."[372]

A tremendous body of case law has developed concerning the question of who is a fiduciary for ERISA purposes. Questions arise, for example, with respect to how much discretion is sufficient to make one a fiduciary, with courts recognizing that some exercises of discretion are too ministerial to give rise to fiduciary status.

---

369 ERISA § 409(a).

370 ERISA § 405.

371 ERISA § 3(21).

372 John H. Langbein, et al., Pensions and Employee Benefit Law 477 (6th ed. 2015).

Litigation also arises with respect to whether service providers, such as attorneys, accountants, actuaries and consultants have acted in such a manner that they should be considered fiduciaries; generally professionals providing services will not be considered fiduciaries so long as they are performing their usual professional functions.

Under ERISA a person is a fiduciary "to the extent" she engages in fiduciary activities.[373] Courts have consistently recognized that a person may be a fiduciary for some purposes and not for others. As the Supreme Court observed in *Pegram v. Herdrich*,[374] "[i]n every case charging breach of ERISA fiduciary duty, then, the threshold question is . . . whether that person was acting as a fiduciary (that is, was performing a fiduciary function) when taking the action subject to the complaint."[375] This means that "people may be fiduciaries when they do certain things but be entitled to act in their own interests when they do others."[376]

This determination has proven difficult at times, particularly when the actor in question is the employer sponsoring a plan. Courts have recognized that employers wear "two hats." Although the employer qua employer owes no fiduciary duties to plan participants, "when employers choose to 'wear two hats,' i.e., act as both employer and plan administrator, ERISA fiduciary duties regarding plan administration attach."[377] Courts have struggled with whether an employer has acted in a fiduciary capacity when making certain representations to employees who are plan participants.[378]

Varity Corporation v. Howe[379] serves as a useful illustration. As part of a corporate restructuring in 1986, Varity transferred part of the operations of its Massey-Ferguson subsidiary to a newly formed corporation. "At best, the restructuring was a last-ditch effort to save Varity from bankruptcy. At worst, it was a ploy to sink most of Varity's liabilities and unprofitable divisions into a corporation that was not expected to last long."[380] To encourage employees to transfer to the newly formed entity, corporate officers told employees that

---

[373] ERISA § 3(21).

[374] 530 U.S. 211 (2000).

[375] Id. at 226.

[376] John Hancock Mutual Life Ins. Co. v. Harris Trust & Savings Bank, 510 U.S. 86, 90 (1993).

[377] Barnes v. Lacy, 927 F.2d 539, 544 (11th Cir. 1991) (quoting Payonk v. HMW Industries, Inc., 883 F.2d 221, 229 (3d Cir. 1989)).

[378] Compare Young v. Washington Gas Light Co., 206 F.3d 1200 (D.C. Cir. 2000) (communication in question was not a fiduciary one) with Mathews v. Chevron Corp., 362 F.3d 1172 (9th Cir. 2004) (statements were made in a fiduciary capacity).

[379] 516 U.S. 489 (1996).

[380] Jayne Zanglein, Divorce, Lies and Pensions: Employee Benefits in the Fifth Circuit, 28 Tex. Tech. L. Rev. 493, 506 (1997).

they would receive the same benefits they were currently receiving as employees of Varity and that their benefits were secure.

After the company went into receivership, the former employees and retirees who lost benefits as a result brought suit alleging fiduciary breach. The first question the court had to address was whether the statements made to employees were made in a fiduciary capacity. The court answered the question in the affirmative, holding that "[c]onveying information about the likely future of plan benefits, thereby permitting beneficiaries to make an informed choice about continued participation" is an act of plan administration.[381]

The Court made clear that it was not saying that Varity was acting as a fiduciary merely because the company made statements about the expected financial prospects of the company or because the decision had an adverse effect on the plan. Rather it was the fact that "Varity *intentionally* connected its statements about Massey Combines' financial health to statements it made about the future of benefits, so that its intended communication about the security of benefits was rendered materially misleading."[382]

5.3.4.2 Fiduciary Standards

Section 404 of ERISA sets out general standards of behavior that must be met by all fiduciaries. It establishes as an overarching principle the notion that everything a fiduciary does in the discharge of her plan responsibilities must be done "solely in the interest of the participants and beneficiaries" of the plan.[383] That broad rule is supplemented with specifically articulated duties on the part of the fiduciary:

(1) a fiduciary of a plan must discharge those duties for the "exclusive purpose of . . . providing benefits to participants and their beneficiaries."[384]

(2) a fiduciary of a plan must act "with the care, skill, prudence and diligence under circumstances then prevailing that a prudent man acting in a like capacity and familiar with such matters would use in the conduct of an enterprise of a like character and with like aims. . . ."[385]

(3) a fiduciary of a plan is required to diversify "the investment of the plan so as to minimize the risk of

---

381 516 U.S. at 502.

382 Id. at 505.

383 ERISA § 404.

384 ERISA § 404(a)(1)(A).

385 ERISA § 404(a)(1)(B).

large losses, unless under the circumstances it is clearly prudent not to do so."[386]

(4) a fiduciary of a plan must act "in accordance with the documents and instruments governing the plan insofar as such documents and instruments are consistent with the provisions of this title and Title IV. . . ."[387]

Challenges to fiduciary actions arise frequently in the context of plan investment decisions, where claims of violation of the duties of prudence and loyalty as well as diversification are common. An increasing area of litigation involves attempts to impose liability for misrepresentation or failure to inform. A common context for such claims is an employee who retires before an employer announces a special retirement incentive program; the claim is that the employer breached a duty by either misrepresenting the company's intention or failing to disclose that such a program was in the works.[388]

ERISA's duty of loyalty is illustrated well by the famous case of *Donovan v. Bierwirth*,[389] a case involving the 1981 attempted takeover by LTV of Grumann Corporation. At the time that LTV made a tender offer for 70% of Grumann's shares (at $45/share), the Grumann pension plan owned 525,000 shares of the company's stock. The trustees of the pension plan, who happened to be officers and directors of Grumman,[390] made two decisions that were challenged: a decision not to tender the shares owned by the plan and a decision to purchase an additional 1,158,000 shares at an average price of $38.27/share. These decisions were made against the backdrop that the corporation had decided to oppose the tender offer and was encouraging its shareholders not to tender.

The conflict of interest is apparent. As officers and directors of the company, the trustees' duty of loyalty was to the corporation and its shareholders. As pension plan trustees, however, their duty of loyalty was to plan participants. Focusing on the purchase decision, the more egregious of the two, whatever may have been the merits of having the plan purchase additional shares of company stock before the tender offer was announced (when the shares were trading at

---

386 ERISA § 404(a)(1)(C).

387 ERISA § 404(a)(1)(D).

388 A seminal case addressing this claim is *Fischer v. Philadelphia Electric Co.*, 96 F.3d 1533 (3d Cir. 1996).

389 680 F.2d 263 (2d Cir. 1982), cert. denied, 459 U.S. 1069 (1982).

390 Section 408(c)(3) of ERISA allows an officer, employee, agent or other representative of a party in interest (a term that includes employers) to be a plan fiduciary. It is this provision which allows pension plans to have in-house trustees. Without § 408(c)(3), an in-house trustee would be a transaction prohibited by ERISA § 406(a)(1)(C), which prohibits the furnishing of services between a plan and a party in interest.

approximately $24–27/share), the purchase of shares during the tender offer (at a prices of approximately $38/share) was clearly not in the best interests of plan participants. A successful tender offer would have left the plan as a minority shareholder in LTV; an unsuccessful tender offer would result in a significant decline in the value of the stock held by the plan. Indeed, when the tender offer failed, the value of the stock purchased at $38/share fell to $28/share.

The court found that the trustees violated their duty to "avoid placing themselves in a position where their acts as officers or directors of the corporation will prevent their functioning with the complete loyalty to participants demanded of them as trustees of a pension plan."[391]

5.3.4.3 Prohibited Transactions

In addition to the general standards of fiduciary behavior set out in § 404 of ERISA, § 406 sets out certain prohibited transactions,[392] essentially transactions that on their face are deemed "likely to injure" the plan. [393]Another way of phrasing it is to say that ERISA prohibits transactions that raise an inference that the fiduciary is not acting in the best interest of plan participants and beneficiaries.

Transactions prohibited by § 406 fall into two categories. First, ERISA prohibits transactions between a plan and a fiduciary that involve self-dealing, such as a fiduciary's dealing in plan assets for his own account or acting on behalf of someone with interests adverse to the plan or its participants and beneficiaries.[394] Second, ERISA prohibits a broad range of transactions between plans and parties-in-interest to the plan, a term that encompasses parties who are related to the employer or to a plan fiduciary, those who provide services to the plan, and others with whom a fiduciary might be tempted to engage in non arm's-length transactions.[395] The categories of transactions that are prohibited are so broadly defined that it would not be hyperbole to say that all transactions between a plan and a party in interest are prohibited except for those specifically permitted by statute or DOL rulemaking.

Section 408(b) of ERISA contains a number of specifically enumerated exceptions to the prohibitions of § 406. In addition, § 408(a) authorizes the DOL to establish an exemption procedure pursuant to which individual or class exemptions may be granted.

---

391 680 F.2d at 271.

392 ERISA § 406(a), (b).

393 Commissioner v. Keystone Consol. Indus., 508 U.S. 152, 160 (1993).

394 ERISA§ 406(b) (prohibiting certain transactions between a plan and a plan fiduciary).

395 ERISA § 406(a).

The DOL has utilized this statutory authority to grant a number of exemptions that facilitate ordinary investment activities by plans.

5.3.4.4 Special Issues Regarding 401(k) Plans

As discussed in Section 5.3.2.1 supra, there has been a marked shift away from defined benefit plans and toward defined contribution plans as the primary means of providing retirement benefits to employees. That makes the fiduciary issues with respect to such plans of increasing importance, something complicated by the fact that the drafters of ERISA had in mind the traditional defined benefit plan when they were considering the statute.

Because in the typical 401(k) plan the participant is making her own investment decisions, the question is to what extent a fiduciary should be liable for losses resulting from those decisions. ERISA says in § 404(c) that there is no liability for such losses to the extent that "a participant or beneficiary exercises control over the assets in his account." Regulations adopted by the Department of Labor establish what it means for a participant or beneficiary to exercise control within the meaning of the statute.[396] The two main things the regulations focus on are the conditions that constitute sufficient participant control, which among other things requires that a participant be given sufficient information to make informed investment decisions, and the requirement that the plan provide a participant or beneficiary with the ability to choose from a broad range of investment alternatives. The latter is typically not an issue, as most plans offer a larger menu of options than what the regulations require.

One of the most problematic issues with respect to 401(k) plans in recent years has been the inclusion of an employer stock fund among a plan's investment options. Because ERISA's diversification requirement does not apply to participant-directed 401(k) plans, where an employer stock fund is offered as an investment option, employees tend to heavily invest in it. The effect on 401(k) account balances from the collapse of companies like Enron and WorldCom has been well publicized, as has been the effect of the financial crisis of 2008. These collapses have given rise to a multiplicity of lawsuits, with plaintiffs alleging breaches of the duty of loyalty based on the continued inclusion of the stock fund in the plan or on misrepresentations or failures to disclose problems with respect to the company's prospects as well as prohibited transactions.

A common theme in cases involving employer stock cases is the claim that under the prudence standard applicable under ERISA, the

[396] 29 C.F.R. § 2550.404c–1.

fiduciary would have known or should have known of the decline in stock price and should have removed the stock from the defined contribution plan. For years, when reviewing such claims courts regularly applied the *Moench v. Robertson* presumption.[397] The presumption held that a fiduciary's decision not to remove employer stock from the options available to the participants was presumed to be consistent with ERISA's prudence requirement, absent rebuttal of the presumption. In 2014, in *Fifth Third Bancorp v. Dudenhoeffer*, the United States Supreme Court rejected application of the *Moench* presumption in ERISA cases.[398] The Court held that employee stock ownership plan fiduciaries are subject to the same duty of prudence generally applicable to all ERISA fiduciaries. Specifically the Court noted that "To state a claim for breach of the duty of prudence on the basis of inside information, a plaintiff must plausibly allege an alternative action that the defendant could have taken that would have been consistent with the securities laws and that a prudent fiduciary in the same circumstances would not have viewed as more likely to harm the fund than to help it,"[399]

5.3.5 Enforcement

ERISA's civil enforcement provisions—"one of the essential tools for accomplishing the stated purposes" of the statute[400]—are contained in § 502.

5.3.5.1 Causes of Action Under ERISA

ERISA § 502 describes what civil causes of action may be brought under the statute and by whom. The three most important subsections are 502(a)(1)(B), 502(a)(2) and 502(a)(3), the first two of which are very specific in what they cover and the third of which is a broad catch all provision.

Section 502(a)(1)(B) authorizes participants or beneficiaries to bring a civil action to recover benefits due under the terms of a plan, to enforce rights under the terms of a plan, or to clarify rights to future benefits under a plan. This is the basic provision allowing a participant to get what is owed under the terms of a plan. It is also the basis for preempting state law claims to enforce benefit entitlements.

---

397 62 F. 3d 553 (3rd Cir. 1995).

398 134 S.Ct. 2459 (2014).

399 Id. at 2472. See also, Amgen Inc. v. Steve Harris, 136 S.Ct. 758 (2016) (reversing the Ninth Circuit Court of Appeals for failing to properly implement the pleading standards for a complaint that alleged breaches of fiduciary duty related to retirement plans' investment in employer stock, as outlined in *Dudenhoeffer*).

400 Pilot Life Ins. Co. v. Dedeaux, 481 U.S. 41, 52 (1987).

Section 502(a)(2) authorizes the Secretary, a participant, beneficiary or fiduciary to bring a claim for appropriate relief under § 409, which is the ERISA section that creates liability on the part of fiduciaries for breaches of their fiduciary duties.

Section 502(a)(3) authorizes participants, beneficiaries or fiduciaries to seek equitable remedies for any act or practice which violates ERISA or plan terms, or to seek other equitable relief to redress such violations or enforce any provisions of ERISA. There is an analogue to 502(a)(3) in 502(a)(5), which allows the DOL to bring a claim in similar circumstances.

In *CIGNA Corp. v. Amara*[401] (discussed in Section 5.3.1.4 and dealing with a discrepancy between a summary plan description (SPD) and the terms of the plan), the Supreme Court had the opportunity to comment on the relationship between sections 502(a)(1)(B) and 502(a)(3). The plaintiffs, which included a class of 25,000 participants, alleged that CIGNA had misrepresented matters related to a conversion of a defined benefit pension plan into a cash balance plan. The plaintiffs sought relief under Section 502(a)(1)(B) for benefits due under the terms of the plan and under Section 502(a)(3) to seeking reformation of plan. The Court held that because the SPD was not part of the plan, the participants were seeking remedies beyond the plan as written and thus Section 502(a)(1)(B) was not applicable.

Section 510 of ERISA prohibits any person from retaliating or otherwise discriminating against any participant or beneficiary of a plan for exercising any rights to which such participant or beneficiary may be entitled under a plan or under ERISA and prohibits interference with the attainment of any right to which a participant may be entitled under a plan or under ERISA. Section 502(a)(3)'s authorization of appropriate equitable relief to remedy ERISA violations includes the ability to grant relief for violations of § 510. Because § 510 speaks in terms of actions taken "for the purpose of interfering" with a participant's rights, the question in suits alleging a violation of § 510 is whether the defendant's action was taken with the specific intent of interfering with ERISA benefits. As one court noted, it is necessary to distinguish between "adverse actions which have an incidental, albeit important, effect on an employee's rights" and actions where depriving a participant of benefits "was a motivating factor."[402] That means that it is not easy for a plaintiff to prevail in action alleging a violation of § 510. Not only will evidence of specific intent almost invariably be circumstantial, but decisions

---

[401] 563 U.S. 421 (2011).

[402] Dister v. Continental Group, Inc., 859 F.2d 1108, 1111 (2d Cir. 1988).

that have an impact on a participant's benefits will quite frequently be made with mixed motives.[403]

One important issue that arises is the extent to which a nonfiduciary may be a defendant in an ERISA action. Relying on the structure of § 502, as well as other provisions of ERISA, the Supreme Court concluded in dicta in *Mertens v. Hewitt Associates*[404] that a claim of breach of fiduciary duty under § 404 may not be brought against a nonfiduciary. However, in *Harris Trust & Savings Bank v. Salomon Smith Barney*,[405] the Court concluded that a plaintiff may bring an action under § 502(a)(3) against a nonfiduciary party in interest who participates in a prohibited transaction.

ERISA says nothing about when jury trials are available under the statute, leaving it to the courts to resolve the question. With few exceptions, courts have disallowed jury trials in ERISA actions on the ground that ERISA is grounded in the law of trusts and that therefore such actions generally seek equitable and not legal relief. This reasoning is not unassailable, as suits to recover benefits due under the plan are probably more accurately thought of as akin to contract actions seeking legal relief. Nonetheless, every circuit court that has faced the question has concluded that there is no right to a jury trial in benefit claims.

Nor does ERISA address the statute of limitations for actions. The approach taken by courts is to apply the most analogous state statute of limitations as a matter of federal common law. Plans can establish different and shorter statutes of limitations than the law so long as the plan's limitations period is reasonable.[406]

5.3.5.2 Remedies

Courts have been rigid in disallowing remedies not authorized under § 502 of ERISA, viewing ERISA's enforcement provisions as an "interlocking, interrelated, and interdependent remedial scheme" that is part of a " 'comprehensive and reticulated statute.' "[407] Since § 502 does not authorize extra-contractual or punitive damages, courts have been unwilling to grant such damages.

---

[403] See Inter-Modal Rail Employees Ass'n v. Atchison, Topeka & Santa Fe Railway Co., 520 U.S. 510 (1997) (finding an employer's action to be a permissible "fundamental business decision").

[404] 508 U.S. 248 (1993).

[405] 530 U.S. 238 (2000).

[406] Heimeshoff v. Hartford Life & Acc. Ins. Co., 134 S.Ct. 604, 612 (2013).

[407] Massachusetts Mutual Life Ins. Co. v. Russell, 473 U.S. 134, 146 (1985) (quoting Nachman Corp. v. Pension Benefit Guaranty Corp., 446 U.S. 359, 361 (1980)).

The Supreme Court established in *Massachusetts Mutual Life Insurance Co. v. Russell*,[408] that remedies under § 502(a)(2) for breach of fiduciary duty may be paid only to a plan and not to plan beneficiaries. *Russell* involved a defined benefit plan and the Supreme Court had occasion in 2008 to consider to what extent the *Russell* holding should apply to defined contribution plans. In *LaRue v. DeWolff, Boberg & Associates, Inc.*,[409] the Court held that "although § 502(a)(2) does not provide a remedy for individual injuries distinct from plan injuries, that provision does authorize recover for fiduciary breaches that impair the value of plan assets in a participant's individual account."[410]

Section 502(a)(3) authorizes courts to award "appropriate" equitable relief. The question of what constitutes equitable relief is one that has been heavily litigated. Prior to the Supreme Court's 2002 decision in *Great-West Life & Annuity Insurance Co. v. Knudson*,[411] many courts had taken an expansive view of the scope of equitable remedies available under § 502(a)(3). However, in *Great-West* the Court signaled a more restrictive view of available remedies, suggesting that relief characterized as restitution may not always be considered to be equitable. The Court might have softened this signal in 2011, in *CIGNA Corp. v. Amara*, (discussed in the prior section). The Court, found that under § 502(a)(3) both reformation and some kinds of monetary relief were appropriate remedies.

5.3.5.3 Preemption

ERISA contains one of the broadest preemption provisions of any piece of federal legislation, preempting, with some exceptions, any and all state laws that "relate to" an employee benefit plan. According to its legislative history, Congress intended the preemption clause to have a broad scope with the aim of eliminating conflicting and inconsistent state laws. The question whether ERISA preempts a particular state law cause of action is perhaps one of the most heavily litigated issues under the statute.

Courts have struggled for many years with the question what it means for a state law to "relate to" an employee benefit plan, and the Supreme Court has decided no fewer than 20 cases interpreting the phrase. Initially, the Supreme Court took a very expansive view, taking an almost literal interpretation of "relate to," speaking of

---

408 473 U.S. 134 (1985).

409 552 U.S. 248 (2008).

410 Id. at 1026.

411 534 U.S. 204 (2002).

ERISA preemption as "deliberately expansive,"[412] "sweeping,"[413] and "conspicuous for its breadth."[414] As articulated by the Court in *Shaw v. Delta Air Lines*, a law "relates to" an employee benefit plan if it "has a connection with" or makes "reference to" an employee benefit plan.[415]

Ultimately, however, the Supreme Court determined that its literal, textual approach to the preemption question was not helpful. In *New York State Conference of Blue Cross & Blue Shield Plan v. Travelers Insurance Co.*,[416] the Court acknowledged that its prior preemption analysis, focusing on the words of the statute, was problematic. Recognizing that if "relate to" is taken to its fullest stretch, everything would be preempted, the Court consciously adopted a more pragmatic approach, suggesting that "we simply must go beyond the unhelpful text and the frustrating difficulty of defining its key term, and look instead to the objectives of the ERISA statute as a guide to the scope of the state law that Congress understood would survive."[417]

In the wake of *Travelers*, courts have taken a more restrictive approach to preemption. Although courts look to a variety of factors in determining whether a state law of general application "relates to" ERISA plans—such as whether the state law affects relations between primary ERISA entities, whether the state law impacts the structure or administration of ERISA plans, and whether the state law provides an alternate cause of action to participants to collect benefits protected by ERISA—the primary focus appears to be on whether the state statute affects the structure or the administration of an ERISA plan. For example, in reviewing a challenge to a state law which required self-insured employee health plans to report claims data, the Court of Appeals for the Second Circuit recognized the narrowing trend in preemption doctrine, but found the law preempted, emphasizing the need to avoid a hodgepodge of state reporting laws.[418]

Section 514(b) of ERISA contains a number of exceptions from the preemptive reach of the statute. The most important of those exceptions is the exception from preemption of state laws regulating insurance. For years, whether a state law regulated insurance and

---

412 Pilot Life Ins. Co. v. Dedeaux, 481 U.S. 41 (1987).

413 FMC Corp. v. Holliday, 498 U.S. 52, 58 (1990).

414 Id. at 58.

415 463 U.S. 85, 96–97 (1983).

416 514 U.S. 645 (1995).

417 Id. at 656.

418 Liberty Mutual Ins. Co. v. Donegan, 746 F.3d 497 (2014), affirmed Gobeille v. Liberty Mutual Ins., 136 S.Ct. 936 (2016).

was therefore saved from preemption was determined with reference to the McCarran-Ferguson Act test, a three part test that examined:

(1) "whether the . . . [state law] has the effect of spreading the policyholder's risk;"

(2) "whether the . . . [state law] is an integral part of the policy relationship between the insurer and the insured;" and

(3) "whether the practice is limited to entities within the insurance industry."[419]

However, in *Kentucky Association of Health Plans, Inc. v. Miller*,[420] the Supreme Court abandoned that approach on the grounds that it failed to provide sufficient guidance to lower courts and did not focus on the central inquiry. In *Miller*, the Court enunciated a two-part test. For a law to regulate insurance, (1) it must be "specifically directed toward entities engaged in insurance" and (2) it must "substantially affect the risk pooling arrangement between the insurer and the insured."[421] A state law "substantially affects the risk pooling arrangement between the insurer and the insured" when it "alters the scope of permissible bargains between insurers and insured" by regulating the substantive terms of an insurance contract.[422]

Under the *Miller* test, so called "any willing provider statutes"[423] and state laws dealing with subrogation[424] have been saved from preemption as state laws regulating insurance. In contrast, bad faith claims are not considered to arise out of a law regulating insurance and thus are preempted.[425]

The insurance savings clause is modified by § 502(b)(2)(B), which provides that no employee benefit plan shall be deemed to be an insurer for the purpose of laws that regulate insurance companies. The effect of this "deemer clause" is that state laws regulating

---

[419] Pilot Life v. Dedeaux, 481 U.S. at 48–49 (quoting Union Labor Life Ins. Co. v. Pireno, 458 U.S. 119, 129 (1982)).

[420] 538 U.S. 329 (2003).

[421] Id. at 341–42.

[422] See Spellman v. United Parcel Service, Inc., 540 F.Supp.2d 237, 246–47 (D. Me. 2008); Standard Ins. Co. v. Morrison, 537 F.Supp.2d 1142, 1151–52 (D. Mont. 2008); American Council of Life Insurers v. Watters, 536 F.Supp.2d 811, 823 (W.D. Mich. 2008).

[423] This was the statute at issue in *Miller*. "Any willing provider statutes" prohibit a health insurer from discriminating against any provider located in the geographic coverage area of the health plan that is willing to meet the terms and conditions for participation established by the insurer.

[424] See, e.g., Singh v. Prudential Health Care Plan, Inc., 335 F.3d 278 (2003).

[425] See, e.g., Barber v. UNUM Life Ins. Co., 383 F.3d 134 (2004).

insurance may not be applied to so-called "self-insured" employee benefit plans. In *Metropolitan Life Insurance Co. v. Massachusetts*,[426] the Supreme Court recognized that the combined impact of the savings and deemer clause had the anomalous effect of allowing state regulation of some (insured) but not all employee benefit plans, but viewed this to be explicitly demanded by the statute.

In a "self-insured" plan there is no real insurance. Essentially, the employer bears the full cost of coverage; if an insurance company is involved at all, it is only to administer claims. One reason larger employers (for whom the risks of self-insurance may be minimal) self-insure is that it may be less expensive for them to bear the risk associated with claims than to pay an insurance company for doing so. The fact that self-insurance has the effect of removing the employer from the reach of state insurance mandated benefits laws obviously provides an additional incentive.

It can be expected that preemption questions, both with respect to the "relate to" clause and with respect to the insurance exception, will continue to plague the courts. This is true for at least two reasons. First, as noted already, the ERISA remedy for a denial of benefits is limited to the benefits due under the plan. This encourages participants to try to re-characterize their benefit denial claims as state law contract, bad faith, or negligence claims so as to avail themselves of extra-contractual and punitive damages.[427] Second, the provision of medical care through managed care entities frequently leads to a blurring of the lines between medical treatment decisions (the appropriate subject of a state malpractice claim) and decisions regarding benefits under a plan (the appropriate subject of an ERISA claim). When an HMO plays multiple roles, it is not always clear whether a claim is a preempted claim of eligibility for benefits or a nonpreempted state law claim.[428]

§ 5.4 Unemployment Compensation

5.4.1 Overview of the Program

The Social Security Act established the unemployment compensation system in 1935.[429] It was designed to provide economic

---

426 471 U.S. 724 (1985).

427 Courts consistently find that claims based on the denial of benefits under an ERISA plan are preempted, regardless of how plaintiffs characterize the claim. See, e.g., McGowin v. ManPower Int'l, Inc., 363 F.3d 556 (5th Cir. 2004); Nester v. Allegiance Healthcare Corp., 315 F.3d 610 (6th Cir. 2003); Hampers v. W.R. Grace & Co., 202 F.3d 44 (1st Cir. 2000).

428 See Kuthy v. Mansheim, 124 Fed. Appx. 756 (4th Cir. 2004).

429 Pub. L. No. 74–27, 149 Stat. 620 (codified as amended in scattered sections of 26 U.S.C. and 42 U.S.C.).

security for employees during times of temporary unemployment, enabling them to support themselves and their families and to make effective job choices.[430] Another goal of the statute was to stabilize the economy during difficult times like the depression by providing individuals with purchasing power. The statute has been amended numerous times but its major structure has remained the same. The system is jointly administered by the federal and state governments and funded by taxes paid by employers based on employee wages. The federal law provides guidelines, standards and regulations, while the system's administration is left to states under state laws.[431] State compliance with federal standards is required in order to obtain federal funds to operate the unemployment compensation systems.[432] Also, if the state meets federal standards, state unemployment taxes paid by the employer are set off against the federal unemployment tax, reducing the amount of federal tax employers must pay. As a result of these incentives, states typically structure their systems to comply with federal requirements. What follows is a basic summary of the provisions of the law. In areas covered by state law, the summary is general and does not reflect the specifics of each state.

5.4.1.1 Coverage

State law determines coverage of unemployment compensation programs. Like most employment statutes, unemployment compensation laws cover only employees, excluding the self-employed and independent contractors.[433] Other common exclusions, some depending on the number workers employed or amount of wages paid, include insurance and real estate brokers working on commission, casual employees, agricultural employees, domestic employees, and students working for the educational institution they attend.[434] Federal law precludes payment to workers who are not lawfully working in the United States.[435] Also, there are separate unemployment compensation systems for federal and railroad employees.[436]

---

430 Walter Nicholson & Karen Needels, Unemployment Insurance: Strengthening the Relationship Between Theory and Policy, 20 J. Econ. Persp. 47 (Summer 2006).

431 For federal statutory standards, see 26 U.S.C. § 3304.

432 See 42 U.S.C. § 503.

433 See Nicholson & Needels, supra note 430, at 53.

434 See 26 U.S.C. §§ 3306(a)(2)–(3), (c)(1)(2), (10)(B); U.S. Dep't of Labor, Employment & Training Administration, Comparison of State Unemployment Laws, Coverage, 2017 at 1–8 to 1–11, available at https://oui.doleta.gov/unemploy/pdf/uilawcompar/2017/coverage.pdf.

435 26 U.S.C. § 3304(a)(14)(A).

436 See 45 U.S.C. §§ 351 et seq. (railroad employees); 5 U.S.C. §§ 8501 et seq. (federal employees).

5.4.1.2 Taxes

The unemployment compensation system is funded by federal and state payroll taxes.[437] Federal taxes are paid into a trust fund which finances the administrative costs of the program, through grants to the states, and the federal share of extended benefits provided during times of high unemployment.[438] Federal taxes are paid at a flat rate on the first $7,000 of income[439] and are offset by state taxes.[440] States can borrow from the federal trust fund if their funds are depleted by high unemployment.

State taxes also go into the Federal Unemployment Trust Fund into accounts allocated by state, and are used to pay benefits to unemployed workers. State taxes are also based on a percentage of wages, but the percentage and the amount of wages subject to tax vary by state.[441] The state taxes are experience-rated, with lower taxes for employers that have fewer employees who are involuntarily unemployed and therefore entitled to benefits.[442] Smaller firms are grouped into classes for rating purposes, while large employers usually have their own rating. Nonprofit organizations are exempt from federal taxes but not from state taxes.[443] However, federal law requires the states to allow nonprofit organizations and governmental entities to reimburse the trust fund for benefits paid, rather than paying state taxes in advance.[444] Employers that choose the reimbursement option do not pay into the system unless they terminate employees who then collect benefits.

5.4.1.3 Benefits

Primary benefits are paid from the regular state program. Subject to federal guidelines, the states decide the following: (1) the qualifying requirements; (2) the amount of benefits; (3) the duration of benefits; and (4) the grounds for disqualification.

5.4.1.3.1 Qualifying Requirements

To qualify for benefits, the employee must show employment by a covered employer during a statutorily defined base period for more

---

437 Nicholson & Needels, supra note 430, at 48.

438 Id.

439 26 U.S.C. §§ 3301, 3306.

440 26 U.S.C. § 3302.

441 Nicholson & Needels, supra note 430, at 49.

442 Id. at 49, 56–57.

443 See, e.g., 26 U.S.C. § 3306(c)(8) (excluding from the definition of employment work for a nonprofit organization); Va. Code Ann. § 60.2–213 (covering employees of nonprofit organizations that employ four or more workers during any part of twenty weeks in a year).

444 26 U.S.C. § 3309.

than one quarter of a year, as well as certain minimum earnings during that time.[445] The base period and minimum earnings requirements are set by the states. Most states use four of the last five completed calendar quarters prior to the filing of the claim for benefits as the base period,[446] and most also require earnings in more than one quarter of the base period.[447] These qualifying requirements are designed to achieve the statutory purpose of providing income in times of temporary unemployment by insuring that benefits are paid only to individuals who have an attachment to the labor force.

5.4.1.3.2 Amount of Benefits

The unemployment compensation payment is a weekly benefit usually determined by formula which is designed to replace about 50% of the employee's average weekly wage.[448] There is commonly a statutory maximum benefit so that employees with higher earnings receive a smaller percentage of prior earnings in benefits.[449] In fact, because of the maximums, very few states replace, on average, half of the beneficiaries' weekly wage.[450] In some jurisdictions there is a dependents' allowance, which is added to the benefit for each employee dependent.[451] In addition, some states allow benefits for partial unemployment.[452] Social Security taxes are not collected on unemployment compensation benefits, but since 1986 benefits have been subject to federal income tax. State and local taxes are imposed on benefits at the option of the states.

5.4.1.3.3 Duration of Benefits

In most states, there is a waiting period for benefits, usually a week.[453] After the waiting period the benefits continue for the duration of unemployment, subject to a statutory maximum.[454] States typically determine the maximum on the basis of the employee's length of prior employment or the amount earned in prior

---

445 Wimberly v. Labor & Indus. Relations Comm'n, 479 U.S. 511, 515 (1987).

446 U.S. Dep't of Labor, Employment & Training Administration, Comparison of State Unemployment Laws, Monetary Entitlement, 2017 at 3–2, https://oui.doleta.gov/unemploy/pdf/uilawcompar/2017/monetary.pdf.

447 Id. at 3–4.

448 See Lori G. Kletzer & Howard Rosen, Reforming Unemployment Insurance for the Twenty-First Century Workforce 11 (2006), available at https://www.brookings.edu/research/reforming-unemployment-insurance-for-the-twenty-first-century-workforce/.

449 Nicholson & Needels, supra note 430, at 54.

450 Kletzer & Rosen, supra note 448, at 11–12.

451 U.S. Dep't of Labor, Monetary Entitlement, supra note 446, at 3–19 to 3–21.

452 Id. at 3–17.

453 Id. at 3–14.

454 Nicholson & Needels, supra note 430, at 54.

employment.[455] In some jurisdictions the maximum is the same for all unemployed workers.[456] Maximums for regular unemployment typically run from ten to twenty-six weeks.[457] In times of high unemployment, supplemental benefits are available through a federal program, with funding split between the state and federal governments.[458] The extended benefits program typically provides for an additional thirteen weeks of benefits.[459] Some states also provide additional supplemental benefits.[460] Congress has periodically provided emergency benefits in times of high unemployment as well.[461] For example, Congress extended benefits for those unemployed as a result of 9/11 and provided benefits to some employees who did not meet the eligibility requirements. Because of the nature of the triggers for the standard extended benefit programs, in recent years temporary emergency benefits have become the more typical funding mechanism for extended benefits, politicizing the process for providing benefits during recessionary times.[462]

5.4.1.3.4 Disqualification for Benefits

The disqualifications stem from the theory that an employee must be unemployed through no fault of his or her own in order to collect benefits. Disqualifications include: (1) voluntary quit; (2) termination for misconduct; (3) refusal to accept suitable work; (4) unemployment due to a labor dispute; and (5) unavailability for work.[463] The application of these disqualifications varies by state. In some states, the disqualification is for a specific time period, while in most the employee is disqualified until he or she has worked for a covered employer and met a specified standard for earnings.[464] The

---

455 Id.

456 Id.

457 Id. Two states have a higher maximum—Massachusetts with thirty and Montana with twenty-eight weeks. Kletzer & Rosen, supra note 448, at 12.

458 Nicholson & Needels, supra note 430, at 55, 62–64.

459 Kletzer & Rosen, supra note 448, at 13.

460 U.S. Dep't of Labor, Employment & Training Administration, Comparison of State Unemployment Laws, Extensions and Special Programs, 2017 at 4–4, https://oui.doleta.gov/unemploy/pdf/uilawcompar/2017/special.pdf.

461 Id.

462 Kletzer & Rosen, supra note 448, at 13; U.S. Dep't of Labor, Extensions and Special Programs, supra note 460, at 4–4.

463 Wimberly, 479 U.S. at 515.

464 U.S. Dep't of Labor, Employment & Training Administration, Comparison of State Unemployment Laws, Nonmonetary Eligibility, 2017 at 5–9, https://oui.doleta.gov/unemploy/pdf/uilawcompar/2017/nonmonetary.pdf. See, e.g., Utah Code Ann. § 35A–4–405(2)(a) (specifying that an individual terminated for just cause is disqualified until he or she earns "an amount equal to at least six times the claimant's weekly benefit amount in bona fide covered employment").

disqualifications have become more stringent over the years as states have looked for ways to reduce the cost of unemployment benefits.

In order to receive benefits, employees must register for employment with the state, be able to work, available for work, and seeking work.[465] In some states, employees must report to the state on their efforts to find work to maintain their eligibility for benefits.[466] They cannot refuse suitable work and remain eligible for benefits. For further discussion of benefit eligibility see Section 5.4.2 below.

The Trade Act of 1974 authorizes benefits for employees unemployed as a result of imports or transfer of their work to another country.[467] These benefits include training, relocation and job search benefits. Individuals unemployed as a result of disasters declared by the President are also eligible for federal unemployment compensation benefits.[468]

5.4.1.4 Administration

Each state has an agency that administers the statute and accepts applications for benefits from unemployed workers.[469] The agency notifies the chargeable employer of the application and offers the employer an opportunity to contest an award of benefits. Whether benefits are denied or awarded initially, an appeal is available to the employee and the employer.[470] Federal law requires the state to offer an opportunity for a fair hearing before an impartial tribunal.[471] A hearing officer typically hears the appeal and in many states the case may be appealed to a board of review or commission.[472] The hearings are relatively informal, often telephonic, and most employees and employers do not use attorneys.[473] All states allow for appeals to the court system after a final decision by the agency.[474]

---

[465] Nicholson & Needels, supra note 430, at 52.

[466] Id.

[467] U.S. Dep't of Labor, Extensions and Special Programs, supra note 460, at 4–7 to 4–8.

[468] Id. at 4–8 to 4–9.

[469] See 42 U.S.C. § 503(a)(2).

[470] U.S. Dep't of Labor, Employment & Training Administration, Comparison of State Unemployment Laws, Appeals, 2017, at 7–1, https://oui.doleta.gov/unemploy/pdf/uilawcompar/2017/appeals.pdf.

[471] 42 U.S.C. § 503(a)(3).

[472] U.S. Dep't of Labor, Appeals, supra note 470, at 7–1 to 7–4.

[473] Ann C. Hodges, The Preclusive Effect of Unemployment Compensation Determinations in Subsequent Litigation: A Federal Solution, 38 Wayne L. Rev. 1803, 1814, 1854–55 (1992).

[474] U.S. Dep't of Labor, Comparison of State Unemployment Laws, Appeals, supra note 470 at 7–4 to 7–7.

The federal statute imposes requirements on the states for timely processing of claims.[475] The Department of Labor monitors the states for compliance.[476] Although the targets for timely processing are not always met, the requirements are designed to speed the award of benefits to accomplish one of the goals of the legislation, which is to slow the downward spiral of the economy in times of recession by providing income to unemployed workers.

5.4.1.5 *Preclusion of Other Claims*

Because unemployment claims are adjudicated more rapidly than most other employment claims, the issue frequently arises of whether a decision in an unemployment compensation proceeding is preclusive in later litigation relating to the termination. A number of states have amended their unemployment compensation statutes to permit further litigation despite unemployment compensation determinations.[477] In states without such statutes, courts have divided over whether such proceedings bar re-litigation of the cause for discharge in later cases alleging discriminatory or wrongful discharge. An important consideration is the rapid and informal nature of unemployment compensation litigation. Allowing preclusion might encourage the parties to use attorneys to try complex discharge cases in the unemployment hearing, adding to the administrative costs of the system and slowing benefit decisions, which could be particularly devastating to unemployed individuals.[478]

5.4.2 Eligibility

The legal issues most often contested relate to the eligibility disqualifications. There are two primary categories of disqualification. The first relates to the circumstances of leaving the prior job, while the second relates to maintaining continuing eligibility through current willingness and ability to work.

5.4.2.1 *Circumstances of Separation*

Individuals leave employment through either voluntary quit or involuntary termination. Because unemployment is designed to compensate employees who are involuntarily unemployed, the burden is on the employee to establish eligibility in the case of a

---

[475] 42 U.S.C. § 503(a)(1); 20 C.F.R. §§ 640.1–640.5.

[476] 20 C.F.R. §§ 640.6–640.8.

[477] U.S. Dep't of Labor, Comparison of State Employment Laws, Appeals, supra note 470, at 7–1.

[478] For a full discussion of the issues relating to preclusion, see Hodges, supra note 473.

voluntary quit and on the employer to establish disqualification in the event of an involuntary termination.

5.4.2.1.1 Voluntary Quit

A voluntary quit does not always result in disqualification for unemployment compensation benefits. Rather, statutes disqualify employees who quit without good cause. Many states add the requirement that good cause must be attributable to the employer. Cases then focus on what is good cause for leaving employment. In determining what is good cause, administrative agencies and courts look to what a reasonable employee desirous of maintaining employment would do under similar circumstances. Statutes may contain specific provisions as to what does and does not constitute good cause, in addition to the general language which is applied where no specific statutory provision applies.[479]

Where the employer changes the employee's job, quitting may be justified. For example, after an Illinois employee was reassigned from regular preschool to working with emotionally disturbed children, work for which she felt unqualified, she quit her employment and was awarded benefits.[480] On the other hand, Indiana denied benefits to an employee whose shift was changed, creating child care and transportation problems.[481] The Indiana court found that the employee's problems were not connected with work, but were personal. Not all states reject personal circumstances as good cause however. In *Raytheon v. Director of Division of Employment Security*,[482] the Massachusetts Supreme Judicial Court awarded benefits to an employee who quit her job when her coworker who had provided her with transportation was laid off and she could not find other transportation or a position on another shift. The court deferred to the administrative agency's finding that the personal reasons made her unemployment involuntary. Despite statutory language specifying that benefits would be denied to employees who quit without "good cause attributable to the employing unit," the court agreed that unemployment need not be the employer's fault to justify an award of benefits.

Leaving employment to follow a spouse may constitute good cause in some jurisdictions,[483] but not others.[484] The same is true of

---

[479] See, e.g., Wash. Rev. Code Ann. § 50.20.050(2).

[480] Davis v. Board of Review, 125 Ill.App.3d 67, 465 N.E.2d 576 (1984).

[481] Gray v. Dobbs House, 171 Ind.App. 444, 357 N.E.2d 900 (1976).

[482] 364 Mass. 593, 307 N.E.2d 330 (1974).

[483] See, e.g., Robinson v. Unemployment Sec. Bd. of Review, 181 Conn. 1, 434 A.2d 293 (1980).

[484] See, e.g., Va. Code Ann. § 60.2–618. For a full list, see U.S. Dep't of Labor, Nonmonetary Eligibility, supra note 464, at 5–6 to 5–7.

leaving employment to follow a significant other.[485] Factors such as the length of the relationship, an engagement to marry, and a child in common may affect the determination. Discrimination or harassment will justify quitting in most states, but the employee's belief that he or she is a victim of discrimination must be reasonable and the employee must take reasonable steps to resolve the problem prior to leaving in order to qualify for benefits.[486] Other common good cause provisions include leaving to join the military, leaving to take another job, and leaving because of illness.[487]

The American Recovery and Reinvestment Act of 2009 provided financial incentives to states to update their laws to take account of employees' increasing need to balance work and family responsibilities. States were encouraged to limit some disqualifications of employees who leave work for family reasons, including domestic violence, to care for an ill or disabled family member, or to follow a relocating spouse. Some states adopted these provisions while others did not.[488]

5.4.2.1.2 Termination

Employees terminated for misconduct are disqualified from receiving unemployment compensation benefits, while those who are simply unable to perform their jobs are not. Some states use the language "termination for just cause," rather than "misconduct" to describe the disqualification.[489] Some state statutes specify that particular behavior by the employee constitutes misconduct, but such definitions are not exclusive.[490] That an employer had a justifiable reason for termination does not determine eligibility for

---

485 Compare Reep v. Commissioner of Dep't of Employment and Training, 412 Mass. 845, 593 N.E.2d 1297 (1992) (awarding benefits), with Davis v. Employment Sec. Dep't, 108 Wash.2d 272, 737 P.2d 1262 (1987) (denying benefits).

486 Compare Umbarger v. Virginia Employment Comm'n, 12 Va.App. 431, 404 S.E.2d 380 (1991) (awarding benefits), with Vick v. Virginia Employment Comm'n, No. 0722–96–2, 1997 WL 117932 (Va. Ct. App. Mar. 18, 1997) (denying benefits). For a list of state provisions, see U.S. Dep't of Labor, Nonmonetary Eligibility, supra note 464, at 5–2 to 5–4.

487 Id. at 5–2 to 5–5.

488 American Recovery and Reinvestment Act of 2009, PL 111–5, February 17, 2009, codified at 42 USC § 1103(f)(3)(B). For lists of states with such provisions, see U.S. Dep't of Labor, Nonmonetary Eligibility, supra note 464, at 5–5 to 5–6,

489 See Utah Code Ann. § 35–4–405(2)(a); Johnson v. Department of Employment Sec., 782 P.2d 965 (Utah Ct. App. 1989) (finding drug use on duty or off to be just cause for termination).

490 See, e.g., Va. Code Ann. § 60.2–618(b) (defining misconduct to include chronic absenteeism or tardiness, intentionally false statements on a job application regarding criminal convictions, and a positive drug test); Utah Code Ann. § 35–4–405(2)(b) (disqualifying for crimes of dishonesty). For a variety of examples of state law provisions, see U.S. Dep't of Labor, Nonmonetary Eligibility, supra note 464, at 5–12 to 5–13.

unemployment compensation benefits, even in states with a just cause standard.[491]

An example will illustrate this principle. An Illinois employee who drove a medical car transporting patients to and from health care facilities had four accidents in three and one half months of employment.[492] Each accident occurred while the driver was backing the vehicle without patients inside, and none caused serious damage. The driver was terminated for violating a company rule providing for discharge after two at-fault accidents. While the unemployment compensation board denied benefits, the court reversed, holding that misconduct required a deliberate breach of a reasonable rule. The court noted that while the discharge may have been proper, there was no evidence of "an intentional or substantial disregard of the employer's interests or of the plaintiff's duties and obligations to his employer."[493] Utah uses a similar formulation for disqualification but in addition, includes discharge for just cause as disqualifying.[494] The test for just cause looks at employee culpability, which includes the seriousness of the offense, employee knowledge of the employer's expectations, and employee control over the conduct.[495] A good faith error in judgment does not meet this test.[496]

Some states provide for greater disqualification penalties for certain serious misconduct. Most disqualifications in this category are criminal acts, but some states include conduct such as use of alcohol at work and insubordination.[497]

Disqualification provisions typically require that the misconduct for which the employee was terminated be connected with work. Disputes over whether such a connection exists are not uncommon. In Arkansas, for example, a press operator was terminated for pleading no contest to a felony domestic violence charge, pursuant to the employer's policy of discharging employees convicted of felonies.[498] The court found no harm to the employer's interests, despite the employer's claimed need to protect employees from violence, and upheld the award of benefits. It bears repeating that

---

491 See Johnson v. Dep't of Employment Sec., 782 P.2d at 969.

492 Pesce v. Board of Review, 161 Ill.App.3d 879, 515 N.E.2d 849 (1987).

493 161 Ill.App.3d at 883, 515 N.E.2d at 852.

494 Utah Code Ann. § 35–4–405(2)(a).

495 See Kehl v. Board of Review, 700 P.2d 1129, 1133 (Utah 1985).

496 Carbon County v. Workforce Appeals Bd., 2013 Ut. 41, 308 P.3d 477 (2013) (finding medical transport employee's failure to comprehend the seriousness of the patient's condition and consequent delay was not culpable).

497 See U.S. Dep't of Labor, Nonmonetary Eligibility, supra note 464, at 5–16 to 5–17.

498 See Baldor Electric Co. v. Arkansas Employment Sec. Dep't, 71 Ark.App. 166, 27 S.W.3d 771 (2000).

the court did not, and indeed could not in this proceeding, question the employer's decision to discharge, but could only review the decision to award unemployment benefits. On the other hand, where an employee left an offensive message on a co-employee's home voice mail because the co-worker had not given her a ride home, the denial of benefits was upheld because of the potential harm to the employer from the adverse impact on employee morale that could result from such hostile language between coworkers.[499] The call was initiated as a result of an incident relating to work and the comments referred to coworkers. Although there was no written rule against such conduct, the court found a written rule unnecessary where the conduct violated standards of behavior that an employer had a right to expect.

Because the standards for disqualification are established by the states, similar conduct can result in different decisions in different states. Often, however, a review of the decisions reveals a difference in facts that might justify the differential treatment. For example, in *Glide Lumber Products v. Employment Division*,[500] the court found that failing a drug test was not disqualifying since there was no evidence of impairment on the job. In *American Federation of Labor v. Unemployment Insurance Appeals Board*,[501] the court upheld the disqualification of a housekeeper on an oil rig who was fired for refusal to take a drug test while on shore leave. In the latter case, however, there was both a history of drug violations and an acknowledgement by the employee that the oil rig was a dangerous place to work, although the employee's own job was not safety sensitive.

5.4.2.1.3 Unemployment Resulting from a Labor Dispute

All states disqualify employees who are unemployed as the result of a labor dispute.[502] The definition of labor dispute is not the same in all states, however. A few states define the term in the statute but most do not, leaving the issue to the courts.[503] Many states allow employees who are locked out by the employer to collect benefits under some circumstances, while all states bar benefits to individuals unemployed because they are striking their employer.[504]

---

[499] Manning v. Department of Employment Sec., 365 Ill.App.3d 553, 850 N.E.2d 244 (2006).

[500] 86 Or.App. 669, 741 P.2d 907 (1987).

[501] 23 Cal.App.4th 51, 28 Cal.Rptr.2d 210 (1994).

[502] Thomas J. Goger, Annotation, General Principles Pertaining to Statutory Disqualification for Unemployment Compensation Benefits Because of Strike or Labor Dispute, 63 A.L.R.3d 88, 94 (1975); U.S. Dep't of Labor, Nonmonetary Eligibility, supra note 464 at 5–20 to 5–22.

[503] Goger, supra note 502, at 104.

[504] See, e.g., Vt. Stat. Ann. tit. 21, § 1344(a)(4) (disqualifying striking employees); Vt. Stat. Ann. tit. 21 § 1344(a)(4)(B) (permitting employees locked out by the employer

Those that allow benefits for locked out employees typically consider that the locked out employees are unemployed through no fault of their own.

Several legal issues have arisen regarding the meaning of the labor dispute disqualification. Suppose for example, that a strike at General Motors causes a layoff of employees at a parts supplier because the lack of production at GM eliminates the need for the parts. Are these employees unemployed as a result of a labor dispute? It would seem so, yet they are unemployed through no fault of their own.

In a few states, the employee is not disqualified unless she is in an employer/employee relationship with the employer directly engaged in the dispute.[505] In such states, if the parts supplier was an independent company, the employees could receive benefits. Some state statutes specify that the disqualification relates only to disputes at the facility where the employee worked.[506] In such case, the employees of that parts supplier could collect benefits, while the GM employees would not. A majority of states also provide that if the claimant is not "participating" in, "directly interested" in, or "financing" the labor dispute that caused the unemployment, the claimant will be eligible to receive benefits.[507] The employees in the example are not participating in the strike, but are they directly interested in or financing the strike? Suppose that they are in the same union as the GM employees? What if their employer follows the GM pattern settlement, meaning that whatever the GM contract provides, their employer will also provide to them? Unless the practice of following the pattern is longstanding, clearly established, and perhaps even a contractual certainty, a finding that such employees are directly interested in the strike is unlikely.[508] In a few states, the term "financing" has been interpreted to include payments into a union strike fund, if the contributions have a "meaningful

---

to collect benefits); Wis. Stat. Ann. § 108.04(10)(a) (disqualifying striking employees but not those locked out). For a full list see U.S. Dep't of Labor, Nonmonetary Eligibility, supra note 464 at 5–20 to 5–22.

[505] See, e.g., Lehigh Navigation Coal Co. v. Unemployment Comp. Bd. of Review, 176 Pa.Super. 69, 74, 106 A.2d 919, 922 (1954).

[506] Thomas J. Goger, Annotation, Construction of Phrase "Establishment" or "Factory, Establishment, or Other Premises" Within Unemployment Compensation Statute Rendering Employee Ineligible During Labor Dispute or Strike at Such Location, 60 A.L.R.3d 11, 18 (1974).

[507] See Thomas J. Goger, Annotation, What Constitutes Participation or Direct Interest in, or Financing of, Labor Dispute or Strike Within Disqualification Provisions of Unemployment Compensation Acts, 62 A.L.R.3d 314, 317 (1975). For a full list see U.S. Dep't of Labor, Nonmonetary Eligibility, supra note 464 at 5–20 to 5–22.

[508] See General Motors Corp. v. Bowling, 85 Ill.2d 539, 543, 426 N.E.2d 1210, 1212 (1981); Aaron v. Ohio Bureau of Employment Serv., 130 Ohio App.3d 376, 393, 720 N.E.2d 159, 172 (1998).

connection" to the strike.[509] Those cases interpreting this requirement have found that payment of regular union dues is not sufficient, however, even if some portion is allocated to a general strike fund.[510]

What about other employees at the struck facility who are not striking, but laid off because the strike has idled the plant? Another requirement of a majority of states is that even if a claimant is involved in a labor dispute, the claimant can receive unemployment compensation benefits so long as he does "not belong to a grade or class of workers of which, immediately before the commencement of a stoppage of work due to a labor dispute, there were members employed at the premises at which the stoppage occurred, any of whom were participating in or directly interested in the dispute."[511] States vary in how they define "grade or class of workers," but there are some general trends. Some courts have found that membership in a union is sufficient, even if the claimant did not go on strike, but was laid-off due to the actions of workers who did go on strike.[512] Of course, some courts have held the opposite.[513] Some courts view membership in the bargaining unit that has the labor dispute with the employer as the determinative factor, i.e., if the claimant is a member of the bargaining unit that is in a labor dispute, even if he is not on strike, he will be in the same "grade or class" as the members that are participating in the labor dispute, and be ineligible to receive unemployment compensation benefits.[514]

Another legal issue is whether the employees are still unemployed as a result of a labor dispute if they have been permanently replaced by the employer as a result of the strike. A number of states have held that permanently replaced workers can

---

509 See General Motors Corp. v. Bowling, 85 Ill.2d at 545, 426 N.E.2d at 1213 (holding that contributions to a strike fund can constitute "financing," but only if the contributions have a "meaningful connection" to the strike, and mere payments to an international union strike fund are not enough); Baker v. General Motors Corp., 420 Mich. 463, 506, 363 N.W.2d 602, 622 (1984) (finding an emergency assessment to union members, paid out several months later to striking workers, to have the necessary "meaningful connection" based on the amount, purpose, and timing). See also James E. Frick, Inc. v. Employment Div., 101 Or.App. 188, 193, 790 P.2d 33, 37 (1990) (holding that contributing to a strike fund can constitute "financing," but that it did not in the instant case, and failing to define a test to determine when contributing to a strike fund does qualify as "financing").

510 See, e.g., Aaron v. Ohio Bureau of Employment Serv., 130 Ohio App.3d at 395, 720 N.E.2d at 174.

511 See Goger, Annotation, supra note 507, at 338. For a full list see U.S. Dep't of Labor, Nonmonetary Eligibility, supra note 464 at 5–20 to 5–22.

512 See, e.g., Bartlett v. Administrator, Unemployment Comp. Act, 142 Conn. 497, 504, 115 A.2d 671, 675 (1955).

513 See, e.g., Davis v. Hix, 140 W.Va. 398, 417, 84 S.E.2d 404, 415–16 (1954).

514 See, e.g., Adams v. Review Bd. of Indiana Employment Sec. Div., 121 Ind.App. 273, 278, 98 N.E.2d 681, 684 (1951).

receive benefits in at least some circumstances.[515] The theory underlying this approach is that the employees are no longer unemployed as a result of a labor dispute, but rather because they have been replaced by the employer.

5.4.2.2 Continuing Eligibility

To maintain eligibility to receive benefits throughout the period of unemployment, the employee must be available for work and seeking work, and must not refuse suitable work without good cause. Registration with the state employment commission is required, as are reports of the search for work in most states. A challenge to the employee's availability is often triggered by the employee's refusal of a job and thus may be accompanied by a claim that the employee refused suitable work.

An employee who is ill or traveling out of the jurisdiction is not available for work.[516] Many states require employees to be able to work full-time.[517] The American Recovery and Reinvestment Act encouraged states to adapt to current employment conditions by making employees available only for part-time work eligible for benefits.[518] Some states amended their laws while others retained the full-time availability requirement.[519] A separated employee cannot be automatically disqualified because she is pregnant,[520] but an individualized determination may find that a pregnant woman is unavailable because of limitations on work caused by the pregnancy.[521]

An employee with restricted availability to work may be found to be unavailable. The test that is often applied is whether the individual remains available to a substantial field of employment. Application of the standard for unavailability will vary by jurisdiction, however. In *Martin v. Review Board*,[522] the Indiana Court of Appeals found that an employee who declined work on the

---

515 See, e.g., Titan Tire Corp. v. Employment Appeals Bd., 641 N.W.2d 752 (Iowa 2002); Bridgestone/Firestone, Inc. v. Doherty, 305 Ill.App.3d 141, 711 N.E.2d 799 (1999); Quincy Corp. v. Aguilar, 704 So.2d 1055 (Fla. Dist. Ct. App. 1997).

516 A few states have special provisions allowing ill or disabled workers to collect benefits for a period of time. U.S. Dep't of Labor, Nonmonetary Eligibility, supra note 464, at 5–23.

517 Id. at 5–24.

518 Id at 5–25; American Recovery and Reinvestment Act of 2009, PL 111–5, February 17, 2009, codified at 42 USC § 1103(f)(3)(A).

519 U.S. Dep't of Labor, Nonmonetary Eligibility, supra note 464 at 5–25 to 5–26.

520 26 U.S.C. § 3304(a)(12).

521 See Wimberly, 479 U.S. 511; Petty v. University of Delaware, 450 A.2d 392 (Del. 1982); Dorsey v. Commonwealth of Pa., Unemployment Comp. Bd. of Rev., 41 Pa.Commw. 479, 399 A.2d 809 (1979).

522 421 N.E.2d 653 (1981).

evening shift due to child care and transportation limitations remained available to work. Similarly, in California a former waitress who refused to work weekends due to child care responsibilities was available.[523] New York, however, found that a claimant was unavailable for work and not entitled to benefits on days that she did not have child care.[524] In *Alexander v. Unemployment Insurance Appeals Board*,[525] an x-ray technologist was found available for work although she restricted her employment search to smoke-free workplaces because of an allergy to smoke, a restriction that was certainly more limiting in 1980 than today. The court found that the agency did not establish that there was an insubstantial field of employment available for the employee, and further concluded that jobs where smoking was permitted were not suitable for the employee and thus, she had good cause to refuse such work.

Students who restrict their availability to work based on school attendance are frequently considered unavailable for work. Some states have statutory provisions that presumptively disqualify students from receipt of benefits.[526] In other states the restrictions on students' availability due to the demands of school will disqualify them.[527] In some states the fact that a student is seeking only part-time work will be disqualifying.[528] In other states, a student may collect benefits if he or she is available to a substantial field of employment despite any educational limitations.[529]

An individual who refuses suitable work without good cause is disqualified. Good cause to refuse work is typically broader than good cause to quit a job, and circumstances that would disqualify an individual initially because of a voluntary quit will not later require terminating benefits due to refusal to consider particular employment.[530] An employee is generally not required to accept substantially different work at significantly lower pay, particularly

---

[523] Sanchez v. Unemployment Ins. Appeals Bd., 20 Cal.3d 55, 569 P.2d 740 (1977).

[524] In re Claim of Pastore, 2 A.D.3d 1172, 770 N.Y.S.2d 177 (2003).

[525] 104 Cal.App.3d 97, 163 Cal.Rptr. 411 (1980).

[526] See, e.g., Shreve v. Department of Economic Sec., 283 N.W.2d 506 (Minn. 1979) (upholding Minnesota statute which presumed that individuals principally occupied as students were unavailable to work unless a majority of their work during the base period was performed during school attendance periods).

[527] See, e.g., In Re Palmer, 265 A.D.2d 787, 697 N.Y.S.2d 391 (1999) (disqualifying student who had refused four jobs as incompatible with school).

[528] See, e.g., Sonneman v. Knight, 790 P.2d 702 (Alaska 1990).

[529] See, e.g., Glick v. Unemployment Ins. Appeals Bd., 23 Cal.3d 493, 591 P.2d 24 (1979) (upholding award of benefits to a California law student who had previously worked many part-time jobs while attending school).

[530] See Martin v. Review Bd., 421 N.E.2d 653, 657 (Ind. Ct. App. 1981); In re Watson, 273 N.C. 629, 640, 161 S.E.2d 1, 10 (1968).

early in a period of unemployment. For example, the Supreme Court of Iowa upheld the administrative agency's award of benefits to an individual who refused to return to work as a nurse's aide at five cents above minimum wage.[531] She had in the interim been working at a much higher paying job at the post office from which she was laid off and to which she hoped to return. Courts are particularly likely to find that an employee did not reject suitable work if the terminating employer offers employment at a significantly lower pay rate, since such action may be an attempt to defeat a claim for unemployment compensation benefits.[532] After some period of unemployment, however, the definition of suitable work may broaden, requiring employees to accept jobs at lower rates of pay.[533] The employee generally is not required to accept work injurious to health.[534] Additionally, federal law bars states from defining suitable work to include jobs available due to a labor dispute, jobs which pay substantially less than similar jobs in the area, and jobs that prevent an employee from being a member of a bona fide union.[535]

5.4.3 Policy Considerations

The percentage of unemployed workers collecting benefits is typically small. In 2014, for example, only 23% of all unemployed workers collected benefits, while 34.7% of short-term unemployed workers received benefits.[536] The main reasons workers do not collect are that they do not meet the eligibility requirements or they do not file for benefits.[537] States that restricted benefits during the Great Recession that began in 2007 had significant decreases in unemployed persons receiving benefits.[538] Evidence also indicates that those who collect benefits are unemployed for longer periods.[539]

---

531 New Homestead v. Iowa Dep't of Job Service, 322 N.W.2d 269 (Iowa 1982).

532 See, e.g., Graves v. Director, 384 Mass. 766, 429 N.E.2d 705 (1981).

533 See Department of Ed. v. Unemployment Comp. Bd. of Review, 890 A.2d 1232 (Pa. Commw. Ct. 2006) (applying a balancing test weighing the length of unemployment against the reduction in pay and indicating that as unemployment grew longer the significance of the reduction in pay decreased); Donnelly v. Unemployment Comp. Bd. of Review, 17 Pa.Commw. 39, 330 A.2d 544 (1975) (finding work with 22% reduction in pay suitable after three and one half months of unemployment).

534 See Alexander v. Unemployment Ins. Appeals Bd., 104 Cal.App.3d 97, 163 Cal.Rptr. 411 (1980).

535 26 U.S.C. § 3304(a)(5)(A), (B), and (C).

536 Will Kimball & Rick McHugh, How Low Can We Go? State Unemployment Insurance Programs Exclude Record Numbers Of Jobless Workers (Employment Policy Institute 2015), http://www.epi.org/files/2015/how-low-can-we-go-state-unemployment-r3.pdf.

537 Nicholson & Needels, supra note 430, at 48–49.

538 Kimball & McHugh, supra note 536, at 6.

539 Nicholson & Needels, supra note 430, at 60–61.

Critics of the current system point out that the eligibility requirements may disqualify growing categories of workers, such as contingent workers or recent entrants to the labor market.[540] They also suggest increasing the duration of benefits, particularly in times of economic recession, in order to provide the intended countercyclical economic stimulus. Supplemental benefits for individuals who obtain employment at reduced wages have also been recommended. In addition, some suggest that the benefits may be too generous in some cases, encouraging workers to remain unemployed. Proponents of benefits, however, point to evidence that indicates that unemployment compensation enables better matches of workers and jobs and keeps workers attached to the labor market.[541] Finally, some critics argue that benefits should be revised to apply to workers and industries in a more targeted way to achieve the goals of the system. Despite the substantial labor market changes since the enactment of the system, however, major changes in unemployment compensation have not been forthcoming.

§ 5.5 Worker Adjustment and Retraining Notification Act

The major employment dislocations that resulted from massive plant closings and relocations in the 1980s led Congress to enact the first statute that limited employer rights to shut down businesses. The Worker Adjustment and Retraining Notification (WARN) Act[542] has perhaps the best acronym of any employment statute, as it requires advance notice to employees and governmental bodies of decisions to terminate businesses or lay off large numbers of employees. This early warning is designed to allow employees and governments to plan for the economic consequences that result.

5.5.1 Coverage

WARN covers employers with 100 or more fulltime employees,[543] thus focusing the notice requirements on events likely to cause major economic disruptions. Government employers are excluded from statutory coverage.

Several events can trigger a notice requirement. First, notice is required of a shutdown, either temporary or permanent, of a single site of employment if fifty or more fulltime employees suffer an

---

[540] For a discussion of many of these issues, see Kletzer & Rosen, supra note 448; Nicholson & Needels, supra note 430.

[541] Kimball & McHugh, supra note 536, at 4.

[542] 29 U.S.C. §§ 2101–08.

[543] 29 U.S.C. § 2101(a)(1).

employment loss during any thirty-day period.[544] An employment loss is defined as a layoff that exceeds six months or a 50% reduction in work hours in each month of a six month period.[545] A mass layoff also requires notice and is defined as an employment loss at a single site of employment within a thirty-day period of either one-third of the employees, if at least fifty are laid off, or 500 employees.[546] WARN contains provisions designed to prevent an employer from timing layoffs to evade liability. Thus, a mass layoff or plant closing has occurred under the law if an employer lays off two or more groups of employees from a single site of employment within a ninety-day period which together exceed the minimum required to constitute a closing or mass layoff, although none alone meets the minimum requirement.[547] To defeat liability, the employer must prove that the employment losses were the result of different causes, and not an attempt to evade the notice requirements.[548]

5.5.2 Notice Required

The law requires sixty days written notice of any closing or layoff to the union representing the employees, or if there is no union, to each employee affected by the action.[549] Notice is also required to the state where the employment loss occurs and the chief elected official of the local government where the employment loss occurs.[550]

5.5.3 Employer Defenses to the Failure to Give Required Notice

The employer may reduce the notice period if, at the time notice was required, it was searching for capital or business that would have delayed or avoided the need to shutdown, and the employer reasonably and in good faith believed that the notice would have prevented the realization of the capital or business.[551] Notice still must be given as soon as practicable, with an explanation for the reduced notice period for this and other lawful reduced notice periods discussed below.[552] This exception was designed to respond to employer concerns that notice would exacerbate the financial problems of businesses trying to survive.

---

544 29 U.S.C. §§ 2101(a)(2), 2102.

545 29 U.S.C. § 2101(a)(6).

546 29 U.S.C. § 2101(a)(3).

547 29 U.S.C. § 2102(d).

548 Id.

549 29 U.S.C. § 2102(a).

550 Id.

551 29 U.S.C. § 2102(b)(1).

552 29 U.S.C. § 2102(b)(3).

The employer also may reduce the notice period if the shutdown or layoff is caused by circumstances that were not reasonably foreseeable when the notice was required.[553] The regulations contain examples, such as the unexpected loss of a major customer or a strike at a major supplier.[554] Furthermore, notice need not be given if the closing or layoff is caused by a natural disaster.[555]

The law does not mandate notice if the number of affected employees is reduced below the statutory minimum by either of the following two circumstances: (1) the employer offers to transfer a sufficient number of employees to a site within reasonable commuting distance with no more than a six month layoff; or (2) a sufficient number of employees accepts transfer to other locations.[556]

No notice is required if the employees were hired with the understanding that they were employed only so long as a temporary facility was operated, or until a project was completed.[557] Also, notice is not required under WARN of a labor strike or lockout or lawful replacement of an economic striker.[558]

If a layoff exceeds six months, it is an employment loss for purposes of the statute. This is true even if it was initially announced as less than six months, unless the extension is a result of business circumstances not reasonably foreseeable and notice is given when it becomes reasonably foreseeable that the layoff will exceed six months.[559] This provision prevents an employer from evading the statutory notice requirements by announcing shorter layoffs knowing that the layoffs will exceed six months.

5.5.4 Enforcement

While the U.S. Department of Labor is authorized to issue regulations for enforcement of the statute,[560] there is no government agency with enforcement authority under the statute nor is there an administrative enforcement forum. Instead, private enforcement by a lawsuit is the sole method of enforcement.[561] Since the WARN Act does not contain a statute of limitations for filing suit, courts use the

---

553 29 U.S.C. § 2102(b)(2)(A).

554 20 C.F.R. § 639.9(b)(1).

555 29 U.S.C. § 2102(b)(2)(B).

556 29 U.S.C. § 2101(b).

557 29 U.S.C. § 2103(1).

558 29 U.S.C. § 2103(2).

559 29 U.S.C. § 2102(c).

560 29 U.S.C. § 2107.

561 29 U.S.C. § 2104(a)(5).

state statute of limitations for causes of action most similar to WARN.[562]

Remedies include back pay for each employee who does not receive the requisite notice for each day of violation, along with benefits lost, which includes any medical expenses that would have otherwise been payable by an employer's health insurance plan.[563] Wages actually paid during the notice period, any voluntary, unconditional severance pay not legally required, and benefit payments made on behalf of the employee such as health insurance premiums can be deducted from the payments owed.[564] The courts have divided over whether the employees are entitled to payment for each calendar day for which notice was not provided, or only for each work day during the notice period. The Third Circuit has read the statutory language, which uses the word "day" in both the provisions requiring notice and the provisions specifying the remedy, as consistently referring to calendar days.[565] A number of other circuits have concluded that employees should only receive pay for days that they would have worked during the notice period, noting that the alternative creates anomalous results that could provide part-time employees who work fewer but longer days with greater benefits than full-time employees.[566]

In another area of disagreement regarding remedies, some courts have held that the employer must compensate employees for certain lost benefits as well as back pay. The WARN statute expressly requires compensation for benefits that employees would have received under an ERISA benefit plan.[567] With regard to non-ERISA benefits, the courts have split. The Ninth Circuit has held that employees are entitled to compensation for tip income and holiday pay that they would have earned during the notice period.[568] Some courts have required payment for benefits like vacation and personal days, while others have refused to award such payments.[569] The

---

562 North Star Steel Co. v. Thomas, 515 U.S. 29 (1995).

563 29 U.S.C. § 2104(a)(1).

564 29 U.S.C. § 2104(a)(2).

565 See UMW v. Eighty-Four Mining Co., 159 Fed. App'x 345, 346 (3d Cir. 2005) (unpublished) (adhering to prior precedents that calendar day approach for computing WARN Act damages is proper).

566 See, e.g., Joe v. First Bank System, Inc., 202 F.3d 1067, 1072 (8th Cir. 2000); Breedlove v. Earthgrains Baking Cos., Inc., 140 F.3d 797 (8th Cir. 1998); Burns v. Stone Forest Indus., Inc., 147 F.3d 1182 (9th Cir. 1998); Frymire v. Ampex Corp., 61 F.3d 757, 771–772 (10th Cir. 1995); Carpenters Dist. Council v. Dillard Dep't Stores, Inc., 15 F.3d 1275, 1282–86 (5th Cir. 1994).

567 29 U.S.C. § 2104(a)(1)(B).

568 Local Joint Executive Bd. of Culinary/Bartenders Trust Fund v. Las Vegas Sands, Inc., 244 F.3d 1152, 1157 (9th Cir. 2001).

569 Compare United Mine Workers v. Midwest Coal Co., No. TH 99–C–141–T/H, 2001 WL 1385893, at *7 (S.D. Ind. Aug. 31, 2001) (requiring pay for vacation and

courts' disagreement on this issue reflects a difference in interpretation of the statute's requirements, with courts ordering broad relief reading the law as providing a make-whole remedy, and those ordering more limited relief viewing the remedy as punitive and deterrent. This same split in views drives the debate over whether the remedial pay is for work days or calendar days. In that case, however, the remedial make-whole view reduces, rather than increases, the pay awarded.

For failure to provide notice to the government, a civil penalty of not more than $500 per day of violation may be assessed, but if employees are paid their back pay and benefits within three weeks of the shutdown, the penalty does not apply.[570] An award of attorneys' fees by the court to a prevailing party is discretionary.[571]

Employer good faith, accompanied by reasonable ground for believing that notice was not required, gives the court discretionary authority to reduce the employer's liability.[572] Because the authority is discretionary, it is difficult to predict when a court will allow such a reduction.[573]

Injunctive relief to prevent or delay closings or layoffs is not available under WARN.[574] Also WARN does not preclude any other rights or remedies provided to employees by state or local legislation

personal days), and United Mine Workers v. Martinka Coal Co., 45 F.Supp.2d 521, 530 (N.D.W. Va. 1999) (awarding vacation and holiday pay), with Jones v. Kayser-Roth Hosiery, Inc., 748 F.Supp. 1292, 1299–1300 (E.D. Tenn. 1990) (providing credit to employer against back pay for vacation pay paid to employees, thereby denying entitlement to vacation pay under WARN), and Ciarlante v. Brown & Williamson Tobacco Corp., No. 95–4646, 1996 WL 741973, at *3 (E.D. Pa. Dec. 18, 1996), rev'd on other grounds, 143 F.3d 139 (3d Cir. 1998) (denying compensation for scholarship program plans, employee stock purchase plans and others).

570 29 U.S.C. § 2104(a)(3).

571 29 U.S.C. § 2104(a)(6).

572 29 U.S.C. § 2104(a)(4).

573 See, e.g., Graphic Commc'ns Int'l Union, Local 31-N v. Quebecor Printing Corp., 252 F.3d 296 (4th Cir. 2001) (instructing the district court to decide whether company acted in good faith and had reasonable grounds to believe that its notice satisfied the WARN Act obligations, justifying reduction in liability); Frymire v. Ampex Corp., 61 F.3d 757, 769 (10th Cir. 1995) (allowing good faith to reduce liability where company provided dismissed employees with generalized notice of impending layoffs months in advance, at least three-weeks pay in lieu of notice and had instituted a "pay in lieu of notice" policy before WARN was even enacted); Roeder v. United Steelworkers (In re Old Electralloy Corp.), 162 B.R. 121 (Bankr. W.D. Pa. 1993) (holding that the employer would owe no damages under the WARN Act when it acted in good faith in notifying its workers of a plant closing). But see Castro v. Chicago Hous. Auth., 360 F.3d 721 (7th Cir. 2004) (finding district court did not abuse its discretion in rejecting good faith defense to WARN liability for failure to warn officers of plan to close CHA police department, where CHA's notice merely indicated it was "contemplating" closure and was sent only to captains, lieutenants, and sergeants).

574 29 U.S.C. § 2104(b).

or by contract.[575] A number of states have laws requiring notice of closings or providing particular benefits to employees affected by plant closings, such as severance payments or continuation of health insurance.[576]

As might be expected given the small amount of damages available to each employee, most lawsuits under WARN have been brought either by unions representing employees or as class actions. While union standing to bring a WARN claim was initially contested, in *United Food and Commercial Workers v. Brown*,[577] the Supreme Court held that unions meet the constitutional standing requirements to sue on behalf of their members adversely affected by a violation of WARN. Although authorized, local governments rarely file actions under WARN.[578]

Cases under WARN frequently contain complex facts. The parties and the courts must sort out the various actions taken by an economically stressed employer to determine whether and when notice was required and to whom. The facts may reveal various layoffs and recalls, as well as actions by employers to obtain and retain financing and customers. The foreseeability of actions causing loss of business must be determined.[579] In addition, determinations as to what is a single site of employment and whether to aggregate

---

[575] 29 U.S.C. § 2105.

[576] See, e.g., Conn. Gen. Stat. § 31–51*o*(a) (requiring continuation of group health insurance for 120 days); Mass. Gen. Laws Ann. ch. 149, § 183(b) (requiring severance pay for employees laid off within two years of a takeover of the employer); Me. Rev. Stat. Ann. tit. 26, § 625–B(1)–(3) (requiring severance pay for employees of employer with 100 or more employees that closes a facility or engages in a mass layoff).

[577] 517 U.S. 544 (1996). The reference to members raises the question of whether unions in right to work states can or must sue on behalf of nonmembers.

[578] U.S. General Accounting Office, Dislocated Workers; Worker Adjustment and Retraining Notification Act Not Meeting Its Goals, GAO/HRD–93–18, at 27–28 (Washington, D.C.: Feb. 23, 1993), available at http://archive.gao.gov/d44t15/148916.pdf [1993 Report]; Richard W. McHugh, Fair Warning or Foul? An Analysis of the Worker Adjustment Retraining and Notification (WARN) Act in Practice, 14 Berkeley J. Empl. & Lab. L. 1, 67 (1993); U.S. General Accounting Office, The Worker Adjustment And Retraining Notification Act: Revising the Act and Educational Materials Could Clarify Employer Responsibilities and Employee Rights 32–37 (Washington D.C.: Sept. 19 2003), available at http://www.gao.gov/new.items/d031003.pdf [2003 Report] (listing cases filed between 1998 and 2002).

[579] See, e.g., Roquet v. Arthur Andersen, LLP, 398 F.3d 585 (7th Cir. 2005) (finding layoffs due to rare criminal indictment of accounting firm and consequent business defections not foreseeable); Calloway v. Caraco Pharm. Labs., Ltd., 800 F.3d 244 (6th Cir. 2015) (finding FDA's seizure of pharmaceutical products, while rare, was not unforeseeable in light of the pattern of company violations and consequent FDA warnings); United Steel Workers of Am. Local 2660 v. U.S. Steel Corp., 683 F.3d 882 (8th Cir. 2012) (finding recession of 2008 unforeseeable because although the employer knew about the economic crisis, it was not aware of the full impact on its business until just before the layoffs).

layoffs for purposes of notice may be required.[580] Another important issue is who is the employer for purposes of notice and coverage, which may be particularly important in these cases where financial resources to satisfy any judgment may be limited.[581] Generalizations about such determinations are difficult as they depend on the facts of the particular case.[582]

5.5.5 Policy Considerations

Critics of WARN have argued that violations are widespread and enforcement inadequate.[583] In addition, both employers and employees find the statute difficult to apply to particular circumstances in many cases.[584] Among the suggested changes are Department of Labor investigation and enforcement, longer notice periods, and altering the thresholds necessary to trigger notice requirements in order to forestall employer evasions of the statutory requirements.[585] Other recommendations include creating a uniform statute of limitations, clarifying damages and simplifying the

---

[580] See, e.g., Morton v. Vanderbilt University, 809 F.3d 294 (6th Cir. 2016) (declining to aggregate layoffs and thus finding no notice required).

[581] See, e.g., Guippone v. BH S & B Holdings LLC, 737 F.3d 221 (2d Cir. 2013) (reversing summary judgment for company related to bankrupt employer because a jury could find that it directed layoffs and thus the two were a single employer).

[582] See, e.g., Allen v. Sybase, Inc., 468 F.3d 642, 649 (10th Cir. 2006) (stating that this particular case "cannot be reduced to broad general strokes" of WARN; rather the court "must sort out the particular facts and determine how they fit within the Act's aggregated mass layoff provision"); Frymire v. Ampex Corp., 61 F.3d 757, 771–772 (10th Cir. 1995) (limiting the decision reducing employer's liability based on good faith to the specific facts of this case, because the determinations to be made about the applicability and implementation of statutory requirements were especially difficult); Carpenters District Council v. Dillard Dep't Stores, 15 F.3d 1275 (5th Cir. 1994); Hotel Employees & Rest. Employees Int'l Union Local 54 v. Elsinore Shore Associates, 173 F.3d 175, 186 (3d Cir. 1999) (stating in analyzing foreseeability "[w]hat is a harbinger of disaster in one context may be an everyday occurrence in another); U.S. General Accounting Office, 2003 Report, supra note 578, at 13–18 (finding that employers, employee representatives, and others reported difficulty applying the statute's provisions when calculating the layoff threshold and determining whether the required number of employees have been laid off within the prescribed time frame to trigger the notice requirements); Tonya M. Cross, Failure to WARN: A Proposal that the WARN Act Provide A Compensatory, Make-Whole Remedy For UnWARNed Employees, 40 San Diego L. Rev. 711, 715 (2003) (arguing that statutory ambiguities make it difficult for an employer to determine what is required for statutory compliance).

[583] See U.S. General Accounting Office, 2003 Report, supra note 578, at 4,19 (indicating that notice is not provided in many covered layoffs and there is much confusion about applicability of the statute); U.S. General Accounting Office, 1993 Report, supra note 578, at 4–6 (also finding that notice is not provided in many layoffs where required and that enforcement is inadequate); McHugh, supra note 578, at 59–64 (noting various enforcement and compliance issues).

[584] See supra note 582.

[585] See McHugh, supra note 578, at 64–70. For example, McHugh suggests a multi-site minimum that would trigger a notice requirement even if single site layoffs were insufficient. Id. at 66–67.

threshold requirements for application of the law.[586] In addition, because WARN does not preempt stronger state laws, a state can enact legislation to address the perceived inadequacies of WARN and many have. For example, New Jersey has enacted its own WARN Act that applies to more job loss situations and has significantly stronger penalties for employer violations.[587]

[586] See U.S. General Accounting Office, 2003 Report, supra note 578, at 20.

[587] See N. J. Stat. Ann. §§ 34:21–1 to 21–7. For a discussion of the New Jersey statute, see Michael Kenny, New Jersey WARN Act Creates New Obligations for Private Employers Contemplating Plant Closings or Mass Layoffs, 34 Em. Rel. L.J. 41 (2008). See also Cal. Lab. Code § 1400 et seq. (applying notice requirements to employers with 75 employees and covering closings, relocations or layoffs affecting fifty employees regardless of the size of the workforce).

Chapter 6

THE REGULATION OF WORKPLACE HEALTH AND SAFETY

Every year, millions of workers experience workplace injuries or occupational diseases. According to the Bureau of Labor Statistics, there were 2.9 million reported cases of nonfatal occupational injuries and illnesses among private industry employers in 2015,[1] and 4,836 fatal work injuries.[2] In this chapter of the book, we focus on the regulation of workplace health and safety. Legislative efforts to address workplace health and safety concerns have focused on (1) compensating workers who become injured or ill as the result of their jobs and (2) preventing the occurrence of workplace injuries and illnesses. We follow this same dichotomy. We begin with a discussion of the state-based system of workers' compensation laws that provide compensation to workers who become ill or injured. The second part of the chapter addresses the Occupational Safety and Health Act, a federal law that aims to prevent workplace injuries and illnesses by requiring employers to provide employees with a safe and healthy workplace.

§ 6.1 Workers' Compensation

6.1.1 Overview

Workers' compensation statutes are intended to provide wage replacement and compensation for employees who suffer work-related injuries or illnesses. Every state has a workers' compensation system under which, except in Texas, employer participation is mandatory.[3] Although each state determines specific aspects of its

---

[1] U.S. Dep't of Labor, Bureau of Labor Statistics, Workplace Injuries and Illnesses in 2015, available at https://www.bls.gov/news.release/archives/osh_10272016.pdf.

[2] U.S. Dep't of Labor, Bureau of Labor Statistics, National Census of Fatal Occupational Injuries in 2015, available at https://www.bls.gov/iif/oshwc/cfoi/cfch0014.pdf. Other research indicates that these numbers may significantly understate workplace injuries and illnesses. See U.S. Dep't of Labor, Does the Workers' Compensation System Fulfill Its Obligations to Injured Workers? 5, n.3, 14 (2016), https://www.dol.gov/asp/WorkersCompensationSystem/WorkersCompensationSystemReport.pdf.

[3] Workers' compensation insurance in Texas is not mandatory for private-sector employers. See Tex. Lab. Code Ann. § 406.002; see also Hernandez v. Jobe Concrete Prods., 282 F.3d 360, 362–63 (5th Cir. 2002) (stating that "[i]f an employer chooses not to carry such coverage [under the Texas Workers' Compensation Act], then the non-subscriber's employees retain the right to sue their employer in state court, and the employer is deprived of traditional common law defenses"). Oklahoma enacted a statute allowing employers to opt out of the workers' compensation system and provide

workers' compensation system, such as employee eligibility requirements and payment schedules, the basic program features are similar from state to state. Employers assume some of the costs of workplace injuries by providing compensation to employees who suffer injuries and occupational diseases that arise out of and in the course of employment. In addition, these laws provide compensation without regard to the negligence or fault of either the employer or employee. Finally, with limited exceptions, if a workers' compensation law covers an injury or illness, the employee may not bring a tort claim against the employer concerning the injury or illness, but instead may seek only the benefits provided under the workers' compensation law.[4]

Although workers' compensation programs operate primarily at the state level, there are several federal programs. The Federal Employees' Compensation Act provides coverage for federal government employees,[5] and the Longshore and Harbor Workers' Compensation Act applies to maritime employees.[6] Other federal workers' compensation schemes include the Jones Act, which covers seamen,[7] the Energy Employees Occupational Illness Compensation Program, which applies to employees in the nuclear weapons industry,[8] the Federal Employers' Liability Act, which provides protection for employees of common carriers by railroad,[9] and the Black Lung Benefits Act, which provides compensation for miners who are disabled by pneumoconiosis or "black lung," a respiratory disease caused by the inhalation of coal dust.[10]

Workers' compensation laws typically exempt from coverage certain categories of workers, most commonly agricultural laborers and domestic service employees. Under some state statutes, however, employers can voluntarily elect to cover these workers.[11] In addition,

---

their own benefit plan for injured workers. 85A Okla. Stat. § 202. It was declared unconstitutional in September 2016 by the Oklahoma Supreme Court, however. Vasquez v. Dillard's, Inc., 2016 OK 89, 381 P.3d 768. For further discussion of efforts to privatize workers' compensation, see Michael C. Duff, Worse Than Pirates or Prussian Chancellors: A State's Authority to Opt-Out of the Quid Pro Quo, 17 Marq. Benefits & Soc. Welfare L. Rev. 123 (2016)

4 See generally Lex K. Larson, Larson's Workers' Compensation Law § 100.01 (2015) [hereinafter Larson]. Larson is the leading comprehensive multi-volume treatise on workers' compensation law.

5 5 U.S.C. §§ 8101 et seq.

6 33 U.S.C. §§ 901 et seq.

7 46 U.S.C. § 30104.

8 42 U.S.C. §§ 7384 et seq.

9 45 U.S.C. §§ 51 et seq.

10 30 U.S.C. §§ 901 et seq.

11 See, e.g., Ga. Code Ann. § 34–9–2(a)(2) (exempting, among others, "farm laborers" and "domestic servants" from workers' compensation "unless such employees and their employers voluntarily elect to be bound"); Mo. Rev. Stat. §§ 287.090.1(1),

these laws usually exclude casual laborers and, as with most employment law statutes, the laws generally apply only to employees and not independent contractors.[12]

Most state workers' compensation laws provide the following benefits:

- Medical benefits to cover the cost of care that is reasonably required to cure or relieve the employee of the effects of the injury or illness;
- Temporary total disability benefits while the employee is off work and recovering from the injury;
- Temporary partial disability benefits while the employee is recovering from the injury and resuming work on a partial or light-duty basis;
- Vocational rehabilitation benefits to cover the costs of services provided to an injured worker who may need retraining or counseling to return to work with the same employer or to find suitable new employment;
- Permanent disability benefits, which the laws provide based on the extent of the disability and whether the disability is scheduled or unscheduled. Permanent total disability benefits are paid when an employee, as a result of injury or illness, has been rendered completely and permanently incapable of engaging in any type of substantial and gainful employment. The laws pay permanent partial scheduled disability benefits when an employee sustains complete or partial loss of use of a body part, such as a limb, due to a job-related injury. Compensation is based on a statutory amount in accordance with a scheduled list of possible disabilities that involve the loss of a body part. Permanent partial unscheduled disability benefits are paid when the employee sustains a permanent partial disability not specifically covered by the schedule.
- Death benefits for surviving family members, notably spouses and dependent children.

The benefits are provided through insurance, which the employer obtains by purchasing from a private insurer, purchasing from a state workers' compensation fund, or providing self-insurance

---

287.090.2 (exempting agricultural and domestic service workers from workers' compensation but allowing their employers to "elect coverage").

[12] See supra Section 1.1.1 ("The Employee Versus the Independent Contractor").

and paying benefits directly. State laws determine which of these options are available, with some states allowing all three and others limiting the choices. The insurance premiums are experience-rated, which means that the rates are higher for employers with more claims, providing an incentive to maintain a safe workplace.

Most states administer benefits through a state agency which adjudicates disputes, such as whether an injury or illness is covered and the extent of resulting disability. Decisions of the agency can be appealed to the state appellate courts.

Analysis by the federal government of workers' compensation systems indicates that in general the systems have become more restrictive since 1990, reducing benefits and making it more difficult for workers to obtain them.[13] As the focus of legislatures shifted from preventing injuries and adequately compensating workers to reducing employer costs and preventing fraud, the costs of workplace injuries have shifted to workers and their families, the community and other benefit programs such as Social Security Disability Insurance and Medicare.[14]

6.1.2 Injuries and Occupational Diseases

State workers' compensation statutes commonly provide coverage for workers who experience a work-related accidental injury or occupational disease. The concept of an accidental injury is often defined by reference to an "unexpected," "unforeseen," or "untoward" event, the occurrence of which is relatively definite as to time and place, and which causes an injury.[15] This definition readily captures specific workplace accidents such as a worker who falls on a

---

[13] U.S. Dep't of Labor, Does the Workers' Compensation System Fulfill Its Obligations to Injured Workers? 13–15, https://www.dol.gov/asp/WorkersCompensationSystem/WorkersCompensationSystemReport.pdf.

[14] Id. at 3, 12–13.

[15] See, e.g., Ala. Code § 25–5–1(7) (defining the word "accident" as "an unexpected or unforeseen event, happening suddenly and violently"); Idaho Code Ann. § 72–102(18)(b) (defining an "accident" to mean "an unexpected, undesigned, and unlooked for mishap, or untoward event, connected with the industry in which it occurs, and which can be reasonably located as to time when and place where it occurred, causing an injury"); La. Rev. Stat. Ann. § 23.1021(1) (defining an "accident" as "an unexpected or unforeseen actual, identifiable, precipitous event happening suddenly or violently, with or without human fault, and directly producing at the time objective findings of an injury which is more than simply a gradual deterioration or progressive degeneration"); Neb. Rev. Stat. § 48–151(2) (defining an accident as "an unexpected or unforeseen injury happening suddenly and violently, with or without human fault, and producing at the time objective symptoms of an injury"). See generally Larson, supra note 4, § 42.02 (stating that the "basic and indispensable ingredient of 'accident' is unexpectedness" and adding that a second ingredient is that the "injury must be traceable, within reasonable limits, to a definite time, place, and occasion or cause").

construction site and breaks his leg or a worker who suffers a back injury after tripping over a power cord.

The literal application of the definition excludes progressive injuries, such as carpal tunnel syndrome, tendinitis, and noise-induced hearing loss, that do not result from a specific and clearly identifiable event but from a repeated trauma caused by a series of events that occur over time. Courts are increasingly willing to provide coverage for repeated trauma injuries, however, even though they do not result from a distinct event.[16] Yet coverage of these injuries raises questions, including how to determine the date of injury. As noted above, the concept of an accidental injury requires the injury to occur at a relatively definitive time. Making this determination is usually straightforward when a specific workplace accident occurs such as a finger injury caused when a worker's hand becomes trapped in a piece of machinery. Establishing the time element for repeated trauma injuries, however, can be difficult given that the onset of such injuries is often gradual. To address this concern, some courts follow Professor Larson's recommendation and hold, in the context of gradual injuries such as repeated trauma disorders, that "the date of accident is the date on which disability manifests itself."[17] Other courts have adopted different tests to determine the time of injury for gradual injuries including the "last exposure" test and the "last day worked" test.[18] Under the "last exposure" test, the time of injury is when the employee is last exposed to the trauma while the "last day worked" test fixes the time of the injury on the last date that the employee is able to work.[19]

---

16 See Larson, supra note 4, § 50.01 (commenting that "most jurisdictions have at some time awarded compensation for conditions that have developed, not instantaneously, but gradually over periods ranging from a few hours to several decades"). See also A.C. & S. v. Industrial Comm'n (Delessio), 304 Ill.App.3d 875, 879, 710 N.E.2d 837, 840 (1999) (commenting, with respect to employee's carpal tunnel syndrome, that the "modern rule allows compensation even when an injury occurs at a time and place remote from the employment if its cause is something that occurs entirely within the time and place limits of employment"). But see Wilson v. Goodyear Tire & Rubber Co., No. 216–57–91, 2005 WL 1033198 at *5 (Va. Workers' Comp. Comm'n Apr. 13, 2005) (observing that except for carpal tunnel syndrome and hearing loss, "job-related impairments resulting from cumulative trauma caused by repetitive motion, however labeled or however defined, are, as a matter of law, not compensable" under the provisions of the Virginia Workers' Compensation Act) (quoting Stenrich Group v. Jemmott, 251 Va. 186, 467 S.E.2d 795 (1996)) (internal quotations omitted).

17 Larson, supra note 4, § 50.05. See also Peabody Galion Corp. v. Workman, 643 P.2d 312, 316 (Okla. 1982) (adopting the manifestation test to fix the date for a repetitive-trauma injury); Meyer v. IBP, Inc., 710 N.W.2d 213, 221 (Iowa 2006) (same).

18 See, e.g., King v. D.C. Dep't of Empl. Servs., 742 A.2d 460, 473 (D.C. 1999) (discussing the alternative tests).

19 Id. These same issues regarding time of injury arise in occupational disease cases, discussed in the following paragraphs, often precluding recovery of benefits in cases where a disease has a long latency period.

Every state statute allows compensation for occupational diseases, with most states treating occupational diseases as a compensable category separate and distinct from accidental injuries.[20] As with repeated trauma injuries, occupational diseases differ from accidental injuries in that they do not result from a distinct and readily identifiable event. Most occupational diseases develop gradually over time. In addition, because their occurrence can often be anticipated, they do not share the unexpected and unforeseen quality that defines accidental injuries. Indeed, far from being unexpected, many occupational diseases such as, for example, black lung disease, are an inherent risk of the particular job or industry.[21]

Both occupational diseases and cumulative trauma injuries pose challenges for a system designed to provide quick and certain, though limited, recovery for accidental injuries. Proving causation may be challenging and the severity of the injury is, for some conditions, difficult to determine. As a result, there is potential for fraud by claimants, doctors and lawyers. At the same time, the restrictions in the system and the difficulties of proof result in few workers receiving compensation, particularly for diseases, regardless of cause.[22]

States differ in their approaches to covering occupational diseases. Some states have statutes that expressly list the conditions that are covered, and include a catch-all provision for diseases not specifically listed,[23] while other statutes provide coverage by adopting a broad definition of the term "injury" that encompasses occupational diseases.[24] Some states also have separate statutes that apply specifically to occupational diseases.[25]

State workers' compensation statutes that define "occupational disease" generally do so by defining it as a disease that is peculiar to the occupation in which the employee was engaged.[26] This definition excludes diseases that qualify as ordinary diseases of life to which

---

[20] See generally Larson, supra note 4, § 52.01.

[21] See, e.g. Larson, supra note 4, § 54 (describing particular protocols for evaluating black lung claims including an irrebuttable presumption of compensability for a particular diagnosis).

[22] See Elinor P. Schroeder & Sidney A. Shapiro, Responses to Occupational Disease: The Role of Markets, Regulation and Information, 72 Geo. L.J. 1231, 1244–48 (1984). Recovery for cumulative trauma injuries is more common but not uniform. See supra note 16 and accompanying text.

[23] See, e.g., N.C. Gen. Stat. § 97–53 (listing specific diseases covered); id. § 97–53(13) (providing a catch-all provision).

[24] See, e.g., Cal. Lab. Code § 3208 (stating that " '[i]njury' includes any injury or disease arising out of the employment").

[25] See, e.g., Pennsylvania Occupational Disease Act, 77 Pa. Stat. Ann. § 1201.

[26] See Larson, supra note 4, § 52.03(2).

the general public is exposed.[27] For example, in *In re Leventer*,[28] the plaintiff, a teacher, claimed that the poor ventilation in her classroom and exposure to noxious fumes from nearby bathrooms injured her vocal cords. Although plaintiff's injury might be compensable as an accidental injury, the court held that it was not an occupational disease as the noxious fumes and poor air quality were specific to the particular classroom in which she taught and not a condition distinctly related to her employment as a teacher. On the other hand, in *Johnson v. City of Winston-Salem*, the court found carpal tunnel syndrome to be an occupational disease based on medical testimony that individuals who do repetitive work with their hands have an increased risk of developing the condition.[29]

Diseases which can also result from nonoccupational causes, such as most cancers, pose particular challenges. Causation may be difficult to establish.[30] Where the public is equally exposed to the disease, it is considered an ordinary disease of life and the employee has a high burden to establish that it was caused by employment.[31] For certain diseases and occupations, some states have reversed the burden with presumptions.[32] Typically these statutes apply to law enforcement officers and firefighters and include heart and respiratory conditions.[33]

Psychological or mental injuries present an additional category of injuries that are frequently at issue in workers' compensation claims. States traditionally denied compensation for such injuries, electing to draw a bright line between physical injuries and mental injuries, and granting compensation only for the former unless the claimed mental injury related to a physical injury. While some

---

27 Id.

28 257 A.D.2d 903, 684 N.Y.S.2d 658 (1999).

29 188 N.C. App. 383, 387–88, 656 S.E.2d 608, 612–13 (2008).

30 See, e.g., Estate of George v. Vermont League of Cities & Towns, 187 Vt. 229, 993 A.2d 367 (2010) (excluding expert testimony about the cause of the employee's cancer after analysis of medical studies on which expert relied).

31 Mark A. Rothstein, et al., Employment Law, § 7.24, at 644 (5th ed. 2015).

32 See, e.g., City of Long Beach v. Workers' Comp. Appeals Bd., 126 Cal. App. 4th 298, 315, 23 Cal. Rptr. 3d 782, 793 (Cal. Ct. App. 2005) (imposing burden on employer to rebut presumption that police officer's cancer arose out of and in the course of employment).

33 Rothstein, supra note 31, at § 7.25, at 650. States are increasingly including other cancers in the presumption laws for firefighters due to exposure to toxins in fighting fires. Louisa Esola, Firefighter cancer presumption a hot issue for workers' comp in 2017, Business Insider (Jan. 18, 2017) http://www.businessinsurance.com/article/20170118/NEWS08/912311446/Firefighter-cancer-presumption-a-hot-issue-for-workers-comp-in-2017-.

jurisdictions continue to follow this approach,[34] others have been more willing to allow compensation for some instances of work-related mental injuries.

Cases involving work-related mental injuries can be usefully grouped into three categories: mental-physical cases in which a mental impact or stimulus, such as extreme fear or nervousness, causes a distinct physical injury;[35] physical-mental cases in which a physical accident or trauma causes a mental injury;[36] and mental-mental cases in which a mental stimulus causes a mental or nervous injury.[37] While the first two categories of injuries are generally compensable, courts are divided over the mental-mental injuries; however a majority of states presently allow compensation for these in some form.[38] Some states have applied heightened requirements to such claims, such as requiring a showing that the stress was unusual or proof that the injury was caused by a sudden stimulus rather than cumulative trauma.[39]

6.1.3 The Course of Employment

For an injury to occur in the course of employment, it must happen within a period of employment at a place where the employee reasonably may be when performing employment duties and while the employee is fulfilling those duties or doing an activity incidental to them.[40] Consider the scenario of a claimant who is working as a mechanic and is injured when he slips in oil and falls while repairing a car. Because the injury occurred while the claimant was at work, during the time he was working, and while he was engaged in a work-

---

[34] See, e.g., Ala. Code § 25–5–1(9) (stating that "[i]njury does not include a mental disorder or mental injury that has neither been produced nor been proximately caused by some physical injury to the body").

[35] See Larson, supra note 4, § 56.02.

[36] See id. § 56.03(1).

[37] See id. § 56.04.

[38] Id. § 56.06 (3).

[39] Id. § 56.06 (5); Transp. Ins. Co. v. Maksyn, 580 S.W.2d 334 (Tex. 1979) (denying benefits to an employee whose anxiety and depression may have resulted from his work, but were not attributable to a specific incident). Henley v. Roadway Express, 699 S.W.2d 150 (Tenn. 1985) (refusing to award benefits to an employee whose anxiety and stress did not result from a specific instance of trauma); Conn. Gen. Stat. Ann. § 31–275 (16)(ii) (excluding from definition of injury mental impairments with limited exceptions for those caused by physical injury or occupational disease or certain defined causes for police and firefighters); Nev. Rev. Stat. Ann. § 616C.180 (excluding from coverage conditions caused by gradual mental stimuli and those caused by stress, unless it is "extreme stress in time of danger" and proved by "clear and convincing medical or psychiatric evidence."

[40] See, e.g., Lavine v. Am. Ins. Co., 179 Ga.App. 898, 902, 348 S.E.2d 114, 118 (1986); Senesac v. Employer's Voc. Res., 324 Ill.App.3d 380, 386, 754 N.E.2d 363, 389 (2001); see also Larson, supra note 4, § 12.01.

related activity, the injury clearly satisfies the course-of-employment requirement.

The wide range of fact patterns involved in workers' compensation claims has prompted the articulation of several concepts to help determine whether a given injury occurred within the course of employment. These concepts include the personal comfort doctrine, the horseplay rule, the going-and-coming rule, and the special mission exception.

6.1.3.1 The Personal Comfort Doctrine

Under the personal comfort doctrine, an employee who is within the time and space limits of employment, and who briefly turns away from work to engage in an activity necessary or convenient to her own personal health or comfort, remains within the course of employment.[41] Courts have routinely applied the doctrine to hold compensable injuries that occurred while employees were engaged in activities such as eating, drinking, smoking, making a personal telephone call, and taking bathroom breaks. These activities, while personal in nature to the employee, are incidental to employment on the theory that "work-connected activity goes beyond the direct services performed for the employer and includes at least some ministration to the personal comfort and human wants of the employee."[42]

In order for a ministerial action to remain within the course of employment, it must represent only a minor deviation or departure from the employee's job duties. If, however, " 'the extent of the departure is so great that an intent to abandon the job temporarily may be inferred, or . . . the method chosen is so unusual and unreasonable that the conduct cannot be considered an incident of the employment,' "[43] the doctrine does not apply and the activity is treated as falling outside the course of employment. Consider, for example, the fact pattern in *Estes*.[44] At the direction of the employer, the claimant drove a van to a gas station to refuel. During the course of the trip, he stopped at a McDonald's drive-thru window and was injured when the van was hit by another vehicle. The Commission concluded that the injury did not fall under the personal comfort

---

[41] See, e.g., Gutierrez v. Petoseed Co., 103 Cal.App.3d 766, 768–69, 163 Cal.Rptr. 313, 314 (1980); Karastamatis v. Industrial Comm'n (Annunciation Greek Orthodox Church), 306 Ill.App.3d 206, 211, 713 N.E.2d 161, 165 (1999).

[42] Gold Kist, Inc. v. Jones, 537 So.2d 39, 41 (Ala. Civ. App. 1988) (citing 1A A. Larson, The Law of Workmen's Compensation, § 20.10 (1985)); see also Sun Ins. Co. v. Boyd, 101 So.2d 419, 422 (Fla. Dist. Ct. App. 1958).

[43] Collins v. Excel Specialty Prods., 347 Ark. 811, 817, n.2, 69 S.W.3d 14, 18, n.2 (2002) (quoting Arthur Larson, The Law of Workmen's Compensation § 21 (2001)).

[44] 9 MOWCLR 1002 (Mo. Lab. Indus. Rel. Comm'n 1996).

doctrine as the stop at McDonald's was not reasonably incidental to the driver's work since the employer had strictly prohibited him from going to McDonald's while refueling vehicles.[45]

6.1.3.2 The Horseplay Rule

Workers' compensation cases frequently involve claims for injuries that occur because of behavior that involves pranks, jokes, rowdiness, showboating, and similar conduct. The case law usually refers to such behavior as horseplay. Although states traditionally denied compensation for horseplay-related injuries, the current trend admits various exceptions as states have increasingly recognized that some level of employee-inspired jokes and pranks is part and parcel of the workplace.[46] Further if employees are not compensated for their injuries through workers' compensation, any recovery is doubtful for the coworkers who caused the injury are unlikely to have sufficient assets to make a tort claim viable. Examples of horseplay that led to injuries include workers firing staples from a staple gun,[47] spraying water from a hose,[48] using box cutters to try and slit each other's water bottles,[49] chasing a supervisor with a bucket of water,[50] arm wrestling on a roof,[51] engaging in rubber band fights,[52] and throwing shingles and nails at each other.[53]

---

[45] Id. See also McLaughlin v. Okaloosa County Road Dep't, 2005 WL 4774074 (Fla. Off. Jud. Comp. Claims Aug. 26, 2005) (because claimant's stop at a gas station for 2 hours and forty-one minutes was an abandonment of his job, the injury he sustained leaving the station did not fall within the course of his job).

[46] See, e.g., Torres v. Parkhouse Tire Serv., Inc., 26 Cal.4th 995, 1007, 30 P.3d 57, 63 (2001) (stating that "[g]iven . . . 'the propensities and tendencies of mankind and the ordinary habits of life, it must be admitted that wherever human beings congregate, either at work or at play, there is some frolicking and horseplay' ") (quoting Pacific Employers Ins. Co. v. Industrial Acc. Comm'n, 26 Cal.2d 286, 294, 158 P.2d 9, 14 (1945)); Yansick Lumber Co., 102 NYWCLR ¶ 1166 (N.Y. Workers' Cop. Bd. 2002) (commenting that "horseplay, in the workplace, is not only common, but injuries resulting from this expected conduct are frequently covered under the law"); Cain v. Travelers Ins., No. 07–05WC, 2005 WL 147737, at *2 (Vt. Dep't Lab. Ind. Jan. 19, 2005) (observing that "[w]hile some, but not all, horseplay is excluded from workers' compensation coverage, it is expected that workers will 'indulge in a moment's diversion from work to joke or play a prank' ") (quoting Clodgo v. Rentavision, Inc., 166 Vt. 548, 550, 701 A.2d 1044, 1045 (1997)).

[47] See Clodgo, 166 Vt. at 549, 701 A.2d at 1045.

[48] See Simmons v. Bonhotel, 40 Conn.App. 278, 670 A.2d 874 (1996).

[49] See In the Matter of the Claim of Alvarez v. Am. Furniture Warehouse and G. E. Young and Co., No. 4–620–148, 2005 WL 2478905 (Colo. Indus. Cl. App. Off. Sept. 28, 2005).

[50] See Doyal v. ITT Baylock Corp., 7 MIWCLR 1428 (Mich. Workers' Comp. App. Comm'n 1994).

[51] See Varela v. Fisher Roofing Co., 253 Neb. 667, 572 N.W.2d 780 (1998).

[52] See Prows v. Industrial Comm'n, 610 P.2d 1362 (Utah 1980).

[53] See Crilly v. Ballou, 353 Mich. 303, 91 N.W.2d 493 (1958).

Injuries caused by horseplay may or may not be compensable. The question in each case is whether the horseplay was of such a character that it served to take the worker out of his or her course of employment. Stated differently, did the horseplay represent a deviation from the job so substantial that the resulting injury should be non-compensable?[54]

In deciding whether to allow compensation for horseplay-related injuries, states typically distinguish between injured claimants who were innocent bystanders versus injured claimants who were active participants or instigators in the horseplay. In the case of the former, courts routinely allow compensation.[55] The latter scenario, however, is more complicated. While many early decisions refused to allow compensation for claimants who initiated the horseplay or were active participants, courts have largely abandoned this approach.[56] Instead, the current approach is to employ a four-factor test, articulated by Professor Larson, to determine whether the horseplay deviated from the employee's course of employment substantially enough to justify a denial of compensation.[57] The test examines: (1) the extent and seriousness of the deviation; (2) the completeness of the deviation (i.e., whether the activity was commingled with performance of work or was a complete abandonment of duty); (3) the extent to which the activity had become an accepted part of the employment; and (4) the extent to which the nature of the employment may be expected to include some horseplay.[58]

6.1.3.3 Recreational and Social Events

Various workers' compensation claims involve injuries that occurred during the course of work-related recreational or social activities such as participation in or attendance at fitness

---

[54] See, e.g., Clodgo, 166 Vt. at 552, 701 A.2d at 1046 (observing, with respect to horseplay, that the "key inquiry is whether the employee deviated too far from his or her duties").

[55] Larson, supra note 4, § 23.02. See, e.g., Coleman v. Armour Swift-Eckrich, 281 Kan. 381, 385, 130 P.2d 111, 115 (2006).

[56] See, e.g., Peet v. Garner Oil Co., 492 S.W.2d 103, 107 (Mo. Ct. App. 1973) (commenting that "reasoned decisions now hold that if the injury is sustained in horseplay which has become an incident or risk of the employment, it is compensable even for the aggressor or voluntary participant") (internal quotations omitted). But see DePuy, Inc. v. Farmer, 847 N.E.2d 160, 164 (Ind. 2006) (finding that participant in horseplay is not entitled to benefits but innocent victim is); Kan. Stat. Ann. § 44–501(a)(1)(E) (disallowing compensation for injury resulting from voluntary participation in horseplay).

[57] Larson, supra note 4, § 23.01.

[58] Id.

programs,[59] company picnics,[60] and games of softball,[61] football,[62] basketball,[63] and ping-pong.[64] Whether such injuries are compensable depends on the extent to which the activities are connected with the employment. As a general rule, injuries sustained as a result of recreational or social activities are within the course of employment when (1) they occur on the premises during a lunch or recreation period as a regular incident of the employment; (2) the employer, by expressly or impliedly requiring participation, or by making the activity part of the services of an employee, brings the activity within the realm of the employment; or (3) the employer derives substantial direct benefit from the activity beyond the intangible value of improvement in employee health and morale that is common to all kinds of recreation and social life.[65] Some states have expressly excluded coverage of recreational or social activities by statute,[66] but these statutes may still be interpreted to cover some injuries resulting from recreational and social activities.[67]

The factual circumstances in *Miller v. UPS*[68] are instructive, as they satisfied two of the three tests mentioned above. The employee, was injured while playing a softball game as part of a UPS-sponsored tournament for its employees to "kick-off" a United Way charity campaign. The Workers' Compensation Commission (Commission) readily found that the premises test was inapplicable to the facts since the game did not occur on the grounds of UPS, nor did it occur during a regular lunch or break period. The Commission, however, concluded that the second and third tests weighed in favor of finding

---

59 See, e.g., Kidwell v. Workers' Comp. App. Bd., 33 Cal.App.4th 1130, 39 Cal.Rptr.2d 540 (1995); Ernst v. Lennox Mfg., Inc., No. 5014455, 2006 WL 3862214 (Iowa Workers' Comp. Comm'n Nov. 30, 2006).

60 See e.g., Smith v. Workers' Comp. App. Bd., 191 Cal.App.3d 127, 236 Cal.Rptr. 248 (1987).

61 See, e.g., Ezzy v. Workers' Comp. App. Bd., 146 Cal.App.3d 252, 194 Cal.Rptr. 90 (1983); Gonzalez v. Workers' Comp. App. Bd., 186 Cal.App.3d 514, 230 Cal.Rptr. 649 (1986); State v. Dalton, 878 A.2d 451 (Del. 2005).

62 See, e.g., Henry v. Lit Bros., 193 Pa.Super. 543, 165 A.2d 406 (1960).

63 See, e.g., City of Stockton et al. v. Workers' Comp. App. Bd., 135 Cal.App.4th 1513, 38 Cal.Rptr.3d 474 (2006); Tensfeldt v. Workers' Comp. App. Bd., 66 Cal.App.4th 116, 77 Cal.Rptr.2d 691 (1998); Briar Cliff Coll. v. Campolo, 360 N.W.2d 91 (Iowa 1984); In the Matter of the Comp. of Karson Gard, 58 Van Natta 1121 (Or. Workers' Comp. Bd. May 3, 2006).

64 See, e.g., McNamara v. Hamden, 176 Conn. 547, 398 A.2d 1161 (1978).

65 See generally Larson, supra note 4, § 22.01.

66 See, e.g., Ill. Comp. Stat. 301/11 (excluding injuries arising from such activities unless the employee was ordered to participate).

67 See, e.g., Michalak v. Liberty N.W. Ins. Corp., 341 Mont. 63, 175 P.3d 893 (2008) (awarding benefits to employee injured riding wave runner at company picnic under statute that excluded injuries from recreational activities if the employee has been relieved of work duties, applying factors similar to those above).

68 No. 1134397, 1999 WL 33619558 (Iowa Workers' Comp. Comm'n Jan. 26, 1999).

that the injury occurred in the course of employment. With respect to the second test, which focuses on whether the employer required or encouraged participation as part of the employee's duties, the Commission observed that *Miller* was not a case where

> a group of employees, completely on their own, organiz[ed] a softball tournament. It was clearly organized by the employer, promoted by the employer, and encouraged by the employer. UPS collected the fees, advertised the event, handled the registrations, arranged for the facility in its name, organized the teams, established the rules, and used an employee to organize the event and maintain a file on it.[69]

The extent of UPS's involvement indicated a high level of employer sponsorship such that an adequate employment connection existed to bring the game within the course of employment.[70] The Commission next turned its attention to the third test to determine whether UPS derived a substantial benefit from the softball tournament. The answer was an unequivocal "yes" since UPS was a major sponsor of United Way and the game allowed the company to foster a positive public image in the community.

6.1.3.4 The Going and Coming Rule

The going and coming rule provides that injuries sustained while an employee is traveling to and from work do not occur in the course of employment. The rationale for the rule is that during travel time to and from work, an employee is not rendering any service to the employer as service begins only when the employee arrives at the place of employment.[71] While this basic rule is straightforward, numerous exceptions have complicated its application. Because the intricacies of the exceptions are far too nuanced to capture fully here, the following provides a useful summary of the more prominent exceptions.

6.1.3.4.1 The Special Mission Exception

The special mission or errand exception applies where an employee suffers an injury while performing an errand in furtherance of her job, although such performance occurs while the

---

69 Id. at *3.

70 See Larson, supra note 4, § 22.04(4)(c) (stating that "[w]hen a clear case is made of outright employer sponsorship, so that it can be said that the activity is part of an employment recreational program, adequate employment connection will usually be found").

71 See, e.g., Santa Rosa Junior Coll. v. Workers' Comp. App. Bd., 40 Cal.3d 345, 351–52, 708 P.2d 673, 676 (1985); Heide v. T.C.I. Inc., 264 Or. 535, 540, 506 P.2d 486, 488 (1973).

employee is traveling to and from work or is otherwise not at her regular place of business. *Bickley v. South Carolina Electric & Gas Co.*[72] illustrates this exception. The employee, an apprentice lineman for the Electric & Gas Company, was "called out" from his home to work around 3:30 a.m. to repair storm damage to electrical wires. As he was driving home later that day, he was killed in a car accident. The court allowed compensation as the employee left his home at the behest of the employer to attend to an emergency situation at a time and place that differed from his usual employment.

6.1.3.4.2 Premise Line Exception

The premise line exception applies to employees who have a fixed time and place of employment, and operates to create a safety buffer before and after official working hours to cover injuries that occur during this time period and while the employee is still on the employer's premises.[73] Many cases applying the exception involve parking lots, and courts generally adopt the view that an injury sustained when an employee falls in an employer-controlled parking lot satisfies the course of employment requirement.[74] In some cases, courts have extended the exception beyond instances where injuries occur in parking lots controlled by employers to situations where employers, while not controlling a lot, encourage use of a particular lot.[75] Where an employee was injured in a car accident on the military base where he worked, the court applied the premise line exception to find he was in the course of employment although he was on his way to work.[76] The court applied the premise line rule rather than the going and coming rule because he accessed the base through a security gate using a pass issued by the military, was one mile inside the base when the accident occurred, and while he had a fixed job

[72] 259 S.C. 463, 192 S.E.2d 866 (1972). See also Straub v. City of Scottsbluff, 280 Neb. 163, 784 N.W.2d 886 (2010) (where employee was found to be in the course of employment when he was injured while off-duty on the way to an MRI his doctor ordered as a result of a work-related injury, with the court noting that failure to submit to medical treatment can cause loss of workers' compensation benefits).

[73] See Larson, supra note 4, § 13.01.

[74] See, e.g., Norpac Foods v. Gilmore, 318 Or. 363, 867 P.2d 1373 (1994); see also Larson, supra note 4, § 13.04(2)(a) (stating that "[a]s to parking lots owned by the employer, or maintained by the employer for its employees, practically all jurisdictions now consider them part of the 'premises' ").

[75] See, e.g., Reynolds v. Collier et al., 2001 DC Wrk. Comp. LEXIS 93, at *13 (DC Off. Emp. Serv. Hearings & Adjudication Sec. Feb. 27, 2001) (commenting that "as a general rule parking lots owned or maintained by the employer for his employees are considered a part of the 'premises' in practically all jurisdictions, whether within the company premises or separated from it. This doctrine is not confined solely to parking lots owned, controlled, or maintained by the employer, but also when the parking lot not owned by the employer, is exclusively used, or used with the owner's special permission, or just used, by the employees of the employer.").

[76] See Schultz v. Workers' Comp. Appeals Bd., 232 Cal. App. 4th 1126, 181 Cal. Rptr. 3d 891 (2015).

location, he also travelled on the base for work using his personal vehicle.[77]

6.1.3.4.3 Employer Conveyance Exception

Another exception to the going and coming rule covers injuries incurred in travel to and from work where the employer owns or controls the conveyance.[78] The exception includes injuries that occur in an employer-owned vehicle,[79] as well as situations where employees are required to furnish their own transportation for use in performing their employment duties. This latter scenario would encompass, for example, a delivery driver who is injured while driving to work in his personal car that the employer requires him to use to make deliveries as part of his job.[80] Tribunals in these cases reason that where the employer benefits from such arrangements, the employee should be covered by workers' compensation.[81] Using that rationale, the Kentucky Supreme Court found an airline pilot killed in a crash commuting to work on a free flight was covered because the employer used the free transportation, provided by a reciprocal agreement among airlines, to induce employees to work for the company.[82]

6.1.3.4.4 Travelling Employee Exception

For some employees, travel is an integral part of their jobs as in the case of a traveling salesperson or a home health care worker who travels from jobsite to jobsite to visit clients at their homes. In these circumstances, ordinary travel hazards become work-related hazards such that injuries that occur while the employee is traveling to and from work fall within the course of employment.[83] *Reynolds v. Home Insurance Co. and Home Indemnity Co.*[84] demonstrates the point.

---

[77] Id. at 1136–38, 181 Cal. Rptr. 3d at 899–901.

[78] Larson, supra note 4, § 15–01.

[79] See, e.g., In the Matter of William B. Ford, 48 Van Natta 581, 582 (Or. Workers' Comp. Bd. Mar. 20, 1996).

[80] See, e.g., Jenkins v. Tandy Corp., 86 Or.App. 133, 738 P.2d 985 (1987).

[81] Id. at 137, 738 P.2d at 987.

[82] Fortney v. Airtran Airways, Inc., 319 S.W.3d 325, 329 (Ky. 2010).

[83] See, e.g., Williams v. Petromark Drilling, LLC, 299 Kan. 792, 795, 326 P.2d 1057, 1059 (2014) (upholding award of benefits to employee required to travel to "ever-changing remote drill sites" although he was injured while riding with another employee to expedite his trip home after work); Cheung v. Wasatch Electric, 136 Idaho 895, 897, 42 P.3d 688, 690 (2002) (stating that "[w]hen an employee's work requires him to travel away from the employer's place of business or his normal place of work, the employee is covered by worker's compensation") (citing Ridgway v. Combined Ins. Cos. of Am., 98 Idaho 410, 411–12, 565 P.2d 1367, 1368–69 (1977)); Leverton v. Mobile Nursing Serv., Ltd., 2006 WL 1374783, at *4 (Iowa Workers' Comp. Comm'n May 15, 2006) (stating that a "traveling employee is within the course of employment for the entire time they [sic] are on the road").

[84] No. 137,392, 1996 WL 103850 (Kan. Workers' Comp. App. Bd. Feb. 23, 1996).

Reynolds worked as a boiler inspector, a job that required him to travel throughout a given geographic region to conduct inspections. He was returning home from a business trip when he was involved in a car accident that resulted in various injuries. The Workers' Compensation Appeals Board concluded that Reynolds' injuries were compensable since travel was an integral part of his job as a boiler inspector, although he was returning home from staff meetings followed by a mandatory holiday party when he was injured in the accident.

6.1.3.5 Substantial Deviations

Where an employee makes a substantial deviation from employment, the employee is not in the course of employment. In *Kindel v. Ferco Rental, Inc.*,[85] the court upheld an award of benefits to an employee who was transported to work in a company vehicle. After work the driver and the employee stopped at a bar for four hours and both were intoxicated when they resumed travel in the company vehicle, in violation of company rules. Nevertheless, the court awarded benefits to the family of the employee who was killed in an auto accident, finding that he had resumed anticipated travel after the deviation, the bar was less than a quarter mile off their route, and the employee violated no laws as he was not driving. In another case, however, West Virginia denied benefits to an employee travelling on employer business who was injured in an accident while being transported home after spending the afternoon and evening bar-hopping.[86] The court found that this deviation varied so substantially in time and activity from normal business that it constituted "abandonment of any business purpose" and thus barred recovery.[87]

6.1.4 Arising out of Employment

In order for an injury to arise out of employment, it must have its origin in an employment-related risk or be incidental to the discharge of employment-related duties.[88] To use a simple illustration, in the case of an employee who falls off a roof while performing roofing work during his employment with a construction company, the resulting injuries arise out of employment because they are a probable consequence of working as a roofer. Likewise, in the context of a delivery driver who is injured in a car accident while driving on behalf of her employer, the injury is properly regarded as

85 258 Kan. 272, 899 P.2d 1058 (1995).

86 Calloway v. Workmen's Comp., 165 W.Va. 432, 268 S.E.2d 132 (W. Va. 1980).

87 Id. at 439–40, 268 S.E.2d at 137.

88 See, e.g., Pintur v. Germann, 183 Ill.App.3d 763, 766, 539 N.E.2d 443, 444 (1989); Hormann v. N.H. Ins. Co., 236 Kan. 190, 198, 689 P.2d 837, 843 (1984).

arising out of employment as it results from a risk associated with employment as a delivery driver.

In contrast to injuries that result from some employment-related risks, injuries that occur because of risks personal to the employee do not arise out of employment unless the employment contributes to the risk or aggravates the injury.[89] Thus, where an employee dies at work as a result of the internal effects of a heart attack that occurred because of an idiopathic condition, the death does not arise out of employment.[90] On the other hand, if a shuttle bus driver experiences an idiopathic seizure while driving and is injured when the bus swerves into on-coming traffic, the injury arises out of employment because the job placed the employee in a position that increased the consequences of having a seizure.[91]

In addition to employment-related risks and personal risks, employees may be injured as a result of so-called neutral risks, "risks of neither distinctly employment nor distinctly personal character."[92] This category of risks includes stray bullets, street attacks by animals, assaults by strangers, and weather-related risks such as lightning.[93]

Courts have used several tests to evaluate "arising out of" causation, especially where the risk appears neutral. The three most popular tests are the increased risk test, the positional risk test, and the actual risk test.

6.1.4.1 Increased Risk Test

The increased risk test is the test used by most states.[94] The test provides that injuries arise out of employment if the employment exposed the employee to a greater degree of risk than members of the general public in the same vicinity.[95] Consider the contrasting outcomes in *Grubbs v. Quality Haulers*[96] and *Spates v. Cook County*

---

[89] See, e.g., S. Convalescent Home v. Wilson, 285 So.2d 404, 407 (Fla. 1973); see also Larson, supra note 4, § 9.02(1) (stating that a "[p]reexisting disease or infirmity of the employee does not disqualify a claim under the 'arising out of employment' requirement if the employment aggravated, accelerated, or combined with the disease or infirmity to produce the death or disability for which compensation is sought").

[90] See Larson, supra note 4, § 9.01(4)(b) (stating that "the purely internal effects of a heart attack in an idiopathic-fall case are not independently compensable").

[91] See id. § 9.02(2).

[92] Id. § 4.03.

[93] See, e.g., Ill. Consol. Tel. Co. v. Industrial Comm'n, 314 Ill.App.3d 347, 353, 732 N.E.2d 49, 54 (2000).

[94] See Larson, supra note 4, § 3.03.

[95] See, e.g., Deffenbaugh Indus. v. Angus, 313 Ark. 100, 104, 852 S.W.2d 804, 808 (1993); Nascote Indus. v. Industrial Comm'n (Beck), 353 Ill.App.3d 1056, 1060–61, 820 N.E.2d 531, 535 (2004).

[96] No. 0415198, 2006 WL 3940369 (S.C. Workers' Comp. Comm'n Apr. 18, 2006).

Hospital.[97] In *Grubbs*, the claimant truck driver injured his back when he stepped out of his truck, slipped on some sand and fell. Based on claimant's testimony that he felt a pop when he stepped down from the truck, the Workers' Compensation Commission concluded that the injury did not arise out of employment as it was caused by the claimant stepping to the ground. Because the act of stepping to the ground is a natural physical function, the risk of the injury was one to which the general public was exposed. In *Spates*, the claimant, a maintenance custodian, was injured when he fainted and fell while performing cleaning duties on the 6th floor of the hospital. At the time of the injury, the temperature was 95 degrees outside and even hotter inside on the 6th floor, which lacked both air conditioning and ventilation. In addition, claimant was solely responsible for cleaning the entire floor, which was as long as a block. The Industrial Commission held that these working conditions placed claimant at a risk of injury far greater than that experienced by the general public.

6.1.4.2 Actual Risk Test

Under the actual risk test, an injury satisfies the arising out of prong as long as the employment subjected the claimant to an actual risk that caused the injury. Stated differently, the employment must have actually contributed to the claimant's injury. The actual risk test is often contrasted with the increased risk test because unlike the latter test's preoccupation with whether the risk was common to the public, this focus is of no concern in the actual risk test. Thus in *Matter of Hughes v. Trustees of St. Patrick's Cathedral,*[98] a case involving an employee who suffered heat prostration while working outdoors, the court observed that "[a]lthough the risk may be common to all who are exposed to the sun's rays on a hot day, the question is whether the employment exposes the employee to the risk."[99] Other states applying the actual risk test, however, require that the risk be "peculiar to the work and not common to the neighborhood."[100] The Virginia Supreme Court found that a truck driver robbed and shot on the road after picking up cash at a truck stop did not show that he was injured by a hazard of the employment since any person on the road could have been robbed.[101]

[97] No. 02WC53146, 2003 WL 22213583 (Ill. Indus. Comm'n Aug. 29, 2003).

[98] 245 N.Y. 201, 156 N.E. 665 (1927).

[99] Id. at 202–03.

[100] See Hill City Trucking v. Christian, 238 Va. 735, 738, 385 S.E.2d 377, 379 (1989) (quoting Baggett & Meador Cos. v. Dillon, 219 Va. 633, 638, 248 S.E.2d 819, 822 (1978).

[101] Id. at 739, 385 S.E.2d at 379–80. Courts in Virginia may be confusing the various risk doctrines. See Steven L. Willborn, et al., Employment Law: Cases and Materials 938 (5th ed. 2012).

6.1.4.3 Positional Risk Test

The positional risk test is more liberal than both the increased risk test and the actual risk test. It incorporates a "but for" element to hold that an injury arises out of employment if it would not have occurred but for the fact that the employee's job required him or her to be in the position where the injury occurred.[102] A growing number of courts and administrators use this test, primarily for the purpose of assessing situations that involve neutral risks.[103] Such risks include those associated with stray bullets, lightning, unexplained falls, and other risks that are neither personal to the claimant nor clearly a product of the employment.[104]

In the Matter of the Claim of Shawn Reese v. Nailbangers, Inc.[105] offers a useful illustration of the positional risk test. The plaintiff, a construction worker, was working at an off-site location where the employer provided its workers with housing in a condominium. After work one day, the plaintiff and a co-worker drove to a restaurant in the only available vehicle. Following dinner, the plaintiff informed his co-worker that he was returning to the condominium. The co-worker did not object, and plaintiff headed back and went to sleep. Later that evening, the co-worker, having returned to the condominium, began assaulting the sleeping plaintiff. The judge concluded that the assault on the plaintiff resulted from a neutral force based on evidence that the co-worker was " 'pissed off' " and " 'needed somebody to beat on.' "[106] The judge also inferred that the positional risk test was appropriate based on a but-for analysis. "[A]ny person then and there present in the condominium would have experienced a similar attack."[107]

6.1.5 The Statutory Defense of Willful Misconduct

As noted above, in Section 6.1.1, as a general matter, workers' compensation benefits are awarded without regard to fault. However, several states have statutorily undermined this proposition by creating a defense of willful misconduct.[108] Although the reach of this defense would appear significant, encompassing any willful act, in

[102] See Larson, supra note 4, § 3.05.

[103] Id.

[104] Id.

[105] No. 4–193–913, 1995 WL 356867 (Colo. Indus. Cl. App. Off. May 30, 1995).

[106] Id. at *3.

[107] Id.

[108] See, e.g., N.H. Rev. Stat. Ann. § 281–A:14; Md. Code Ann., Lab. & Emp. L. § 9–506(e); Tenn. Code Ann. § 50–6–110; Utah Code Ann. § 34A–2–302.

fact it is usually limited to intentional violations of safety regulations designed to protect employees from serious bodily injury.[109]

Mills v. Virginia Electric & Power Co.[110] provides a straightforward illustration of the defense. The employee, who was injured when he came in contact with an energized wire, filed a workers' compensation claim. The employer defended on the ground that the employee's injury was proximately caused by his willful misconduct in violating a workplace safety rule. The evidence indicated that the employee was an experienced worker who knew of and violated the employer's rule that required him to wear rubber gloves for his own safety when he worked with energized wires. The court ruled in favor of the defendant because the employee intentionally violated a reasonable safety rule enacted for his benefit.

An employee can rebut the defense of willful misconduct by proving that the rule was not consistently enforced[111] or by demonstrating that there was a valid reason for failing to comply with the rule.[112] An employee can also rebut the defense by establishing that he lacked actual notice of the rule and the danger involved in violating it.[113]

6.1.6 The Exclusivity Principle

Employees who suffer workplace injuries may want to avoid the workers' compensation system and pursue a tort claim against their employers because of the possibility of recovering greater damages, including punitive damages. Yet if an injury or illness falls within the scope of a workers' compensation statute, the statute provides the exclusive remedy for the employee except in limited circumstances. This exclusivity feature was an integral element of the legislative compromise needed to facilitate the enactment of workers' compensation statutes.

As the United States transitioned from an agrarian economy to an industrial economy, increasing numbers of employees were the victims of industrial injury. Unfortunately, many employees were unable to obtain redress from their employers because of common law

---

[109] See Larson, supra note 4, § 34.01 (commenting that the defense is relatively unimportant); id. § 34.02 (stating that "[t]he most impressive thing about the defense is the variety of situations in which it has *not* succeeded") (emphasis in original).

[110] 197 Va. 547, 90 S.E.2d 124 (1955).

[111] See, e.g., Daniel v. Dep't of Corrections, 468 Mich. 34, 46–47, 658 N.W.2d 144, 151 (2003) (stating that the defense of willful misconduct "does not operate to preclude benefits where an employee was injured while violating a work rule that had not been enforced by the employer"); Buzzo v. Woolridge Trucking, Inc., 17 Va. App. 327, 332, 437 S.E.2d 205, 208 (1993); see also Larson, supra note 4, § 35.03.

[112] See Larson, supra note 4, § 35.04.

[113] See id. § 35.02.

rules relating to contributory negligence, fellow servant negligence, and assumption of risk. The unavailability of adequate and predictable remedies eventually led states to consider the enactment of workers' compensation laws that would allow employees to receive compensation for workplace injuries without having to prove employer negligence.[114] Employers were reluctant to agree to a no-fault system, however, without assurances that they would not face further liability for injuries suffered by employees at work. Under workers' compensation laws, employees sacrifice the opportunity to pursue tort claims against their employer that might yield a wide range of remedies, including full compensatory and punitive damages, in exchange for the relatively certain payment of lesser benefits. Employers, on the other hand, assume liability without regard to fault in exchange for predictable moderate payments and immunity from suit by employees.[115]

There are several exceptions to the exclusivity of the workers' compensation remedy, including intentional injury by the employer and injuries governed by the dual capacity doctrine and the dual persona doctrine. In addition, in some states an employee may be able to sue in tort when the injury is not one covered by workers' compensation.[116] Finally, employees may sue third parties such as the manufacturer of a defective machine that caused injury.

In most jurisdictions, however, the workers' compensation bar applies to tort actions against fellow employees, including supervisors, managers and corporate officials.[117] A few states allow injured individuals to sue fellow employees, including managers and corporate officials, whose actions cause injury.[118] Even in these jurisdictions, employees cannot sue company owners who do not personally act to cause injury based on their ownership status, however.[119]

---

[114] See Rothstein et al., supra note 31, at § 7.1, at 544; § 7.3 at 588.

[115] See generally id. § 7.3, at 588–89 and Larson, supra note 4, § 100.01(1).

[116] See, e.g., Snead v. Harbaugh, 241 Va. 524 404 S.E.2d 53 (1991) (finding defamation claim not barred by exclusivity provision because reputational injury not within the definition of injury in workers' compensation act). Not all courts agree, however. See, e.g., Becker v. Automatic Garage Door Co., 156 Wis. 2d 409, 418–19, 456 N.W.2d 888, 891–92 (Ct. App. 1990).

[117] See Rothstein, supra note 31, at 676. In order to be protected from suit, however, the employee causing the injury must be acting in the course of employment. Id.

[118] Id.

[119] Id.

6.1.6.1 Intentional Conduct

The most straightforward application of workers' compensation laws is in the context of accidental work-related injuries.[120] The exclusivity principle applies to negligent, grossly negligent and reckless conduct. It does not include intentional employer misconduct in most states. Consequently, an employee injured by an employer's intentional act has the option of claiming compensation or suing the employer at common law.[121]

Most jurisdictions adopt the view that a tort-based claim against an employer for intentional conduct must allege actual intent. Conduct that falls short of the actual intent standard includes reckless, wanton and willful misconduct.[122] A handful of states, however, allow an exception based on either intentional conduct or conduct indicating that an employer knew with "substantial certainty" its actions would cause injury.[123] An employee can satisfy the substantial certainty standard by demonstrating that a reasonable person in the employer's position would have known that its actions were substantially certain to result in injury.[124] The Supreme Court of Connecticut explains the distinction between the intent standard and the substantial certainty standard as follows: "Under the former, the actor must have intended both the act itself and the injurious consequences of the act. Under the latter, the actor must have intended the act and have known that the injury was substantially certain to occur from the act."[125]

---

[120] See supra Section 6.1.2.

[121] Larson, supra note 4, § 103.02.

[122] See, e.g., Van Biene v. Era Helicopters, 779 P.2d 315, 318 (Alaska 1989); Johnson v. Kerr-McGee Oil Indus., 129 Ariz. 393, 398, 631 P.2d 548, 553 (Ariz. App. 1981); Johnson v. Mountaire Farms of Delmarva, Inc., 305 Md. 246, 254–55, 503 A.2d 708, 712 (1986).

[123] See, e.g., Sorban v. Sterling Eng'g Corp., 79 Conn.App. 444, 830 A.2d 372 (2003); Bakerman v. Bombay Co., 961 So.2d 259 (Fla. 2007); see generally Larson, supra note 4, § 103.04(2)(e) (listing states).

[124] See, e.g., Sorban, 79 Conn.App. at 455, 830 A.2d at 379 (stating that "[t]o satisfy the substantial certainty test, the employee must show that a reasonable person in the position of the employer would have known that the injury or death suffered by the employee was substantially certain to follow from the employer's actions"); see also Woodson v. Rowland, 329 N.C. 330, 340–41, 407 S.E.2d 222, 228 (1991) (stating that "when an employer intentionally engages in misconduct knowing it is substantially certain to cause serious injury or death to employees and an employee is injured or killed by that misconduct, that employee, or the personal representative of the estate in case of death, may pursue a civil action against the employer").

[125] Suarez v. Dickmont Plastics Corp., 242 Conn. 255, 280, 698 A.2d 838, 851 (1997); see also Sorban, 79 Conn.App. at 450, 830 A.2d at 377 (noting that an employee can prevail on an intentional tort claim against an employer by proving "either that the employer intended to injure the plaintiff (actual intent standard) or that the

Rovasio v. Wells Fargo Armored Servs. Corp.[126] provides a straightforward illustration of the substantial certainty standard. *Rovasio* involved a security employee who sued his employer for injuries sustained when a presumed robber shot him on the job. The employee claimed that the employer had refused to supply him with a bulletproof vest even though the employer mandated that its employees wear such vests. In dismissing the employer's motion for summary judgment, the court observed that the danger of an employee shooting was foreseeable and that employees without vests were substantially certain to incur harm.

6.1.6.2 The Dual Capacity & Dual Persona Doctrines

The dual capacity doctrine and the dual persona doctrine may also remove the exclusivity of the workers' compensation remedy. Under the former doctrine, an employer normally shielded from tort liability by the workers' compensation exclusivity principle may become liable in tort to an employee if the employer occupies, in addition to its capacity as an employer, a second capacity that confers obligations on it independent of those imposed on it as an employer.[127] The dual capacity doctrine recognizes that a single legal entity may have many capacities, each with a different set of obligations. In addition to an employment relationship, an employer might, for example, have a relationship with an employee as a medical provider, vendor, landowner, or products manufacturer.[128]

Consider the fact pattern in *Sturtevant v. County of Monterey.*[129] The plaintiff in the case worked at a medical center when she fell and sustained several injuries including a wrist injury. She sought treatment at the center and had surgery performed on her wrist by a doctor employed at the center. Plaintiff received workers' compensation for her original injuries and later filed suit against the center and the doctor for medical malpractice, alleging that the medical care received had aggravated her wrist injury. In concluding that the dual capacity doctrine was applicable, the court noted that at the time of the initial injury, plaintiff's relationship with the center was solely that of employer and employee. When the plaintiff later

employer intentionally created a dangerous condition that made the plaintiff's injuries substantially certain to occur (substantial certainty standard)").

[126] 47 Conn.Supp. 30, 767 A.2d 1288 (2001); see also Woodson, 329 N.C. 330, 407 S.E.2d 222 (holding that there was sufficient evidence for a reasonable juror to conclude that the conduct of the subcontractor and its owner in failing to properly maintain a trench was substantially certain to cause serious injury or death, and that such conduct was tantamount to an intentional tort).

[127] See, e.g., Ritchie v. Bridgestone/Firestone, Inc., 621 So.2d 288 (Alaska 1993); Jones v. Kaiser Indus. Corp., 43 Cal.3d 552, 737 P.2d 771 (1987).

[128] See generally Larson, supra note 4, § 113.01(2).

[129] 228 Cal.App.3d 758, 279 Cal.Rptr. 161 (1991).

became a patient at the center, however, the center assumed the additional duties of a medical care provider. Because the center breached those duties, the plaintiff was entitled to sue it for medical malpractice.

The dual capacity doctrine is frequently confused with the more stringent dual persona doctrine. Whereas liability under the dual capacity doctrine requires that an employer occupy more than one capacity in its interactions with an employee, the dual persona doctrine requires that an employer possess "a second persona so completely independent from and unrelated to its status as employer that by established standards the law recognizes that persona as a separate legal person."[130] Professor Larson argues that the doctrine should ordinarily apply only to "situations in which the law has already clearly recognized duality of legal persons, so that it may be realistically assumed that a legislature would have intended that duality to be respected."[131] Cases that readily illustrate this type of duality include those where the duality flows from a corporation since the corporate entity is a separate legal persona by statute.[132]

Consider, for example, *Kimzey v. Interpace Corp.*[133] In *Kimzey*, an employee suffered a workplace injury while operating a machine that was manufactured by a company that was merged into a corporation that later merged into the employer, Interpace. In the merger agreement, Interpace agreed to assume all debts, liabilities, restrictions, duties, and obligations of the manufacturer. After receiving workers' compensation benefits, the employee sued Interpace for product defects and negligence with respect to the machine he was operating at the time of his injury. The court allowed plaintiff's tort claim to go forward. The court observed that plaintiff's suit was "essentially an attempt to recover from a third-party manufacturer of a defective machine through a suit against its successor corporation. . . ."[134]

To date, most jurisdictions considering the dual capacity doctrine have rejected it in favor of the dual persona doctrine. The dual capacity doctrine is subject to overextension given that an employer can potentially have many "capacities."[135] If extended to reach all the possible capacities that an employer might occupy, the doctrine would undermine the exclusivity of the workers' compensation system. The doctrine would allow an employee to avoid

---

[130] Larson, supra note 4, § 113.01(1).

[131] Id. § 113.01(2).

[132] Id. § 113.01(3).

[133] 10 Kan.App.2d 165, 694 P.2d 907 (1985).

[134] Id. at 170, 694 P.2d at 912.

[135] See Larson, supra note 4, § 113.01(2).

the system as long as she sues her employer in a capacity other than that of the employment relationship, and the additional capacity imposed obligations on the employer separate from those imposed by the employment relationship. By contrast, the dual persona doctrine is narrower than the dual capacity doctrine and consequently allows fewer exceptions to the exclusivity of the workers' compensation system. The dual persona doctrine renders an employer vulnerable to a tort suit by an employee only in the extremely limited circumstance when the employer possesses a distinct legal persona.

§ 6.2 Occupational Safety and Health Act

Various federal and state statutes exist to promote safe and healthful working conditions by regulating workplace hazards. The most important of these statutes is the federal Occupational Safety and Health Act of 1970 (OSH Act).[136] The OSH Act's purpose is to "to assure so far as possible every working man and woman in the Nation safe and healthful working conditions . . . by providing that employers and employees have separate but dependent responsibilities and rights with respect to achieving safe and healthful working conditions."[137] Unlike workers' compensation laws,[138] which compensate employees for work-related illnesses or injuries, the OSH Act aims to prevent workplace injuries and illnesses from occurring. Also unlike workers compensation laws, the OSH Act does not provide a cause of action to employees for compensation for injuries. Rather, the act is enforced through fines payable to government.

6.2.1 Coverage

The OSH Act covers most private-sector employers engaged in a business affecting commerce.[139] This coverage extends to agricultural businesses although it excludes farms that employ only immediate members of the farmer's family.[140] The OSH Act also excludes self-employed persons.[141] In addition, it does not cover federal, state or local government employees[142] nor does it regulate working conditions where another federal agency has exercised its statutory

[136] 29 U.S.C. §§ 651 et seq.

[137] Id. § 651(b).

[138] See supra Section 6.1.

[139] 29 U.S.C. § 652(5).

[140] 29 C.F.R. § 1975.4(b)(2).

[141] 29 U.S.C. § 652(6) (stating that "[t]he term 'employee' means an employee of an employer who is employed in a business of his employer which affects commerce").

[142] Id. § 652(5).

authority to regulate health and safety[143] as, for example, in the case of mining operations covered by the Federal Coal Mine Safety and Health Act.[144] The U.S. Postal Service is subject to enforcement as a private employer, with some modifications. The Act also requires the United States as an employer to provide safe and healthful places and conditions of employment consistent with OSHA standards.[145] The OSH Act authorizes states to establish their own safety and health programs,[146] and requires approved state plans to cover state and local government employees.[147] State plans must provide for the development and enforcement of safety and health standards which are at least as effective as those promulgated pursuant to the OSH Act.[148] Twenty-two states and territories operate plans covering both the public and private sectors, and four states operate public employee only plans.[149]

6.2.2 Procedural Overview

The Occupational Safety and Health Administration (OSHA) of the Department of Labor handles enforcement and administration of the OSH Act at the federal level.[150] OSHA is responsible for setting standards[151] and conducting workplace inspections carried out by compliance officers.[152] OSHA and its state partners together employ approximately 2100 inspectors, along with engineers, physicians, educators, standards writers, and other support employees in more than 200 offices across the country.[153]

The OSH Act provides that an OSHA compliance officer may "enter without delay"[154] any place of employment to perform an inspection. There are two types of inspections. Programmed inspections occur on the basis of administrative plans developed by OSHA. For example, inspections might be scheduled for any employer exceeding a preset threshold on a particular safety metric (e.g., days away from work due to injury).[155] Unprogrammed

---

143 Id. § 653(b)(1). See S. Ry Co. v. OSHRC, 539 F.2d 335, 336 (4th Cir. 1976), cert. denied, 429 U.S. 999 (1976) (interpreting 29 U.S.C. § 653(b)(1)).

144 30 U.S.C. § 801.

145 29 U.S.C. § 668; 29 C.F.R. § 1960.

146 29 U.S.C. § 667(b).

147 Id. § 667(c)(6).

148 Id. § 667(c)(2).

149 Occup. Safety and Health Law: Comp. & Prac. § 2:1 (2016).

150 Id. § 651(b)(3).

151 Id.

152 Id. § 657(a).

153 Occup. Safety and Health Law: Comp. & Prac. § 2:1 (2016).

154 29 U.S.C. § 675(a).

155 Occup. Safety and Health Law: Comp. & Prac. § 5:15 (2017).

inspections, on the other hand, are initiated following specific complaints, or after an event resulting in a fatality.[156]

Although the OSH Act does not state whether the government must obtain a search warrant before entry, the Supreme Court in *Marshall v. Barlow's, Inc.*[157] held that employers have the right to require compliance officers to obtain an inspection warrant before entering the worksite.[158] *Marshall* involved an employer who refused an OSHA inspector's request to search the working areas of the employer's business unless the inspector presented a search warrant. The Court rejected the Secretary of Labor's argument that warrantless inspections to enforce OSHA are reasonable within the meaning of the Fourth Amendment.[159] " 'The businessman, like the occupant of a residence, has a constitutional right to go about his business free from unreasonable official entries upon his private commercial property.' "[160] That said, the Court, while refusing to allow OSHA to conduct warrantless searches absent consent by the employer, concluded that the government, in order to secure a warrant, did not have to demonstrate criminal probable cause to believe that the premises contained conditions in violation of the OSH Act. Distinguishing between criminal law searches and administrative searches, the Court held that for purposes of an administrative search pursuant to the OSH Act, probable cause to justify the issuance of a warrant may be based on a showing that " 'reasonable legislative or administrative standards for conducting an . . . inspection are satisfied with respect to a particular [establishment].' "[161]

The Act authorizes the compliance officers to enter at reasonable times and to inspect within reasonable limits, and in a reasonable manner.[162] The physical scope of the search depends on the reason for the inspection. Searches conducted as part of an administrative plan (i.e., programmed inspections) can be wall-to-wall inspections. For other searches, the scope of the search is limited by the scope of the warrant. For example, when the warrant is obtained pursuant to

---

156 Id. at § 5:16.

157 436 U.S. 307 (1978).

158 For a useful discussion of *Marshall v. Barlow's, Inc.*, see generally Mark A. Rothstein, OSHA Inspections after Marshall v. Barlow's, Inc., 1979 Duke L. J. 63.

159 See also Concrete Constr. Co., 15 OSH Cas. (BNA) 1614, 1616 (1992) (observing that because the Fourth Amendment only protects against intrusions into area where employer has reasonable expectation of privacy, it does not require a warrant for nonconsensual inspection of workplace to the extent the workplace is open to public).

160 Marshall v. Barlow's, 436 U.S. at 312 (quoting See v. Seattle, 387 U.S. 541, 543 (1967)).

161 Id. at 321 (quoting Camara v. Municipal Court, 387 U.S. 523, 538 (1967)).

162 29 U.S.C. § 657(a)(2)

a specific complaint about a localized condition, the scope is limited to the area of that condition.[163]

Based on the inspection, the compliance officer may issue an employer a citation that describes the OSHA requirements allegedly violated, fixes a reasonable time for the violations to be abated (corrected), and lists any proposed penalties.[164] OSHA must issue the citation within six months of the violation's occurrence.[165] When an employer receives a citation, it is required to post the citation at or near the alleged place of violation.[166]

The issuance of a citation initiates the prosecutorial process.[167] If a violation is found during the inspection, a citation will follow. That is, there is no warning once a violation is found to exist. However, employers commonly challenge citations, and it is not uncommon for OSHA to scale back the penalty when a citation is contested.[168]

The OSH Act provides for the following categories of violations: de minimis, nonserious, serious, repeated, willful, failure to abate, and failure to post.[169] The proposed penalties may range from zero for violations classified as de minimis, nonserious, failure to abate, and failure to post, to a maximum of $70,000 for willful and repeated violations.[170] In addition to these civil penalties, the OSH Act provides for criminal penalties for a willful violation that causes the death of an employee. For individuals, a conviction for such a violation is punishable by a fine of not more than $20,000 or by imprisonment for not more than six months, or by both.[171] If convicted, a corporation may be fined for up to $500,000.

Commentators have noted that the fines imposed by the OSH Act are ineffective in reducing workplace injuries or increasing employer compliance. The argument is that the low likelihood of inspections combined with the small amount of the fines, creates a

---

163 Donovan v. Sarasota Concrete Co., 693 F.2d 1061 (11th Cir. 1982).

164 See 29 U.S.C. §§ 658–59.

165 Id. § 658(c).

166 Id. § 658(c).

167 Occup. Safety and Health Law: Comp. & Prac. § 6:1 (2017).

168 Id.

169 Id. §§ 658(a), 666(a)–(d), (i).

170 29 U.S.C. §§ 658(a), 666(a)–(d), (i). See also 29 U.S.C. § 666(j) (granting the Occupational Safety and Health Review Commission the authority to reduce penalties based on an employer's good faith, inspection history, and size of business). The Federal Civil Penalties Inflation Adjustment Act Improvements Act of 2015, increased the fine for a repeated violation up to $126,749.00.

171 29 U.S.C. § 666(e) (providing further that if the conviction is for a violation committed after a first conviction of such person, "punishment shall be by a fine of not more than $20,000 or by imprisonment for not more than one year, or by both").

situation in which the cost of violating the act is smaller than the cost of compliance.[172]

Under the Severe Violator Enforcement Program, OSHA aims to focus enforcement on recalcitrant employers who demonstrate indifference to the health and safety of their employees through willful, repeated, or failure-to-abate violations of the OSH Act. Employers characterized as severe violators, are subject to mandatory follow-up inspections, corporate-wide agreements, enhanced settlement provisions, and federal court enforcement under Section 11(b) of the OSH Act.[173]

Even after taking into account these heightened enforcement efforts, the chances of any particular employer being subject to an inspection are small. In 2016, OSHA conducted just short of 32,000 inspections.[174] While that number might seem large, when one considers that there are over seven million workplaces covered under the OSH Act, the limited reach of the inspections become apparent.

6.2.3 Employer Duties

To reduce workplace hazards, the OSH Act imposes two main substantive duties on employers. First, under the Act's specific duty clause, employers must comply with safety and health standards promulgated by OSHA pursuant to the OSH Act.[175] Specific OSHA standards, which appear in the Code of Federal Regulations,[176] fall into four broad categories: general industry, construction, maritime and longshoring, and agriculture.[177] The "general industry" standards apply to all industries not included in construction, maritime and longshoring, or agriculture.[178] The standards cover a range of workplace issues and conditions including, for example, exposure to toxic substances,[179] fall and trip hazards,[180] the need for

---

172 Sidney A. Shapiro & Randy S. Rabinowitz, Punishment Versus Cooperation in Regulatory Enforcement: A Case Study of OSHA, 49 Admin. L. Rev. 713 (1997).

173 Severe Violator Enforcement Program, Directive number CPL 02–00–149 (June 18, 2010).

174 Occupational Safety and Health Administration Enforcement, available at https://www.osha.gov/dep/2016_enforcement_summary.html (2016).

175 29 U.S.C. § 654(a)(2).

176 29 C.F.R. § 1910.

177 Id. §§ 1910–28.

178 See County Concrete Corp., 16 OSH Cas. (BNA) 1952, 1954 (1994) (stating that "general industry standards apply if there is no specific construction, maritime and longshoring, or agricultural standard governing the hazardous condition") (citing Dravo Corp. v. OSHRC, 613 F.2d 1227, 1234 (3d Cir. 1980)).

179 29 C.F.R. § 1910.119.

180 See, e.g., 29 C.F.R. §§ 1918.85(j)(1)(iii), 1926.503(a)(1), 1926.760(a)(3).

protective equipment such as hard hats,[181] fire prevention,[182] exit signs,[183] and ventilation devices.[184]

In addition to complying with specific standards, employers must comply with the OSH Act's general duty clause.[185] As it is impossible to anticipate and develop standards to guard against all of the many hazards that may exist in the workplace, the OSH Act imposes on employers a general duty to keep their workplaces "free from recognized hazards that are causing or are likely to cause death or serious physical harm to . . . employees."[186] In effect, the general duty clause functions as a catch-all provision that kicks in when a hazard is identified but OSHA has not promulgated a specific standard that applies to it.[187]

6.2.4 Standards Promulgation

Section 3(8) of the OSH Act defines a health and safety standard as one that is "reasonably necessary or appropriate to provide safe or healthful employment and places of employment."[188] The OSH Act provides for the promulgation of three types of OSHA standards: national consensus, emergency temporary, and permanent. OSHA was authorized to promulgate national consensus standards during the two-year period after the OSH Act became effective.[189] Section 6(a), which governs national consensus standards, allowed OSHA to adopt the standards of any nationally recognized "standards producing" organizations without resorting to a lengthy rule-making process.[190] The adoption of such standards enabled OSHA to provide workers with safety and health protection soon after the OSH Act became effective.[191] OSHA's authority to promulgate a national consensus standard under § 6(a) ended in 1973.[192]

---

181 29 C.F.R. § 1910.135.

182 Id. § 1910.39.

183 Id. § 1910.36.

184 Id. § 1910.94.

185 29 U.S.C. § 654(a)(1).

186 Id.

187 See, e.g., Reich v. Mont. Sulphur & Chem. Co., 32 F.3d 440, 445 (9th Cir. 1994) (noting that the " 'general duty clause applies when there are no specific standards' ") (quoting Donovan v. Royal Logging Co., 645 F.2d 822, 829 (9th Cir. 1981) (internal quotations omitted), cert. denied, 115 S.Ct. 1355 (1995)).

188 29 U.S.C. § 652(8).

189 Id. § 655(a).

190 Id. § 652(9).

191 See Mark A. Rothstein, OSHA After Ten Years: A Review and Some Proposed Reforms, 34 Vand. L. Rev. 71, 73–74 (1981) (discussing OSHA's national consensus standards).

192 See 29 C.F.R. § 1910.4(b).

Section 6(c) of the OSH Act allows OSHA to issue emergency temporary standards (ETS) without going through the notice and comment process required for permanent standards.[193] In order to implement an ETS, which lasts only six months,[194] OSHA must establish that the standard is necessary to protect employees from a "grave danger."[195] Judicial interpretations indicate that a "grave danger" exists when a hazard is life threatening.[196]

OSHA's authority to issue permanent standards derives from § 6(b) of the OSH Act. Section 6(b) provides procedures for modifying or revoking existing standards, or issuing new standards.[197]

The majority of all OSHA standards currently in existence are the national consensus standards that OSHA enacted during the first two years of the Act pursuant to § 6(a).[198] This reality reflects in part the "protracted, detailed, cumbersome, and adversarial" character of OSHA's rulemaking process.[199] Promulgating a new standard under § 6(b) can take years.[200] Stringent judicial interpretations of OSH Act provisions have often exacerbated the difficulties that OSHA encounters in trying to engage in successful rulemaking under § 6(b).[201]

The Supreme Court's decision in *Industrial Union Department, AFL-CIO v. American Petroleum Institute* (the Benzene Case)[202] illustrates the burden of proof that OSHA must establish in order to act pursuant to § 6(b). The case involved OSHA's attempt to reduce

---

193 29 U.S.C. § 655(c)(1).

194 Id. § 655(c)(3).

195 Id. § 655(c)(1)(A); see also International Union, United Auto., Aerospace, & Agric. Implement Workers of Am., UAW v. Donovan, 590 F.Supp. 747, 749 (D.D.C. 1984) (stating that an ETS must address a grave danger, even though a permanent standard may address merely significant risk).

196 See, e.g., Fla. Peach Growers Ass'n v. U.S. Dep't of Labor, 489 F.2d 120, 132 (5th Cir. 1974) (defining "grave danger" as the potential for "incurable, permanent, or fatal consequences").

197 29 U.S.C. § 655(b).

198 See U.S. Dep't of Labor, OSHA at 30: Three Decades of Progress in Occupational Safety and Health, available at https://www.osha.gov/as/opa/osha-at-30.html.

199 Mark A. Rothstein, Substantive and Procedural Obstacles to OSHA Rulemaking: Reproductive Hazards as an Example, 12 B.C. Envtl. Aff. L. Rev. 627, 698 (1985).

200 Henry H. Drummonds, The Sister Sovereign States: Preemption and the Second Twentieth Century Revolution in the Law of the American Workplace, 62 Fordham L. Rev. 469, 595 (1993) (citing Mark Rothstein et al., Employment Law 601–28 (2d ed. 1991)).

201 Wendy Wagner, The "Bad Science" Fiction: Reclaiming the Debate over the Role of Science in Public Health and Environmental Regulation, 66 Law & Contemp. Probs. 63, 82 n.75 (2003) (collecting sources critical of the Benzene Case, described infra).

202 448 U.S. 607 (1980).

employee exposure to benzene from ten parts per million to one part per million. In defense of OSHA's modified benzene standard, the Government argued that in setting a standard under the OSH Act, OSHA was required to impose a standard that "guarantee[s] workplaces that are free from any risk of material health impairment, however small, or that come[s] as close as possible to doing so without ruining entire industries."[203] The Court disagreed with this interpretation and concluded that the OSH Act's mandate of "safe" workplaces was not the equivalent of " 'risk-free.' "[204]

> There are many activities that we engage in every day—such as driving a car or even breathing city air—that entail some risk of accident or material health impairment; nevertheless, few people would consider these activities "unsafe." Similarly, a workplace can hardly be considered "unsafe" unless it threatens the workers with a significant risk of harm.[205]

Writing for a plurality of the Court, Justice Stevens held that before OSHA acted pursuant to § 6(b) it had to first demonstrate, through the use of substantial evidence, that it was more likely than not that the current exposure level for benzene presented a "significant risk" of harm.[206] OSHA, the Court held, had failed to undertake this risk assessment.

The American Petroleum Institute, on behalf of itself and member companies, argued that OSHA not only had to perform a risk assessment but also a cost-benefit analysis to ensure that the benefits to be gained from promulgating the modified standard would be reasonable relative to the costs that industries affected by the standard would incur in complying with it. Although the Court did not address this issue in the Benzene Case, it did so later in *American Textile Manufacturers Institute v. Donovan* (the Cotton Dust Case).[207] In *American Textile*, the Court held that the plain language of the OSH Act did not require a cost-benefit analysis.

6.2.5 Establishing a Violation of an OSHA Standard

6.2.5.1 Specific Duty Clause Violation

To prove a violation of a specific standard, OSHA must show that (1) the cited standard applies to the employer and to the claimed

[203] Id. at 641.
[204] Id. at 642.
[205] Id.
[206] Id. at 639–40.
[207] 452 U.S. 490 (1981).

hazard; (2) the employer failed to comply with the standard; (3) the employees were exposed to the hazard; and (4) the employer had actual or constructive knowledge of the hazardous condition.[208]

Establishing that a standard applies to an employer may require OSHA to prove that the employer belongs to a particular industry group. For example, if the cited standard is a maritime standard, OSHA must prove that the employer operates within the maritime industry in order for the standard to apply. Whether a cited standard applies also depends on the specific circumstances surrounding the claimed hazard. Thus if the cited standard requires that "exit routes" must be "free and unobstructed,"[209] OSHA must show that the route in question was indeed an exit route.

Demonstrating that an employer failed to comply with a cited standard involves, in many cases, a straightforward determination. If, for example, the cited standard prohibits employees from working on scaffolds during storms or high winds,[210] OSHA can show noncompliance through evidence indicating that employees were in fact working on a scaffold during a storm.

Proving the existence of non-complying conditions may involve a more substantial judgment call, however, especially in instances where the question of compliance turns substantially on employee training. *Superior Custom Cabinet Co.*[211] illustrates the point. The case involved an employee who fell to his death while walking backwards on a stairwell that lacked guardrails. OSHA cited the employer for failing to comply with a standard that required employers to instruct employees "in the recognition and avoidance of unsafe conditions. . . ."[212] The issue of noncompliance in the case required an evaluation of whether the employer's training was sufficiently specific to inform the employees of the hazards involved in their work and how to avoid them. Superior's employees testified that Superior instructed them to watch out for " 'dangerous situations' " and to avoid unsafe conditions.[213] The Occupational Safety and Health Review Commission (OSHRC) held that this level of instruction was far too general because it gave employees too much

208 See, e.g., Access Equip. Sys., Inc., 18 OSH Cas. (BNA) 1718, 1720 (1999); Wheeling-Pittsburgh Steel Corp., 16 OSH Cas. (BNA) 1780, 1782 (1994); Astra Pharm. Prods., Inc., 9 OSH Cas. (BNA) 2126, 2129 (1981).

209 29 C.F.R. § 1910.37(a)(3).

210 Id. § 1910.28(a)(18) ("Employees shall not work on scaffolds during storms or high winds.").

211 18 OSH Cas. (BNA) 1019 (1997).

212 Id. at 1020.

213 Id.

discretion in determining whether a given condition was safe or unsafe.

The third element of a specific standard violation requires proof that the employees were exposed to the hazard. OSHA can prove this element by showing either actual exposure to an unsafe working condition or that access to the hazard was reasonably predictable.[214] For example, if the hazard is a stairwell that lacks guardrails, actual exposure exists if an employee uses the stairwell. In the absence of such exposure, proof of access is sufficient where it is reasonably predictable either by operational necessity or otherwise (including inadvertence) that employees have been, are, or will be in the zone of danger.[215] Thus, in the illustration above, OSHA could establish exposure if the stairwell was in an area of the facility accessible to employees, making it reasonably predictable that they might use it, even if no employee used the stairwell.[216]

The final element to sustain a violation under the specific duty clause requires that the employer had actual knowledge or constructive knowledge of the hazardous condition. This element necessitates a showing that the employer either knew, or with the exercise of reasonable diligence could have known, of the violative condition.[217] In assessing reasonable diligence, the courts and the OSHRC have relied on various factors, " 'including the employer's obligation to have adequate work rules and training programs, to adequately supervise employees, to anticipate hazards to which employees may be exposed, and to take measures to prevent the occurrence of violations.' "[218]

A lack of reasonable diligence may be shown where the employer fails to take measures to prevent foreseeable hazards.[219] *Donohue Industries, Inc.*[220] illustrates the point. In *Donohue*, OSHA cited the employer after an experienced electrician failed to ground equipment in violation of a "basic tenet" of the electrical trade.[221] The OSHRC vacated the citation, holding that because the employer's work rules,

---

[214] See, e.g., Donovan v. Adams Steel Erection, 766 F.2d 804, 811–12 (3d Cir. 1985).

[215] Id.; Mineral Indus. & Heavy Constr. Group v. OSHRC, 639 F.2d 1289, 1294 (5th Cir. 1981).

[216] The illustration mirrors the facts in *S. Masonry Constr., LLC*, 2005 OSHD (CCH) P32,919 (2007) (concluding that employees were actually exposed to the danger of an unprotected stairwell and that they had access to the hazard which was reasonably predictable).

[217] See, e.g., Atlantic Battery Co., 16 OSH Cas. (BNA) 2131, 2138 (1994).

[218] Precision Concrete Constr., 19 OSH Cas. (BNA) 1404, 1407 (2001).

[219] See, e.g., Pride Oil Well Serv., 15 OSH Cas. (BNA) 1809, 1814 (1992).

[220] 20 OSH Cas. (BNA) 1346 (2003).

[221] Id. at 1350.

training, and supervision were adequate, there was no basis to conclude that the employer knew or had reason to know that an experienced employee would act contrary to the standard.

Issues at times might arise in cases in which an employer is cited for a condition under a general standard (applicable to all employers), which is also subject to a specific industry standard, which the employer arguably has satisfied. Is the more general standard applicable? Usually, the more general standard will not apply if the specific industry standard and the general standard apply to the same hazard and if the specific standard requires the employer to take one action and the more general standard require the employer to take a different action.[222]

6.2.5.2 General Duty Clause Violation

As noted above, under the general duty clause—§ 5(a)(1) of the OSH Act—employers must keep their workplaces "free from recognized hazards that are causing or are likely to cause death or serious physical harm to . . . employees."[223] In order to prove a violation of the clause, the Secretary of Labor must show that (1) a condition or activity in the workplace presented a hazard to employees; (2) either the employer or the industry recognized the condition or activity as a hazard; (3) the hazard was likely to or actually caused death or serious physical harm; and (4) a feasible means to eliminate or materially reduce the hazard existed.[224]

Case law under the OSH Act defines a hazard "in terms of conditions or practices deemed unsafe over which an employer can reasonably be expected to exercise control."[225] In *Pepperidge Farms*,[226] for example, carpal tunnel syndrome and other musculoskeletal disorders were hazards of workplace tasks involving repetitive motion and lifting of heavy objects. In *Noble Drilling Services, Inc.*,[227] the employer's use of a personnel basket, which lacked an inside grab rail, to lift employees into the air more than 100 feet in order to transport them from a dock to a boat constituted a hazard.

A hazard is recognized when the potential danger of a condition or practice is either actually known to the employer or generally

[222] Occup. Safety and Health Law: Comp. & Prac. § 7:20 (2016).

[223] 29 U.S.C. § 654(a)(1).

[224] See, e.g., Fabi Constr. Co. v. Sec'y of Labor, 508 F.3d 1077, 1081 (D.C. Cir. 2007).

[225] See, e.g., Morrison-Knudsen Co./Yonkers Contracting Co., A Joint Venture, 16 OSH Cas. (BNA) 1105, 1121 (1993).

[226] 17 OSH Cas. (BNA) 1993 (1997).

[227] 19 OSH Cas. (BNA) 1869 (2002).

known in the industry.[228] Industry standards and guidelines are useful evidence of industry recognition.[229] In *Kokosing Construction Co., Inc.*,[230] the OSHRC found that the employer recognized the hazard of climbing a support wall without protection. The OSHRC relied on two industry standards, in existence prior to the citation, that regarded such an act as unacceptable. Similarly, in *SeaWorld of Florida v. Perez*, a killer whale was ruled to qualify as a "recognized hazard" for trainers at an aquatic theme park for purpose of general duty clause.[231] Notice, however, that in cases involving an obvious hazard, the employer cannot avoid liability by asserting that it and its industry were ignorant of the hazard.[232]

The third element, causing or likely to cause death or serious physical harm, focuses not on the likelihood of an accident or injury but on whether, if an accident or injury does occur, the result is likely to cause death or serious harm.[233] In *Waldon Health Care Center*,[234] for example, a nursing home operator contested a citation for violating § 5(a)(1), based on employee exposure to the Hepatitis B virus (HBV). The employer argued that the hazard of HBV transmission was not likely to cause death or serious physical injury because its nursing staff seldom came into contact with the blood of residents. The OSHRC disagreed and held that this element was satisfied because if an employee contracted the virus, the result was likely to be death or serious physical harm even if the risk of the transmission was minimal.

The final element of a § 5(a)(1) violation, a feasible means to eliminate or materially reduce the hazard must exist, has often sounded the death knell of such violations in the employer's favor. In assessing a proposed abatement method, the OSHRC considers if a reasonable person familiar with the conditions of the industry would have instituted it.[235] *Pepperidge Farm* illustrates this element. As noted above, the case involved hazards in the form of various

---

[228] See, e.g., Kelly Springfield Tire Co. v. Donovan, 729 F.2d 317, 321 (5th Cir. 1984); St. Joe Minerals v. OSHRC, 647 F.2d 840, 845 (8th Cir. 1981).

[229] See, e.g., Cargill, Inc., 10 OSH Cas. (BNA) 1398, 1402 (1982) (commenting that "[i]t is well established that voluntary industry standards . . . are probative evidence of industry recognition of hazards").

[230] 17 OSH Cas. (BNA) 1869 (1996).

[231] 748 F.3d 1202 (D.C. Cir. 2014).

[232] Safeway, Inc. v. OSHRC, 382 F.3d 1189 (10th Cir. 2004).

[233] R.L. Sanders Roofing Co., 7 OSH Cas. (BNA) 1566, 1569 (1979), rev'd on other grounds, 620 F.2d 97 (5th Cir. 1980); Waldon Health Care Ctr., 16 OSH Cas. (BNA) 1052 (1993).

[234] Id.

[235] See, e.g., Fluor Constructors Int'l, Inc., 17 OSH Cas. (BNA) 1947 (1997).

musculoskeletal disorders that stemmed from workers engaging in repetitive motion tasks and lifting heavy objects.[236]

The Secretary of Labor proved all of the elements to sustain a § 5(a)(1) violation except for the abatement issue. Pepperidge Farm had already taken several steps to lessen the occurrence of the disorders, especially with respect to its assembly line employees whose job included the packaging of cookies. The Secretary insisted, however, that additional steps were warranted, such as adding workers to the line, reducing the line speed, and rotating workers out of highly repetitive jobs to less repetitive ones.[237] Intuitively these steps would appear to help reduce the hazard. The Commission concluded, however, that the Secretary had not introduced any evidence to demonstrate that these steps would in fact materially reduce or eliminate the hazard. In addition, there was no evidence to conclude that the proposed steps would not adversely affect the quality of the cookies manufactured by Pepperidge Farm.

6.2.5.3 Employer Defenses

When challenging an OSHA citation or penalty, employers may be able to raise procedural defenses such as the failure of OSHA to follow inspection procedures and the issuance of a citation without reasonable promptness.[238]

An employer also has a fixed and limited amount of time in which to respond to a citation—generally, 15 working days.[239] The OSH Act allows employers to contest OSHA citations or penalties before an administrative law judge of the OSHRC.[240] At the OSHRC hearing, the Secretary of Labor has the burden to establish the elements of the alleged violation as well as the propriety of the proposed abatement order and any proposed penalty.[241]

If an employer is unable to comply with an OSHA standard, the OSH Act provides that the employer can submit an application for a variance. A variance allows an employer to avoid complying with some part of an OSHA safety-and-health standard.[242] Although four

---

236 17 OSH Cas. (BNA) at 1995.

237 Id.

238 See, e.g., Walter B. Connolly, Jr. & Donald R. Crowell, II, A Practical Guide to the Occupational Safety and Health Act § 12.02 (2005) (discussing procedural defenses); Occupational Safety and Health Law 158–161 (Randy S. Rabinowitz ed. 2d ed. 2002) (discussing procedural defenses).

239 Occup. Safety and Health Law: Comp. & Prac. § 6:1 (2016).

240 Id. § 661.

241 Id. § 651(b)(3).

242 Id. § 655(d).

types of variances are possible,[243] the two most common are temporary and permanent variances. A temporary variance allows employers a short-term exemption from a standard either when they cannot comply with OSHA requirements in a timely fashion because the necessary construction or alteration of the facility cannot be completed in time or when personnel, materials, or equipment are temporarily unavailable.[244] Eligibility for a temporary variance requires the employer to implement an effective compliance program as quickly as possible. In the meantime, the employer must demonstrate that it is taking all available steps to safeguard employees.[245] By contrast, to obtain a permanent variance, an employer must prove that its methods, conditions, practices, operations, or processes provide workplaces that are as safe and healthful as those that follow the OSHA standards.[246]

In addition, employers have at their disposal several affirmative defenses including "unpreventable employee misconduct," "infeasibility," and "greater hazard."

6.2.5.3.1 Unpreventable Employee Misconduct

Unpreventable employee misconduct, also referred to as unavoidable employee misconduct, isolated occurrence, isolated misconduct and employee misconduct,[247] is the most important of the affirmative defenses. The defense is based on the adage that " 'a cowboy can lead his horse to water, but the horse may not drink.' In certain situations, the horse may not drink even if water was brought to the horse."[248] In other words, when an employer does everything reasonably within its power to protect the health and safety of its workers, and " 'an employee nonetheless fails to use proper equipment or otherwise ignores firmly established safety measures, it seems unfair to hold the employer liable.' "[249]

---

243 See U.S. Dep't of Labor, OSHA Fact Sheet (2002), available at http://www.osha.gov/OshDoc/data_General_Facts/VarianceFactS.pdf (listing the four variances as temporary, permanent, experimental, and national defense). Experimental variances are authorized under 29 U.S.C. § 655(b)(6)(C) (allowing a variance that "is necessary to permit an employer to participate in an experiment approved by him or the Secretary of Health and Human Services designed to demonstrate or validate new and improved techniques to safeguard the health or safety of workers"). OSHA issues national defense variances "to avoid serious impairment of the national defense." 29 C.F.R. § 1905.12(b)(4).

244 29 C.F.R. § 1905.10(b)(7)(i).

245 Id. § 1905.10(b)(7)(ii)–(iii).

246 Id. § 1905.11(b)(4).

247 See Occup. Safety and Health Law: Comp. & Prac. § 9:10 (2016)

248 Id.

249 P. Gioioso & Sons, Inc. v. OSHRC, 115 F.3d 100, 107–08 (1st Cir. 1997).

To prevail on this defense, an employer must demonstrate that it (1) established a work rule to prevent the reckless behavior and/or unsafe condition from occurring; (2) adequately communicated the rule to its employees; (3) took steps to discover incidents of noncompliance; and (4) effectively enforced the rule whenever employees transgressed it.[250] The success of the defense generally depends heavily on the employer's training and supervision of employees, as an inadequate training program and a lack of supervision suggest that the employer could have taken reasonable steps to prevent the danger from occurring.[251]

6.2.5.3.2 Infeasibility

Employers may also defend against a charge of violating the OSH Act by demonstrating that compliance was infeasible. The defense of infeasibility requires an employer to satisfy the following elements: (1) that it would be technologically or economically infeasible to comply with the standard's requirements or that compliance would have rendered necessary work operations technologically or economically infeasible; and (2) that the employer used alternative means of protection not specified in the standard, or that alternative means of employee protection were unavailable.[252]

6.2.5.3.3 Greater Hazard

A third affirmative defense is the greater hazard defense. The defense allows employers to avoid sanctions for violating an OSHA standard if they can prove that complying with the standard would impose an even greater threat to the health and safety of their employees.[253] To use this defense, an employer must establish three basic elements: (1) that compliance with a standard would result in greater hazards to employees than non-compliance; (2) that there are

---

[250] Frank Lill & Son, Inc. v. Sec'y of Labor, 362 F.3d 840, 846 (D.C. Cir. 2004).

[251] See, e.g., Danis-Shook Joint Venture XXV v. Sec'y of Labor, 319 F.3d 805, 812 (6th Cir. 2003) (concluding that the employer's defense of unpreventable employee misconduct failed because in order to assert the defense, the employer was required to have a thorough safety program, which it did not).

[252] See, e.g., V.I.P. Structures, Inc., 16 OSH Cas. (BNA) 1873, 1874 (1994); see also Brock v. Dun-Par Engineered Form Co., 843 F.2d 1135, 1139 (8th Cir. 1988) (observing that "[w]here the employer determines that the specified means of compliance [are] infeasible, it must affirmatively investigate alternative measures of preventing the hazard, and actually implement such alternative measures, to the extent feasible"); Harry C. Crooker & Sons, Inc. v. OSHRC, 537 F.3d 79, 22 O.S.H. Cas. (BNA) 1298, 2008 O.S.H. Dec. (CCH) P 32971 (1st Cir. 2008) ("To prevail on an infeasibility defense, the employer must prove (i) that compliance with a particular standard either is impossible or will render performance of the work impossible; and (ii) that it (the employer) undertook alternative steps to protect its workers (or that no such steps were available).")

[253] Dole v. Williams Enter., Inc., 876 F.2d 186, 188 (D.C. Cir. 1989).

no alternative means of employee protection available; and (3) that a variance was unavailable or inappropriate.[254]

One case in which the defense was successful involved a situation where the employer was charged with a serious violation for a failure to have employees wear safety lanyards when removing steel trusses between columns of the building being demolished.[255] The employer had a safety rule requiring employees to wear safety lanyards. The employees complied except in one instance when they refused to tie-off the safety lines while removing the last four bolts and safety pins holding a truss in place. There was testimony to the effect that the truss was likely to spring free and uncontrolled when the tension holding it in place was removed. The employees involved stated that it was much more hazardous to tie-off than to remain unfettered so as to enable them to dodge an out-of-control truss. Finding that the employees would "be endangered rather than protected by compliance with a standard in light of the operative facts," the Commission vacated the citation and penalty imposed on the employer.[256]

Despite the successful pleading of the greater hazard defense in this case, the Commission and reviewing courts have been hesitant to find in favor of employers in these cases.[257]

6.2.6 Employee Rights and Responsibilities

6.2.6.1 Overview of Rights

The OSH Act provides employees with a range of rights and responsibilities. Many of the employee rights encourage employees to play an active role in ensuring that their workplace is safe and healthful. Some of the more important rights include the following:

- the right to be informed by the employer of applicable OSHA standards[258] and worker injuries and illnesses;[259]
- the right to petition for the adoption of a standard;[260]

---

254 See, e.g., E & R Erectors v. Sec'y of Labor, 107 F.3d 157, 163 (3d Cir. 1997); Williams Enter., Inc., 876 F.2d at 188. To receive a permanent variance permitting noncompliance with a standard, an employer must prove that its methods, conditions, practices, operations, or processes provide workplaces that are as safe and healthful as those that follow the OSHA standards. 29 C.F.R. § 1905.11(b)(4).

255 Sec'y of Labor v. Industrial Steel Erectors, Inc., 6 OSAHRC No. 703 (1974),

256 Id. at 2.

257 See 3 West's Fed. Admin. Prac. § 2615 (2017).

258 29 U.S.C. § 657(c)(1).

259 29 C.F.R. § 1904.35(b)(2)(v)(a).

260 29 U.S.C. § 655(b)(1).

- the right to seek judicial review of a standard;[261]
- the right to request an OSHA inspection if the employee believes that hazardous conditions or violations of standards exist in the workplace;[262]
- the right to accompany an OSHA compliance officer during a workplace inspection, or to have an authorized employee representative do so,[263] and to be informed of any dangers found during an inspection;[264]
- the rights to be free from retaliation;[265]
- the right to be notified if an employer applies for a variance from an OSHA standard, and to have an opportunity to participate in a variance hearing;[266] and
- the right to gain access to relevant employee exposure and medical records.[267]

6.2.6.2 The Right to Be Free from Retaliation

Section 11(c) of the OSH Act provides employees with a right not to be discharged or discriminated against for filing a complaint, testifying, or engaging in any other right under the Act.[268] While formal complaints to OSHA are clearly protected under § 11(c), so are informal communications.[269] Protection is also available in a situation where an employee contacts OSHA but later declines to file a formal complaint.[270] Protection also extends in situations where

---

[261] Id. § 655(f).

[262] Id. § 655(b)(1).

[263] Id. § 657(e). Three important cases that address this right are *Chamber of Commerce v. OSHA*, 636 F.2d 464, 467 (D.C. Cir. 1980) (invalidating a federal OSHA regulation that required employers to pay employees for time spent participating in an inspection); *Stephenson Enter., Inc. v. Marshall*, 578 F.2d 1021, 1025–26 (5th Cir. 1978) (employers are not entitled to access the notes of an OSHA compliance officer that contains notes of employee statements made during the inspection); and *Trinity Industries, Inc. v. Martin*, 963 F.2d 795, 799 (5th Cir. 1992) (upholding OSHA's policy prohibiting employer representatives from attending employee interviews during inspections).

[264] 29 U.S.C. § 662(c).

[265] Id. § 660(c)(1).

[266] Id. § 655(d).

[267] Id. § 657(c)(3).

[268] Id. § 660(c)(1).

[269] See, e.g., Reich v. Skyline Terrace, Inc., 977 F.Supp. 1141, 1146 (N.D. Okla. 1997); Donovan v. George Lai Contracting, Ltd., 629 F.Supp. 121, 122 (W.D. Mo. 1985); Donovan v. Freeway Constr. Co., 551 F.Supp. 869, 879 (D. R.I. 1982).

[270] See Kennard v. Louis Zimmer Commc'n, Inc., 632 F.Supp. 635 (E.D. Pa. 1986).

employees file complaints with other federal agencies[271] as well as with state agencies.[272] In addition, protection has been afforded to an employee who communicated with a newspaper reporter about alleged OSH Act violations.[273]

While the OSH Act does not provide an employee the right to refuse to perform an unsafe or unhealthful job-related activity, an OSHA regulation provides that an employee may refuse to work when faced with an imminent danger of death or serious injury.[274] The Supreme Court's decision in *Whirlpool Corp. v. Marshall*,[275] upholding the regulation, indicates that an employee's refusal to work in such a situation is a limited right that should be undertaken only as a last resort.[276] If time permits, an employee should first report the unsafe or unhealthful condition to OSHA.[277]

The following conditions must be present in order to justify an employee's refusal to engage in work that threatens health or safety: the employee must have no reasonable alternative to refusing; the refusal must be in good faith; the worker must have a "reasonable" fear that the working conditions present a danger of death or serious injury; there must be insufficient time to utilize the normal remedies that exist under the OSH Act; and the worker must have made an attempt to remedy the hazard through consultation with the employer.[278]

As the OSH Act does not permit a private cause of action,[279] rights protected by the Act, including the right of hazardous work refusal, can only be enforced through an action brought by the Secretary of Labor. An employee who believes that she has been discriminated against in violation of the OSH Act must file a complaint with the Secretary alleging such discrimination within 30 days of the alleged violation. The Secretary then investigates the complaint, and, upon a determination that the employer has violated

---

271 See Marshall v. Commonwealth Aquarium, 469 F.Supp. 690, 693 (D. Mass. 1979) (employee filed complaint with the National Institute of Occupational Safety and Health).

272 See Donovan v. Peter Zimmer Am., Inc., 557 F.Supp. 642, 651–52 (D. S.C. 1982) (ordering the employer to pay back pay and interest to employees wrongfully discharged under the OSH Act in retaliation for filing complaints with the state occupational safety agency alleging violations of the OSH Act).

273 See Donovan v. R.D. Andersen Constr. Co., 552 F.Supp. 249, 253 (D. Kan. 1982).

274 29 C.F.R. § 1977.12(b).

275 445 U.S. 1 (1980).

276 Id. at 10–11.

277 Id. at 11.

278 Id. at 4 n.3.

279 See, e.g., George v. Aztec Rental Ctr., Inc., 763 F.2d 184, 186 (5th Cir. 1985); Taylor v. Brighton Corp., 616 F.2d 256, 264 (6th Cir. 1980).

the anti-discrimination provision of the OSH Act, § 11(c), the Secretary can sue in federal district court.[280] If the Secretary declines to bring a § 11(c) suit on behalf of an employee, that decision is not judicially reviewable.[281] In exercising jurisdiction over a § 11(c) action, federal district courts, upon petition of the Secretary, can issue an injunction to restrain violations of § 11(c),[282] and order "all [other] appropriate relief" on behalf of an employee including rehiring or reinstatement to the employee's former position with back pay.[283]

Even though the OSH Act does not provide for a private cause of action, employees who suffer retaliation as the result of complaining about health and safety issues, might bring a claim of wrongful discharge in violation public policy.[284]

6.2.6.3 Employee Responsibilities

Although the OSH Act is primarily concerned with the conduct of employers, it does require that employees "comply with occupational safety and health standards and all rules, regulations, and orders issued pursuant to this chapter which are applicable to his own actions and conduct."[285] Courts have held, however, that the OSH Act does not give OSHA the power to sanction employees because the enforcement scheme is clearly aimed at employers.[286] That said, an employee's failure to live up to his or her responsibilities may aid an employer in defending against a violation on the ground of unpreventable employee misconduct.

---

[280] 29 U.S.C. § 660(c)(2).

[281] See, e.g., Wood v. Dep't of Labor & Elaine Chao, 275 F.3d 107 (D.C. Cir. 2001).

[282] 29 U.S.C. § 662(a).

[283] Id. § 660(c)(2).

[284] See e.g., Pytlinski v. Brocar Products, Inc., 760 N.W. 2d 385, 94 Ohio St. 3d 77 (2002) (finding that an at-will employee who is discharged for filing a complaint with OSHA concerning matters of health and safety in the workplace is entitled to maintain a common-law tort action against the employer for wrongful discharge in violation of public policy). See also supra Section 2.5.1.

[285] Id. § 654.

[286] Atlantic & Gulf Stevedores, Inc. v. OSHRC, 534 F.2d 541, 553 (3d Cir. 1976) (making this observation with "considerable misgivings"); see also United Steelworkers of Am., AFL-CIO-CLC v. Marshall, 647 F.2d 1189, 1231 (D.C. Cir. 1980) (describing the requirement that employees comply with the Act as a mere "exhortation"); United States v. Doig, 950 F.2d 411, 415 (7th Cir. 1991) (commenting that subjecting employees to liability under the OSH Act is inconsistent with the Act's legislative purpose).

Chapter 7

PRIVATIZATION OF EMPLOYMENT DISPUTE RESOLUTION

For many years unions and employers have resolved disputes over the meaning of collective bargaining agreements using labor arbitration. Arbitration of disputes in the nonunion workplace was rare, however, until the late 20th century. Arbitration is touted as quicker and cheaper than litigation. It is also private, while litigation takes place in a public process. While not all statutory schemes allow substitution of arbitration for judicial or administrative resolution, courts often enforce mandatory arbitration provisions that require employees to waive their right to go to court and instead, arbitrate any claim that they have against the employer. Accordingly, cases involving statutory as well as contractual claims are being heard in the arbitral forum. Yet there is continued resistance to mandatory arbitration by employees and their attorneys. Litigation over the enforceability of arbitration agreements is common and opponents have advocated for and in some cases succeeded in obtaining limits on arbitration.

§ 7.1 Historical Background and Scope of Arbitration

The use of arbitration as a private process to resolve disputes has been a common practice in the United States. Soon after the American Revolution, state legislatures adopted statutes affirming the practice of arbitration.[1] While not going back as far as 1776, arbitration in the unionized workplace also has a long tradition. The use of arbitration in labor contracts (i.e., in contracts negotiated between labor unions and employers) dates back to the early 1900s. Over the ensuing century, arbitration became the most common method of resolving disputes over the meaning and application of labor agreements.[2] In 1960, the Supreme Court, in a series of cases known as the *Steelworkers Trilogy*, decided to enforce labor

---

[1] See Carli N. Conklin, Introduction: Beyond the FAA: Arbitration Procedure, Practice, and Policy in Historical Perspective, 2016 J. of Disp. Res. 1.

[2] See generally Dennis R. Nolan & Roger I. Abrams, American Labor Arbitration: The Early Years, 35 U. Fla. L. Rev. 373 (1983).

arbitration agreements in order to discourage strikes and lockouts as a method of dispute resolution.[3]

Despite encouraging labor arbitration, courts were reluctant to enforce arbitration agreements in many other contexts. While the Federal Arbitration Act (FAA) made agreements to arbitrate enforceable, courts refused to compel arbitration of claims based on statutory rights.[4] In the 1980s, however, the Supreme Court's view of arbitration began to change, and it overruled earlier decisions denying enforcement of agreements to arbitrate statutory claims.[5] In the early 1990s, this trend moved into employment law. In *Gilmer v. Interstate Johnson/Lane Corp.*[6] the plaintiff filed suit against the employer arguing that he had been terminated because of his age in violation of the Age Discrimination in Employment Act. Relying on an arbitration provision found in the plaintiff's registration application with the New York Stock Exchange, the employer filed a motion to compel the plaintiff to arbitrate his claim. The plaintiff opposed the motion, arguing in part that arbitration was an inadequate forum to protect an employee's statutory rights. The Court agreed with the employer and concluded that an agreement to arbitration was merely an agreement to use a different forum, not a waiver of substantive rights.[7] Unless the statute creating the claim explicitly barred arbitration, the Court would order arbitration.

Ten years later in *Circuit City v. Adams,*[8] the Court opened the door to widespread adoption and enforcement of arbitration agreements in employment. Because in *Gilmer* the arbitration provision was included in a securities registration application, and not in an employment contract, the Court did not need to determine the scope of the exclusion for employment contracts in the Federal Arbitration Act (FAA).[9] The FAA, the statutory basis for enforcing arbitration agreements, states "nothing herein contained shall apply to contracts of employment of seamen, railroad employees, or any other class of workers engaged in foreign or interstate commerce."[10] In *Circuit City*, the Court read that exclusion very narrowly, holding

---

3 United Steelworkers of America v. American Mfg. Co., 363 U.S. 564 (1960); United Steelworkers of America v. Warrior & Gulf Navigation Co., 363 U.S. 574 (1960); United Steelworkers of America v. Enterprise Wheel & Car Corp., 363 U.S. 593 (1960).

4 See, e.g., Wilko v. Swan, 346 U.S. 427, 74 S. Ct. 182, 98 L. Ed. 168 (1953).

5 See Mitsubishi Motors Corp. v. Soler Chrysler Plymouth Inc., 473 U.S. 614 (1985); Shearson/American Exp. Inc. v. McMahon 482 U.S. 220 (1987); Rodriguez de Quijas v. Shearson/American Exp. Inc., 490 U.S. 477 (1989).

6 Gilmer v. Interstate Johnson/Lane Corp., 500 U.S. 20 (1991).

7 Id. at 29.

8 532 U.S. 105 (2001).

9 See 9 U.S.C. § 1.

10 Id.

that it excluded from arbitration only contracts of transportation workers like those specifically mentioned.[11] As a result, employers could impose agreements to arbitrate all claims relating to employment on most employees as a condition of employment, with limited exceptions.

Subsequent to the *Circuit City* decision, many employers began requiring employees to agree to arbitrate all claims arising out of employment, waiving their right to go to court to enforce their legal rights. The Civil Rights Act of 1991, which added compensatory and punitive damages to the remedies available under Title VII, made arbitration particularly appealing to employers worried that juries would award employees substantial damages. There is no comprehensive data on the number of employees who are covered by arbitration agreements. Estimates are that more than half of the civilian nonunion workforce, constituting about 60 million employees, is covered by such agreements.[12] High-level executives and other powerful employees may voluntarily negotiate arbitration agreements with their employers. In most cases, however, the agreements are imposed on employees as a condition of employment, often with limited notice. Many employees are surprised to learn when a dispute arises that they have agreed to arbitrate their claims against the employer. Some employers adopt comprehensive dispute resolution systems, however, which include substantial training of employees and managers, efforts to resolve disputes at the lowest possible level, and often include mediation preceding arbitration.[13] Such systems appear to be designed to establish an effective and fair system for resolving disputes rather than simply to move disputes to a forum more favorable to the employer.[14]

§ 7.2 Enforceability of Arbitration Agreements

There are two basic types of legal challenges likely to arise with respect to arbitration: challenges to the arbitration provision itself and challenges to an arbitration award.

7.2.1 Challenges to the Arbitration Agreement

In the first type of challenge, one party seeks to invoke an arbitration provision included in a contract, while the other party refuses to arbitrate. The party seeking to enforce the arbitration

---

[11] 532 U.S. at 119.

[12] Alexander J.S. Colvin, The Growing Use of Mandatory Arbitration 2 (Economic Policy Institute 2017). See also note 59 infra.

[13] See Richard A. Bales & Jason N.W. Plowman, Compulsory Arbitration as Part of a Broader Employment Dispute Resolution Process: The Anheuser-Busch Example, 26 Hofstra Lab. & Emp. L.J. 1, 12–24 (2008).

[14] Id. at 5–7, 22–28, 29–32.

provision files suit to enforce the arbitration provision or, alternatively files a motion to compel arbitration in a case filed in court by the other party. In the employment context, it is usually the employer seeking to compel arbitration and the employee who seeks to avoid that obligation.

Employees resist arbitrating claims for many reasons. Conventional wisdom suggests that employees fare better before juries and the employee may want a jury trial for claims where a jury is permitted. In most cases, the arbitration system is unilaterally designed by the employer. Arbitration agreements may shorten statutes of limitation and/or limit discovery, which could make it more difficult for employees to bring and win their cases. Additionally, arbitration agreements may limit the remedies available to the employee, reducing them from what a court could order under the particular statute at issue. Further, the agreement might provide for the employee to pay some or all of the cost of the arbitrator, a cost that would not be incurred in court where the judge is paid by tax dollars. Some have argued that the employer has an advantage in arbitration against an individual employee, even where the arbitrator is mutually selected, since the employer may be a repeat player in arbitration while the employee almost certainly will not.[15] Thus employers may be able to secure more favorable arbitrators, because they are more knowledgeable about their qualifications, and more favorable decisions, because the arbitrator will want to ensure future business.[16] Finally, arbitral agreements may preclude class actions, making it difficult for employees with small claims to pursue them because of the cost of individual arbitration.

Although the Supreme Court has found that agreements to arbitrate statutory and common law claims are enforceable, there remain limited avenues for employees to challenge their application. The argument that the employee's lack of bargaining power alone is a defense to enforcement is unavailing, however.[17] One possible defense to an employer effort to compel arbitration is that the statute that gives rise to the dispute does not allow such agreements.[18] Most employment statutes were enacted before such agreements were enforceable, however, and do not include language barring arbitration. Congress has failed to amend any statute to preclude

---

[15] Alexander J.S. Colvin, An Empirical Study of Employment Arbitration: Case Outcomes and Processes, 8 J. Empirical Leg. Stud. 1, 11–16, 20 (2011).

[16] Id.

[17] Gilmer, 500 U.S. at 33.

[18] Gilmer, 500 U.S. at 27–28.

arbitration, although in 2010 it did ban pre-dispute agreements to arbitrate whistleblower claims under the Dodd-Frank Act.[19]

Another defense that appears more theoretical than real is a claim that the agreement to arbitrate prevents effective vindication of statutory rights. The Supreme Court recognized the defense in *Green Tree Financial Corporation v. Randolph* but found the plaintiff failed to meet it in that case.[20] Subsequent to that decision, courts applied the doctrine to bar arbitration. For example, in *Morrison v. Circuit City Stores, Inc.*, the plaintiff in a race and sex discrimination claim under Title VII of the Civil Rights Act, argued that the cost-splitting, remedies, discovery, and limitations provisions of the agreement prevented vindication of statutory rights.[21] The cost-splitting required a payment of $1622 within 90 days of the arbitrator's award to avoid payment of half the cost of the arbitration, while the remedies provision limited back pay, front pay and punitive damages compared to what would be available in a judicial action. Discovery was limited to twenty interrogatories and three depositions absent a showing of substantial need for more, and there was a one-year statute of limitations. The court found that the cost-splitting and remedies provisions prevented effective vindication of statutory rights. After considering data on average arbitration costs, the plaintiff's salary, and the fact that she was terminated yet had ongoing expenses, the court determined that the cost-sharing provision "would deter a substantial number of similarly situated persons from attempting to vindicate their statutory rights in the arbitral forum."[22] Similarly the court found that the extensive reductions in available remedies from what was available in court undermined both the make whole and deterrence goals of Title VII.[23]

---

[19] See Dodd-Frank Act, Pub. L. No. 111–203, § 922(c)(2), 124 Stat. 1376 (2010) codified at 18 U.S.C. § 1514A(e).

[20] Green Tree Fin. Corp. v. Randolph, 531 U.S. 79, 90 (2000).

[21] 317 F.3d 646 (6th Cir. 2003).

[22] Id. at 669. Other courts prior to *Italian Colors*, discussed infra, developed tests to determine whether arbitration costs prevent effective vindication of statutory rights. It is not clear whether such tests survive the *Italian Colors* decision. For example, the Sixth Circuit looks at whether the average costs of arbitration as compared to litigation would deter individuals situated similarly to the employee from vindicating their statutory rights. See Mazera v. Varsity Ford Mgmt. Servs., LLC, 565 F.3d 997, 1003–04 (6th Cir. 2009) (finding a $500 deposit required within ten days for employees making about $20,000 per year was a sufficient deterrent to make the agreement unenforceable, but because the cost provision offered a waiver option the court remanded to provide the employer an opportunity to waive the requirement to make the agreement enforceable). The Fourth Circuit looks at the plaintiff's ability to pay and whether any difference between the projected costs of arbitration and litigation in the case would deter a claim in arbitration. See Bradford v. Rockwell Semiconductor Sys., Inc., 238 F.3d 549, 556 (4th Cir. 2001).

[23] Id. at 673.

In *American Express Co. v. Italian Colors Restaurant*, however, the Supreme Court cast doubt on the effective vindication defense, enforcing a class action waiver in an arbitration agreement between merchants.[24] The Court found that the law did not ban class action waivers in antitrust cases nor guarantee the right to bring a class claim, even if an individual claim would cost more to litigate than was available in damages.[25] The Court suggested that the defense is limited to situations where the arbitration provision precludes the statutory claim altogether or imposes fees so excessive that access to the forum is effectively barred.[26]

Other defenses to arbitration appear somewhat more viable depending on the facts. According to the FAA, the generally applicable defenses to the enforcement of any contract apply to arbitration agreements.[27] Employees may argue that there was no agreement to arbitrate. In addition, they may defend against arbitration in the ground that the agreement is unconscionable.

A defense of lack of agreement to arbitrate may be based one of two arguments. The employee may claim that the particular dispute is not encompassed in the arbitration agreement or that there was no agreement to arbitrate any dispute. An example of the former is *Jones v. Halliburton Co.*, where the court found the arbitration provision did not cover a claim that an employee filed against her employer, a contractor in Iraq, for a sexual assault that occurred after work hours in the employee's bedroom in employer-provided housing.[28] The claims did not relate to her employment or occur in or around the workplace and thus were outside the scope of the arbitration provision.[29] This defense is challenging, however, because courts frequently apply a presumption in favor of arbitration.[30]

Lorenzo v. Prime Communications[31] is an example of a case where the employee argued that she did not agree to arbitrate her state and federal wage claims against the employer. In *Lorenzo*, the arbitration provision was in an employee handbook and the acknowledgement form for the handbook drafted by the employer and signed by the employee disclaimed any intent to create a contract. The Fourth Circuit held that because the parties expressly agreed

---

24 133 S.Ct. 2304 (2013).

25 Id. at 2310–11.

26 Id.

27 9 U.S.C. § 2 (requiring enforcement of arbitration agreements except "upon such grounds as exist at law or in equity for the revocation of any contract.")

28 583 F.3d 228, 240 (5th Cir. 2009).

29 Id. at 241.

30 See id. at 235; United Steelworkers v. Warrior & Gulf Navigation Co., 363 U.S. 574, 582–83 (1960).

31 806 F.3d 777 (4th Cir. 2015).

that the handbook was not a contract, there was no agreement to arbitrate.[32] Courts in these cases look to see whether the elements necessary to form a contract are met. In *Seawright v. American General Financial Services, Inc.*, for example, the court found that the parties agreed to arbitration where the employer sent a letter informing the employees that "[s]eeking, accepting or continuing employment" constituted an agreement to arbitrate employment disputes and the employee continued employment, thereby accepting the offer.[33] In *Walker v. Ryan's Family Steak Houses, Inc.*, the court refused to enforce an arbitration agreement that applicants were forced to sign in order to be considered for employment.[34] The court found a promise to consider the plaintiff's application to be inadequate consideration under Tennessee law. Further, because the arbitration provider reserved the right to change the rules and procedures of arbitration at any time without notice to the employees or their consent, any promise by the provider in exchange for the agreement to arbitrate was illusory. The court in *Hooters of America, Inc. v. Phillips* offers another application of the doctrine of substantive arbitrability.[35] There the court found that the employer promulgated rules so overwhelmingly biased that it materially breached the arbitration agreement, and thus it was not enforceable.[36]

Typically, the question of whether there is an enforceable agreement to arbitrate is for the courts. But in *Rent-A-Center, West, Inc. v. Jackson*, the Supreme Court held that when an arbitration provision delegates the authority to the arbitrator to decide questions of enforceability, that delegation is an enforceable agreement in the absence of a specific challenge to the delegation provision itself.[37] A challenge to the agreement to arbitrate is then decided by the arbitrator.

Challenges to arbitration based on differences between arbitral and judicial procedure frequently argue unconscionability. Unconscionability is a state law concept, and cases vary in their application. In *Ingle v. Circuit City Stores*, a claim for employment discrimination and harassment under state and federal law, the court found an arbitration provision unconscionable.[38] It was procedurally unconscionable because it was offered on a "take it or

---

[32] 806 F.3d at 781–82 (finding under North Carolina law the express contract negated any implied assent to the arbitration provision).

[33] 507 F.3d 967, 971–73 (6th Cir. 2007) (applying Tennessee law).

[34] 400 F.3d 370 (6th Cir. 2005).

[35] 173 F.3d 933 (4th Cir. 1999).

[36] Id. at 940.

[37] 561 U.S. 63, 71–4 (2010).

[38] 328 F.3d 1165 (9th Cir. 2003).

leave it" basis to employees with far less bargaining power than the employer.[39] The court found a number of substantively unconscionable provisions in that arbitration agreement including a one-year statute of limitations, a prohibition on class actions, a confidentiality clause, a provision that the employer need not arbitrate claims against employees, cost-shifting and fee-splitting provisions, and limitations on remedies.[40] By way of contrast, in *Caley v. Gulf Stream Aerospace Corp.*, involving claims under the Fair Labor Standards Act, Age Discrimination in Employment Act, Title VII and the Employee Retirement Income Security Act, the court enforced a similar arbitration agreement.[41] Although there was a disparity in bargaining power and acceptance was a condition of employment, the court found no procedural unconscionability.[42] And the employer's reservation of its right to litigate, prohibition on class claims, confidentiality provision, limits on discovery, exhaustion requirements, short deadlines, and limitations on counsel in the early steps of the procedure did not make the agreement substantively unconscionable.[43]

A later decision from California, which has been a leader in refusing to enforce arbitration provisions, found an agreement unconscionable in a case based on California wage and hour laws.[44] In *Chavarria v. Ralph's Grocery Co.*, the court found the agreement procedurally unconscionable because it was imposed on all applicants unilaterally. Further, the actual terms of the agreement were not supplied until the employee orientation. It was substantively unconscionable because the arbitrator selection provisions ensured that the employer would select the arbitrator for all employee claims. In addition, the employee's share of the arbitrator fees alone constituted more for one day of arbitration then the employee's claim was worth. The court considered the Supreme Court's decision in *Italian Colors*, but determined that the situation in *Ralph's* met the test articulated there—the cost was so high that access to the forum was effectively precluded.

Where a court finds unenforceable provisions in the agreement, it may refuse to order arbitration, particularly if it finds that the provisions are not easily severable.[45] On the other hand, a court

39 Id. at 1172.

40 Id. at 1172–79.

41 428 F.3d 1359 (11th Cir. 2005).

42 Id. at 1377.

43 Id. at 1378–79.

44 Chavarria v. Ralph's Grocery Co., 733 F.3d 916 (9th Cir. 2013).

45 See Armendariz v. Found. Health Psychcare Servs., Inc., 24 Cal. 4th 83, 125, 6 P.3d 669, 697 (2000) (refusing to enforce agreement with multiple unconscionable

might sever the unenforceable provisions or construe ambiguous provisions to make the agreement enforceable.[46]

Federal preemption has played an important role in enforcement of arbitration provisions. The Supreme Court has read the Federal Arbitration Act broadly to preempt state law that interferes with the statute's purpose of ensuring enforcement of arbitration agreements.[47] Accordingly, state law defenses to arbitration may be invalidated on preemption grounds. The FAA does not preempt all state law defenses, however. In *Chavarria v. Ralph's Grocery Co.*, the court found that the defense applied to all contracts, not just to arbitration agreements and did not disproportionately disfavor arbitration.[48]

For many years *Alexander v. Gardner-Denver Co.*, decided in 1974, was interpreted to prohibit unions from waiving the rights of employees to litigate legal claims.[49] In 2009, however, without reversing the earlier decision, the Supreme Court held that a union's agreement with an employer to arbitrate disputes arising under discrimination laws barred an employee from suing the employer for discrimination.[50] To be enforceable, however, the agreement must clearly and unequivocally waive the employees' right to litigate.[51] Additionally, the Court did not decide whether the employee was bound to arbitration if the union refused to arbitrate the employee's claim, which is commonly the union's right under collective bargaining agreements.[52]

The Supreme Court has also held that employees with arbitration agreements can still file claims with administrative enforcement agencies, which may litigate on the employee's behalf despite the arbitration agreement.[53] The employee's arbitration

---

provisions, finding it could not cure the problems with severance and declining to reform the agreement).

[46] See Little v. Auto Stiegler, Inc., 29 Cal. 4th 1064, 1075–76, 1082–85, 263 P.3d 979, 986–87, 991–93 (2003) (enforcing agreement in case alleging wrongful termination in violation of public policy after severing unconscionable provision and requiring employer to pay for arbitration where agreement was silent on payment of costs).

[47] See, e.g., AT&T Mobility LLC v. Concepcion, 563 U.S. 333 (2011) (preempting state law that deemed waivers of class claims unconscionable where contained in contracts of adhesion where claims predictably involve small amounts of damages and allegations are that party with greater bargaining power has engaged in scheme to cheat individuals of small amounts of money); Allied-Bruce Terminix Cos. v. Dobson, 513 U.S. 265 (1995).

[48] 733 F.3d at 927.

[49] Alexander v. Gardner-Denver Co., 415 U.S. 36, 51 (1974).

[50] 14 Penn Plaza LLC v. Pyett, 556 U.S. 247, 274 (2009).

[51] Wright v. Universal Marine Service Corp., 525 U.S. 70, 79–80 (1998).

[52] 14 Penn Plaza, 556 U.S. at 249.

[53] EEOC v. Waffle House, 534 U.S. 279, 297–98 (2002).

agreement does not bind the agency, which has a public interest to vindicate.[54] Government agencies file suit in a very small number of cases, however.[55]

7.2.2 Challenges to the Award

Challenges to the arbitration award involve situations in which the parties go through the arbitration process and obtain a decision, but then the losing party refuses to comply with the award or decides to challenge the award. In both labor and employment cases, courts have been very deferential to arbitration awards. In the labor context, the U.S. Supreme Court has held that courts must enforce the arbitrator's award, so long as the award "draws its essence from the collective bargaining agreement."[56] Similarly, on the employment side the Federal Arbitration Act provides for very narrow grounds on which a court can vacate an award.[57] Because of the limited grounds for challenging an award, arbitration is not without risk for employers, leading some to eschew arbitration despite its other benefits. Arbitration of class claims poses a particularly significant risk because of the potential for a large damage award that is unlikely to be reversed on appeal.

§ 7.3 Class Actions

Class and collective actions are available under many employment laws. Class cases are expensive, time-consuming and frequently draw media interest, pressuring companies to settle.[58] In addition, they allow individuals to join together, sharing the cost of litigating small claims that might be too expensive to litigate individually compared to the potential recovery. One example involves collective actions under the Fair Labor Standards Act, which as discussed supra in Chapter 5, have become increasingly common.

---

[54] Id. at 295–96.

[55] For example, in 2015 the EEOC received 89,385 charges of discrimination and brought suit in only 174 cases. Charge Statistics FY 1997 Through FY 2015, http://www.eeoc.gov/eeoc/statistics/enforcement/charges.cfm; EEOC Litigation Statistics FY 1997 through FY 2015, http://www.eeoc.gov/eeoc/statistics/enforcement/litigation.cfm.

[56] United Steelworkers of America v. Enterprise Wheel & Car Corp., 363 U.S. 593, 597 (1960).

[57] Section 10 of the Federal Arbitration Act limits orders to vacate to situations: "(1) where the award was procured by corruption, fraud, or undue means; (2) where there was evident partiality or corruption in the arbitrators, or either of them; (3) where the arbitrators were guilty of misconduct in refusing to postpone the hearing, upon sufficient cause shown, or in refusing to hear evidence pertinent and material to the controversy; or of any other misbehavior by which the rights of any party have been prejudiced; or (4) where the arbitrators exceeded their powers, or so imperfectly executed them that a mutual, final, and definite award upon the subject matter submitted was not made." 9 U.S.C. § 10.

[58] Deborah A. Sudbury, et al., Keeping the Monster in the Closet: Avoiding Employment Class Actions, Emp. Rel. L.J. at 20–23 (Autumn 2000).

Arbitration agreements offer an appealing vehicle to limit class claims.[59]

In 2010, the Supreme Court ruled that a party could not be ordered to arbitrate class claims unless the arbitration agreement specifically provided for class arbitration.[60] Then in 2011, the Court found that the Federal Arbitration Act preempted a state law that invalidated adhesive arbitration agreements precluding class actions imposed by powerful business on consumers with small claims.[61] Finally, in a 2013 decision, the Court enforced a class action waiver in an arbitration agreement between merchants, finding that the law did not guarantee the right to bring a class claim even if an individual claim would cost more to litigate than was available in damages.[62]

The National Labor Relations Board and several federal courts of appeals have held that the National Labor Relations Act (NLRA) prohibits class action waivers because the right to bring a class or collective action is a form of concerted activity protected by Section 7 of the NLRA.[63] Other courts of appeals have found that the NLRA does allow class action waivers,[64] however, and the Supreme Court will decide the issue in the October 2017 term.

The Fair Labor Standards Act has been a particular focus of opponents to waivers of collective claims because individual claims under that statute may be small relative to the cost of arbitration.

---

[59] A 2017 study of the 100 largest U.S. companies found that 80% of them have used arbitration for workplace disputes since 2010 and 39 have employed agreements containing class action waivers. Imre S. Sazlai, The Widespread Use of Employment Arbitration Among America's Top One Hundred Companies 2 (Employee Rights Advocacy Institute for Law and Policy, 2017). Another 2017 study found that 24.7 million employees have waived their right to class action claims. Colvin, supra note 12, at 2.

[60] Stolt-Nielsen S.A. v. AnimalFeeds International Corp., 559 U.S. 662. Where the parties agreed to allow the arbitrator to decide whether a class action was permissible under a contract that was silent on the issue, however, the Court followed its general policy of deference and refused to set aside the arbitrator's interpretation that the agreement allowed class actions. Oxford Health Plans v. Sutter, 133 S.Ct. 2064 (2013). Although the cases were not employment law cases, because they were decided under the Federal Arbitration Act they apply to employment arbitration.

[61] AT&T Mobility v. Concepcion, 563 U.S. 333.

[62] American Express Co. v. Italian Colors Restaurant, 133 S.Ct. 2304.

[63] See, e.g., D.R. Horton, 357 NLRB No. 184 (2012); Murphy Oil, USA, 361 N.L.R.B. No.72 (2014); Lewis v. Epic Sys. Corp., 823 F.3d 1147 (7th Cir. 2016) (refusing to order individual arbitration of employee's collective action claim under the Fair Labor Standards Act because provision requiring individual arbitration violated NLRA); Ernst & Young LLP v. Morris, 834 F.3d 975 (9th Cir. 2016) (same). The NLRA, however, does not cover government employees, agricultural employees, employees of railroads and airlines, 29 U.S.C. §§ 152(2), (3), supervisors, or managers. 29 U.S.C. §§ 152(2), (3), (11); NLRB v. Bell Aerospace Corp., 416 U.S. 267 (1974).

[64] See D.R. Horton v. NLRB, 737 F.3d 344 (5th Cir. 2013); Sutherland v. Ernst & Young, LLP, 726 F.3d 290, 297 n.8 (2d Cir. 2013)

Most courts have upheld the waivers, however, particularly after the decision in *Italian Colors*.[65]

§ 7.4 Comparing Arbitration and Litigation

Because arbitration is a private process unless the parties to the agreement agree otherwise, obtaining empirical evidence to evaluate its effectiveness as a substitute for litigation has been challenging. Further it is difficult to precisely compare arbitration and litigation because individual cases vary widely on a range of metrics. Nevertheless, some studies of the process exist.

Evidence shows that arbitration is on average quicker than litigation, although still time-consuming.[66] The cost of arbitration relative to litigation will depend on the provider used and who pays. Under the American Arbitration Association (AAA) rules for employer-promulgated arbitration systems, the employee pays a $175 filing fee and the employer pays almost all remaining costs.[67] AAA costs for individually negotiated arbitration agreements are not capped and can be substantially higher, including larger filing fees and half of the arbitrator's fees which average $700 per day.[68] Other arbitration providers do not cap up front fees for employees and they can be well over one thousand dollars depending on the size of the claim.[69] Other costs that are not present in litigation include the fees and travel expenses of the arbitrator, and hearing room rentals.[70] One study found arbitration expenses significantly exceeded the cost of litigation.[71]

Employees do win arbitration cases, although research indicates that employee victories are more common in cases based on contracts negotiated individually by high level employees than in cases where arbitration is imposed on employees as a condition of employment.[72]

---

[65] See, e.g., Sutherland v. Ernst & Young LLP, 726 F.3d 290, 295–99 (2d Cir. 2013); Owen v. Bristol Care, Inc., 702 F.3d 1050, 1052–53 (8th Cir. 2013). But see Killion v. Ke He Distrib., LLC, 761 F.3d 574, 591–92 (6th Cir. 2014) (refusing to uphold a waiver where there was no arbitration agreement).

[66] Alexander J.S. Colvin & Kelly Pike, Saturns & Rickshaws Revisited: What Kind of Arbitration System Has Developed, 29 Ohio St. J. on Disp. Resoln. 59, 73 (2014) (finding arbitration cases took about one year to hearing while court cases average two years); Colvin, supra note 15, at 8 (same).

[67] Michelle Eviston & Richard Bales, Capping the Costs of Consumer and Employment Arbitration, 42 U. Tol. L. Rev. 903, 910 (2011).

[68] Id.

[69] Id. at 911.

[70] Id.

[71] Id. at 911–12.

[72] Mark Gough, The High Cost of an Inexpensive Forum: An Empirical Analysis of Employment Discrimination Claims Heard in Arbitration and Civil Litigation, 35 Berk. J. Emp. & Lab. L. 91, 97–99 (2014); Colvin & Pike, supra note 66, at 74 (finding employee win rates of 24.7% in employer-promulgated arbitrations and 64.6% under

Labor arbitrators deciding cases under union contracts rule for employees more often than employment arbitrators.[73] Evidence regarding whether employees prevail more frequently in court or in arbitration is mixed,[74] and the validity and significance of this evidence is debated.[75] The most recent research, however, particularly on employer-promulgated arbitration, shows lower win rates for employees in arbitration.[76] The evidence also indicates that employees receive greater monetary damages in court than in arbitration.[77] Some have questioned the studies, however, as well as studies on case outcomes, because they do not consider cases that settle prior to litigation, which might change the relationship of litigation and arbitration outcomes.[78]

Research indicates that repeat players, almost always employers in employment arbitration, fare better in arbitration. Employers who have arbitrated previously win more frequently and when they have arbitrated before the same arbitrator, they are even more likely to win.[79] Additionally, employees recover less when the employer is a repeat player.[80]

As for legal representation, employees represent themselves more frequently in arbitration than in court.[81] When they use

---

individually negotiated arbitration agreements); Douglas M. Mahony & Hoyt N. Wheeler, Adjudication of Workplace Disputes in Labor and Employment Law and Economics 361, 380 (Kenneth G. Dau-Schmidt et al., eds. 2009).

[73] Id. at 380, 387, 390.

[74] See id. at 373 (showing mix of research results); Gough, supra note 72, at 97–99 (same).

[75] Mahony & Wheeler, supra note 72, at 373; Gough, supra note 72, at 101–02.

[76] Gough, supra note 72, at 104 (presenting survey of plaintiffs' lawyers showing significantly higher win rate in court); Colvin & Pike, supra note 66, at 29 (showing win rates lower than litigated cases, particularly when the individually negotiated agreements of high level employees are separated from employer-mandated arbitration); Alexander J.S. Colvin, Mandatory Arbitration and Inequality of Justice in Employment, 35 Berkeley J. Emp. & Lab. L. 71, 79 (2014) (showing lower win rates in arbitration).

[77] See Mahony & Wheeler, supra note 72, at 383–385; Colvin & Pike, supra note 66, at 29 (showing damage awards lower in arbitration than litigated cases, particularly when the individually negotiated agreements of high level employees are separated from employer-mandated arbitration); Gough, supra note 72, at 104 (showing higher average awards in litigation than in arbitration).

[78] See Mahony & Wheeler, supra note 72, at 383–385; Colvin, supra note 15, at 6.

[79] Lisa B. Bingham, On Repeat Players, Adhesive Contracts, and the Use of Statistics in Judicial Review of Employment Arbitration Awards, 29 McGeorge L. Rev. 223, 234, 238 (1998); Mahony & Wheeler, supra note 72, at 379–80; Colvin, supra note 15, at 9. But see Samuel Estreicher, Saturns for Rickshaws: The Stakes in the Debate over Predispute Employment Arbitration Agreements, 16 Ohio St. J. on Disp. Resol. 559, 566 (2001) (citing later research by Bingham finding a substantially reduced benefit from being a repeat player).

[80] Bingham, supra note 79, at 234.

[81] Colvin & Pike, supra note 66, at 69.

attorneys in arbitration, they are less likely to be experienced employment attorneys than those representing management.[82] Representation in arbitration is a significant predictor of employee win rates and higher damage recovery.[83] It is more difficult for employees to find attorneys for representation in arbitration than litigation.[84]

While supporters of arbitration have argued that low wage employees may have more opportunity to pursue their claims in arbitration than in court, available data do not show widespread use of arbitration by low wage employees.[85]

§ 7.5 Critical Perspectives

Employment arbitration has been far more controversial than labor arbitration. Critics complain that these agreements deprive unsuspecting employees of important rights like a jury trial.[86] Further they argue that arbitration is used to limit legal rights by discouraging employee claims.[87] Employees are less likely to prevail in arbitration, less likely to find legal representation, and less likely to bring smaller claims because they are prevented from proceeding collectively.[88] To the extent arbitration is more costly than litigation, employees may be further dissuaded from proceeding.[89] Opponents also worry that arbitration will limit public exposure of legal violations, decreasing the deterrent effect of the laws and allowing patterns of violations of employee rights to continue.[90] A related concern is that development of the law may be suppressed, with fewer judicial opinions interpreting statutes.[91] Others are concerned that

---

[82] Id. at 70.

[83] Id. at 78.

[84] See Jean Sternlight, Disarming Employees: How American Employers Are Using Mandatory Arbitration to Deprive Workers of Legal Protection, 80 Brooklyn L. Rev. 1309, 1334–40 (2015).

[85] See Mahony & Wheeler, supra note 72, at 385, 390; Gough, supra note 72, at 110; Colvin & Pike, supra note 66, at 80.

[86] Jean R. Sternlight, The Rise and Spread of Mandatory Arbitration as a Substitute for the Jury Trial, 38 U.S.F. L. Rev. 17, 34–35 (2003).

[87] Sternlight, supra note 84, at 1313–1315.

[88] Id.

[89] Colvin & Pike, supra note 66, at 81–82 (stating that based on the empirical research often "bringing cases in employment arbitration will not be economically viable and the system will not be readily accessible to employees").

[90] See, e.g., Katherine Van Wezel Stone, Mandatory Arbitration of Individual Employment Rights: The Yellow Dog Contract of the 1990s, 73 Denv. U. L. Rev. 1017, 1042–43, 1047 (1996).

[91] Myriam Gilles, The Day Doctrine Died: Private Arbitration and the End of Law, 2016 U. Ill. L. Rev. 371, 420–21.

arbitration may provide a kind of second-class justice, especially where there is no control over arbitrator quality.[92]

Proponents of arbitration suggest that a quicker, cheaper method of dispute resolution may benefit employees, particularly those with small claims that are unattractive to the plaintiffs' bar because of the small legal fees generated.[93] While some employees may win large jury verdicts in a litigation system, many others cannot get to court because of the cost of litigation.[94] Arbitration's advocates point to employee victories in arbitration. They argue that while employees may trade off certain rights such as extensive discovery or larger damages, they gain benefits from agreeing to arbitration and it should be permissible.[95] In response to the complaint that arbitration should be the employee's option rather than imposed by the employer, arbitration's fans assert that voluntary arbitration is impractical and unlikely to occur.[96] Proponents also claim that there are many incentives for complying with the law, and the prospect of a large and public jury verdict is only one; most employers will comply because of the risk of arbitration claims, bad publicity and administrative enforcement, as well as employee morale and retention. Finally, some commentators have suggested that arbitration is less beneficial for employers than may initially appear.[97]

Efforts to enact a comprehensive federal statute to prohibit imposition of arbitration agreements on employees as a condition of employment have thus far been unsuccessful. Limited restrictions on arbitration have been imposed for certain employee claims.[98]

---

[92] See Harry T. Edwards, Where Are We Heading with Mandatory Arbitration of Statutory Claims in Employment?, 16 Ga. St. U. L. Rev. 293, 298, 309 (1999). This concern has abated in the courts but not among arbitration's critics.

[93] See Estreicher, supra note 79, at 562; Theodore J. St. Antoine, The Changing Role of Labor Arbitration, 76 Ind. L.J. 83, 91 (2001).

[94] See id.

[95] See id.

[96] See id. at 91–92; Estreicher, supra note 79, at 567–69.

[97] Michael Z. Green, Debunking the Myth of Employer Advantage from Using Mandatory Arbitration for Discrimination Claims, 31 Rutgers L.J. 399, 421–440 (2000).

[98] See Department of Defense Appropriations Act, Pub. L. 111–118, Section 8116(a), Dec. 19, 2009 (prohibiting defense contractors from requiring arbitration of employee claims under Title VII and tort-related claims of sexual harassment or assault). President Obama issued an Executive Order limiting the ability of federal contractors to require arbitration of such claims but the order was revoked in 2017 by Congress.

Table of Cases

Index

References are to Pages